T0334621

A Cultural History of Climate Change

Charting innovative directions in the environmental humanities, this book examines the cultural history of climate change under three broad headings: history, writing and politics. Climate change compels us to rethink many of our traditional means of historical understanding, and demands new ways of relating human knowledge, action and representations to the dimensions of geological and evolutionary time. To address these challenges, this book positions our present moment of climatic knowledge within much longer histories of climatic experience. Only in light of these histories, it argues, can we properly understand what climate means today across an array of discursive domains, from politics, literature and law to activism and neighbourly conversation. Its chapters identify turning points and experiments in the construction of climates and of atmospheres of sensation. They examine how contemporary ecological thought has repoliticised the representation of nature and detail vital aspects of the history and prehistory of our climatic modernity.

This groundbreaking text will be of great interest to researchers and postgraduate students in environmental history, environmental governance, history of ideas and science, literature and eco-criticism, political theory and cultural theory, as well as all general readers interested in climate change.

Tom Bristow is a Postdoctoral Research Fellow at the ARC Centre of Excellence for the History of Emotions, University of Melbourne, Australia.

Thomas H. Ford is a Lecturer in English at Monash University, Australia.

The *Routledge Environmental Humanities* series is an original and inspiring venture recognising that today's world agricultural and water crises, ocean pollution and resource depletion, global warming from greenhouse gases, urban sprawl, overpopulation, food insecurity and environmental justice are all *crises of culture*.

The reality of understanding and finding adaptive solutions to our present and future environmental challenges has shifted the epicentre of environmental studies away from an exclusively scientific and technological framework to one that depends on the human-focused disciplines and ideas of the humanities and allied social sciences.

We thus welcome book proposals from all humanities and social sciences disciplines for an inclusive and interdisciplinary series. We favour manuscripts aimed at an international readership and written in a lively and accessible style. The readership comprises scholars and students from the humanities and social sciences and thoughtful readers concerned about the human dimensions of environmental change.

"As Gro Harlem Brundtland famously observed, "Current environmental problems require that we move beyond compartmentalization to draw the very best of our intellectual resources from every field of endeavor." This valuable collection of essays from a globally diverse group of historians and cultural scholars expands those resources in valuable ways by revealing new dimensions of the discourses surrounding climate change and the Anthropocene."

—*James Rodger Fleming, Charles A. Dana Professor of Science,*
Technology, and Society, Colby College, Maine, USA

"Understanding the way climate change is altering the world – imaginatively as much as materially – requires the serious engagement of humanities scholars who can bring with them great depths of insight about how and why humans reason and imagine. This volume is the first to bring together leading contemporary humanities scholarship about climate change into a single coherent setting. The chapters help us to think together about what changes in our climates mean. They show that the humanities are not simply a late-arriving appendage to Earth System science, to help merely in the work of translation. Their distinctive insights necessarily alter the ways in which the idea of climate change can be conceptualized and acted upon."

—*Mike Hulme, King's College London, UK*

A Cultural History of
Climate Change

**Edited by Tom Bristow and
Thomas H. Ford**

LONDON AND NEW YORK

from Routledge

First published 2016
by Routledge

2 Park Square, Milton Park, Abingdon, Oxfordshire OX14 4RN
711 Third Avenue, New York, NY 10017

Routledge is an imprint of the Taylor & Francis Group, an informa business

First issued in paperback 2017

British Library Cataloguing-in-Publication Data
A catalogue record for this book is available from the British Library

Library of Congress Cataloging-in-Publication Data
Names: Bristow, Tom (Cultural historian), editor. | Ford, Thomas H. (Literary historian), editor.
Title: A cultural history of climate change / edited by Tom Bristow and Thomas H. Ford.
Description: Abingdon, Oxon ; New York, NY : Routledge, Earthscan, 2016. | Includes bibliographical references and index.
Identifiers: LCCN 2015045018| ISBN 9781138838161 (hardback) | ISBN 9781315734590 (ebook)
Subjects: LCSH: Climatic changes—Social aspects. | Climatic changes—History. | Human ecology—Cross-cultural studies. | Anthropology.
Classification: LCC QC903 .C865 2016 | DDC 363.738/7409—dc23
LC record available at http://lccn.loc.gov/2015045018

ISBN: 978-1-138-83816-1 (hbk)
ISBN: 978-0-8153-5589-2 (pbk)

Typeset in Bembo
by diacriTech, Chennai

Contents

PART II
Climates of writing 109

PART III
Climates of politics 175

Figures

Contributors

Deb Anderson is an oral historian and writer based in Melbourne. Born in North Queensland, she spent more than a decade working as a journalist in Australia and overseas, principally for *The Age*, before becoming a lecturer in the School of Media, Film and Journalism at Monash University. She is the author of *Endurance: Australian Stories of Drought* (CSIRO, 2014).

Tom Bristow is a research fellow at the Australian Research Council Centre of Excellence for the History of Emotions, University of Melbourne, and a key contributor to the Mellon HfE (Humanities for the Environment) Observatory at the University of Sydney. His book, *The Anthropocene Lyric: An Affective Geography of Poetry, Person, Place*, was published by Palgrave Macmillan in 2015.

Dipesh Chakrabarty is the Lawrence A. Kimpton Distinguished Service Professor in History, South Asian Languages and Civilizations at the University of Chicago. His publications include *The Calling of History: Sir Jadunath Sarkar and His Empire of Truth* (Chicago, 2015), *Rethinking Working-Class History: Bengal 1890–1940* (Princeton, 1989, 2000), *Provincializing Europe: Postcolonial Thought and Historical Difference* (Princeton, 2000; second edition, 2008), and *Habitations of Modernity: Essays in the Wake of Subaltern Studies* (Chicago, 2002). He is currently working on two books, provisionally entitled *The Climate of History* (Chicago) and *History and the Time of the Present* (Duke).

Thomas H. Ford is a Lecturer in English at Monash University. A literary historian of British Romanticism, Ford has also published on critical and literary theory, the environmental humanities, and contemporary poetics. His translation of Boris Groys's *The Communist Postscript* was published by Verso in 2010.

Roslyn Jolly is an Honorary Research Associate in English at the University of New South Wales. Her research focuses on narrative and its theory, travel writing, and literature and empire. Jolly's publications include *Henry James: History, Narrative, Fiction* (Oxford, 1993) and *Robert Louis Stevenson in the Pacific: Travel, Empire, and the Author's Profession* (Ashgate, 2009).

Jayne Lewis is Professor of English at the University of California, Irvine, where she teaches seventeenth- and eighteenth-century British literature. She is the author of *The English Fable: Aesop and Literary Culture, 1650-1740* (Cambridge, 1995), *Mary Queen of Scots: Romance and Nation* (Routledge, 2000), and, most recently, *Air's Appearance: Literary Atmosphere and British Fiction* (Chicago, 2012). She has published numerous articles on eighteenth-century literature and culture and co-edited several volumes of essays, including two on John Dryden. Now editing an anthology of anglophone religious writing, 1660–1750, she is pursuing research into Enlightenment conceptions of the aura.

Nick Mansfield is Professor of Critical and Cultural Studies and Dean of Higher Degree Research at Macquarie University in Sydney. His books include *Masochism: The Art of Power* (Greenwood, 1997), *Theorizing War: From Hobbes to Badiou* (Palgrave Macmillan, 2008), and *The God Who Deconstructs Himself: Subjectivity and Sovereignty Between Freud, Bataille and Derrida* (Fordham, 2010). He is one of the founding general editors of the journal *Derrida Today* (Edinburgh UP), and is currently working on a book called *Sovereignty and Violence: Recalling the Politics of the Future*.

Timothy Morton is Rita Shea Guffey Chair in English at Rice University. He gave the Wellek Lectures in Theory in 2014 and has collaborated with Björk. He is the author of *Dark Ecology: For a Logic of Future Coexistence* (Columbia, forthcoming), *Nothing: Three Inquiries in Buddhism* (Chicago, forthcoming), *Hyperobjects: Philosophy and Ecology after the End of the World* (Minnesota, 2013), *Realist Magic: Objects, Ontology, Causality* (Open Humanities, 2013), *The Ecological Thought* (Harvard, 2010), *Ecology without Nature* (Harvard, 2007), eight other books and 150 essays on philosophy, ecology, literature, music, art, design and food. He blogs regularly at www.ecologywithoutnature.blogspot.com.

S. Romi Mukherjee is *maître de conférences* in Religion and Politics at *l'Institut d'Etudes Politiques de Paris* (Sciences-Po). Since 2009, he has been affiliated with UNESCO in various research capacities where his work has focused, amongst other topics, on the ethics of climate change and the social implications of the Anthropocene. He has published widely, mostly in political theory and the history of religions. Recent books and edited volumes include *Durkheim and Violence* (Blackwell, 2010), *The Political Anthropology of the Global*, (Blackwell, 2011), and *Nouveaux visages du religieux dans un monde sécularisé* (with Lionel Obadia, Karthala, 2015).

Harry Nankin is a photographic artist and educator who has, for over two decades, explored the meaning of 'place' and 'nature' at a time of ecological crisis.

Noted for his poetic evocations of the abject, ambient, transient and invisible in nature, Nankin uses the landscape as the camera to enact the speculative 'space' between wonder and tragedy, which he calls an 'ecological gaze'. His photomedia works can be viewed at; www.harrynankin.com

Chris O'Brien is a historian and Postdoctoral Research Fellow with the Northern Research Futures Collaborative Research Network based at Charles Darwin University and ANU's North Australia Research Unit. He is currently working on a history of weather and climate across the Indonesian Maritime Continent and the Arafuru/Timor region (including northern Australia), post 1600 CE, tentatively called *Chasing the Winds*.

Karen Pinkus is Professor of Italian and Comparative Literature at Cornell University. She has published widely on climate change, environmental theory, Italian literature and cinema and visual culture. She is a member of the Faculty Advisory Board of the Atkinson Center for a Sustainable Future. Her speculative dictionary, *Fuel* (University of Minnesota Press, 2016) explores the distinction between energy as system and fuel as substance. She is completing a new digital project titled *Terranes of Climate Change: Subsurface, Surface, Atmosphere*.

Nicole Rogers is a Senior Lecturer in the School of Law and Justice at Southern Cross University, NSW. Her research interests include the intersection of performance studies theory and law, and climate change law, with a particular emphasis on climate change litigation. She has worked as a solicitor in private practice in Sydney and Lismore and as a research officer for the National Aboriginal and Islander Legal Services Secretariat.

Jerome Whitington is a Senior Research Fellow at the National University of Singapore. An anthropologist, his current research project, *Accounting for Atmosphere: Climate Change, Quantification and the Second Life of Carbon*, is an ethnographic study of carbon accounting as a mode of exploring the anthropological significance of climate change. Recent publications include 'Carbon as a Metric of the Human' (*Political and Legal Anthropology Review*, 2016) and 'Fingerprint, Bellwether, Model Event: Climate Change as Speculative Anthropology' (*Anthropological Theory*, 2013).

Linda Williams is Associate Professor of Art, Environment and Cultural Studies at RMIT University. She has published widely in cultural history and the environmental humanities, and acknowledges the support of the ARC (Australian Research Council) Centre of Excellence for the History of Emotions (CE110001011) in researching her chapter for this book. She is a key researcher at the HfE Mellon Pacific Observatory for the environmental humanities at the University of Sydney, and also recently led an international ARC project *Spatial Dialogues: Public Art and Climate Change*, discussed in Hjorth, L; Pink, S; Sharp: K; Williams, L. *Screen*

Ecologies: Art, Screen Culture and the Environment in the Asia-Pacific Region, to be published by MIT Press in 2016.

Andrea Witcomb is Director, Cultural Heritage Research Centre for Asia and the Pacific and Deputy Director (Governance), Alfred Deakin Institute for Citizenship and Globalisation. She is the author of *Re-Imagining the Museum: Beyond the Mausoleum* (Routledge, 2003) and with Chris Healy, the co-editor of *South Pacific Museums: An Experiment in Culture* (Monash e-press, 2006). Additionally, Andrea has co-written *From the Barracks to the Burrup: The National Trust in Western Australia* (University of NSW Press, 2010) with Dr Kate Gregory, and she is the volume editor of *The International Handbooks of Museum Studies* (Wiley-Blackwell).

Acknowledgements

Research for this book was supported through an Australian Research Council grant, "Nineteenth-Century Climate Change: Atmosphere, Culture and Romanticism," by an Early Career Researcher grant from the University of Melbourne, and by the Australian Research Council Centre of Excellence for the History of Emotions.

The editors would like to acknowledge the assistance and support of the following people and institutions: Lindy Allen, Rebecca Brenan, Dipesh Chakrabarty, Charles Dawson, Debjani Ganguly, Tom Griffiths, Christine Hansen, the Humanities Research Centre at the Australian National University, Adeline Johns-Putra, Museum Victoria, Richard Kerridge, Harry Nankin, Libby Robin and Khanam Virjee.

Special thanks to Auntie Di Kerr, Cousin Ron Jones, Annette Xiberras and Wurundjeri Council, and the Taungurung Clans Aboriginal Corporation, with respect to referencing the experiences of Martha Nevin and Brian Paterson (in Chapter 4).

The editors would also like to thank Peter Cudmore and Helen Bell for their continual support and outstanding input throughout this project.

Foreword

Dipesh Chakrabarty

Anthropogenic climate change that is now perceived globally as portending serious danger to humanity has had the welcome effect of revitalizing the ongoing conversation between the humanities and the physical and biological sciences. Climate change, considered on its own, is a geophysical phenomenon and, as an object of study, belongs squarely to the province of the physical sciences. But *"dangerous climate change"*, as the historian Julia Adeney Thomas has remarked, is not something that can be defined by scientists alone, for our understanding of what constitutes danger, and to whom and how and when, entails some crucial value-judgments.[1] Climate change, therefore, promotes debates on human perspectives, values, and priorities – issues that ultimately express the arbitrariness of human signs. Public discussions of anthropogenic climate change, for this reason, have always involved humanities issues.

Yet it has been difficult for scholars in the humanities – who do not speak in the "practical" diction of social scientists who advise governments on policy-related matters – to secure a place in larger debates on global warming. I can see two important reasons for this. The first is, of course, that reading and understanding even the basics of the complex science of climate change is not easy. Climate science is not one discipline. It involves specialists from many different disciplines such as physics, chemistry, geology, and biology, as well as specialists from interdisciplinary areas of science, such as earth systems sciences. Scholars in the humanities need to come to terms with the basics of the findings and arguments of specialists in these areas. It is, of course, only to be welcomed that many leading climate scientists have themselves written several general books and articles on the topic, thus helping to make their specialist knowledge comprehensible to a more general reading public. The second problem that scholars in the humanities face in bringing their observations and inference in the public domain is a more complicated one, and it relates to certain differences that mark and distinguish the cultures of "knowledge" in the humanities and the natural sciences. When a particular field of a scientific discipline is full of opinions that clash with one another, we think

---

1 Julia Adeney Thomas, "History and Biology in the Anthropocene: Problems of Scale, Problems of Value," *American Historical Review*, December 2014, pp. 1587–1607.

of that particular branch of science as "unsettled." Indeed, it is for this reason that climate deniers have sometimes succeeded in blowing up differences between the positions of particular climate scientists to claim that the science of climate change was still "unsettled." The human sciences, on the other hand, are constituted by – and thrive on – differences and arguments that, for the field as a whole, never get settled! Of course, a group of scholars subscribing to a particular point of view may consider debates and positions "settled" from their own point of view, but others will still vigorously disagree. Given this perennially-unsettled nature of the humanities – the fact that arguments within the humanities are always on the boil – it is impossible for humanities scholars to take to the public the kind of nuanced and provisional "consensus" that climate scientists seek to arrive at, however tentative and temporary such consensus may be. Climate scientists can issue statements like "ninety five per cent of scientists hold at a confidence interval of ninety per cent that ...," but it is impossible for humanities scholars to make a statement of this kind. Take, for instance, the question that attracts a lot of debate in the humanities – whether or not we can blame global warming squarely on global capitalism. All kinds of differences of opinion will be expressed over the very understanding of the term "capitalism" itself and they will never be resolved to everybody's satisfaction.

Such indeed is the nature of the humanities. In valuing arguments over consensus, the human sciences only reflect the fact that human values and perspectives remain irreducibly plural. But this is an important insight, for nothing of significance can be achieved for humanity as a whole by riding roughshod over these differences of values. Whatever the hard won consensus of scientists on the causes of global warming and on the means of meeting its challenges, policies and actions, addressing their findings will not follow in a straightforward way from what those findings may suggest. Consider the "climate deal" worked out between about 200 nations in Paris in December 2015. Its success is dependent on the good will and commitment of many important political leaders. A powerful nation can undo the deal if its leaders happen to take the view that it is not in their national interests (as happened with the Kyoto protocol of 1997). Humanities teaches us the skills we need today to stay with the conflicts of values and perceived interests that make for conflicts between different groups of humans, for the only way forward is to be found by humans working through – and not by ignoring or bypassing – the contradictory values that give rise to these conflicts. The agreements we achieve will always be vulnerable to present and future clashes of perspectives.

Questions of empathy and understanding – the ability to look at the world through the points of view of others (including those of non-human animals, plants, or even things) – gains in importance everyday when a planetary crisis calls humanity to a certain kind of self-awareness that, we know, cannot be realized if we ignore either the differences among humans or the multifarious networks that connect us to non-humans. The patience one would require to undertake this work of understanding in the political-public sphere – assuming that the politics of climate change would be sensitive to those most at risk from it – is not very different in quality from the patience a scholar in the humanities needs to be able to read a text closely or to inhabit a point of view radically different from his or her own. These are skills that only the humanities can impart.

This collection brings together some splendid essays from established and emergent scholars whose analyses move deftly between the world and the word, between facts about climate, politics, history, and their discursive constructions. They discuss historical cases, philosophical issues, literary readings of the biosphere, the place of law and religion in climatic issues, and, not least, the linguistic-political differences between the expressions "global warming" and "climate change." This conversation is still in its early days. But the insights garnered here deserve to be disseminated widely.

Dipesh Chakrabarty
Chicago, January 3, 2016

Climates of history, cultures of climate

Tom Bristow and Thomas H. Ford

The first topic addressed in Robert Boyle's *The General History of the Air*, pre-pared posthumously for the press by John Locke and published in 1692, was not what air is, but rather 'What We Understand by the Air' (1692, p. 1). As Jayne Lewis has recently argued, by approaching the history of air via the question of its understanding, Boyle was able to draw a critical distinction between his empirical study of the material atmosphere, and that long philosophical tradition which had investigated the metaphysical qualities of a super-sensible, immaterial æther, from Aristotle to Descartes. 'Boyle's "common air,"' Lewis writes, 'will have nothing to do with that. It is all about *us*. The syntax of the sentences within which Boyle said as much would put the emphasis on the preposition – the air is all *about* us' (2012, p. 48). This ambiguity in the way air is 'about us', Lewis goes on to suggest, formed a recurrent trope in subsequent English writing on atmosphere. By asking how air is understood, Boyle reconceived of it as an immersive material medium available to experimental investigation. And yet – and in part because of its ambi-ent ubiquity – air's recognisability here was also made to depend on its media-tion in discourse. In modern atmospheric knowledge, these two media – air and writing – have shown a troubling propensity to mimic and echo one another, and to function as metaphors and figures for each other (Connor, 2010; Favret, 2009). Atmosphere became so semantically intertwined with discursive self-reflection that the two often appeared to be indistinguishable, particularly when it came to ques-tions of what air meant.

Writing in the present day, it would seem as if climate change is what is now all about us, and it is about us in more than one sense, as Lewis might suggest. It is cer-tainly about us, all around us, to be found on every side, active wherever attention is turned, from the troposphere to the mediasphere to the oceanic depths of the hydrosphere. The language of climate change powerfully informs recent attempts to conceive of the present as history. It is motivating new proposals for dating and periodizing the history of the present, most notably that of the Anthropocene, the contested geological present of transgressed planetary boundaries (Crutzen, 2002). Climate change appears increasingly all-pervasive in contemporary public culture – often backgrounded, yet always relevant. With climate change, old meta-phors, such as 'the economic climate' or 'the climate of opinion', have taken on a stark and suddenly literal and material reference. The field of oppositions that once allowed these formulations to function metaphorically, with economics, opinions, politics and culture over here, and physical climates over there – tenor and vehicle drawn from clearly distinct existential realms – no longer holds. Climate change is all about us because it concerns an immersive set of environmental conditions that shape all human activities, indeed almost all planetary life. And it is also all about us because these climatic conditions are changing meaningfully as an effect of human activity, of the totality of our actions and everyday lives considered at some collective, global and species level. So climate change is about us in the sense in which a narrative or discourse is about its theme or subject; in the sense of its presenting an ambient experienced world, the surrounding conditions of a unique historical atmosphere or ecology; but also in the self-implicating sense in which a narrative is always about its author – or, as a post-structuralist might qualify, about its author's death.

In the context of the Anthropocene ('the age of the human'), an epoch based on the realisation that human practices profoundly influence a suite of global and local biophysical systems, a potentially mobilising sense of cultural consciousness might be haunted by a narcissistic flaw, where 'to be radical is to grasp things at the root. But for man the root is man himself' (Marx, [1843] 1975, p. 251). Critics then face a double risk: in 'reducing the future to climate' (Hulme, 2011), we might both flatten out the effects of climate change – disproportionately impacting the global south – and neglect to critique the unequal means of anthropogenic climate change production (Nixon, 2011). Secondly, there are dangers inherent to species thinking, recognition of which has motivated calls for a more-than-human ethics beyond ecomodernist technofixes to our predicament. 'To think like a planet' requires thinking of the survival of all species, and degrees of dependencies on humans changing ethics, lifestyles, energy choices, and critical frameworks, as Libby Robin (2013) has argued: 'living with altered biophysical circumstances requires major reconceptualisation of the place of humans on Earth at every scale.'

When it comes to histories of climate change, it is important, both methodologically and ethically, to distinguish between these different senses of being about, and to be clear what manner of narrative it is that one is telling. Historical understanding of climate change rests on critical distinctions between causes and effects; between human subjects and environmental conditions; between anthropogenic warming and natural variability; between different kinds of acts, scenes, agents, agencies and purposes; between ecological interconnectedness and discursive intentionality. But climate change can also blur these distinctions, making them difficult to draw with any finality. There is a further sense in which climate change is all about us, which involves the way 'about' can be used to express approximation or indefiniteness, registering a fuzzy margin of numerical error or residual uncertainty. Virginia Woolf played on this sense of 'about' in her famously indeterminate dating of literary modernism: 'on or about December 1910 human character changed' (2008, p. 38). Climate change appears to demand similarly imprecise historical dating; the Anthropocene, for example, has been said to begin on or about 1800.[1] And that date is only one of a penumbral cloud of proposed points of origin for the Anthropocene that have ranged from prehistory to not quite yet. 'About', in this sense, suggests an ineliminable vagueness rather than sharp lines and pinpoint precision. The quest for consensus on a single synchronous spike – the search for the unique flash of the Anthropocene starter's gun, so to speak – may even militate against a more culturally nuanced sense of climate change as involving the conjunction of vastly heterogeneous practices and processes, so that retracing its career requires a discontinuous chronology. The diachronous character of the many proposed physical strata of the Anthropocene suggests how its onset and impact have been spread out over time. These multiple breakdowns and error conditions in the Earth's systems mirror the ways in which environmental catastrophe plays out in our period: damage and suffering is distributed in space and time; crisis is a complex of catastrophes not reducible to a single instant, date, or even chronological schema. 'Aboutness' is then also relevant in this sense too, for climate change couples prehistoric hydrocarbons with modern capitalist cultures. It has dispersed beginnings that are often inscribed in distant locations and radically disparate time-scales. As an object of historical understanding, climate change keeps shifting about; it seems hard to hold in focus – a 'hyperobject', perhaps, to draw from Timothy Morton's lexicon. With climate change, a lengthening series of ontological and temporal categories unravel; distinctions between natural history and human history grow hazy; the historical thresholds of modernity, and of the present, blur into increasing unrecognizability. Limits and borderlines become uncertain and unreliable.

Climate change shares this semantic quality of vagueness or 'aboutness' with many other terms from the environmental vocabulary – such words as ambience, immersion, or indeed environment itself, which all similarly refer to what exists about us. This vocabulary, as Morton and others have suggested, implicitly codes for a human subject who organises his or her peripheral surroundings, so that the ontological dualisms these terms were thought to overcome are in fact reinstated at a more structural but elusive level: 'The very word *environmentalism*,' Morton writes, 'is evidence of wishful thinking… a case of some "thing" that surrounds us, that environs us and differs from us' (2007, p. 141). This wishful thinking is in evidence whenever we speak of a person and his or her environment. The history of climate change courts a similar criticism, particularly when approached from a cultural perspective that might appear to be inescapably anthropocentric. And the vague universalism of some climate change discourse also covers for other more purely human acts of conceptual and material exclusion.[2] As chapters in this book remind us, collective first-person formulations – all about *us*, what *we* understand by climate change – often work to obscure what are in fact starkly unequal distributions of climatic agency and threat across very different communities, whether they be cultural, geographic, generational, or indeed biological. But the chapters of this book also point, more speculatively, to an indeterminate fraternity of climate change, made up of all those potentially included in climate's reach and influence. That is to say, climate change is all about us only if we can conceive of our community of fate as including not only living humans, but also the unconceived and the dead, and not only humans too, but also such other climatically sensitive life forms as lichens, butterflies, and the dinoflagellate symbionts of coral reefs. Climate being all about us might then invite a fundamental redefinition of who 'we' are.

As Steven Poole (2006) has shown, 'climate change' is not a politically neutral term, but one whose historical emergence and present dominance reflect a complex struggle over meaning (p. 42–49). Through the 1980s and into the early 1990s – the years in which climate change was first widely discussed in the public sphere, and then established as a vital issue on the international political agenda – the term appeared roughly as frequently in the published language as did 'global warming'. If anything, 'global warming' was slightly more common, and, perhaps as a result, was rhetorically associated with those who had first recognised in climate a new and dangerous object of concern: scientists, and, somewhat later, activist groups and environmentalists.[3] In *The Sea and Summer*, George Turner's early and important climate change novel (1987), for instance, the phrase 'climate change' does not actually appear. The key term there is 'greenhouse' – 'Greenhouse Culture', 'Greenhouse Effect'. By the middle of the 1990s, however, 'climate change' had become the hegemonic term, the received phrase of scientific, public and political debate. The pattern holds in other European languages: in German, for instance, *Klimawandel* supplanted *globale Erwärmung* in these same years. Far from being driven purely by a desire for transparently scientific terminology, this lexical shift was in fact impelled, Poole suggests, by the material interests of petro-capitalism. As a term, climate change was seen to be usefully vague: it 'worked to support the notion… that there is controversy about whether there is warming, and if there is, whether humankind is to blame at all' (2006, p. 45). Climate change retained a space for manufactured uncertainty; it was code for no change, for business as usual.

And yet, as Poole also notes, 'climate change' invites more local and particularist perspectives than does 'global warming'. In so doing, it can help to articulate some of the complexity and multifariousness of what it names. It more easily accommodates discussion of such related phenomena as oceanic acidification, for instance. And its semantic flexibility and vagueness correspond to some of the ambiguous ways in which climate change is all about us. The 'change' of climate change is about the present, but even more about the future. Our understanding of it is premised on a model of knowledge as inherently provisional and contestable. Its likely scale, as it reorganises planetary life over tens of millennia, far exceeds our normal patterns of historical comprehension, almost entering mythic time. Its uncertainty is inherent; radical doubt cannot be eliminated from what we understand by climate change. This imbues the term with a generative semantic potential, enabling speculative uses that seek to articulate what lies at the dissolving limits of historical self-understanding. The inherent uncertainty of climate change can always be misrecognised or misrepresented. But the term also captures some of the genuine conceptual difficulties of apprehending our present circumstances, of coming to terms with this historical moment.

Epistemic climates

This book examines what we understand by climate change. It follows recent studies that have approached climate change as a discursive event and object of public concern, studies that have explored how our current climatic crisis has been constructed, mediated and processed by the culture at large. Needless to say, within contemporary public culture, what we know about climate change is deeply politically contested. But whatever one's position in this debate (and it is the editors' hope that readers on all sides will find something of interest and value in this volume), the sheer presence of climate change as a social fact, as an event in the discursive history of globalization, and as a fault-line in the contemporary politics of knowledge, would seem to merit study. How has climate change become so vital an object of political contention in the last two decades or so? Why have scientific practices and institutions become items of such widespread anxiety, specifically in relation to climate? Why is climate change disagreeable, so intractable, so frustrating?

Questions like these have oriented scholarly inquiry to the recent scientific, technological and social histories of climate change, and equally to the recent history of climate politics and media (Fleming, 2005; Hulme, 2009). They are questions that directly concern the contemporary construction of scientific knowledge, and its mediation in the public sphere. But they are also questions that have been addressed in more affective and intimately experiential terms, in studies, for example, of the forms of environmental consciousness that are embodied in the atmospheres of everyday sociability (Anderson, 2009; Adey, 2010; Choy, 2012). And they are questions, too, that invite looking farther back into the past, and into the histories and prehistories of modernity. Historians of science, for instance, have shown how meteorology was reconstructed as a modern scientific discipline around 1800 through a complex process of drawing boundaries that were as institutional as they were terminological, matters of social as well as linguistic practice (Janković, 2000; Anderson, 2005). The late eighteenth-century chemical analysis of the atmosphere has long served as an object lesson for theories of the structure of scientific revolutions (Engels, 1956; Kuhn, 1996). 'Heat-death' and nineteenth-century planetary thermodynamics, meanwhile, have been studied for the broader cultural implications of the irreversibility and finitude they attributed to cosmological time. As a rubric, the cultural history of climate change potentially brings these accounts together with histories of climate as a mediating framework of public discussion, and with accounts of democracy, and ideology, understood as atmospheres (Golinski, 2007; Latour and Weibel, 2005; Ross, 1991). It links histories of literary and aesthetic atmospheres to histories of climate as an experienced matrix of thought, feeling, and life, and to the intervolved histories of climatic determinism and ecological understanding (Markley and Wood, 2008; Menely, 2012).

These and related studies have illuminated climate's place in the universe of contemporary knowledge, and its historical conjunctures with other determining conditions of our cultural present – global, technological, postcolonial and material. And although they have often sought to restrict their scholarly focus to climate considered as culture – to climate as a discursive or social construct, so to speak – in practice this has proven possible only by radically expanding the conceptual limits of the cultural field far beyond human discourse and society, traditionally conceived. Paradoxically, accounts of climate as culture or as discourse have tended to dissolve any conventional sense of culture as a bounded human universe of symbolic meaning. As they track changes in the meaning of climate, historical propositions come to drift indeterminately between climate and culture, between literal and figurative registers, between environmental conditions and their symbolic mediation and interpretation.

In its most basic scientific definition, climate is the statistical abstraction of weather over a set period of time, conventionally thirty years. What we understand by climate in these terms is the yield of an interrelated array of practices of recording, adjusting and synthesizing; of apparatuses, instruments, and computational processes; of protocols for the validation and communication of scientific information; of the negotiations and frictions between scientific and public cultures. Climate is the creation of a 'global knowledge infrastructure', in Paul Edward's phrase (2010, p. 8). And climate change, which involves shifting to an Earth systems perspective that also incorporates social processes, represents a whole further stage of complex and non-deterministic mediation. For many, this hyper-mediation of climate change knowledge drives a wedge into the historical understanding of the present. Climate change appears to detach knowledge from meaning, distancing received scientific facts from the thick textures of lived experience (Moser and Dilling, 2007; Howell, 2011; Whitmarsh, 2009b). The heat of a summer's day, felt on the skin, is not climate change, nor is being caught in unseasonal rain, nor the sudden chill of an autumn wind that springs up when you have forgotten to bring a jacket. As Sheila Jasanoff has written, our knowledge of climate change relies on 'techniques of aggregation and deletion, calculation and comparison that exhaust the capacities of even the most meticulously recorded communal memories' (2010, p. 237). Scientific representations of climate change, Jasonoff concludes, 'have become decoupled from most modern systems of experience and understanding' (p. 249).[4] Whatever public consensus exists when it comes to climate change rests on a vast and contested architecture of discursive practice. And yet these many layers of mediation – from the construction of scientific facts to their communication and wider publicity – can often appear to be failing to achieve any significant material impression. Climate change, that is to say, marks an acute disjunction between what we know and how we feel, between our affective, discursive and epistemological selves. Climate change seems to be everywhere and nowhere: it appears at once cognitively and discursively ever-present, and yet experientially and even materially invisible, at least in any direct form. There is in consequence an 'impasse', Richard Kerridge suggests, 'between our awareness of climate change and our inability to act on that awareness… One knows something and yet does not behave as if one knows it' (2013, pp. 358, 360).

The disciplines of cultural history – literary history, art history, the history of material cultures, and so on – are usually seen to have first acquired their modern intellectual formation around the end of the eighteenth century. From our perspective, this historical coincidence of modern disciplinarity with climate change and with the Anthropocene (at least on certain datings of it) implies that the received forms of disciplinary knowledge can no longer be taken for granted. For the humanities, thinking about climate change involves sometimes uncomfortable aspects of scholarly self-reflection. Inherited styles of thought must be re-examined in a vastly expanded environment of ideas. For cultural history, this felt need is one way climate change is being experienced materially and directly, as it were, precisely in its hyper-mediation. Like lichens and coral reefs, the disciplines of the humanities may also be considered as climatically sensitive forms. Climate change is all about us not least as a cascade of collapsing and outmoded philosophical and scholarly categories. Understanding proceeds here by catachresis. In the conceptual resistance or friction that attends approaching climate change from the point of view of culture, the sense appears of as yet inarticulable truths of our planetary circumstances. Glimmers of a new way of apprehending our situation can emerge from these fractures and gaps between knowledge and feeling, between fact and experience. At the blurred limits of the planet's writability, we encounter climate as it exceeds our efforts at representation.

Time, representation, agency

The cultural history of climate change presents particularly acute challenges to our traditions of historical understanding and historical method. It unsettles traditional notions of the historical period, of the narrative forms of historiography, and of collective and individual agency. It demands new ways of relating the existential and historical moments of human knowledge, action and representation to the dimensions of geological and evolutionary time. Each of the chapters in this volume addresses the histories of these intertwined questions of time, representation and agency as they now appear in a changing climate.

The book's first section, 'Climates of History', brings together essays on climatic modernity, describing practices and processes that have shaped the present-day atmospheric environment. Through the history of the settler culture of far North Australia, Chris O'Brien reconnects our contemporary climatic crisis to colonial experience. O'Brien explores how colonial settlements encountered new climatic conditions via existing beliefs and expectations – norms that were entwined with culturally distinct ideas of memory and destiny, of past and future collective life. Recounting the histories of nineteenth-century climate change as those of misperception and ecological imperialism, O'Brien reminds us that histories of profound environmental misunderstanding continue to shape present-day landscapes and social practices. But they also point, more positively, to a potential flexibility and adaptability of climatic understanding, presenting climate as a vital matrix through which cultures mark, negotiate and share time, as O'Brien's account of indigenous experiences of seasons attests. Climate, in this account, emerges as a critical medium for practices of cultural transmission – not least including history – across and between different forms of temporal experience.

Linda Williams takes up the recent proposal that the Columbian Exchange marks a critical turning point in the history of the Anthropocene. Tracing out diverse and even contradictory intellectual traditions in this period, Williams reconnects present-day concerns with a much longer history of climatic experience, positioning the history of ideas as a critical resource for coming to terms with the paradoxes of climatic historiography. Jerome Whitington identifies a comparable conceptual and aesthetic openness – and again, one that has been largely overlooked to date – in the history of climate science. Re-reading Joseph Fourier's 1827 paper on planetary and interplanetary temperatures, Whitington shows how central speculative practice was to this important document in the development of the scientific conception of a global climatic system. When it comes to climate change and the history of climate change, both Williams and Whitington suggest, theoretical speculation and aesthetic wonder have long operated as critical modes for the production of knowledge.

In taking an example of a contemporary Australian museum, Tom Bristow and Andrea Witcomb reflect upon an array of interconnected issues that highlight the difficulty of visualising climate change in history. In dialogue with O'Brien's attention to indigenous experience of seasons, Bristow and Witcomb's close reading of the enacted connections between disparate peoples, materials and events – seasons and fire, colonialism and ancient continents – invokes the 'dialogic interactivity' of the museum space as a complex emotional terrain of conflict and confluence. The living gallery's exhibition syntax and aesthetic strategies elicit a range of emotions towards changing ecosystems and their relationship to cultural practices, especially indigenous and European practices that relate to fire. Empathy is a principle that Dipesh Chakrabarty (2002) called a performative understanding of citizenship, with significant consequences for how we understand the pedagogical work of museums. From the impacts of colonisation and the indigenous witnessing of seven seasons (marked by flora and fauna, and their life cycles), to the shaping of the landscape by water and fire, Melbourne Museum's multi-dimensional treatment of time illuminates one way that the politics of representation can shift into a pedagogy of feeling via sensitive curatorial practices.

Like the other authors in this section, Deb Anderson identifies climate as a means of cultural self-definition. In her oral history of recent drought in the Mallee wheat-belt of southeast Australia, Anderson explores ways in which climatic stories have functioned to bind generations together in what she calls 'a dynamic process of cultural retraditionalisation'. Anderson's archive holds out an ambiguous promise: it presents a story of impasse, misunderstanding and self-defeat, even as it describes cultural resources that will be critical for addressing the climatic present – resources of solidarity, pity and fear, of historical self-reflection and, as with all the authors of this section, of speculative wonder.

Cultures represent and mediate climates. But climate change entails that contemporary societies are now also making natural history, allowing us to recognise in climate the inscriptions of human culture. As such, sociogenic climate change invites interpretation and decipherment, the techniques of textual criticism.

Literary representations of climate change often tend to be discussed in terms of public awareness, scientific literacy and pro-environmental behaviour. In effect, this is to understand literature as a sub-branch of science communication. The chapters collected in our volume's second section, 'Climates of Writing', take a different tack, re-examining our present literary moment in the terms of a much longer literary history of climatic experience. Literature has often reflected on climate as a cultural dimension of thought and feeling, positing atmospheres of sensation that hover in a conceptually undecidable position between environmental condition and literary construct. In this way, literature can come to mediate the climatic experience of the past – experience that takes on a new significance and urgency in our contemporary climatic moment.

Jayne Lewis investigates the conceptual and historical crosscurrents that linked Enlightenment practices of literary fiction with Enlightenment atmospheric science. Both were discourses that sought to represent atmospheric environments; as such, both constructed micro-climates, or what Lewis calls 'bubbles of mediated reality'. This genealogy, Lewis argues, is reworked in an ironic register in Helen Simpson's recent short fiction collection *In-Flight Entertainment*. By reviving this historical dialectic between the macro-level of climate and the intimate atmospheres of personal and fictional experience, Simpson, in Lewis's reading, potentially intervenes in the scalar impasses of our present climatic crisis. Roslyn Jolly examines literary reworkings of nineteenth-century medical theories that apprehended physical and mental illnesses in climatological terms, locating in texts from Henry James and Robert Louis Stevenson the medical practice of therapeutic changes of climate reimagined from the perspective of its dark reverse, the foreign grave. In these literary explorations of the underside of modernising schemes that harnessed climatic technologies for purposes of social and individual improvement, Jolly discovers notable precursors to some of the ambiguities of present-day climatic anxieties and concerns. Literary writing opens up a potential movement between distant climates – those distant in place and those in time.

The disjunctive temporalities and wider conceptual disarray brought about by climate change are shown by Karen Pinkus to problematize oppositions so foundational in our thinking as to be almost invisible – in particular, those between fuel and human life, between the geological forms of past life and the organised political life of human communities. Excavating a rich seam of fossil fuel literature, from Zola's *Germinal* to Upton Sinclair's *King Coal*, Pinkus re-conceives reading in the speculative context of time spans that are measured in millions of years. Beyond the limits of their individual case studies, each of these chapters claims a critical role for the literary imagination in the age of climate change – a claim which, crucially, these authors see to be advanced by the literature of the past as much as that of the present. Literature provides fuel for thinking about climate change, in these chapters, thanks to its modern history as a self-reflective medium for the communication of climatic existence and atmospheric states of being. Thomas H. Ford adopts a second-order perspective on literary climates, addressing the history of climate as a concept within the discipline of literary history, rather than in literary texts directly.

Returning to some key moments in the disciplinary construction of literary history, Ford shows how climate emerged as a central category of cultural understanding in the naturalist model of literary history proposed by Hippolyte Taine – a model that continues to inform literary studies today, if in often unrecognised ways. Both in terms of disciplinary self-understanding and in terms of the interpretation of individual texts, the chapters presented in this section reveal climate to be at once inside and outside writing; it is a framework of feeling and thought that can be inscribed on the page and yet also drifts out to encompass the speculative totality of planetary life.

There is a vast and ever-expanding literature on climate change as a problem of politics and public policy. In its final section, 'Climates of Politics', our volume adopts a more reflective position, investigating ways in which climate has figured historically in the construction of the field of politics. Nick Mansfield examines the problems climate change poses for existing systems of political thought from the point of view of sovereignty. The scalar challenge of climate change exceeds the capacities of any political settlement that could be negotiated by sovereign nation-states. Instead, in its unmanageable gravity and scale, climate change points to a nature out of proportion not only with existing political actors, but also even with our human languages of care and purpose. For Mansfield, what is required involves the deconstruction of sovereignty, refiguring the term so that it can address the particularities of climate change while remaining humble in its aspiration to oversee them. S. Romi Mukherjee turns to the political and ethical implications of an array of contemporary 'para-religions', from Gaia to post-natal ethics to voluntary human extinction movements. In seeking to apply strict post-religious ethical logics to climate change, these movements nihilistically welcome it as an Armageddon of human self-extinction. Identifying this para-religious apocalypticism as a 'liminal strategy for liminal times', Mukherjee reveals how those idiosyncratic movements can illuminate the ideological dimensions of the climatic present. The 'extinction daydreams' they offer reflect the absence of any existing political community capable of undertaking the hard work of adaptation and mitigation: they are expressions of a growing 'collective anxiety about the end', but their desire to trump actual political impotence with imagined extinctions 'undermines the real horizon of the disaster'.

Timothy Morton and Nicole Rogers consider how climate change repositions political life in relation to other domains of social practice – in particular, that of aesthetics. Climate change links new forms of political injustice to concerns about climate change as visually and discursively unrepresentable in its enormity. This entails that, with climate change, aesthetic experience enters into a new and critical relationship with politics. Aesthetics, in effect, comes to figure a praxis of engagement with a catastrophe that is present and yet hidden, at once everywhere and nowhere. Morton relates the onset of climate change, on or about 1790, to the Kantian revolution in western philosophy, which established the essentially modern philosophical principle that we could not talk directly about the real, which was posited as unknowable in itself, but only about our access to that real. In the history of philosophy, modern aesthetics has often been presented as the bridge – or, perhaps, the exploratory placeholder – that overleaps the breach Kant thereby opened in the unity and knowability of historical experience. For Morton, art indeed comes to serve as a platform for thinking about climate change, a means to coax thought beyond its existing conceptual limits so as to approach the temporal and spatial scales of the Anthropocene. Rogers takes up the aesthetic dimension of climate change activism as it manifests in the context of the law, particularly in performative practices of imposture, role-swapping, farce and paradox. Examining recent cases in Australia, Britain and the USA, Rogers outlines modes of activism that have creatively targeted the conceptual instabilities of our cultural and political codes as they are formalised in legal discourse. Could this be the political art – the clima-political art – called for by Morton?

Taken collectively, these chapters demonstrate how the cultural history of climate change impels a rethinking of the limits of the present moment. Much contemporary climate change discourse remains polarised in terms of the timescales it employs: it struggles to connect the perspectives of deep time, ranging from 100,000-year ice cores to 1,000-year futures, with those of the short political present or the immediate news cycle. This intellectual impasse contributes to our general public sense of climatic failure, of ecological malaise and political drift. We have sought alternative measures of the present as potential critical ways of intervening in present debates. In the temporality of climate change, those alive today are effectively geological contemporaries with those living two centuries ago. Our present extends back climatically into its own cultural prehistory. Revisiting this long present allows the construction of a more extended and more nuanced understanding of climate, and of climate change.

Enduring bad faith

In climate change activism, as Rogers shows, paradox often functions as an aesthetic and political medium. Climate activists need to be adept practitioners of paradox, for they tend to be aware that their activities against climate change enrol them in a performative contradiction. Climate change, we understand, is all about us; all contemporary human activities contribute to it, although to vastly varying degrees. Organising, speaking and acting against climate change are all practices that involve carbon emissions; arguing that emissions need to be lowered itself emits carbon. Perversely, even fighting climate change contributes to it – although this is not sufficient reason, it should be affirmed, to cease fighting. The same irony afflicts books such as this. The cultural history of climate change is clearly implicated in its subject matter, particularly when we take into account the material practices required for its emergence and continued existence: campuses, publishers, research time, libraries, archives, academic lifestyles – not to mention international conferences, the activity in which this book, like so many others, was first conceived. Read on a page or on a screen, the carbon budget of these words is not inconsiderable. The environmental humanities are by no means immune to the universal bad faith of climate change: namely, the fact that, however good our intentions, we contribute to it simply by virtue of being alive today, whatever we do.

Whether this delegitimises these disciplines is not a question they can ultimately answer themselves. But they can help call attention to the sense in which, in climatic bad faith, we might begin to register the atmospheric materiality of current-day discourses. The professional anxieties and unease that surround climate change – as the conceptual frameworks that once organised our thinking and shaped our disciplinary landscape dissolve – can be traced to otherwise invisible pressures of a changing climate. Climatic bad faith, in its universality and inescapability, registers the new weight words are taking on in the present, when what we say is directly and materially the stuff not only of climates of opinion but also of climate. Cultural materialism, the medium as the message, the materiality of the signifier: these and other well-worn phrases of critical theory are now acquiring a technical and palpable reality. Via self-implication and conceptual blur, and through bad faith and the collapse of inherited categories, a newly climatic understanding of the materiality of cultural inscription is taking shape. Climate change guarantees our actions, symbolic and otherwise, an inhuman indelibility, imbuing them with a lifetime that far exceeds the spans of recorded history. Insignificant as our acts may be individually, they nonetheless mean something very real once extrapolated, climatically, to the unimaginable level of humankind, of the species considered as a whole. Long after the readers of this book will have died, the traces of its production will still be contributing their miniscule and yet measurable portion to a changed climate. What we understand by climate change will be there to be read and lived by other readers with other eyes – alienated and enduring messages, all about us.

Notes

1   'The Anthropocene began around 1800 with the onset of industrialization, the central feature of which was the enormous expansion in the use of fossil fuels' (Zalasiewicz et al., 2010). More recently, it has been proposed that the Anthropocene be defined 'to begin historically at the moment of detonation of the Trinity A-bomb at Alamgordo, New Mexico, at 05:29:21 Mountain War Time (+-2 s) July 16, 1945' (Zalasiewicz et al., 2015).
2   This argument was first articulated in a postcolonial context by Sunita Narain and Anil Agarwal Narain (1991). For a more recent account, see Nixon (2011).
3   The term 'global warming' has been found to evoke more concern than the term 'climate change'. See Whitmarsh (2009a).
4   See also Lowe (2006).

References

Adey, P. (2010). *Aerial Life: Spaces, Mobilities, Affects*. Oxford: Wiley-Blackwell.
Anderson, B. (2009). Affective atmospheres. *Emotion, Space and Society*, 2 (2), 77–81.
Anderson, K. (2005). *Predicting the Weather: Victorians and the Science of Meteorology*. Chicago: University of Chicago Press.
Boyle, R. ([1692] 2012). *The General History of the Air*. London: Awnsham and John Churchill.
Chakrabarty, D. (2002). Museums in late democracies. *Humanities Research*, 9 (1), 5–12.

Choy, T. (2012). Air's Substantiations. In K. S. Rajan (Ed.), *Lively Capital: Biotechnologies, Ethics, and Governance in Global Markets.* Durham, NC: Duke University Press.

Connor, S. (2010). *The Matter of Air: Science and Art of the Ethereal.* London: Reaktion Books.

Crutzen, P. J. (2002). Geology of Mankind. *Nature, 415* (6867), 23.

Edwards, P. N. (2010). *A Vast Machine: Computer Models, Climate Data, and the Politics of Global Warming.* Cambridge, MA: MIT Press.

Engels, F. (1956). Preface. In *Karl Marx, Capital: A Critique of Political Economy* (Vol. 2). Moscow: Progress Publishers.

Favret, M. A. (2009). *War at a Distance: Romanticism and the Making of Modern Wartime.* Princeton, NJ: Princeton University Press.

Fleming, J. R. (2005). *Historical Perspectives on Climate Change.* Oxford: Oxford University Press.

Golinski, J. (2007). *British Weather and the Climate of Enlightenment.* Chicago: University of Chicago Press.

Howell, R. (2011). Lights, camera …action? Altered attitudes and behaviour response to the climate change film The Age of Stupid. *Global Environmental Change, 21* (1), 177–187.

Hulme, M. (2011). Reducing the future to climate: A story of climate determinism and reductionism. *Osiris, 26,* 245–66.

Hulme, M. (2009). *Why We Disagree About Climate Change: Understanding Controversy, Inaction and Opportunity.* Cambridge: Cambridge University Press.

Janković, V. (2000). *Reading the Skies: A Cultural History of English Weather, 1650–1820.* Chicago: University of Chicago Press.

Jasanoff, S. (2010). A new climate for society. *Theory, Culture & Society, 27,* 233–253.

Kerridge, R. (2013). Ecocriticism. *The Year's Work in Critical and Cultural Theory, 21,* 345–374.

Kuhn, T. S. (1996). *The Structure of Scientific Revolutions (3rd edition).* Chicago: University of Chicago Press [1962].

Latour, B., & Weibel, P. (2005). *Making Things Public: Atmospheres of Democracy.* Cambridge, MA: MIT Press.

Lewis, J. E. (2012). *Air's Appearance: Literary Atmosphere in British Fiction, 1660–1794.* Chicago: University of Chicago Press.

Lowe, T. (2006). *Vicarious experience vs. scientific information in climate change risk perception and behaviour: a case-study of undergraduate students in Norwich, UK.* Norwich: Tyndall Centre for Climate Change Research Technical Report 43.

Markley, R., & Wood, G. D. (Eds.). (2008). Climate and crisis. *Journal for Early Modern Cultural Studies, 8* (2).

Marx, K. ([1843] 1975). *Contribution to a Critique of Hegel's Philosophy of Right.* (R. Livingston, Trans.) Cambridge, MA: MIT Press.

Menely, T. (2012). 'The present obfuscation': Cowper's task and the time of climate change. *PMLA, 127* (3), 477–492.

Morton, T. (2007). *Ecology without Nature.* Cambridge, MA: Harvard University Press.

Moser, S. C., & Dilling, L. (Eds.). (2007). *Creating a Climate for Change: Communicating Climate Change and Facilitating Social Change.* Cambridge: Cambridge University Press.

Narain, S., & Agarwal, A. (1991). *Global Warming in an Unequal World: A Case of Environmental Colonialism.* New Delhi: Centre for Science and Environment.

Nixon, R. (2011). *Slow Violence and the Environmentalism of the Poor.* Cambridge, MA: Harvard University Press.

Poole, S. (2006). *Unspeak: How Words Become Weapons, How Weapons Become a Message, and How That Message Becomes Reality.* New York: Grove Press.

Robin, L. (2013). Histories for Changing Times: Entering the Anthropocene? *Australian Historical Studies, 44* (3), 329–340.

Ross, A. (1991). *Strange Weather: Culture, Science, and Technology in the Age of Limits.* London: Verso.

Turner, G. (1987). *The Sea and Summer.* London: Faber.

Whitmarsh, L. (2009a). What's in a name? Commonalities and differences in public understanding of 'climate change' and 'global warming'. *Public Understanding of Science,* *18*, 401–420.

Whitmarsh, L. (2009b). Behavioural Responses to Climate Change: Asymmetry of Intentions and Impacts. *Journal of Environmental Psychology, 29,* 13–23.

Woolf, V. (2008). Character in fiction. In *Selected Essays.* Oxford: Oxford University Press.

Zalasiewicz, J., Waters, C., Williams, M., Barnosky, A., Cearreta, A., Crutzen, P., et al. (2015). When did the Anthropocene begin? A mid-twentieth century boundary level is stratigraphically optimal. *Quaternary International, 383,* 196–203.

Zalasiewicz, J., Williams, M., Steffen, W., & Crutzen, P. (2010). Response to 'The Anthropocene forces us to reconsider adaptationist models of human-environment interactions'. *Environmental Science & Technology, 44* (16), 6008.

Part I

Climates of history

1 Voices of endurance

Climate and the power of oral history

Deb Anderson

Sheep scatter as a little blue car burls past a stubble-lined paddock, where barely a century ago someone's predecessors staked out an isolated existence by rolling and burning their 'block' of mallee scrub.[1] It's 39 degrees, it's February. Earlier in the day I had embarked on what felt like a drive to the end of the Earth to reach this blip on the map of Victoria's northwest – a now-memorable point on a learning curve through the band of semi-arid country that demarcates the inner edge of Australia's commercial cropping zone, the Mallee. Scooting west of the wheatbelt town of Ouyen, from my car window I note the outward signs of ecosystems in flux: patches of dryland salting, wind erosion and sand-drift bringing fence-posts to their knees. Then abruptly the sand hills slope away and flatten into a vast, quiet expanse of earth.

By the hour I reach Hubie Sheldon's farm, my thoughts have turned to an infamous account of the Mallee. In 1878, a Royal Commission into Crown Land described it as 'sand, scrub and mallee below, the scorching sun and bright blue sky above, and not a sound of life to break the solemn silence' (Blainey, 2006, 147). Such words formed the narrative bed, so to speak, for colonial engineer Alfred Kenyon's futuristic 1912 *Story of the Mallee*, a pioneering battle saga of Australian rural establishment – of men with 'hearts like lions' (Bromby, 1986, 55), new methods and evermore-advanced machines who would make this country 'profitably productive' (Kenyon, [1912] 1982, 1–2). But that story has been retold with time. As Australian environmental historian Tom Griffiths wrote towards the end of the twentieth century, the word 'Mallee' became 'synonymous for heroic, even bloody-minded settlement' (1994, 21).

Unlike Kenyon with his evocative oratory, or Griffiths with his compelling environmental history – or me, here with a voice recorder to capture snippets of the past in the present – Sheldon knows the Mallee as 'home'. Tellingly, he calls this country 'forgiving' (Sheldon, 2005).[2] Not far from Ngallo ('a spring') and a shearing shed shy of the South Australian border lies the remote wheat-sheep property where Sheldon lives on his own. He has spent most of his life here, as did his father and mother before him – and his father's parents before them, having selected their block before the First World War, in 1910. Almost a century later, across an old kitchen table in an ageing farmhouse on the edge of a colossal swathe of tilled soil, Sheldon picks up the threads of *his* story of the Mallee. He draws upon a multigenerational 'archive' of memories – oral testimony of a way of life, preserved on grounds of enduring cultural, historical and evidentiary value – to speak of the lived experience of drought.

The story begins in an all-too-familiar Australian saga of rural pioneering endurance. This is a boom-and-bust tale of backbreaking work, told with grim humour. Anchored in that wide-brown-horizon version of the past, this becomes a survivor narrative through sporadic environmental extremes: severe droughts, monster dust-storms, 'nasty' frosts, 'hellishing' heatwaves and plagues of rabbits and mice. The tale twists into a period of rural decline – of crisis so commonplace as to seem clichéed (Bourke & Lockie, 2001, 1) – to depict an agro-industrial present clouded by economic uncertainty, amplified by prolonged drought and heightened by public debate on global climate change. Then, the plot thickens. The scene itself, of climate in the wheatbelt, shifts in ways that defy generations of lived experience. That final straw, so to speak, prompts a reflexive idealisation of history *as* the future, and of 'a new generation of pioneers' who will 'survive' by learning to 'pull back' (Sheldon, 2005, 2007).

'When you look at Australia and its history,' Sheldon says, 'while we've been here a coupl'a hundred years, we've probably only really developed the country in the last hundred, and more particularly in the last fifty.' He looks at me intently:

> That's a very, *very* brief time. And we've altered this landscape a hell of a lot in a short period o' time. And if that's gonna change our weather patterns – which it, well, it looks like it *is* – we need to look at what we've done in the past and try and learn (Sheldon, 2005).

Valuing oral history

Cultural engagement with climate is under constant renegotiation – as oral historical research is apt to reveal. Oral history has already challenged the historical enterprise, if not the hegemony of scholarly authority, generating heated debate over the relationship between memory and history, past and present (Perks & Thomson, 2006). Amid the groundswell of interest in recent decades among humanities scholars in addressing ecological issues and crises, oral historians have been 'listening on the edge' (eg. Cave & Sloan, 2014), gathering discourse on social-environmental problems grounded in stories of lived experience. The documentation and interpretation of life narratives can be viewed as instrumental, insofar as they shed light on the significance of storytelling context. As historian Stephen Sloan wrote:

> [M]oments of crises or disaster can offer an environment when the larger weaknesses or strengths of a society are quite visible … rendering quite clearly societal, political, cultural and economic realities that may not be as obvious during periods of comparative tranquillity (Sloan, 2014, 265).

My research explores moments of extreme weather experience and climate perception in a bid to illuminate not only how climate shapes culture, but also how culture shapes climate. Through the spontaneity of oral narrative, the animated interchange of dialogue and the compulsion to 'share authority' when working with living memory (Frisch, 1990), how might we broaden and deepen the national climate conversation 'beyond' the science?

This chapter argues for the significance of the cultural and historical dimensions of climate (cf. Hulme, 2015), while exploring the power and application of oral history to shed light on the interpretive problems of climate change.[3] Such problems have been branded 'wicked', a term anthropologist Steve Rayner (in Hulme, 2009, xxi–xxii) qualifies as 'a way of describing problems of mind-bending complexity, characterized by "contradictory certitudes" and thus defying elegant, consensual solutions'. In this respect, oral history research can help us understand the tensions implicit in the ways experience, memory and history act on lives over time. For even as oral history can mediate change or promote a more widely shared historical consciousness, oral tradition may form a source of resistance to it (Frisch, 1990). This facet alone serves as a constant reminder of the density of life stories as cultural artefacts – and, arguably, it affords opportunity. As historian Marjorie Shostak notes: 'It is just this tension – the identifiable in endless transformation – that is the currency of personal narratives, as they reveal the complexities and paradoxes of human life.' (2006, p. 392)

Indeed if, as Australian historian Tim Sherratt wrote, 'climate and culture create each other across a shifting, permeable frontier' (2005, 4), then those words form a near-maxim for the dynamics of research on which this writing draws. An extensive oral history collection was conducted in rural Australia for Museum Victoria, the state's premier cultural institution, from 2004 to 2007 – a series of annual recordings with twenty-two members of wheatbelt communities dotted across the semi-arid Victorian Mallee.[4] This was a period that became known as the millennium drought, which peaked in 2006–7 and some scientists deemed the 'worst drought in 1,000 years' (Vidal, 2006). Discursive themes emerged early in these history recordings: of drought anchored in the celebratory remembrance of past survival; of uncertainty as ongoing change in the Australian countryside posed a threat to Mallee livelihoods; and of putative adaptation as local communities sought solace in a historicized capacity to cope with trying social-environmental conditions.

Meaning is seldom static, however, for memory is innately revisionist. Fortuitously, the timing of the research coincided with a momentous shift in Australian public awareness of climate change. That shift, to me, formed a moment of big history – elevating how people *live with* stories over time. The Mallee Climate Oral History Collection thus captured significant moments of reflection and self-reflexivity on the meaning of drought, revealing contestation over expertise and experience as inherently partial forms of knowledge, exposing the core interpretive problems of climate change. Despite shifts in climate change perception, each Mallee oral history represented a historical, battler narrative of endurance – revealing both livelihoods and identities at stake.

Thus, this chapter examines the notion of the self-preservative power of narrative and oral tradition for a rural culture under threat. Framed by discourse analysis and the ethnographic techniques of cultural journalism and anthropology, each of which seeks to comprehend the world in the interviewees' own terms (Bird, 2005), it allows space for the richness of detail that oral history offers – illuminating the *other* types of history that oral stories can tell, and their distinctive transference at the interstices of history, biography, culture and place. Amid divisive debate over rural futures in Australia, this work underscores how strongly conceptions of climate are shaped by historical narratives of identity, in this case forming both a cultural legacy and a shield from anxieties about the future. In the face of imminent and immense change, many people in the dryland Mallee have been gearing up to endure more.

Endurance

In the late twentieth century, the development of climate science has brought undeniable evidence that global warming is altering the Earth's climate. Attempts to assemble a 'big picture' of global risk has manifested as a polarising moral and political dispute over human agency, both within and outside of the scientific community. Since the 1980s at least, as historian William Stevens noted (1999), public debate over whether global warming was human-induced was cast as a dispute between two positions: the doubters and the believers. Early in the twenty-first century, across the globe there appeared to have been a rapid rise in the number of believers. This 'history of the present' formed the backdrop for this research.

Ideas of aberrance have been common to most ways of thinking about drought throughout the modern period of Western culture – and formed the forefront of the research. Insofar as ideas about nature represent an interplay of physical and social forces, the social construction of drought in Australia has been shaped by an at-times brutal social and environmental history that commenced on this continent at the climax of the Industrial Revolution – a 200-year struggle to 'green' a drought-prone, brown land (Barr & Cary, 1992). In that context, drought has been apprehended as a temporal shock, exciting horror, alienation and dread. As art historian Roslynn Haynes wrote, 'memories of drought and fear of its recurrence have stalked the collective memory for two hundred years' (1998, 251).

Despite a growing awareness of Australia in biophysical terms, the drama of aridity still grips the popular imagination: drought makes national news headlines today much as it did a century ago (West & Smith, 1996). Commonwealth Bureau of Meteorology records since the 1860s can show a 'severe' drought has occurred in Australia, on average, once every eighteen years (Lindesay, 2003); conversely, the longest sequence of years Australia has been relatively free of drought is but eleven years (Heathcote, 2000). Yet as government scientist John Williams lamented during the millennium drought, the Australian psyche remains 'dominated by dreams of water' and drawn to notions of drought-proofing the land (Williams, 2003, 40). The editors of *Beyond Drought*, Australia's foremost anthology on the topic, took that idea one step further. Linda Courtenay Botterill and Melanie Fisher argued a more sophisticated climate literacy was an overdue aspect of 'learning to be Australian'. 'Ideally,' they wrote, 'the term "drought" itself should be struck from the national language and replaced with "climate variability" – or perhaps not be the subject of discussion at all!' (2003, 3)

In contradistinction, exploring life stories about drought as cultural artefacts can open the door to a nuanced historical approach. Droughts – like floods, bush-fires and cyclones and yet distinct in terms of time, space and mythology – have 'punctuated' Australian rural, regional and national cultural histories (West & Smith, 1997). 'Drought' has played a role in the construction of a 'harsh' and 'unpredict-able' climate and in the mythologising of rural battlers, shaping foundational nar-ratives of struggle and hope. As sociologists Brad West and Philip Smith wrote, drought retains 'a unique place among Australian natural disasters as the generator of a national solidaristic narrative' (1997, 205). The concept of drought to which I refer, therefore, is a *cultural* term. Through an examination of how the past shapes present understandings of climate, drought can be viewed as a concept whose pri-mary connotations are less related to rainfall than to an overarching, mythic narra-tive of endurance.

Remarkably, for a country where the effects of isolation, landscape and colonialism have been invoked repeatedly as explanations of Australian character (Gillen, 2002), there was little published on drought as a cultural concept when I began this research in 2003 – in stark contrast to the swell of interest in the topic since (eg. Botterill & Fisher, 2003; McKernan, 2005; Sherratt, Griffiths & Robin, 2005). Sherratt (2005) wrote that, until recently, even historians neglected to take seriously the topic of Australian climate. He noted Geoffrey Blainey's lament in 1971 that although climatic events such as drought have shaped 'some of the most dismal eras of our history', the influence of climate on Australian history has been 'largely unstudied' (3). Climate, Sherratt continues, was instead 'often imagined as the back-drop against which history is played out'. Further, in *Cultural History in Australia*, Griffiths outlined a dominant sense of causality in Australian historiography, which runs *from* nature *to* culture. Nature has often been thought to be the 'hard, physical, earthy, empirical reality against which culture defines itself' (Griffiths, 2003, 67).

Recording oral histories on drought puts ways of thinking about climate and identity front and centre. Indeed, the approach I took to the Mallee was concerned first with how meaning is created, rather than simply what the meaning is. Perhaps it was an approach born of necessity, for there was and remains but a handful of ethnographic studies on the Australian lived experience of climate (the prominent exception is Stehlik, Gray & Lawrence, 1999). Yet where recollections of a 'golden age' of agriculture still loom large in Australian rural historiography (Davison & Brodie, 2005), oral history presents a means to explore the tensions between the rural past and present.

Drought 'makes who we are'

In Victoria, the most intensively settled of Australian states, the northwest corner is the most sparsely populated region, with the lowest annual rainfall (Lumb, 1987). In counterpoint, it is an ultra-productivist landscape – a region driven by forces of capital accumulation and engaged in ever-larger-scale industrial agriculture. The Victorian Mallee covers 39,300km^2, or about one-sixth of the state.[5] Up to one million hectares is put in dryland (or rain-fed) crops each year, 'fed' on an annual 'average' of 200 to 500 millimetres of rain (Department of Primary Industries Victoria, 2007). Here 'productive land' is considered 'the backbone of the economy' and about 2,000 dryland farmers produce half of Victoria's annual cereals crop, mostly wheat (Mallee Catchment Management Authority, 2003, 36).

If it is through narrativity that we constitute social identity (Somers, 1994), then stories of drought have been integral to the making of the Mallee. As one Mallee interviewee put it, drought 'makes who we are' (Hogan, 2005). Rural histories of the region have represented spirited sagas of community struggle, endurance and hope in 'battling' a harsh climate. 'Settled' from the mid-1800s with the establishment and subsequent collapse of pastoralism, the region was 'opened up' in the wholesale clearing of mallee forest and advance of dryland agriculture in the twentieth century. European occupation of the Mallee has been narrated predominantly as an ongoing struggle on a frontier beset by environmental extremes, 'where coping with disastrous drought was part of the pioneer lifestyle' (van Veldhuisen, 2001, cover; cf. Torpey, 1986; Bate, 1989). Drought has tempered the triumphalism of 'modern' Mallee land settlement, at times culminating in disaster and strife ('Is the Mallee Blowing Away?' cried *The Australasian* newspaper in January 1941). 'Disastrous drought' has even led to bleak periods of exodus – as Griffiths noted, of 'failure' so distressing that families abandoned their holdings 'in the middle of the night' (1994, 22). But for *those who stayed* and their ardent successors who remain determined to stay put, stories of drought survival have been elevated into historical terms.

Although Mallee histories form selective dedications to pioneers 'who succeeded because they never admitted defeat' (Nixon, 1965, cover), the region's name derives from bushland considered by local indigenous people to be a supporter of life – for the water in mallee roots (Hopgood, 1989). In this sense, 'the Mallee' marks an historical 'frontier' – an imagined geographical, temporal feature that represents the limits of knowledge and of 'disposability over history' (Thomas, 1996, 66). Occupying the region for 40,000 to 60,000 or more years before European invasion were traditional custodians of eight language groups (Mallee Catchment Management Authority, 2003).[6] Koori history here, especially near the Murray River, is significant because that water source and local quarries allowed relative permanency; the region today is among the nation's richest cultural heritage areas (Mallee District Aboriginal Services, 2013). About 3 per cent of the region's current population is of indigenous origin and their retention of physical, spiritual, social and cultural ties to land is evidenced in the fact all public land in the Victorian Mallee has been claimed under Native Title (Australian Bureau of Statistics, 2009).

So too the Mallee has formed a boundary between 'settlers' and an 'extreme' nature-as-wilderness. The term 'mallee' applies to eucalypts with a multi-stemmed habit. This makes the bush especially hardy: at the base of the stems is a woody structure, or lignotuber, that actually enables vegetative recovery after fire or other ecological stress (Brooker, et al., 2002). In contrast, mallee bushland was documented by nineteenth-century newcomers as 'useless scrub' (Parkes & Cheal, 1989, 7). *That* term was a form of linguistic overkill, for in Australian English the word 'scrub' already denotes a plant species liable to be considered as having little value (Arthur, 2003). The denotation was manifest in its wholesale clearance. In northwest Victoria, about three-quarters of the original mallee lands were cleared to make way for industry (Griffiths, 1994). Profoundly, then, 'the Mallee' is a place-name founded upon absence. To gaze out across the Mallee today is, on occasion, to see no mallee trees at all.

Weathering loss

Conversations on the weather can be relegated to the task of space-filler, or viewed as mere 'chatter', replete with the elements of phatic small talk. But a round of Mallee oral histories in spring 2004 and summer 2005 procured fascinating tales of optimism amid hardship, of enduring vulnerability and of rural community *as* resilience – and more.

Although oral history does not provide an exacting document about historical or categorical 'real' events, I soon learnt that oral testimony in effect defied 'reality' by challenging accepted categories of history. The stories people shared in fact complicated dominant ideas on drought – narratives of endurance that have enabled a more singular version of Australian history – with the memory and experience of rural modernity. These were stories grounded in *totalizing* biographical narratives of place, labour, family and community – multigenerational understandings historically linked in rural culture, if hardened through crisis, which constitute cultural artefacts. The scale and scope of the life-interviewing process quickly underlines how stories function as sites of self-expression and communal interpretation. Historian Alessandro Portelli concretizes this idea in his assertion that oral stories 'communicate what history means to human beings' (1997, 42).

The beauty of working with oral history feels personal, for it lends the listener a sense of raw immediacy, an appreciation of direct experience. Let me share a moment from September 2004.

This first excerpt is deliberately presented in original transcript to illustrate challenges in form and interpetation. Lynne Healy, a health worker then in her mid-40s, had grown up on a farm near the outpost of Culgoa (population today: 250) in the southern Victorian Mallee. The farm had belonged to her father's family. She was the eldest child, and all she'd wanted to do was be a farmer: 'I was always out the farm with Dad' (Cooke & Healy, 2004). Over the years, like most farmers in an era of farm expansion, her Dad went into debt to buy more land – up to a total of about 2,500 acres (or 1,000 hectares). But then he bought half a block of land 'at the wrong time', she said:

> During the 1980 drought which was really really severe, um, we actually lost our farm. Um. And, it had a *huge* impact on our family. Um, I can remember my mother ended up in hospital; um, she had a breakdown. Um, I can remember, Dad sitting at the table at night, drinking, and um just, not even

communicating – or when he did, you know there was, um, arguments and things like that, it was just so tense in the, in the family. Um. And Dad then was in his, well into his 60s, um, so I mean there was nothing that he could do, no you know no other job that he could do anyway – not that he wanted to do anything else. And, um. Yeah so, through the finance companies and the banks, they um foreclosed on the property, and um, and we lost our farm. Um. [pause]

And I suppose, one of the hardest things about that was that, the following year was a really good year (in Cooke & Healy, 2004).

Oral histories involve *oral* sources. As Portelli (1998) reminds us, oral histories contain bearers of cultural meaning that are different to the segmentary traits of writing (even in Western societies, where literacy and self-consciousness arguably permeate culture). Transcription, however, turns the aural object into visual text, where punctuation tends to be redefined by grammatical rules, making the transcript 'readable'. Presenting an unedited transcript, as above, conveys a sense of how meaning is carried in the rhythm and pause of speech, spotlighting emotion and affect – even conjuring an image of Healy's body language, as she pushed at her own instinctive hesitancy to recount a traumatic experience.

Oral history, therefore, gives the researcher an appreciation of the way events affected people then as well as how the recollection affects them now. Indeed, the rising anger and volume in Healy's voice seemed to be biting back at the past. This personalized form of 'anti-history' spoke of an attachment to her special place – marked out with boundaries, clearing, working and 'the physical presence of being' (Read, 1996, 8) – now 'lost' to the inexorable logic of capital, while the social custom of endurance, of holding on for the next 'good year', prevailed.

Interview materials are, as Frisch argues, 'unique in themselves being documents *about* the past' (1990, 81). Whatever their limits as history in traditional terms, he writes, oral histories are 'fascinating in what they reveal about historical memory patterns as cultural documents' (1998, 36). Where Healy gives voice to despair, making her story public draws into play the cultural politics embodied in the problem of collective memory – raising questions about historical issues of pride, shame and resilience in rural communities. Farm families rarely sought professional counselling during the early 1980s droughts in southeast Australia; research confirms the prevailing rules for behaviour among farm families, such as 'keeping it in the family' and 'keeping a stiff upper lip', often meant the problems they faced were obscured by myths of harmony, independence and self-reliance (Craig & Killen in Lawrence, 1987, 44). When local farmers ended up buying Healy's parents' property, her father found it tough to 'then turn around and watch someone bring wheat into the silo off his land' (Healy in Cooke & Healy, 2004). Her parents ended up leaving the district.

Narrative framing also sheds light on a greater story of rural past and present – of *loss*, writ large in living memory: of the impacts of global capital restructuring since the 1970s, of rural decline amid shifts in the political economy of agriculture, of socio-economic hardship amid the transformation of agricultural technologies and industries, reformation of government policy and ongoing depopulation of rural Australia. 'The control was taken away from the farmers,' Healy said bluntly (2004), recalling bank practices in the 1980s. 'I mean, they put the interest rates up from like 5–7 per cent up to 25 per cent and all this rubbish.' In telling *that* story, she shared a perception common to this oral-history collection – of unresolved national and global tensions being displaced onto local people. She continued: 'It was like the government was just saying, *Well, basically we've got too many farmers here, we've got too much debt between 'em all, okay there's gotta be a cut-off line … We'll cull them.*'

Where Healy's story denotes division within the community and differentiation from the state in the interests of maintaining livelihood *and* identity, we gain rare insight into the ways agrarian ideology enables farm communities to legitimise local interpretations of global misfortune. As geographers Ian Gray and Geoffrey Lawrence wrote, agrarianism could be seen to have 'facilitated the exploitation of farming families by capital' (2001, 91), yet if we factor in farmers' self-reflexivity, we find they themselves have used agrarian ideology to 'justify' self-exploitation too.

Dwelling in uncertainty

With a bundle of transcript and audio files, I intended to wrap up the oral-history collection in 2005. Things changed quite rapidly within the research timeframe, however. By autumn of that year, about half of Australia's arable land was drought-affected. As reports of rural hardship began to flood into the public realm, farm lobby groups stressed this was 'no normal drought' (Peters in Pash, 2005, 3). By mid-May, economic forecasters were predicting 'catastrophic' consequences, including wiping up to a third off Australia's forecast economic growth (Lee, 2005). By June, as the National Climate Centre released its forecast for little rain in sight, the federal Bureau of Agricultural Resource Economics forewarned that the drought could wipe up to a half a percentage point from Australia's Gross Domestic Product growth in the coming financial year (Waldon, et al., 2005, 1–2). As the dry conditions lingered, the Australian historical and meteorological record books were rewritten. Some Mallee farmers were telling the media of having endured nearly nine dry years (Khadem & Marino, 2005, 3). Much as droughts in the twentieth century had been apprehended as 'unexpectedly severe' in intensity or duration (West & Smith, 1996, 94), the nation was pronounced as suffering one of the worst droughts on record – 'in our history', stated Australia's conservative prime minister of the day, John Howard (Schubert, 2005, 4).

This prolonged drought was discursively intensifying as an indicator of a new narrative of social-environmental destiny, however. In July, the Australian Government's Greenhouse Office released *Climate Change Risk and Vulnerability*, its first high-level strategic assessment of such issues in Australia. That report deemed the agricultural sector a top priority, with widespread drought, heatwaves, bushfires and storms driving home the nature of the key stresses ecosystems faced under conditions of climate change (Allen Consulting Group, 2005). Public discourse on 'weird weather' began to fuse with that on the greater problems posed by global warming – 'wicked' problems that defied rational and optimal solutions (Christoff, 2005). As a public issue in Australia, anthropogenic climate change owed much to the scientific community for its rise to prominence, which, as political scientist Mark Lutes noted, has the effect of reinforcing 'the idea that scientists should play the lead role in structuring debates around what appears as their natural territory' (1998, 162). Yet problems of interpretation remained, and lay at the core of the global warming 'debate' that persisted. As political scientist Peter Christoff wrote, doubts and anxieties framing such debate took shape as 'issues of public concern' – questions over the veracity of perceived change in weather patterns, its causes and timing, and who to turn to for answers (2005, 13). He continued: 'The instability of "modern" ways of constituting time, knowledge and risk runs through the heart of global warming as an issue' (13). The concurrent millennium drought was no mere temporal shock; it began to represent a *cultural* shock with a 'new', intergenerational temporality in tow.

Compelled to extend my fieldwork, I began to develop a longitidunal study. By the summer of 2006, I was back out on the Mallee Highway, criss-crossing the region – where talk of uncertainty about climate change now peppered discussion of drought. The same interviewees began reflecting on their earlier observations. Some doubted themselves. Others doubted the climate science. All doubted the politicians, who had weighed in heavily on climate change debate in Australia – emphasising how, as sociologist Rosemary McKechnie argues, the 'local' has assumed 'new significance' in place- and identity-based responses to global change (1996, 126). Indeed most of the interviewees showed little interest in questions about climate that could be answered purely in the abstract.

I revisited Des and Maree Ryan and their son Andrew in February 2006. Des was a third-generation Mallee farmer on their wheat-sheep property near Manangatang, in the eastern Mallee. His side of the family had spent nearly a hundred years on the property, in which time it had grown from one block (640 acres) to nine (5,760). In this sense, the Mallee landscape was also a 'timescape', a term sociologist Barbara Adam (1998, 131–2) used to explain how, in agricultural landscapes, the future is imagined in a way that allows people to conceive of themselves upon a multigenerational continuum. Maree said of their farm, 'It's got that continuity. It's also got that history ... Our family *created* that' (Ryan, et al., 2006). This was a dimension of the socialisation of place, in that the history of their landholding was not only material but also cultural, entailing a social and emotional geography that strengthened their attachment to place (cf. Read, 1996).

Evidence of that cultural history was voiced in folkloric discourse on weather and climate 'cycles' – an idea handed down through generations of oral tradition, 'performed' here as Mallee farm talk. In fact, cycles dominated the Ryans' interpretation of patterns of Mallee climate, on interannual and interdecadal scales. This historical idea of cycles was documented in Australia as early as the 1830s; such faith in weather lore had its roots in the eighteenth century, a time when farmers and mariners became most interested in and skilled at reading the 'signs' of the weather (Keating, 1992). Although science ushered in a new form of statistical regulation of Australian droughts in the twentieth century, the idea of cycles lingers today – so much so that the Bureau of Meteorology still finds the need to discredit it (Crowder, 1995).

When I first met the Ryans, two years previously, in 2004, they had quickly described drought as part of a Mallee climate cycle; their district was then experiencing a 'drier cycle' (Ryan, et al., 2004). But they understood that the cycle would turn in time. 'The old-timers used to say *one in about ten* ... but in recent times it's been sorta *three year in ten*,' Des had chuckled. 'But I've no doubt that it will turn around back to the one in ten ... when the cycle turns again.'

By 2006, talk of climate change prompted discourse of uncertainty, however. Like all interviewees involved in this oral history collection, the Ryans began reconciling local knowledge of climate, gained through lived experience, with more abstract ideas received through science and the media:

Do you believe in climate change?

Andrew: Well it's pretty hard not to ... if you take on board the evidence ... It does look like there is going to be some definite climate change but to what degree ... who knows? ...

Des: I'm not sure ... Might be climate change to a certain degree but it's also just one of them cycles. I dunno whether I've learnt, or I just hope, that's what it is.

Maree: Unfortunately, I think it is climate change as well. It's cyclical, but yes, there is climate change ...

Des: Every time there's been some extreme in weather, one way or the other, we hear this 'climate change' come up.

Maree: But historically even, I think I can remember our parents saying, 'the climate ... it used to be hotter', or 'it used to be ...' – you know?

Des: Yeah. I think if we go back to the '40s or something, well the climate's probably changed for the better to what it could've been then! (Ryan, et al., 2006)

Uncertainty is far from novel in farming culture. Rather, Carla Roncoli and a team of anthropologists noted in a study of farming 'meteorological meanings' that uncertainty forms 'a building block of local systems of thought' (Roncoli, et al., 2003, 188). This was evident in the Ryans' oral history, where expertise and experience were considered inherently partial forms of knowledge on climate, conceived as a multi-generational work-in-progress that unfolds through time. Talk of 'vicious' cycles could form the subject of grim humour, while the memory of a cycle 'turning' could invoke a generic discourse of hope.

On that note, the above excerpt of the Ryans' story shares detail that, again, cannot be read off the page: people generate distinctive ways of articulating and interpreting their own (extra)ordinary lives. Through narrative structure as well as voice, intonation and delivery, grim humour was evident in Des's speech. This was gendered – most common to the stories of drought gathered from Mallee farming men for this collection. Intriguingly, a 1960s American study found grim humour was also common in the stories of farming men in the Dust Bowl region of the Great Plains, considered in climatic and some historical respects to be comparable to Australia's Mallee.

That study tabulated grim humour by area, revealing three of the driest counties had greater numbers of farmers exhibiting the personality trait, which geographer Thomas Saarinen surmised served 'to relieve the anxiety brought about by facing a fickle and harsh environment' (1966, 113). Of course, Australian humour – with its self-mockery, anti-authoritarian outlook and dark sense of irony – has a history that many writers have traced to colonisation and the response to a new environment; the nation state has a web page on the topic (Big Black Dog Communications and Australian Government, 2007). Some even argue Australian humour is a manifestation *of* the climate: dry and full of extremes (Little, [2003] 2009). There is that sense of causality of which Griffiths wrote, running from nature to culture.

Insofar as humour derives from *perception* of predicament and risk, grim humour about drought may form a coping strategy that aids adjustment to arduous and exhausting circumstances, yet it is also, surely, composed with a sense of intended audience. Perhaps grim humour masks the pathos of troubling contemplations of an evaporating future, forming resistance to dominant discourse on climate change and the capacity of modernisation to construct people *as* risk communities (or at-risk communities). As cultural scholars Warwick Mules, Tony Schirato and Bert Wigman have noted, in Australian society, drought 'is a symbolic event that involves strategic positioning of meanings about what it is to be a farmer' (1995, 243).

Returning year upon year to extend the oral-history collection in the Mallee, meantime, was illuminating the fixity of traditional methods of historical research. As historian William Schneider (2008) has argued, the act of *re*telling is a critical narrative act, for stories reflect current understanding through their retelling. In this project, time and again I was challenged to allow for a change in the weather and in people's minds too.

Listening for change

The power of time and chance cannot be underestimated as agents in oral historical research. By late 2006, the national gaze had fixed upon climate change – and, reflexively, to Australian public discourse on global warming. The spring of 2006, in particular, brought a dramatic shift in public discourse on climate (startling even for a scholar immersed in talk of weather extremes). The Climate Institute of Australia reported by March 2007 that concern about climate change was at 'an all time high'; its survey showed climate change ranked as more important than housing afford-ability and national security. The 'vast majority' of Australians no longer doubted climate change was 'real' or attributable to human activity (Climate Institute of Australia, 2007). The contemporary experience of extreme weather had sharpened the public interest in climate change, affording people a sense they were 'seeing' the effects now. Scientist Snow Barlow also highlighted the power of popular culture, in particular the film *An Inconvenient Truth*, as a medium for mainstream climate science:

> The record maximum temperatures and the accompanying bush fires of early spring 2006 dramatically underlined to the community that this is not just a

severe drought – it is climate change. At the same time we had the Stern report providing credible economic analysis of the costs of continued inaction and Al Gore's Oscar-winning 'slide-show' bringing the science of climate change to millions in Australia and internationally (in Hannink, Scott & Sim-Jones, 2007, 4).

Although the global politics of climate change appeared to be turning a corner (see Rootes, 2008), in Australia a federal election loomed – and the interpretation of climate change seemed entrenched in the politics of climate. In a moralising 'debate' over scientific certainty, predictions of runaway climate change were alternately feared or dismissed as a grand narrative of apocalypse (see Christoff, 2008).

When I returned to the Mallee to record a final round of oral histories in February 2007 (how could I not?), the shift in broader awareness of climate change was apparent. Certainly, dialogue on the reinterpretation of drought in the context of global warming highlighted the intensity of global environmental risks pervading society. However, the interviews also drew attention to the mediation of those risks through abstract systems, and to the significance of people's sense of trust in, or distrust of, the media and politicians at that time.

One of the 'surest' parts of the Mallee for dryland farming was a pocket of land near Walpeup in the western Mallee. That's how Merle and Robert Pole, wheat-sheep farmers in their 60s, had described their farm when I first met them in 2005. Walpeup rainfall was 'patchy', Robert said: one farm, one *paddock*, could get soaked while the neighbours missed out (Pole, et al., 2005). But for the past twenty years, their property 'Seven Pines' had been blessed with a few points of rain at the right time, almost every year. Might not get much, they said, but always got some. Thus, the Poles' interpretation of drought was anchored in remembrance of lived experience, of what they and previous landholders here (Robert's forebears) had survived. 'The good thing about the droughts that I can remember,' said Robert, 'is they only lasted one year, and the following year they bounced back with record yields and record prices.' Although the grain price outlook was 'not brilliant', he added, 'we just hope that can happen perhaps again this year coming – that we can bounce back with a good crop.' It seemed historical narratives of labour and place were crucial to beliefs in providential climate in 'next year' country. As Robert explained: 'In the back of your mind you always think, *Oh well, next year'll be good* … And even if it's not, *Well, the next year will definitely be alright.*'

Two years later, a follow-up interview with the Pole family proffered unique insights into the utility of an old idea of climate (cf. Hulme, 2015). In 2007, Robert and Merle reflected openly on their earlier perceptions and subsequent shift in interpretation:

Robert: Last year, when we knew we were in for a drought, we just thought, *Oh well, this is just a bloody good drought* – and didn't think too much about climate change … We sort of talked with me old father … In the '30s and '40s, they went through some very dry years and we just thought, *Oh this is the return of some of that* – we have a few years of up and down … Didn't think much of climate change until perhaps the media picks up on it, or the politicians pick up on it, and then you start thinking of it a bit more. And watch a few documentaries on it, of Al Gore's –

Merle: Yeah, *The Inconvenient Truth*. And when you see films like that, it really does make you think. And when you see the icebergs –

Robert: The icebergs, that's what really hit home to me. When you see what's happening on the South and the North Pole and the ice melting away … you think perhaps something really is happening (Pole & Pole, 2007).

While foregrounding social (familial) dynamics, the above excerpt reveals a multi-scalar negotiation of meaning. Where local climate is measured against experience, 'global' change is *understood* to be mediated by politics and representation. As environmental sociologists Phil Macnaghten and John Urry have pointed out, contemporary risks transcend the senses and extend to the distant and the extraordinarily long term, hence people have become dependent on increasingly global 'expert systems' of knowledge. At the same time, they proposed, the unrelenting reporting of global disasters has heightened people's sense of powerlessness. Thus the abstraction of global risks such as climate change through science and the media affected personal identity and ontological security (1998, 99–100).

For the Poles, risk had sharpened long-term commitment. Like most Mallee dryland farmers, their commitment to landholding was multigenerational, constituting a precondition for long-term agricultural survival. As Merle said: 'If it *is* climate change, we've still paid good money for the land. You're committed; you're *here* … You're in for the long haul, so you've really got to make the best of it' (Pole & Pole, 2007). In lieu of that commitment, she pondered how projections of rapid climate change disrupted established ways of thinking about locality. Further, time itself had shrunk:

You think, *How can it happen that quickly?* Like, there's been droughts and that in the past, and then you get some good years – and so on … You know, *Can things change this quickly that we can actually see it happening before our eyes?* (Pole & Pole, 2007)

Certainly, the 2006 agricultural season gave Australian farmers plenty to question. It turned out to be just the 'evidence' that another interviewee in the Mallee Climate Oral History Collection, harvesting contractor Brent Morrish, needed to accept that something 'bigger' than drought was happening on the land. I managed to catch up with him and his wife Melissa only twice, in 2005 and 2007. They were farmers in their 30s whose contracting work kept them travelling most of the year, harvesting thousands of hectares of crop across eastern Australia – through South Australia and Victoria, up the coast through New South Wales and into southern Queensland. What the pair had witnessed of Australian agriculture in 2006 was unlike anything they'd seen before, Brent said. He had initially thought 'it was a bit of a drought', but the fact he had secured contracts for harvesting indicated 'things were gonna be okay'. On reflection, he wondered if he'd been 'a little bit naïve':

> I'd driven for about seven-and-a-half hours and driven through most of New South Wales. There was some areas there that I've never seen in my life – in my career as a contractor – *failed* … It was dirt, barren; there was nothing. There was stock in poorer condition up there that I've never seen before. It was pretty disheartening all around. That's when it sorta sunk in to me that, you know, things aren't looking very good (Morrish & Morrish, 2007).

They'd seen similarly dismal yields across Victoria and Queensland; the business was nearly 10,000 hectares short on the previous year's harvest. Brent called the season 'probably one *not* to remember'. I asked him whether this shaped his thoughts on climate change. He didn't flinch: 'Oh, up until six months ago, I would have said no.'

That acceptance of climate change hinged on what was seen and *heard* – in the intergenerational transfer of memories through oral tradition. To help understand dry seasons, Brent said he relied on older generations' stories of climate norms and past extremes. The 2006 season defied generations of lived experience – prompting a search for meaning. 'Through my travels, I've sorta in the last six months … spoken to as many older men – you know, the older the better – to try and find out a little bit of history of past droughts and tough times,' he said. 'They don't know. *They're* not sure.' When they began to doubt, he did too.

Rayner notes that in the 'selective' incorporation of scientific ideas about climate into social practice, 'we tend to incorporate new information that is compatible with our existing views' (2003, 288). As the above excerpt of oral history reveals, competence in Mallee farming, thus coping with drought, was tied to lived experience of local practice and culture, which lingered as expertise on climate and change. In turn, the *cultural* idea of climate enabled local people to live with their weather. In this case, Brent questioned his very capacity *to know* climate (as an index of weather), especially when it came to the Mallee farming environment. 'I'm not old enough perhaps,' he said, 'to know what a good season is' (Morrish & Morrish, 2007).

Living with future drought

Memory is not only a living, active engagement between past and present; memory making is a critical way of engaging with imagined futures. Australian historian Alistair Thomson observes that memory making can be conceived of as an act of 'composure'. 'We make or repress memories of experiences which are still painful and "unsafe" because they do not easily accord with our present identity,' he wrote, 'or because their inherent traumas or tensions have never been resolved. We seek composure: an alignment of our past, present and future lives' (1998, 301). In that light, these oral histories on drought are as much about documenting memory, or its use as a didactic tool, as they are about what people want to remember *as* history.

Further, while the events of our pasts are unchangeable, the stories we recount of our lived experiences change with time. Each time, people deploy a process of amplification and screening. In that sense, the Mallee Climate Oral History Collection came to represent a shifting terrain of stories and storytelling, an ongoing process of destabilizing the way things were ordered in the immediate past. In the shifting politics of history and memory, a climate of uncertainty and risk persisted – retold in stories of cycles and endurance. The idea of climate had acquired new powers yet continued to reflect established ways of thinking about nature, encompassing tensions between the past, present *and* future, about Australian relationships to land and water that have never been resolved.

Sociologists have argued that a near-exclusive focus on 'expert' knowledge in late modern responses to perceived environmental threats has limited our understanding of the very concept of risk (see Lash, Szerszynski & Wynne, 1996; especially Wynne 1996). In that vein, political scientist Sheila Jasanoff noted that climate change has been driving 'wedges' between people's fact-making and meaning-making faculties, tending to erase local specificity and mask the value people place upon solidarity and experience in narrating eco-social relations (2010, 243). In this respect, there is critical value in oral history, in allowing time and space for a deeper and more sustained dialogue – as Frisch (2003) argues, for 'talking and really listening across diverse realms of experience'.

Recording oral history on drought enabled the capture of contemplations both unifying and divisive, profoundly troubling *and* optimistic, of a past, present and future way of life under conditions of climate change. This uncovered a moral framework: these were narratives of *the way it was*, retold, re-imagined and relived in depictions of *the way it is* and, significantly, *the way it could be* in an increasingly globalized, 'detraditionalized' and ever-warming world. Indeed, where these oral histories attest to the power of battler narratives of endurance, perceptions of climate change (of global forces *per se*) complicate the very idea of drought having an end. Critically then, these stories reveal something of the subjectivity of climate change – itself a dialectical image, oscillating between purposive reason and avoidance of the unimaginable (Dibley & Neilson, 2010). These stories offer us a glimpse of the 'identifiable in endless transformation', to return to Shostak's phrase, thus of the complexities and paradoxes of becoming the political subjects of climate crisis.

Adam offers a cautionary note to the historicisation of change, however – that 'tradition constitutes renewal at every moment of active reconstruction of past beliefs and commitments' (1996, 137). The oral histories at the heart of this chapter form a case in point. As environmental historian Donald Worster wrote, 'change is never all there is in nature'; stories of change lead somewhere, he argued, and possess 'a discernible direction, conventionally called Progress' (1995, 69–70).[7] In the interconnected narratives of humans and non-human nature 'going somewhere' in the Mallee, a parable of change brings with it a potent yearning for tradition. In turn, this prompts us as researchers to take seriously the ways social and environmental risks are inextricably linked – how and why human interpretations of disaster endure due to their usefulness in social and cultural systems, even if at the peril of the environments of which humans are a part.

Notes

Material in this chapter was first published in *Endurance: Australian Stories of Drought* as detailed in the end notes and works cited. This book can be found at the CSIRO Publishing website: http://www.publish.csiro.au/pid/7245.htm.

1   The botanic phenomenon, 'mallee' (eucalypts with a multi-stemmed habit), gives its name to the region. Mallee 'blocks' are 640 acres, roughly a square mile, but can stretch to 700 acres or 280 hectares (Nickolls & Angel, 2003).

2   The archives for *The Lived Experience of Drought in the Mallee* and *Perceptions of Climate Change in the Mallee* projects are stored at Museum Victoria's Melbourne Museum building in Carlton North, Victoria. The oral histories are stored in audio form on MP3s, have been uploaded and catalogued to MV's collections as digital audio files, and are kept in printed form as a big bound volume of transcripts.

3   This chapter draws upon and updates material written by the author and published in the book *Endurance: Australian Stories of Drought* (2014) and the journals *Hecate* (2012), *Cultural Studies Review* (2010), *Rural Society* (2009), *Australian Humanities Review* (2008) and *Traffic* (2007).

4   The research was supported by a Melbourne Research Scholarship, co-sponsored by the University of Melbourne's Australian Centre and the Technology and Sustainable Futures division of Museum Victoria. Participants were advised their oral histories would be utilised in my doctoral research, then stored as a public resource at Museum Victoria. I sought a cross-section of perspectives from people in a number of industries and public services. This resulted in a group of twelve women and twelve men who typically wore several 'hats' in life: farmers, health workers, members of poverty action and social welfare groups, members of local government, a newspaper editor, a nurse, educators, administrators, agronomists, researchers and people involved in various community-driven organisations dedicated to social and environmental sustainability. Interviews were primarily conducted face-to-face, on average once a year for three years, between September 2004 and December 2007.

5   The Victorian Mallee (representing 17.3 per cent of Victoria's total area) is but a portion of Australian Mallee country. The semi-arid region also covers parts of New South Wales and South Australia, and extends across the Nullarbor through Western Australia.

6   This includes the Latji Latji, Wadi Wadi and Wemba Wemba peoples who made extensive use of the Murray River, the Wotjibolik people whose main language was Wergaia and who occupied most of the southern Mallee, and the Yupagalk people who lived in the southeast Mallee.

7   Worster (1995) argued Darwinism had turned biology into history, such that a story of 'change' *became* that of Progress in nature.

References

Adam, B., 1996. Detraditionalisation and the Certainty of Uncertain Futures. In: P. Heelas, S. Lash & P. Morris, eds. *Detraditionalisation: Critical Reflections on Authority and Identity*. Oxford: Blackwell, 134–48.

Adam, B., 1998. *Timescapes of Modernity: The Environment and Invisible Hazards*. London: Routledge.

Allen Consulting Group, 2005. *Climate Change Risk and Vulnerability: Promoting an Efficient Adaptation Response in Australia – Final Report to the Australian Greenhouse Office*. [Online] Available at: www.allenconsult.com.au/publications/download.php?id=298&type=pdf&file=1 [Accessed 22 October 2006].

Anderson, D., 2007. Weathering the Storm: A Tale of Timing, Loss and Learning from Cyclone Larry. *Traffic*, Issue 9, 15–33.

Anderson, D., 2008. Drought, Endurance and 'The Way Things Were': The Lived Experience of Climate and Climate Change in the Mallee. *Australian Humanities Review*, Issue 45, 67–81.

Anderson, D., 2009. Enduring Drought Then 'Coping' with Climate Change: Lived Experience and Local Resolve in Rural Mental Health. *Rural Society*, 19(4), 340–52.

Anderson, D., 2010. Drought, Endurance and Climate Change 'Pioneers': Lived Experience in the Production of Rural Environmental Knowledge. *Cultural Studies Review*, 16(1), 82–101.

Anderson, D., 2012. Climate Lived and Contested: Narratives of Mallee Women, Drought and Climate Change. *Hecate*, 38(1 & 2), 24–41.

Anderson, D., 2014. *Endurance: Australian Stories of Drought*. Collingwood(Victoria): CSIRO Publishing.

Anon., 1941. Drifting Sands: Is the Mallee Blowing Away? *The Australasian*, 18 January, 42–3.

Arthur, J. M., 2003. *The Default Country: A Lexical Cartography of Twentieth-Century Australia*. Sydney: University of New South Wales Press.

Australian Bureau of Statistics, 2009. *National Regional Profile: Mallee (Statistical Division)*. [Online] Available at: www.abs.gov.au/ausstats/abs@nrp.nsf/lookup/230Main+Featu res12005-2009 [Accessed 8 July 2015].

Barr, N. & Cary, J., 1992. *Greening a Brown Land: The Australian Search for Sustainable Land Use*. Crows Nest(NSW): MacMillan Education Australia.

Bate, W., 1989. *Having a Go: Bill Boyd's Mallee*. Melbourne: Museum Victoria.

Big Black Dog Communications and Australian Government, 2007. *Australian Humour*. [Online] Available at: http://australia.gov.au/about-australia/australian-story/austn-humour [Accessed 8 July 2015].

Bird, S. E., 2005. The Journalist as Ethnographer? How Anthropology Can Enrich Journalistic Practice. In: E. Rothenbuhler & M. Coman, eds. *Media Anthropology*. Thousand Oaks(CA): Sage, 301–8.

Blainey, G., 2006. *A History of Victoria*. Melbourne: Cambridge University Press.

Botterill, L. & Fisher, M. eds., 2003. *Beyond Drought: People, Policy and Perspectives*. Collingwood (Victoria): CSIRO.

Botterill, L. & Fisher, M., 2003. Introduction. In: L. Botterill & M. Fisher, eds. *Beyond Drought: People, Policy and Perspectives*. Collingwood(Victoria): CSIRO, 1–7.

Bourke, L. & Lockie, S., 2001. Rural Australia: An Introduction. In: S. Lockie & L. Bourke, eds. *Rurality Bites*. Annandale(NSW): Pluto Press, 1–13.

Bromby, R., 1986. *Unlocking the Land: The Saga of Farming in Australia*. Melbourne: Lothian.

Brooker, M. I. H., Slee, A. V. & Connors, J. R., 2002. *Habit*. [Online] Available at: www.anbg .gov.au/cpbr/cd-keys/Euclid/sample/html/habit.htm [Accessed 8 July 2015].

Cave, M. & Sloan, S. M. eds., 2014. *Listening on the Edge: Oral History in the Aftermath of Crisis*. Oxford: Oxford University Press.

Christoff, P., 2005. Weird Weather and Climate Culture Wars. *Arena Journal*, Issue 23, 9–16.

Christoff, P., 2008. The End of the World as We Know It. *The Age*, 15 January, 13.

Climate Institute of Australia, 2007. *Climate of the Nation: Australians' Attitudes to Climate Change and its Solutions*. [Online] Available at: www.climateinstitute.org.au/cia1/publication.php?content_id=80 [Accessed 18 May 2007].

Cooke, G. & Healy, L., 2004. *Interview, D. Anderson, Ouyen*, Carlton North: Museum Victoria.

Crowder, B., 1995. *The Wonders of the Weather*. Canberra: Bureau of Meteorology, Commonwealth of Australia.

Davison, G. & Brodie, M., 2005. *Struggle Country: The Rural Ideal in Twentieth Century Australia*. Melbourne: Monash University ePress.

Department of Primary Industries Victoria, 2007. *Mallee: Climate*. [Online] Available at: www.dpi.vic.gov.au/dpi/vro/malregn.nsf/pages/mallee_climate[Accessed 8 July 2015].

Dibley, B. & Neilson, B., 2010. Climate Crisis and the Actuarial Imaginary: The War on Global Warming. *New Formations*, 69(8), 144–59.

Frisch, M., 1990. *A Shared Authority: Essays on the Craft and Meaning of Oral and Public History*. Albany: State University of New York Press.

Frisch, M., 1998. Oral History and 'Hard Times': A Review Essay. In: R. Perks & A. Thomson, eds. *The Oral History Reader*. New York: Routledge, 29–37.

Frisch, M., 2003. Working-Class Public History in the Context of Deindustrialisation: Dilemmas of Authority and the Possibilities of Dialogue. *Labour*, Issue 51, 153–64.

Gillen, P., 2002. Telling the Nation: Current Australian Configurations. *Cultural Studies Review*, 8(2), 157–78.

Gray, I. & Lawrence, G., 2001. *A Future for Regional Australia: Escaping Global Misfortune*. Cambridge: Cambridge University Press.

Griffiths, T., 1994. Mallee Roots: A Brief History of Victoria's Northwest. *Park Watch*, Issue 178, 21–23.

Griffiths, T., 2003. The Nature of Culture and the Culture of Nature. In H.-M. Teo & R. White, eds. *Cultural History in Australia*. Sydney: University of New South Wales Press, 67–80.

Hannink, N., Scott, R. & Sim-Jones, J., 2007. The Big Shift. *The University of Melbourne Voice*, 1(1), 4–5.

Haynes, R. D., 1998. *Seeking the Centre: The Australian Desert in Literature, Art and Film*. Melbourne: Cambridge University Press.

Heathcote, R., 2000. 'She'll Be Right, Mate': Coping with Drought – Strategies Old and New in Australia. In: D. Wilhite, ed. *Drought: A Global Assessment*. London: Routledge, 59–69.

Hogan, A., 2005. *Interview, D. Anderson, Hopetoun*, Carlton North: Museum Victoria.

Hopgood, D., 1989. Foreword. In: J. C. Noble, P. J. Joss & G. K. Jones, eds. *The Mallee Lands: A Conservation Perspective*. Adelaide: CSIRO, v–vii.

Hulme, M., 2009. *Why We Disagree About Climate Change: Understanding Controversy, Inaction and Opportunity*. Cambridge: Cambridge University Press.

Hulme, M., 2015. *Climate and Its Changes: A Cultural Appraisal*. [Online] Available at: http:// onlinelibrary.wiley.com/doi/10.1002/geo2.5/full [Accessed 8 July 2015].

Jasanoff, S., 2010. A New Climate for Society. *Theory, Culture & Society*, 27(2–3), 233–53.

Keating, J., 1992. *The Drought Walked Through: A History of Water Shortage in Victoria*. Melbourne: Department of Water Resources Victoria.

Kenyon, A., [1912] 1982. *The Story of the Mallee: A History of the Victorian Mallee Read before the Historical Society of Victoria, 18 March 1912*. Rainbow (Victoria): Brentwood.

Khadem, N. & Marino, M., 2005. Canberra Control Urged as Drought Hits Meat Prices. *The Age*, 17 May.

Lash, S., Szerszynski, B. & Wynne, B. eds., 1996. *Risk, Environment and Modernity: Towards a New Ecology*. London: Sage.

Lawrence, G., 1987. *Capitalism and the Countryside: The Rural Crisis in Australia*. Sydney: Pluto Press.

Lee, T., 2005. *Forecasters Offer Alternatives to 'Dry Winter' Prediction*. [Online] Available at: www.abc.net.au/landline/content/2005/s1377788.htm [Accessed 8 July 2015].

Lindesay, J., 2003. Climate and Drought in Australia. In: L. Botterill & M. Fisher, eds. *Beyond Drought: People, Policy and Perspectives*. Collingwood (Victoria): CSIRO, 21–47.

Little, M., [2003] 2009. *Aussie Rules! Mark Little on Australia's Comedy Heritage*. [Online] Available at: www.chortle.co.uk/features/2009/03/22/8577/aussie_rules [Accessed 8 July 2015].

Lumb, M., 1987. Introduction. In: D. Connor & D. Smith, eds. *Agriculture in Victoria*. Parkville (Victoria): Australian Institute of Agricultural Science.

Lutes, M. W., 1998. Global Climatic Change. In: R. Keil, D. Bell, P. Penz & L. Fawcett, eds. *Political Ecology: Global and Local*. London: Routledge, 157–75.

Macnaghten, P. & Urry., J., 1998. *Contested Natures*. London: Sage.

Mallee Catchment Management Authority, 2003. *Regional Catchment Strategy 2003–8*. [Online] Available at: www.malleecma.vic.gov.au/resources/corporate-documents/ rsc_2003-08.pdf/view?searchterm=%2522the%20backbone%20of%20the% 20economy%2522 [Accessed 14 July 2015].

Mallee District Aboriginal Services, 2013. *Cultural History: Mildura, Swan Hill, Kerang*. [Online] Available at: www.mdas.org.au/page.php?id=29 [Accessed 9 July 2015].

McKechnie, R., 1996. Insiders and Outsiders: Identifying Experts on Home Ground. In: A. Irwin & B. Wynne, eds. *Misunderstanding Science? The Public Reconstruction of Science and Technology*. Cambridge: Cambridge University Press, 126-51.

McKernan, M., 2005. *Drought: The Red Marauder*. Crows Nest(NSW): Allen & Unwin.

Morrish, B. & Morrish, M., 2007. *Interview, D. Anderson, Tiega*, Carlton North: Museum Victoria.

Mules, W., Schirato, T. & Wigman, B., 1995. Rural Identity within the Symbolic Order: Media Representations of the Drought. In: P. Share, ed. *Communication and Culture in Rural Areas*. Wagga Wagga(NSW): Centre for Rural Social Research, 239-57.

Nickolls, J. & Angel, A., 2003. *Mallee Tracks: A Wanderer's Guide to the South Australian and Victorian Mallee*. 2nd ed. Pinnaroo(SA): Jill Nickolls and Ann Angel.

Nixon, W.M., 1965. *While the Mallee Roots Blaze: The Story of Berriwillock*. Berriwillock(Victoria): Back to Berriwillock Committee.

Parkes, D. M. & Cheal, D. C., 1989. Perceptions of Mallee Vegetation. In: J. C. Noble, P. J. Joss & G. K. Jones, eds. *The Mallee Lands: A Conservation Perspective*. Adelaide: CSIRO, 3-7.

Pash, R., 2005. Howard Admits to Farmers More Help is Needed. *The Age*, 18 May.

Perks, R. & Thomson, A., 2006. Introduction to Second Edition. In: R. Perks & A. Thomson, eds. *The Oral History Reader*. London: Routledge, ix–xiv.

Pole, M. & Pole, R., 2007. *Interview, D. Anderson, Walpeup*, Carlton North: Museum Victoria.

Pole, M., Pole, R. & Pole, M., 2005. *Interview, D. Anderson, Walpeup*, Carlton North: Museum Victoria.

Portelli, A., 1997. *The Battle of Valle Giulia: Oral History and the Art of Dialogue*. Madison(WI): University of Wisconsin Press.

Portelli, A., 1998. What Makes Oral History Different. In: R. Perks & A. Thomson, eds. *The Oral History Reader*. London: Routledge, 63–74.

Rayner, S., 2003. Domesticating Nature: Commentary on the Anthropological Study of Weather and Climate Discourse. In: S. Strauss & B. S. Orlove, eds. *Weather, Climate, Culture*. New York: Berg, 277–90.

Read, P., 1996. *Returning to Nothing: The Meaning of Lost Places*. Melbourne: Cambridge University Press.

Roncoli, C., Ingram, K., Jost, C. & Krishen, P., 2003. Meteorological Meanings: Farmers' Interpretations of Seasonal Rainfall Forecasts in Burkina Faso. In: S. Strauss & B. S. Orlove, eds. *Weather, Climate, Culture*. New York: Berg, 181–202.

Rootes, C., 2008. The First Climate Change Election? The Australian General Election of 24 November 2007. *Environmental Politics*, 17(3), 473–80.

Ryan, M., Ryan, D. & Ryan, A., 2004. *Interview, D. Anderson and L. Dale-Hallett, Manangatang*, Carlton North: Museum Victoria.

Ryan, M., Ryan, D. & Ryan, A., 2006. *Interview, D. Anderson, Manangatang*, Carlton North: Museum Victoria.

Saarinen, T. F., 1966. *Perception of the Drought Hazard on the Great Plains*, Chicago: Department of Geography, University of Chicago.

Schneider, W., ed., 2008. *Living with Stories: Telling, Retelling, and Remembering*. Ogden(UT): Utah State University Press.

Schubert, M., 2005. $250m Rescue Package for Farms. *The Age*, 31 May.

Sheldon, A., 2005. *Interview, D. Anderson, Ngallo*, Carlton North: Museum Victoria.

Sheldon, A., 2007. *Interview, D. Anderson, Ngallo*, Carlton North: Museum Victoria.

Sherratt, T., 2005. Human Elements. In: T. Sherratt, T. Griffiths & L. Robin, eds. *A Change in the Weather: Climate and Culture in Australia*. Canberra: National Museum of Australia Press, 1–17.

Sherratt, T., Griffiths, T. & Robin, L. eds., 2005. *A Change in the Weather: Climate and Culture in Australia*. Canberra: National Museum of Australia Press.

Shostak, M., 2006. What the Wind Won't Take Away: The Genesis of Nisa – The Life and Words of A !Kung Woman. In: R. Perks & A. Thomson, eds. *The Oral History Reader*. London: Routledge, 402–13.

Sloan, S. M., 2014. The Fabric of Crisis: Approaching the Heart of Oral History. In: M. Cave & S. M. Sloan, eds. *Listening on the Edge: Oral History in the Aftermath of Crisis*. Oxford: Oxford University Press, 262–74.

Somers, M., 1994. The Narrative Constitution of Identity: A Relational and Network Approach. *Theory and Society*, 23(5), 605–49.

Stehlik, D., Gray, I. & Lawrence, G., 1999. *Drought in the 1990s: Australian Farm Families' Experiences*. Rockhampton(Queensland): Rural Industries Research and Development Corporation.

Stevens, W. K., 1999. *The Change in the Weather: People, Weather, and the Science of Climate*. New York: Delacorte Press.

Thomas, J., 1996. Heroic and Democratic Histories: Pioneering as a Historical Concept. *The UTS Review: Cultural Studies and New Writing*, 2(1), 58–71.

Thomson, A., 1998. Anzac Memories: Putting Popular Memory Theory into Practice in Australia. In: R. Perks & A. Thomson, eds. *The Oral History Reader*. London: Routledge, 300–10.

Torpey, D., 1986. *The Way It Was: A History of the Mallee 1910–1949*. Ouyen(Victoria): Local History Resource Centre.

Van Veldhuisen, R., 2001. *Pipe Dreams: A Stroll through the History of Water Supply in the Wimmera-Mallee*. Horsham(Victoria): Wimmera Mallee Water.

Vidal, J., 2006. *Australia Suffers Worst Drought in 1,000 Years*. [Online] Available at: www .guardian.co.uk/world/2006/nov/08/australia.drought [Accessed 9 July 2015].

Waldon, S., Hopkins, P. & Marino, M., 2005. Drought Tipped to Slash Grain Production. *The Age*, 8 June.

West, B. & Smith, P., 1996. Drought, Discourse and Durkheim: A Research Note. *Australian and New Zealand Journal of Sociology*, 32(1), 93–102.

West, B. & Smith, P. L., 1997. Natural Disasters and National Identity: Time, Space and Mythology. *Australian and New Zealand Journal of Sociology*, 33(2), 205–15.

Williams, J., 2003. Can We Myth-Proof Australia?. *Australasian Science*, 24(1), 40–42.

Worster, D., 1995. Nature and the Disorder of History. In: M. Soule & G. Lease, eds. *Reinventing Nature? Responses to Postmodern Deconstruction*. Washington, DC: Island Press, 65–85.

Wynne, B., 1996. May the Sheep Safely Graze? A Reflexive View of the Expert-Lay Knowledge Divide. In: S. Lash, B. Szerszynski & B. Wynne, eds. *Risk, Environment and Modernity: Towards a New Ecology*. London: Sage, 44–83.

2 Rethinking seasons

Changing climate, changing time

Chris O'Brien

Our concepts of time infuse our understandings of weather, climate and seasons. Western notions of time are the invisible moulds shaping and structuring modern efforts to grasp the dynamics of the ocean of air in which we are immersed. This nexus between conceptions of time, season, weather and climate has helped make intelligible processes that otherwise may have evaded us. But these insights have come at the cost of moments of blindness, obscuring other possibilities of historical and ecological legibility. Examining the weather history of the northern third of Australia's Northern Territory – what happened, as well as how it was understood – I will show that this nexus has been blind to a crucial aspect of this region's climate: its temporal variability. I will then reflect on the implications of this for how we might better conceptualise climate, and tease out consequences for reading and dealing with the signs of anthropogenic climate change.

Before this, however, a sketch of western notions of time and their relationship to weather and climate is in order. This is an exercise in rendering the familiar strange. Habitual and transparently sensible as our ways of understanding weather, climate, seasons and time may seem, they are still the result of manifold historical and cultural contingencies. An intriguing result of historical contingency is that since the British invasion of north Australia two cosmologies have co-existed there. Even a brief exploration of indigenous understandings of climate and season shows just how peculiar western and indeed dominant contemporary understandings of climatic experience can be. Such vastly different epistemologies, such starkly contrasting cosmologies encompass remarkably different phenomena. Each makes sense of atmospheric dynamics in particular ways. More particularly, Aboriginal notions of season are not fused to time and manifestations of particular ideas of time such as the Gregorian Calendar. For nearly 150 years, people along the far north of Australia have experienced a common weather but starkly different climates, and possess strikingly distinct understandings of its climate and seasonal regimes.

Indigenous seasons

Long before digital displays, long before the repeated cycles traced by analogue machines replicating apparent cycles of the sun, humans noticed the cycles of the seasons. Aboriginal societies in Australia's far north related weather to the appearance of the sky, and distinct stages in the life cycle and behaviours of plants and animals. Indispensable to adaptation and survival these understandings have resisted the onslaughts of colonial invasion. Depicting an annual cycle of observable constellations of coinciding events in non human nature, they are not bound by the western calendar. They instead incorporate a temporal flexibility that allows for seasons which don't happen at an exact time, but come nonetheless in a cyclical sequence, though occasionally a season does not come at all.[1]

Aboriginal people reckon seasons in an entirely different way from Europeans. Anthropologists, linguists and geographers in collaboration with various Aboriginal communities across northern Australia have revealed the ideas of season, signifiers of season and seasonal regimes for particular communities. Beginning in the 1970s these led to a modest number of publications during the 1980s and 1990s that showed how Aboriginal people integrate phenomena of land, seas and skies in their understanding of nature. In the 1990s this collaboration went beyond academia to include conservation groups, national parks authorities and local government. Indigenous people have lived along and near Australia's north coast for upwards of 40,000 years. Only in the last forty, though, have non-Aboriginal people come to learn that, in indigenous cosmologies, this region has a mosaic of micro-climates and seasonal variations. Many elements recur across the region. However, while some places have five seasons, others have six, others seven. The same event – a crocodile laying eggs – can mean one thing in one locale and something quite different in another. Yet, still-dominant western notions define climate by latitude and so classify all of Australia's north coast and its hinterland as having the same climate and seasonal regime. In recent decades, members of Aboriginal communities have worked with western researchers to create Indigenous Seasonal Calendars and share indigenous knowledge with the wider community. These now appear in public places such as the visitors' centre at the World Heritage listed Kakadu National Park and in Darwin's Smith Street Mall. They feature in academic treatments of weather in Australia such as *Windows on Meteorology*, and they are commonly created for use in Northern Territory schools. As linguists Robert Hoogenraad and George Jampijina Robinson have argued (1997), the charts often and unwittingly force one way of knowing into another by making the rich web of knowledge inherent in indigenous concepts of season conform to the template of the western calendar. In trying to blend two different epistemologies they have often bent indigenous understandings into shapes set by western ideas of the relationship between seasons and time. The Gurruwilyun Yolgnu Seasonal Chart (Guthadjaka, et al., 2012) (see Figure 2.1) has just recently gone into broader public circulation in the Northern Territory and arguably overcomes this. Certainly, its intricacies warrant detailed examination. Furthermore, it illustrates a radically different means of identifying seasons to that which European and neo-European societies take for granted.

A wealth of local knowledge is concentrated in this chart. Produced in collaboration between senior elder and educator Kathy Guthadjaka (known as Gotha), Merri Creek Productions and Charles Darwin University, it is a distillation of oral knowledge formed from assiduous observation and passed from custodian to custodian through performance over centuries, perhaps millennia. The locale it represents is

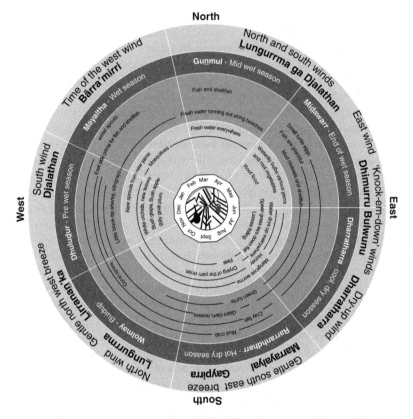

Figure 2.1 Gurruwilyun Yolŋu seasons – Gäwa Gurruwilyun Seasons Poster. © Gotha
(Kathy Guthadjaka), not to be reproduced without permission.

Gawa, along Australia's far north coast in northeast Arnhem Land, some 500 kilo-
metres east of Darwin.

Freezing something so dynamic into a static image means some inevitable loss;
nevertheless, the result is rich and illuminating. The centre comprises a rendering
of traditional motifs of the community of Gawa. This is ringed by a 12-sided poly-
gon, each side marked by a western calendar month. From this 'circle' seven lines
emanate delineating seven seasons, uncoupling these from precise calendar dates.
The lines come down at different points in the various months of change. Since
these points are vague – middle of the month, during the first half, at the turn of
two months – they give the impression of fuzzy boundaries between seasons. Given
the widespread convention in calendars, including some other Aboriginal calendars,
to anchor seasons to precise calendar dates I aver that this absence here can reason-
ably be read as deliberate. It is more likely a conscious break from convention than
an oversight to overcome the near impossibility of representing the dynamic in
static images on paper or on the two-dimensional space of a screen. Nothing else in
the document disputes this reading.

Seasonal events on the land are depicted in the next circle. Where the presence of certain plants or animals transcends particular seasons, this too is indicated. From this we learn much about the life cycles of salient organisms. Encircling this is a ring depicting aquatic activity across the seasons. On land and in the water, activity is explicitly defined positively – by what is present rather than what is absent. Reading across all seasons, though, we implicitly see the absences. In the next circle the seasons are named. The first turn of season in the western calendar year is to *Mayaltha*, translated as the wet season. This is followed by *Gunmul* – the mid wet season and then *Midewarr*, the end of the wet season. *Dharratharra*, the cool dry season is next, then *Rharranhdharr*, the hot dry season. *Wolway* – the build-up, is next in the sequence and then *Dhuludur* – the pre-wet season. Only with the outermost circle is season tied to weather. The ring of seasons is enclosed by a circle in which the local names of dominant winds appear. These align not to specific seasons but to general times of year when certain winds most commonly blow. In some cases, for example, *Barra'mirri*, the time of the West Wind, these correspond to a season – *Mayaltha*. In others – *Lugngurrma ga Djalathagn* (North and South Winds) – they straddle two seasons – *Gunmul* and *Midawarr*. Different again, the period of *Djalathagn* (South Winds) is just a portion of a season: the latter part of *Dhuludhur*. Indicating the variability of the elements, these periods of winds are not tied to precise dates but appear in a sequence that can be read from any time of the year.

Some indications of how people in Gawa distinguish one season from another can be given by describing one season more fully. At the start of *Dhuludhur*, the gentle northwest sea breeze known as *Lirragnan'ka* blows. During the season, *Djalathagn*, a more vigorous south wind, becomes more common, giving a sense of atmospheric turbidity. A bounty of mud crabs and crayfish can be seen in the waters, continuing their activity from the two preceding seasons. Fish and shellfish are abundant. Coral spores appear and then disappear. Black tip sharks and stingrays abound and remain through the following season. On land, new yams sprout. This is a pivotal time for mosquitoes, which are present in Gawa from the preceding two seasons, through *Dhuludhur*, to the two following seasons. Unique to *Dhuludhur* are blooms of white orchids, new leaves, bush grape, bush apple and billy goat plum. The seasonal conception of *Dhuludhur* involves a breathtaking constellation of interconnecting ecological signs. It corresponds to an ecological sense of atmospheric time.

Western seasons: the weather, climate, calendar nexus

The contrast with how colonial newcomers to the north have understood the same atmospheric dynamics is stark. Newcomers saw the climate as working like a clock, with extraordinary precision. In 1902, J. A. G. Little – Darwin's Postmaster and Superintendent of Telegraphs, and a most diligent observer of Darwin's weather from 1872 through to 1906 – said of the Top End's climate and seasons that there are two each year – the Wet and the Dry – and that 'the different changes of these seasons are so uniform and regular that they may be predicted to almost a day' (Taylor, 1918, p. 70). Newspapers, government reports and almanacs during the period 1880–1940 did just this, defining the Wet as either October through March, or November through April, and the Dry as the balance of the calendar year. Curiously they disagreed on the actual timing but were solidly unified behind the notion that the seasons changed with clockwork precision. Indeed, this sense of regularity seemed to be supported by meteorological analysis. During this period and throughout the twentieth century, the mean monthly figures for various weather elements such as rainfall, temperature, humidity and atmospheric pressure were the main way weather watchers read the dynamics of the skies. Although other statistical techniques, such as standard deviation, came into use during this period in other disciplines, Australian meteorologists almost always relied solely on means. Means were what appeared in reports, studies and books. Look at the average monthly rainfall figures for the period 1870–1942. Starting with January they are 393.2mm, 329.7mm, 257mm, 102.6mm, 14.3mm, 3mm, 1.3mm, 1.6mm, 12.8mm, 51.6mm, 124mm and 241.8mm (Commonwealth Bureau of Meteorology, Australia, 2015a). Such numbers seemingly confirm the received understanding: distinct periods of wet and dry alternate with an orderly, predictable progression between the peaks and troughs, year after year. This goes a long way to explaining the endurance of the idea, since this sense of regularity and linearity has a long and compelling pedigree in western thinking.

When the ancient Greeks noticed the cycle of the seasons, they linked the appearances of stars to the weather. Hesiod's delightful poem *Works and Days*, dating from the eighth century BCE, is also the oldest surviving farmers' almanac. It is replete with links between weather and the regular, and even then utterly predictable, movements of the stars. Here are just three examples: 'When the Pleiades, Atlas' daughters, start to rise begin your harvest; plough when they go down' (Hesiod, 1973, p. 71); 'Gales of all winds rage when the Pleiades, Pursued by violent Orion, plunge into the clouded sea' (p.78); 50 days after the autumn equinox a period of gentle breezes is displaced by "Notos" – awful blasts' (p. 80). Herodotus' *The Histories*, still a foundational text in historical scholarship, conveys a comparable sense of nature as regular, calendrical, and stellar. Reporting a fabled discussion between Croesus (King of Lydia) and Solon (Statesman and Lawmaker) about happiness and the good life, Herodotus (1973, p. 15) quotes Solon as saying:

> Take seventy years as the span of a man's life: those seventy years contain 25,000 days, without counting intercalary months. Add a month every other year, to make the seasons come around with proper regularity.

Seasons were thought to be regular, and the system for marking time was designed to ensure this calendrical regularity. Between Hesiod and Herodotus came Ionian natural philosophy. Described by Arthur Koestler (1959, p. 22) as a 'Promethean quest for natural explanations and rational causes', it sought physical causes for physical phenomena. This conception of seasons as astronomically regular in fact lies at the root of our word 'climate'. Climate (κλίμα), in classical geography, named the distinct cultural and ecological zones of the planet, as determined by the inclination of the sun's rays on the surface of the Earth – climate and inclination sharing a common etymology. Another famous classical almanac poem, Virgil's *Georgics*, repeatedly reinforces this relationship and its inherent regularity. By Virgil's time (the mid first century BCE) the notion of the four seasons, four annual seasons of practically equal length, each arriving on a particular date and departing on another, was widely held in Greco-Roman society. The seasons, understood to refer to weather and climate, were tied to the calendar and also the stars. To quote Virgil (1999, p. 59):

> [it is] Well for us that we watch the rise and fall of the sky-signs And the four seasons that divide the year equally.

The year 46BCE was 445 days long. This anomaly was part of the most enduring product of the time–season relationship of that era: the Julian Calendar. Calendar and seasons were so out of sync that one nominal year of unique length had to be intercalated to recalibrate the system of time reckoning before the new calendar was introduced. It took many centuries before the new calendar became noticeably out of time with seasons and weather. Nearly 16 centuries passed before the situation became so bad as to warrant the imposition of a new calendar, during which, Europeans came to live a fairly rigid time discipline. Benedictine monks worked and prayed to a factory-like time discipline; books of devotions based on Benedict of Nursia's Table of Hours set out how each hour of each day would be spent. As Lawrence Wright notes, books were commonly organised by season, defined by precise, predetermined dates of equinoxes and solstices. Beyond the walls of the monastery, demands of markets, trade, government, bureaucracy and the church ensnared many into living a form of time discipline. Time became the measure of so much in life. Nature was ordered; so was society, or at least many aspects of public life, like clockwork, before the invention of the clock. But this was far from total, or uniform. As British Historian E P Thompson notes, between 1300 and the Industrial Revolution a variety of times coexisted in the same places: 'nature's' time and clock time, 'merchant's' time and 'church' time (1967, p. 56). This changed as the monumental, imperious demands of industrialisation compelled synchronisation of labour on a grand scale. This required time discipline characterised by exactitude. By the 1820s this economic revolution bequeathed a cultural revolution that did nothing less than change how people lived (ibid.). For industrialised people, society, nature and the universe not only worked to time, it had come to do so with the utmost precision and to an encompassing, uniform sense of time that had completely colonised nature.

Calendars came to have almost ontological force. With the advent of the BC/AD dating system, calendars could not only set out each day of a year or period: they now, it seemed, could map the entire timescape. Being so stable a technology – the only update since 46BCE came in 1582CE – calendars have been taken to be natural rather than cultural artefacts, as if they do nothing less than embody time, providing an independent and external measure of nature, life and society. With the invention (circa 1270CE) and spread of the clock came both a finer, more precise delineation of time and a powerful metaphor for nature. It was 1377 when the French philosopher Nicole Oresme first described the universe as an eternally working clock, an idea that has resonated ever since.

Subsequent revolutions in astronomy and physics certainly reinforced these powerfully cosmic clockworks. They also presented this sense of time and its proxy – the calendar – as profoundly natural phenomena, aiding our forgetting of their deeply cultural natures. The painstaking work of Copernicus, Galileo and Tycho Brahe showed just how pervasive order in the skies is. Celestial movements were demonstrated as so regular and orderly as to allow precise prediction. Kepler's laws of planetary motion strengthened this, and his correct explanation of the tides extended this sense of interstellar order to terrestrial spheres.

From 1687 time took on a life of its own. With Newton's *Principia*, the mechanics of observable motion were explained, from planetary motion to gravity and acceleration. Newton's laws were testable. When tested and retested they proved reliable. At the core of Newtonian physics and the order and harmony they explained is a particular view of time as 'absolute, true and mathematical time, [which] of itself, and from its own nature, flows equably without relation to anything external' (Newton, [1687] 1962, p. 7). According to the most powerful systems of scientific explanation both at the time and since, time is independent of all other physical processes, a yardstick against which all else can be measured, especially phenomena that regularly repeat in time, such as seasons, which define climates and provide expectations for weather. This is the basic understanding of time for scientific and scholarly knowledge, but also that in which people live and dwell, operationalised as it is through calendars: the working week, seasonal holidays, 24/7, the billable hour, births, deaths and marriages. Time was thought of and lived as purely natural. As time's proxy, calendars took on the same aura. With printing and the profusion of almanacs and navigational directories that circulated through Europe and its colonies, this became even more steadfast.

So, Westerners became conceptually blind to vital aspects of the climate of places such as northern Australia. Almanacs have been produced since antiquity. During the middle ages they combined information about ecclesiastical feasts and observances with details of eclipses, and the movement of planets and constellations. In 1448 an almanac was among the first items off the Gutenberg Press. Almanacs were among the first publications in colonies such as Massachusetts and New South Wales; by the eighteenth century a huge variety of almanacs were published and circulated in Britain. According to Maureen Perkins (1996, p. 14) 649,000 authorised almanacs were printed in 1839 in Britain alone with a great many more unauthorised editions circulating. In common, across location and time, almost all of these featured calendars, calendrical definitions of seasons and, increasingly, sections relating typical weather to the month of the year. Such weather lore is most revealing. Where weather was thought to be fickle, rules for forecasting were supplied. As Jan Golinski showed (2007, p. 92–93), even where variability was evident ideas about forecasting were still structured by the calendar. In eighteenth century England, Scotland and Ireland, weather was popularly thought and spoken of as belonging to a month of the year. So when, for example, 'March days' occurred in April (or indeed any such untimely weather) they were considered 'borrowed days'.

In time the natural order was expected to correct such imbalances – perhaps 'May days' following 'March days' in April.

Interviewed about a heatwave besetting western Queensland in November 2012, and asked 'What happens when we get to summer?' one of Birdsville's publicans said: 'We are sort of getting January weather now in November' (Weatherzone, 2012a). A meteorologist from the Australian Bureau of Meteorology's Williamtown (Newcastle) office stated (Weatherzone, 2012b) about imminent heat: 'summer does not really start until over the weekend'. For all of the cleavages between folk weather and natural philosophy, and between non-scientific and scientific weather communities, both domains continue to organise weather by the month. Hooke's 'Method for Making a History of the Weather' set the standard for collecting weather data in 1667: one page per calendar month, a format followed by official weather observers ever since. Certain weather was related to months, and seasons to particular dates. This is how weather often remains both measured and lived.

With European imperialism this thinking washed ashore at numerous points along Australia's coastline. Almanacs from colonial Australia evince this sense of a local clockwork climate, different in many ways from that of Europe but identical in the key respect of temporal regularity. Even where colonial Australians innovated – as when the *NSW Pocket Almanac and Colonial Rememberancer* (George Howe, 1806) unhitched the seasons from the skies and first defined the four seasons not by the solstices and equinoxes but by the periods between the first of March, June, September and December – a calendrical notion of precise, regular timing from one year to the next was retained.

The Northern Territory did not have its own almanac until 1885. Since the NT was part of South Australia between 1863 and 1911, South Australian almanacs, in which various farmers' and gardeners' calendars featured prominently, circulated in the NT from the founding of Darwin in 1869. These all portrayed nature as perfectly rhythmic and ordered. By the 1860s, tables of the weather, organised by each month, accompanied precise, calendrical definitions of the seasons. Even where weather is not discussed explicitly, instructions for the garden were imbued with a sense of the weather's perceived regularity. The *Royal South Australian Almanack* for 1839 (Robert Thomas, 1838, p. 7) issued the following command for February:

> Finish planting of potatos; prepare the ground for turnips, sow cauliflower, broccoli, cabbage, peas, broad beans, celery, artichokes and seakale…

In the almanacs each respective month was the same year after year. Moreover, they often tell a story of orderly, linear progression from one month to the next. Andrew Murray's *Almanac* for 1862 speaks of gradual, incremental declines in temperature between March and May. Yet weather records for Adelaide show that it is not uncommon for periods of 4–7 days in May to be warmer than equivalent periods in March (Commonwealth Bureau of Meteorology, 2015b). March days in May perhaps?

For the Northern Territory, the climate is defined as a flipping between Wet and Dry. This prevailed in almanacs, newspapers, government reports and scientific studies into the last quarter of the twentieth century. Remarkably, this sense of a calendrically defined clockwork climate also circulated long before Europeans invaded northern Australia. It pervades the writings of those who undertook the four earlier failed attempts at colonising the far north. It infuses reports of the various expeditions to and across the far north coast and its hinterland. Journals of the mariners who sailed around Australia's northern coastline abound with references to regular flipping of Wet and Dry and expectations based on this. It is in fact an idea dating to Edmund Halley's account of the trade winds and monsoons, first published in 1686. Based on records from East India Company ships, Halley imposed this climatic interpretation on what we now know as far northern Australia and Indonesia. It was a conception transmitted and disseminated through a plethora of navigational guides and nautical almanacs through the eighteenth and nineteenth centuries (O'Brien, 2012). Seaborne European colonists came to the Top End with a largely predetermined temporal framework of seasons, a sense of climatic time that was set in place long before they had actually gained experience of Northern Australia's distinctive climatic rhythms. Weather and climate remained rigidly defined by calendrical time. There is a long European history of representing the tropics as climatically 'other', an exotic space culturally and ecologically alien to the 'normality' of the temperate places of the mid-latitudes.[2] But underlying this sense of tropical otherness, however, was an unchanged climatic schema of clockwork cosmic time.

The idea vs history

While the clockwork climate has endured in tropical Australia, it does not accord with weather history.[3] This is particularly the case with rainfall, as Figures 2.2 to 2.5 illustrate.

A closer look at rainfall figures for the threshold or transition months of April and October in Darwin destabilises the simple notion of wet and dry. Throughout the period 1869–1941, volumes of rain during both months fluctuate wildly. There are two Aprils when under 2mm fell and thirteen when less than 25mm fell. On the other hand, there were nine Aprils when over 200mm fell. This suggests that there are years when the wet ends before April and others when it does not. Examination of daily rainfall records indicates that this is indeed the case. In 1870, 1874, 1887, 1891 and 1911 there were fewer rain days, longer dry spells, and less rainfall in March than in April. On more than a dozen occasions, rain fell most days in March but on very few in April. Yet, in 1872, 1881, 1918, 1923, and 1931, rain fell on as many days, if not more, in May than in April. Some Aprils are wet, some are dry, some both – as the seasons turn.

Similarly, examples abound of the wets that neither began in earnest on a particular date, nor intensified in an orderly linear fashion. Owing to its ecological importance, the onset of the wet has attracted considerable research. As Nicholls et al. (1982) and Garnett and Williamson (2010) demonstrated, the coming of rain in northern Australia is highly variable across time and space. A brief history of the onset of rain bears this out. Between 1869 and 1941 the Octobers of 1870, 1873,

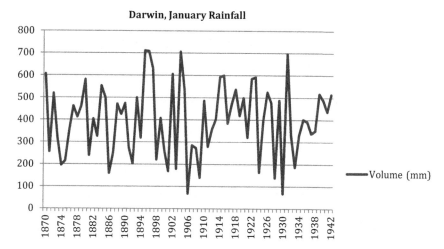

Figure 2.2 January Rainfall, Darwin, 1870–1942.

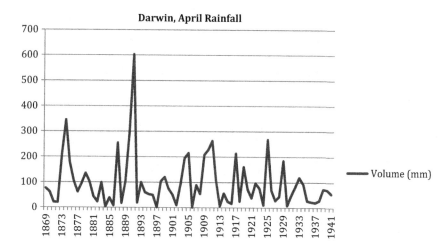

Figure 2.3 April Rainfall, Darwin, 1869–1941.

1877, 1879, 1880, 1890, 1914, 1916, and 1921 recorded more rain than the respective November. Of these, 1870, 1873, 1877, 1914 and 1921 experienced a particularly dry November in Darwin. 1873, 1880, and 1914 were especially wet Octobers, with up to 213mm recorded at Darwin Post Office in October 1914. In 1877, both months were particularly dry, consistent rains not arriving until December 23 and an accumulation of 100mm of rain for 'the season' not being reached till December 17. In contrast, the 100mm cumulative was reached as early as 6/10 in 1931. Some years the Octobers are wet and the Novembers dry. Other years both are wet. Of these, a few of the Octobers are wetter. During the period 1896–1941

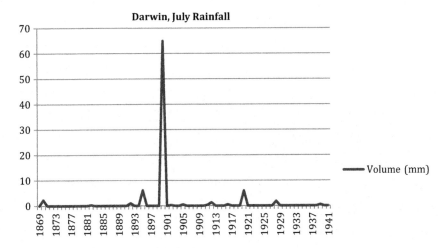

Figure 2.4 July Rainfall, Darwin, 1869–1941.

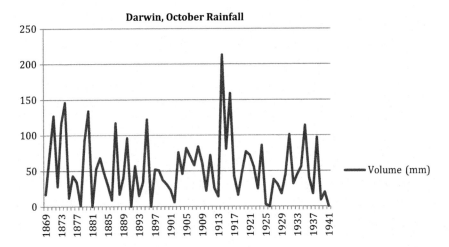

Figure 2.5 October Rainfall, Darwin 1869–1941.

no fewer than five Octobers – 1881, 1891, 1896, 1926 and 1941 – recorded no rainfall at all in Darwin. One of these completely dry Octobers was followed by a November recording of just 46mm of rain (1926); another (1891) preceded a November deluge of 370mm. The timing of the first rains varies from year to year. So too does the pattern of rainfall that follows them. Such a variable temporal pattern of weather and seasons undermines the traditional wet/dry dyad defined by the calendar. Even if we acknowledge a distinct transitional season, meteorological records make clear that its timing varies across the years.

Clearly, the timing of wet and dry vary within a substantial range from year to year. While the dominant conceptualisation of climate has been of two seasons of six months changing in a timely fashion from year to year, we can see from the 73 years of rainfall records taken at Darwin Post Office from 1869 to 1942 that in only eight occasions has Darwin experienced as many as five straight months without rain. Moreover there are many occasions during what is called 'The Wet' when rain does not fall for nearly a week at a time. This happened in Darwin on no fewer than 45 occasions during the Januaries and Februaries between 1870 and 1941. This of course is taking the extreme, conservative case of no rain. If you include periods of light rains these drier spells are even more numerous.

The wet/dry dichotomy is further destabilised when the history of elements such as heat and humidity are examined. Although the locale around Darwin and much of Australia's north coast almost experiences virtual drought conditions during the middle of the year, the nature of this 'Dry' is not the same from year to year. First, as already shown, its length varies remarkably. Even more crucially, the quality of this time with little or no rain, that is to say, how it feels to those who experience it, differs from year to year and between months that are considered in the dominant western understanding to be of the same season. Temperature records for Darwin only survive for the period post 1885. If we examine temperature records first for July between 1885 and 1916 we see that mean 3 p.m. temperatures for the warmest five Julys clustered around 31 degrees Celsius.[4] During the five coolest Julys the 3 p.m. mean was 28°C. While a three-degree difference in absolute temperature is not especially significant, a three-degree difference in means is. If we look at wet bulb temperatures − temperatures levels that indicate atmospheric moisture − it is clear that some Julys are decidedly unlike others. With wet bulb temperature, the higher the reading, the higher the combination of heat and humidity. Geographer Griffith Taylor determined that the threshold above which a 'white' labourer could not comfortably and healthily undertake physical work was a mean wet bulb temperature of 21.1°C (70 degrees Fahrenheit). The warmest five 3 p.m. means during this period way surpassed this level, ranging from 22°C and 24.5°C. In contrast, the coolest was a brisk 18.7°C and the four next coolest were all below 20°C. Griffith Taylor's line was somewhat arbitrary and subjective. In reducing comfort to a number, it was certainly quasi-scientific. If, however, we take it as a differentiation between warm and dry conditions on the one hand and hot and humid weather on the other, it shows that even deep in 'The Dry', the weather is variable between years. Between 1885 and 1916, nineteen years fell below the threshold and twelve exceeded it. July, one of the only months with a reliably recurring absence of rain from year to year, does not experience the same weather each year. Instead, the pattern tends to one of three types. It can be cool and dry, warm and dry, and warm/hot and humid. Across the so-called 'Dry' season these can appear in a meteorological mosaic. From data on a decadal scale it is clear that the temporal patterns vary markedly across the years. During the 31-year period from 1885 it looks like humidity levels were so high in each calendar month of the years 1885, 1915 and 1916 that 'The Dry', arguably, did not come. During other years, people in the north have experienced two months or longer of cooler dry weather.

Just as rainfall patterns have undermined the neat wet/dry dichotomy, so the vicissitudes of humidity in far northern Australia show that there is no one unified dry season. We need, rather, to talk about dry seasons. We also need to accommodate the reality that not all seasons come every year. Colonial north Australia sought its economic viability on the land, so it is no surprise that water – its presence and availability – would matter so much that its presence or absence even defined the seasons. This notion, while geared to human needs, implicitly took humans out of the equation, treating its fundamental sense of time as natural, not cultural, and obscuring even the basic experience of what weather felt like. An idea of seasons that incorporates human experience – reactions to humidity or its lack, for instance – begins to return us to weather's other times, and so help us identify vital dimensions in the variability of climatic experience.

Without detailed weather histories, this variability has been missed. Where weather clearly did not conform to the orderly template, it was seen as strange, abnormal and deviant. Even though there was variation, this did not undermine the resonance and strength of the received understanding of the region's climate. Where it was strange, it was part of the strangeness of the place, not part of the inherent variability of the region's climate. In a community of the clockwork climate, seasons could only be early, late or on time, but not normally liable to such temporal flux. Where variation was noted, variability was simply invisible. The wet/dry dyad has broken down in recent decades in both popular and more formally scientific meteorology with the emergence of a third season, the 'Build-up', but the same template of temporal regularity remains.

Climate change and the seasons

This brings us to the significance of this moment in the cultural history of climate change. Even as the fact that climate is changing is now generally acknowledged, there has also been growing recognition that how climate has often been understood in terms of seasons is grossly inadequate. So at the very time that physical dynamics are being transformed, our conceptual models also need to be updated, to accommodate the past as well as the changing present and future. Climate change requires examining just how regular purportedly stable climates have been, even in recent history. And this is a question not only about averaged quantities such as rainfall and temperature, but also, and importantly, about the timing of patterns of weather that usually recur each year. It is a question of particular salience for much of Australia, Indonesia and the Arafura/Timor regions, where the ebbing and flowing of the El Nino Southern Oscillation (ENSO) has an enormous influence on weather and seasons. ENSO is a massive flux in ocean temperature, convection, air pressure and winds across the entire Pacific basin south of the equator. It brings alternating periods of drought and flood, not only throughout this region but also far beyond, for example to India and North America. ENSO's mercurial atmospheric flows mean that understanding the climates of Australia cannot be accomplished merely by means of the calendar year, but rather requires review of longer spans of time. One reason the nexus between calendar months and weather has endured is that it has been very useful. It answers many important questions.

It captures vital aspects of weather and climate. Yet, it is blind to many others. Now that the variability of climate in Australia is clear, this connection must be used in a more sophisticated fashion to capture the range of variation in seasonal durations and, indeed of seasons, as well of the elements of weather for different times of the year, variation that occurred long before anthropogenic climate change/ global warming began to change weather and seasons. Of course, one crucial aspect of climate change could well be changes in the very variability of climates across Australia. Here we really do need to understand the past to understand the present and to properly anticipate the future.

In the Top End, the predominant understanding of the clockwork climate is deficient for understanding the region's weather. Looking at historical records suggests that, rather than wet and dry, the region in and around Darwin arguably experiences three annual dry seasons and three annual wet seasons, but not always. Of course, this schema is contestable, and is certainly complicated by the fact that elements of different seasons can be present simultaneously. But it is reasonable and useful to distinguish within broader periods of rain times when rain comes from different sources: thunderstorms of the early and late 'The Wet', to use the traditional parlance, that broadly come from the east and southeast, and the monsoonal rains from the west and northwest. These patterns break 'The Wet' down into three periods of distinct kinds of weather events, in a regular sequence. With respect to the 'The Dry', it is also reasonable and useful to distinguish the distinctly drier and cooler periods during the middle of the year from the time of no rain and high but lowering humidity preceding it and the rainless part of the build-up that follows.

Concepts are meant to be general, and the concept of 'season' is very difficult to set in concrete. However, it should not be so broad as to be meaningless. This is especially important because we have various concepts of season that serve particular purposes. Commonly, seasons are metaphors that structure the timelines of human lives. Seasons are used to structure narrative and drama. As both metaphor and structuring device, seasons can be rich and illuminating, if a bit hackneyed when used unimaginatively. Season as a concept helps people structure and make sense of weather. In literary terms, people commonly use seasons as a metanarrative that structures sequences of weather events, that gives them coherence and allows us to identify the larger patterns that make climate. Various 'scientific' seasons are different from one another too: we've seen that astronomical and meteorological seasons often do not correspond. Meteorological seasons are themselves just one aspect of ecological seasons. When we think about seasons and talk about them, we must be clear about what we mean and how we are applying the concept. Concepts of season geared to illuminating weather and climate need to reflect the complexity of the reality they try to encompass; they require a broad ecological grounding, incorporating things that matter to plants and animals such as the timing, nature and intensity of rainfall. Historically legible patterns of heat, humidity, cooling, dryness, winds and tempest resemble the models developed by local Aboriginal people who have long studied this environment with a most diligent empiricism. Unbound by the calendar, they saw the temporal variability that is largely still invisible to most.

Although this revision of the seasons may seem confusing, more nuanced ideas of season that incorporate variability can give us a better sense of what global warming might be doing now. Understandably and importantly, the debate about global warming is focused on mean temperatures. And yet there is so much else to weather, and to climate and climate change. For example, if there are typically six turnings of season in a year, change might manifest in the timing of these turnings. Perhaps the range may expand; it may contract. It may not change at all, but rather the quality of the seasons might change. Most years the monsoons might be more intense. On decadal scales it might be that monsoons are more intense than before. Monsoons might become both more numerous and intense. They might become less frequent but more intense. Or monsoons might become less frequent, more intense and last longer. There are many permutations that are simply invisible if we study weather on the scale of the year. What I call the Monsoonal Wet season of Darwin is a series of monsoonal episodes punctuated by brief, drier breaks. Occasionally the breaks are so long as to give a sense of two Monsoonal Wets in a given year. This happened in 1937 when no heavy rain was recorded at Darwin PO between 17/1 and 23/2 and there were two periods of over a week when no rain at all fell (Commonwealth Bureau of Meteorology, 1937). With climate change these breaks might become more frequent, or they could disappear. But these are questions that could only be assessed over decadal time scales, or longer.

Other time scales matter. Think about how weather and climate can differ on smaller slices of time: by the day, the hour, or the minute (or to move away from clocks, from moment to moment). Climate change for a place might mean the changes in daily temperature or humidity profile, historically measured from hour to hour and now measured continuously. Rather than change in mean maximums, change might happen on this scale – it might warm earlier, or cool later. This might happen at particular times of year, which might change from year to year. Temperatures might be close to the maximum for a much larger portion of the day. With rising air temperatures, sea breezes in a locale might start to blow much earlier in the day, increasing levels of humidity for the rest of the day or night. In another locale higher sea surface temperatures could suppress sea breezes till later in the day. The feedback between higher atmospheric temperature and higher sea temperature might effect a major change in daily temperature and humidity of a place. This might change typical winds at particular times – dynamics not captured by a focus on daily maximum and minimum temperatures. Counterintuitively, higher sea surface temperatures might lead to more evaporation and then more rain in a region. This might even prevent a rise in maximum temperatures for locations under these influences. We should also think about how climate change could alter the constellation of events imbued in indigenous understandings of season. The behaviour of an animal, or the appearance of plants, associated with one season could become integral to another season. Some seasons might actually be accompanied by new happenings on land and in the water. Seasons might become associated with new signs. Thinking of climate this way need not lead into an epistemological quagmire. Rather, it could offer a challenge to the sensitivity and creativity with which climate is currently sensed and conceived. Both the ever-growing knowledge of western meteorology and also the content and methods of indigenous knowledge can offer new ways of seeing climate, and so improved possibilities for understanding its complexities and those of climate change.

Climate change changes the time of weather and the timing of weather, as well as what we understood as taking place in those times. We can identify compelling alternatives to our dominant climatic temporal understanding by revisiting historically quantified measures, as well as in indigenous modes of ecological knowledge. The kinetics of the atmosphere happen in time, but how we experience and understand that timing is not pre-given. It is cultural, and so changeable, open to contestation, alteration, invention and recovery. Variability itself is one of many factors that climate change may alter. Unless we critique the nexus between time, weather and climate, important facets of this vital aspect may remain invisible to us.

Notes

1   For more on Aboriginal seasons see Webb (1997), Chapters 1–6.
2   For a more detailed account see O'Brien (2014).
3   For thorough discussion, see Driver and Martins (2005).
4   Unless otherwise stated, all subsequent data comes from Adelaide Observatory for 1869–1907 and the Commonwealth Bureau of Meteorology, Australia from 1908 onwards.

References

Commonwealth Bureau of Meteorology, Australia, 2015a. *Climate Data Online, Darwin Post Office, Station Number 014016.* [Online] [Accessed 12 June 2015].

Commonwealth Bureau of Meteorology, A., 2015b. *Climate Data Online, Adelaide, Station Number 023090.* [Online] [Accessed 17 June 2015].

Driver, F. & Martins, L. eds., 2005. *Tropical Visions in an Age of Empire.* Chicago: University of Chicago Press.

Garnett, S. & Williamson, G., 2010. Spatial and Temporal Variation in Precipitation at the Start of the Rainy Season in Tropical Australia. *The Rangelands Journal,* Volume 32, p. 215–226.

George Howe, 1806. *NSW Pocket Almanac and Colonial Rememberancer.* Sydney: George Howe.

Golinski, J., 2007. *British Weather and the Climate of Enlightenment.* Chicago: University of Chicago Press.

Guthadjaka, K., Garrawurra, G. & Miller, M., 2012. *Seasonal Chart: Gurruwilyun Yolŋu Seasons – Gawa.* Darwin: Merri Creek Productions and Charles Darwin University.

Herodotus, 1973. *The Histories.* London: Penguin.

Hesiod, 1973. *Works and Days.* London: Penguin.

Hoogenraad, R. & Robertson, G. J., 1997. Seasonal Calendars from Central Australia. In: E. K. Webb, ed. *Windows on Meteorology.* Melbourne: CSIRO Publishing.

Koestler, A., 1959. *Sleepwalkers: A History of Man's Changing Vision of the Universe.* London: Penguin.

Newton, I., [1687] 1962. *The Mathematical Principles of Natural Philosophy.* Berkeley: University of California Press.

Nicholls, N., McBride, J. L. & Ormerod, R. J., 1982. Predicting the Onset of the Australian Wet Season at Darwin. *Monthly Weather Review,* Volume 110, p. 14–17.

O'Brien, C., 2012. *A Clockwork Climate?*. Canberra: PhD Thesis, Australian National University.

O'Brien, C., 2014. Imported Understandings. In: J. Beattie, E. O'Gorman & M. Henry, eds. *Climate, Science and Colonisation: Histories from Australia and New Zealand*. New York: Palgrave Macmillan.

Perkins, M., 1996. *Visions of the Future: Almanacs, Time and Cultural Change, 1775–1870*. Oxford: Clarendon Press.

Robert Thomas, 1838. *Royal South Australian Almanack for 1839*. Adelaide: Robert Thomas and Co.

Taylor, T. G., 1918. *The Australian Environment (Especially as Controlled by Rainfall)*. Melbourne: Australian Government Printer.

Thompson, E. P., 1967. Time, Work-Discipline and Industrial Capitalism. *Past and Present*, Volume 38, p. 56–97.

Virgil, 1999. *The Eclogues, The Georgics*. Oxford: Oxford University Press.

Weatherzone, 2012a. *Weather News*. [Online] Available at: Weatherzone.com.au [Accessed 29 November 2012].

Weatherzone, 2012b. *Weather News*. [Online] Available at: Weatherzone.com.au [Accessed 29 November 2012].

Webb, E. K. ed., 1997. *Windows on Meteorology*. Melbourne: CSIRO Publishing.

3 The terrestrial envelope

Joseph Fourier's geological speculation

Jerome Whitington

Introduction: poiesis of other worlds

'On the Temperatures of the Terrestrial Sphere and Interplanetary Space' is a beautifully crafted work with remarkable clarity interspersed with the turns of phrase that one might expect from Jean-Baptiste Joseph Fourier (1768–1830), a Baron, Governor of Egypt under Napoleon Bonaparte and Prefect of Grenoble and Lyon under Bonaparte and then during the First Restoration of the monarchy. Edward Said (2003) announces the first part of *Orientalism: Western Conceptions of the Orient* with Fourier's words: 'the restless and ambitious genius of Europeans ... eager to use new instruments of their power' (30).[1] The power of Egypt's exotic grandeur heralded what Said describes as Fourier's dramatic *coup* according to which, again in Fourier's words, 'Egypt was the theatre of [Napoleon's] glory' (85–6). The very model of an empire of Reason, Fourier's *preface historique* to the publication of the famous orientalist text *Description de l'Egypte* was written on pages one metre by one metre square (86).

For Auguste Comte, Joseph Fourier was the preeminent citation with which to introduce his *Course in Positive Philosophy*, the text that secured the monumental project of French positivism on its publication in 1830. After introducing and then passing over the scientific projects of Francis Bacon and Johannes Kepler, it is Joseph Fourier's work that first receives Comte's unqualified praise. 'Fourier, in his fine series of the researches on Heat, has given us all the most important and precise laws of the phenomena of heat, and many large and new truths, without once inquiring into its nature, as his predecessors had done when they disputed about calorific matter and the action of a universal ether' (Comte, 1875, p. 5). At stake was Fourier's rejection of questions related to the metaphysical essence or substance of heat, to discover laws on the basis of observation and reason alone. Fourier's research antedates Comte's positivism and was not prone to making general claims about the project of Reason. Yet like the grand gestures of colonial occupation, it preserves his place at the centre of Enlightenment projects of universal knowledge, not least of all for his mathematical and scientific achievements, namely the analytical theory of heat, techniques for solving partial differential equations, and development of the Fourier series.[2]

And yet there is an imaginative dimension that is irreducible. William Thomson (Lord Kelvin), who identified the temperature of absolute zero, described Fourier's work as a 'great mathematical poem' (Fleming, 2005, p. 55). By invoking the poetic I claim an opening for thinking about specificity, language and imaginative practice in the heart of a topic that is explicitly devoted to mathematical analysis and scientific rigor. This imaginative dimension is integral to mathematical and experimental practice and, as I will show, is especially relevant concerning Fourier's attempt to imagine the temperature of interplanetary space. Thus, Fourier can be said to have initiated a practice of planetary and geological speculation. I take *speculation* to be a material practice, a kind of reasoned extrapolation and a manner of exploring possibilities. In general, one might say that Fourier's interest in Earth as such can be interpreted in light of James Fleming's question concerning the cultural history of climate change, namely, 'How do people (scientists included) gain awareness and understanding of phenomena that cover the entire globe, and that are constantly changing on timescales ranging from geological eras to centuries, decades, years and seasons' (1998, p. 161)? Fourier's geological speculation provides a partial answer to that question, not because it fulfilled deterministic Enlightenment expectations about climate and history, but because it provided an avenue for rupturing those expectations through the mathematical potential for imagining different worlds.

Fourier described the outer shell of the globe surrounded by an ephemeral atmosphere as the 'terrestrial envelope', as if one could see the fragile, shimmering surface of the globe's biosphere. I find this to be a powerful image of Earth prefiguring by more than fifteen decades the photos of Earth from space continually invoked in an effort to grasp the planetary stakes of climate change. Yet Fourier did not achieve this partial, privileged perspective by technological prosthesis (Haraway, 1988). There was no mechanical apparatus by which he found it possible to place a roving eye far above the Earth's surface. The Archimedean imagination was achieved by mathematical displacement in apprehending Earth, *qua* planet, as an abstract sphere that could be understood speculatively. Robert Friedman, a historian of Fourier's science, argues that for Fourier, 'Algebra is capable of advancing knowledge better than any other language; for once an algebraic equation for a problem is formulated, a solution can be arrived at by manipulation of signs without reference to what they represent' (1977, p. 92). In Fourier's own words, there is a supplementary excess to mathematical reasoning: 'mathematical analysis has outrun observation, it has supplemented our senses, and has made us in a manner witnesses of regular and harmonic vibrations in the interior of bodies' ([1878] 2009, p. 24). As techniques that emerge in historical time, and with implications sometimes beyond anticipation, the poetics of analytical technique therefore invoke an older sense of poiesis as that which transforms the world and qualifies its continuation.

The modern statement of the problem of greenhouse gases in the atmosphere is commonly attributed to Svante Arrhenius, who published a calculation of the effect on Earth's temperature of a doubling of atmospheric carbon dioxide in 1896. However, the theoretical problem of identifying the factors that determine Earth's temperatures was posed in the early 1800s, and appeared in its full, speculative form in Joseph Fourier's 1824 paper, available in a modern translation by noted geophysicist Raymond Pierrehumbert (Fourier, [1827] 2011; hereafter identified as *TS*).[3] Fourier is sometimes credited with having 'discovered the greenhouse effect', an argument which is spurious if by that one means by it to link Fourier's actual discoveries, and the authority of his legacy, to the modern discourse of anthropogenic climate change (Fleming, 2005, p. 56; Fleming, 1999).[4] And yet there is a link, recognizable in the way some contemporary scientists invoke his scientific legacy and especially his inspiration for a certain kind of imaginative planetary thinking. Raymond Pierrehumbert is only one striking case. A translator of Fourier's for the contemporary climate science community, Pierrehumbert is a theoretical geophysicist at the University of Chicago whose research concerns among other things the conditions in which Earth may have been completely covered in ice, a hard snowball Earth hypothetically possible under as-yet undiscovered atmospheric mechanisms (e.g. Pierrehumbert, 2005). In this chapter I identify a genealogy that links together Fourier's research on the role of Earth's atmosphere, his experimental mathematics, and the contemporary imaginative or speculative approach to climate change. My approach addresses the problems scientists set for themselves, and a description of the continuity of those problems compared to the discontinuity of their solutions (see Rabinow, 1994). Fourier's inheritance for contemporary climate science stems not from inaugurating a steady accumulation of scientific discoveries, but from posing questions for which his answers were inadequate and proposing techniques whose implications could not be determined.

There is a kind of science fiction at stake in the possibility of other worlds, and it is my contention that the imaginative potential of fictive worlds is directly at work in how science is sometimes done. Fourier's theoretical analysis of heat transfer can be viewed as the original formulation of the problem of what governs the temperature of the surface of the Earth, given a definite amount of energy from the sun and presumably far colder interplanetary temperatures. Given a constant flux of energy, the planet will warm until the energy escaping Earth is equal to the energy it receives. It is a relatively simple calculation to show that, if Earth had no atmosphere, its average temperature would be about 33°C colder than it is now known to be (Archer, 2012, p. 14).[5] The fact that this contemporary calculation rests on important simplifying assumptions does not change what was pivotal about Fourier's work, namely that it became possible to ask such a shocking question – what would Earth's temperature be without an atmosphere? One can imagine the existential drift that accompanied the view of a vulnerable planet floating in a deathly cold space.

Science studies and imagination

The science of climate change is a remarkable achievement of the late twentieth century, on a par with the development of genomics, and I would argue that we have only barely begun to understand the implications of its predictive claim that we can expect several degrees of warming by the end of the century. That predictive or anticipatory dimension is essential to the mode of expectation which permeates scientific and political debates about climate change. Expectation is a question about what might happen in the future, but it is also a question of the demands we place on our knowledge about the Earth. Even the most serious climate modelling efforts have a speculative dimension in the development of multiple climate 'storylines' or scenarios which simulate diverse potential futures. Thus the Intergovernmental Panel on Climate Change recently explained the need to use many different models simultaneously in this way: 'the sampling of possible futures is neither systematic nor comprehensive. [...] it is not yet clear which aspects [...] should guide our evaluations of future model simulations' (IPCC, 2013, p. 1036). My use of the term 'speculation' is not pejorative; rather it indicates an imaginative (reasoned) dimension of knowledge practices oriented toward the plausible demonstration of current expectations.

Unlike a foundationalist epistemology, speculative epistemology asks not 'On what grounds is truth necessary?' but rather, 'What might these definite, real relationships make possible?' Speculation grasps at possibility rather than resting on necessity, and attempts to underscore the generative conditions of uncertainties surrounding anthropogenic climate change. What concerns me here, in part, is to trace one element in a genealogy of this kind of quantitative, imaginative reasoning. From complex socio-technical systems, to the concerted development of new energy technologies, to the cultural production of climate fiction or futuristic visualization techniques, the exploratory dimension of future climates is imaginative, reasoned and deeply materialist. The question is how quantitative technique or the manipulation of mathematical relations can provide for practices of imagining different worlds.

Shapin and Schaffer (1986) demonstrate the rise of probabilistic reasoning in the 17th century, which does not demand 'geometrical' proof or reasoning from first principles. Instead, through the demonstration of experimental facts, using sophisticated experimental devices before a community of observers, the rise of modern science hinged on a critique of the ideal of complete certainty that might derive from a logical demonstration from first principles. Instead of axiomatic proof, experimental practice rests on what Shapin and Schaffer call moral certainty, that is, the adequate confidence produced within the social space defined by an experimental apparatus and a community of qualified observers. This approach to the social and material interactions in which reliable truths are produced has enabled a complete re-ordering of questions about the relative comparison of truth claims and even belief systems. Furthermore, it has rightly focused research on the materialist practices of the laboratory, moral expectations of scientific witnessing, and the material-semiotic knowledge infrastructures through which facts and truth claims are composed.

However, there is an additional level of imaginative reasoning that goes beyond the experimental demonstration of fact. Later work following in the tradition of actor network theory explicitly avoided questions of reason (see Rabinow, 1996; Hacking, 1994). But in contrast to the supposition of a singular universal reason, it is possible to view reason*ing* as a public, plural and materially extensive activity embedded and embodied in objects, technologies and social relations through which knowledge practices are made possible and produce results. Experts manipulate all sorts of relationships, from genomes to visualizations and mathematical sign systems, in order to explore ideas, many of which may not work out. That is to say, I view imaginative extrapolation as deeply invested in specific techniques for exploring logical outcomes. Just as climate change science is inescapably dependent on supercomputers capable of running General Circulation Models – whose calculations are physically impossible to do by hand – analogically, the emergence of complex socio-technical systems like carbon accounting may generate new ideas for reducing emissions and, through their definite socio-technical infrastructure, make it possible to imagine different relationships to the atmosphere. Whereas imagination is often contrasted with rationalism and a materialist outlook, I view an imaginative, speculative approach as extending materialism in the exploration of concrete possibilities whose outcomes cannot be anticipated in advance. As Harris puts it, 'if you can steal ideas then they are real. Every mathematician knows ideas can be and often are stolen' (Harris, 2008, p. 971).[6] Such a speculative materialism invites an exploratory practice of reasoning or 'modelling' possible futures, rather than a narrow, purportedly universal rationalism committed to foundational demonstrations of truth.

A generative ethos prevalent in contemporary science can thus be identified in Fourier, through which climate change is understood as a problem of imagining indeterminate futures. If Fourier is important to contemporary understandings of climate change, it is because he posed questions he could not adequately answer, using techniques that proved extremely generative. Fourier did not imagine a future of climate change; rather, he imagined logically divergent worlds based on the manipulation of specific variables related to the temperature of the terrestrial globe. Today, the imagination of indeterminate futures runs right through most climate change practices, and takes on transformative potential through specific material infrastructures. What real possibilities are entailed in new material-semiotic relations? The generativity of climate change and its manifold uncertainties, moreover, is a function of pervasive fossil energy emissions. By the 1950s, the terrestrial envelope, increasingly saturated by industrial fossil fuel emissions, enabled novel material and semiotic possibilities for imagining a new, anthropogenic Earth. But for that to occur, the surface of the Earth must have been displaced as the given horizon of human experience. That displacement was mathematical.

Fourier's demonstration

> One thus sees that the surface of the Earth [*le superficie du globe terrestre*] is located between one solid mass, whose central heat may surpass that of incandescent matter, and an immense region whose temperature is below the freezing point of mercury. (TS 5)

Fourier's unique concern is to provide a vantage on the limited context in which the Earth is lived and experienced; the metaphor of the 'terrestrial envelope' captures well the thin sliver of physical space in which humans reside between the heavens and the depths of Earth. His mathematical analysis manifests the singular truth of the universe's immensity and Earth's position in that vast secular condition. A rhetoric of scale is continuous throughout the text. He claims the dimensions of the planetary system are 'incomparably smaller than the distance separating the system from the radiant bodies distributed throughout the universe' (TS 10). In one thought experiment, he estimates 200,000 years must pass 'before one could observe even a single degree of temperature increase at the surface' (TS 21). The interior of the Earth must be as hot – possibly hotter – as the surface of the sun, and yet it ceased long ago to have any sensible effect on the temperature of the surface. The interior retains its heat for an immense period of time; he ventures in conclusion that, in their origin, the planetary bodies 'were made from the mass of the sun' (TS 21). In addition to the temperature of interplanetary space, a principle concern is 'the heart of the Earth itself, which it possessed at epochs when the planets were formed' (TS 13).

The rhetoric of scale is therefore also durational. '[T]he interior masses, whatever their state and temperature may be, communicate only an insignificant quantity of heat to the surface over immense stretches of time' (TS 20). The problem of the secular cooling of the globe, on which Fourier had previously published, is a question of Earth's origins in the context of a vast universe. Unlike the English, the French *séculaire* evokes historical time, the duration of a century, and cyclical periods of civilizations or astronomical variation. Repeatedly Fourier brings the surface conditions in which we live into the perspective of the boundary conditions provided by the primordial heat of the globe, the interiority of an immense planet, and the vastness of 'the region of the heavens presently occupied by the solar system' (TS 9).

These three coordinates – secular time; the exteriority of planetary space; and the interiority of the *globe terrestre* – therefore position the diversity of climates. For Fourier, the depth of space and time dominate. In contrast, the diversity of climates for Montesquieu was a feature of the surface of the Earth in relation to the incidence of the rays of the sun. 'Drunkenness predominates throughout the world, in proportion to the coldness and humidity of the climate. Go from the equator to the North Pole, and you will find this vice increasing together with the degree of latitude' (Montesquieu, [1748] 1970, p. 228). *Earth's climate* in the singular was simply not a question. Fourier's opening gambit expands that simple relation radically, for he is to analytically separate and describe each source of Earth's heat in turn to raise the general question of what determines the broad features of the planet's temperatures. Fourier identifies three distinct sources:

> It is first necessary to distinguish the three sources from which the Earth derives its heat:
> 1 The Earth is heated by solar radiation, the unequal distribution of which produces the diversity of climates;

2 It participates in the common temperature of interplanetary space, being exposed to irradiation by countless stars which surround all parts of the solar system;

3 The Earth has conserved in the interior of its mass, a part of the primordial heat which it had when the planets originally formed. (TS 3)

Planetary average temperature is raised as a potential question when considering the importance of atmosphere, and with the full demonstration of his speculative reasoning. 'As for the mean temperature caused by the action of the Sun on each of these [other planets], we are in a state of ignorance, because it can depend on the presence of an atmosphere and the state of the surface. One can only assign, in a very imprecise manner, the mean temperature which the Earth would acquire if it were transported to the same position as the planet in question' (TS 6).

Even so, Earth's 'diversity of climates' is not a major theme. The term appears sporadically, and usually in the context of a statement of inference. In a sense, his goal is to abstract away from the appearance of surface conditions to every extent possible. He begins his geological analysis with a single empirical claim from which mathematical analysis follows: 'If one places a thermometer at a considerable depth below the surface of the solid Earth, for example at 40 meters, this instrument indicates a fixed temperature. One observes this fact at all points of the globe. This deep subsurface temperature is constant for any given location; however, it is not the same in all climates' (TS 6). Effectively he peels away the outer layers of the Earth to consider the constant state of the interior temperature, taken as an abstract sphere.

One can imagine that the state of the mass has varied continually in accord with the heat received from the heat source. This variable temperature state gradually alters, and more and more approaches a final state which no longer varies in time. At that time, each point of the solid sphere has acquired – and conserves – a fixed temperature, which depends only on the position of the point in question (TS 6).

He then proceeds analytically to 'restore the upper envelope of the Earth, for which points are not sufficiently deep for their temperatures to be time-independent' (TS 7).[7] This allows him to consider the periodicity of annual and diurnal variations in temperature as the solar heat penetrates the surface of the Earth to varying extents. Indeed this analysis is the main demonstration of his trigonometric technique of decomposing heat flux into sinusoidal wave forms (Fourier refers readers to his *Analytical Theory of Heat* (i.e. Fourier [1878] 2009) for the full analysis). The amplitude of these annual pulses of energy decreases with depth, yet '[t]he mean annual temperature of any given point of the vertical, that is, the mean of all values observed at this point in the course of a year, is independent of depth' (TS 8). Another consequence is that the interior does not warm at the same time of year as the surface, but rather a flux of heat penetrates the surface only to escape again in the winter months. 'One eighth of a year before the temperature of the surface rises to its mean value, the Earth begins to accumulate heat; the rays of the Sun penetrate the Earth for six months. Then, the movement of the Earth's heat reverses direction; it exits and expands through the air and outer space' (TS 8). Here again climate is the occasion for specifically planetary reasoning rather than its consequence. 'Our goal in choosing this example of the application of the formulae is to show that there exists a necessary relation between the law of periodic variations and the total quantity of heat transfer which accompanies this oscillation; once this law is known from observations of one given climate, one can deduce the quantity of heat which is introduced into the Earth and which later returns to the air' (TS 8). This calculation would be an estimate of the total, annual planetary heat flux.

He doesn't attempt it. He recognizes that he doesn't know the true empirical values of certain coefficients. The numerical evaluations are given as examples only; 'however inexact, […] they serve to give a more correct idea of the phenomena than would general mathematical expressions bereft of numerical application' (TS 7).

Given the incidental consideration of climate in his text, his view nonetheless reconciles with the prevailing understanding of human influence over climatic conditions, by way of introducing a distinction between fundamental causes and accessory causes that is important for understanding his view of the atmosphere.

> The movements of the air and the waters, the extent of the oceans, the elevation and form of the surface, the effects of human industry and all the accidental changes of the Earth's surface modify the temperature of each climate. The basic character of phenomena arising from fundamental causes survives, but the thermal effects observed at the surface are different from those which would be seen without the influence of these accessory causes. (TS 11)

But this particular passage, often quoted, is a conventional view of climate common to his time, and is not derived from his analysis. The accessory causes that do garner special attention are the communication of heat established by ocean currents and the atmosphere, in particular the capacity of transparent fluids to trap infrared radiation. I will turn to the role of the atmosphere in a moment, but for now I want to single out the kind of problem Fourier has happened upon. Fourier's concern was not the diversity of climates in the deterministic traditions of natural history (Herivel, 1975, p. 128; Fleming, 1998, p. 48–50). Later – and throughout most of the nineteenth century – the question of climate would revolve around explaining periodic ice ages – but that, too, was not his problem. Fourier's concerns were rather more general and more global. He has little concept of a global climate (in the singular), which would not emerge in the contemporary sense until the late twentieth century (Miller, 2004), yet clearly his problematic anticipates such a singular, planetary-scale object characterized by an average Earth temperature. He claims that terrestrial temperature is 'the most important application of the theory of heat' (TS 20) because it demonstrates the necessary mathematical relations of his theory while proving the usefulness of scientific reason. His career included no other comparable application of his theory, which he considered to be an examination of unvarying laws equivalent to Newton's laws of motion. His objective was to speculate, analytically, on the immensity of the geological and interplanetary conditions that influence *la superficie du globe*. He stops short of deterministic claims, calling attention to the preliminary stage of understanding and the role of the accessory causes, such as the heating of the atmosphere, which can 'totally change the results' (TS 17).[8]

Notwithstanding the accidental character of Earth's superficial condition, his conclusion is ultimately conservative. The juxtaposition of scale repeats a constant paradox concerning this secular predicament: 'if one were to imagine that the portion a few leagues below the surface were replaced by either ice or the very substance of the Sun having the same temperature of that star, a great number of centuries would flow by before one observed any appreciable change in the surface temperature' (TS 21). The truth of that paradox is the very recognition of stability. 'Here one again encounters the stable character presented by all great phenomena of the universe' (TS 15). Fourier's geological speculation imagined mathematically hypothetical planets, not radically different potential futures.

The scene of imagination

What was the mise-en-scène of Fourier's 'extended body'?[9] How was Fourier's imagination extended throughout his instrumentation, his laboratory space, his visual technologies and practices of scientific sociality? Only an indication of the materialism of his practice can be given here. However astute his mathematical innovations, it is clear that that they demanded precise but limited experimental measurement of the transmission of heat within solid bodies. The description of his experiments was written up in his 1807 *Memoire sur la Propagation de la Chaleur*, published without translation in Grattan-Guinness (Fourier, [1807] 1972), who mentions that further experiments were carried into the 1820s. Three central experiments occupied Fourier's attention. The first concerned the transmission of heat within an iron ring about a foot in diameter. By applying heat at one point on the ring with an Argand lamp, he allowed the iron ring to achieve a steady state temperature, which alone took four hours and 24 minutes. The objective was to precisely measure the temperature difference at various points along the ring during this steady state. For this purpose the ring was drilled in the appropriate locations with 1.45cm holes, and these holes were fitted with mercury thermometers; the remaining space was filled with mercury. The thermometers used the Reaumur scale graded in ¹⁄₁₂-degree increments; the air temperature in the room was controlled to 17° ⅔ (22°C or about 72°F) by regulating air from an adjacent, heated room. The experiment was varied by measuring the rate of cooling of the iron ring over a period of three hours after it had been heated in the initial manner, a task requiring a small team of assistants. Indeed, this seems to be the only passing reference to other people involved in or witnessing his experiments. It is only appropriate that the question of care and disciplined observation is raised precisely in connection with multiple witnesses: with four thermometers fitted to the ring and the ring heated to a steady temperature, 'We then began to measure temperatures with the utmost care. Each person watched a single thermometer;

all were notified at the same time by the one watching the clock. We immediately noticed the mercury in the thermometer position, and we took note' (Art. 162, Grattan-Guinness 1972, p. 422).

Thermometers were expensive and hard to come by; Fourier referenced that only four suitable thermometers could be found, and his ring was drilled for more instruments had he been able to find them (for the experiment, these holes were filled with mercury). He also spent considerable effort developing a mathematical analysis of the thermometers he used – effectively conducting experiments on his thermometers – in what would later be called a re-analysis of his instruments (Arts. 108–110, Grattan-Guinness 1972, p. 320–322). Chang (2008) gives an extended description of the travails of the development of temperature measurement, much of the work for which preceded Fourier's labour and on which he depended. Fourier was concerned with the differences in measurement between thermometers as well as the time required to heat or cool a thermometer during a measurement, the tendency for a thermometer to register different temperatures when being heated rather than being cooled, and the effect of the thermometer's heat on the medium to be measured. More broadly, all sorts of difficulties with the experiments crop up in his prose.

One final experiment should be noted because it directly concerns an Earth analogue, in the form of a polished iron sphere, 5.52cm in diameter, drilled with a 1.5cm hole to a depth of 3.8cm in order to accommodate a thermometer to measure the temperature of its centre. As he claimed in his essay on the temperatures of the terrestrial sphere and interplanetary space, the experiment involved determining the variable temperature of the iron sphere, having been heated in a medium, which was then moved to a colder space. The experiment was varied when the sphere 'having been plunged successively and for some time in two or more media of different temperatures, should undergo a final cooling in a medium of constant temperature' (Fourier, [1824] 1837, p. 15). The various media included a bath of mercury, fine sand and heated filings. 'Sometimes we covered the body in a black coating, resulting in almost twice the rate of cooling' (Art. 166, Grattan-Guinness 1972, p. 438). These experiments provided him with an empirical understanding of the logarithmic distribution of heat during the process of cooling, and with experimental confirmation of the trigonometric functions and their approximations that formed the basis of his mathematical technique. Indeed, Herivel (1975, p. 151) claims Fourier's trigonometric innovations would scarcely have been believed except for the experimental confirmation.

Almost no discussion of Fourier's experimental practice can be found in the existing historical studies of his work, nearly all of which are concerned with his innovative calculative techniques (an exception being Grattan-Guinness 1972, p. 421–423 and passing references in Herivel 1975). There is little experimental description in his lengthy prepared manuscripts. In Fourier's words, his practice combined twin components of theoretical physics, 'precise observation' and 'exact calculation', which link together material and mathematical assemblages in an exploratory mode. An iron sphere, as an Earth analogue, is plunged into media of various temperatures in order to understand how heat radiates from that body.

I would like for these thinly described experiments to do some of the work of experimental demonstrations that Shapin and Schaffer expect from Robert Boyle's air pump. For the mise-en-scene of Boyle's experimental apparatus encapsulated the material problems of measurement, empirical confirmation, and public witnessing essential to the emergence of experimental procedure.

And yet Fourier's experiment also captures his mathematical imagination of Earth's temperature problem. At the core of his mathematical practice was his demonstration of how to treat heat propagation as a wave by decomposing the complex pattern into simpler sine wave functions – that is to say, not an axiomatic proof from first principles but the elaboration of a technique of manipulating signs in ways that had not been previously explored. Moreover, at the level of mathematical technique Fourier's work became fully public. Herivel (1975) describes at length the complex debates surrounding acceptance of his work by the leading scientists of his time, and has published many of the letters in which Fourier defended, explained and even sometimes pleaded for acceptance of his unorthodox methods. Before these distant and demanding witnesses, the numbers and their technical manipulation introduced surprising possibilities not previously under consideration.

At the core of his imagination of Earth's temperatures are oscillating pulses of energy that permeate Earth's surface seasonally and daily, and then release that energy in turn. As Earth spins on its axis, and as it rotates around the sun, these are variables that can be treated speculatively. 'If the speed of rotation of the Earth about its axis were to become incomparably greater, and if the same were to occur for the movement of the planet about the Sun, one would no longer find diurnal and annual temperature variations ...; the points of the surface would attain and conserve [a] fixed [...] temperature' (TS 8). One could find seeds of a science fiction here, with its roots in the mathematical decomposition of relations into sinusoidal waveforms, helping compose a cultural history of the present. 'A light wave rings like a bell,' writes David Archer (2012, p. 10) in a textbook on climate science. 'A blackbody is like a musical instrument with all the notes.' In no small sense, this is Fourier's imagination. This technique of reasoning takes on definite material-semiotic forms that can be described not as a habitus or 'logic of practice' but rather as a practice of logical reasoning that is generative and exploratory. If one takes an iron sphere and alternately plunges it into media of different temperatures in order to simulate an imagined Earth – or if one mathematically allows the planet's periodicity to approach infinity – it is a short step to a science fiction of imagining different worlds.

Infinite cold

At the grand scale of the planetary, Fourier worked in the Copernican tradition of undermining the givenness of Earth's condition. His experimental apparatus provided specific insights into the relation of interior temperature with surface conditions and the role of solar radiation in maintaining Earth's temperature. However, these two factors are inadequate to explain the relatively minor variation of surface temperatures. Why aren't nights and winters colder? What explains the relative warmth of the poles, when compared with calculated values? He cannot imagine that 'the solar system [could be] located in a region deprived of all heat. [...] The polar regions would be subject to intense cold, and the decrease of temperature from equator to pole would be incomparably more rapid and more extreme than is observed' (TS 9). What could it mean to be exposed to a region of space deprived of all heat whatsoever?

Consider such a premise. 'Under this hypothesis of absolutely cold space, if such a thing is possible to conceive of [...] the alternation of day and night would produce effects both sudden and totally different from those we observe. The surface of bodies would be exposed all of a sudden, at the beginning of night, to an infinitely intense cold. The living world, both animal and vegetable, could not survive such a rapid and strong action, which repeats in the opposite sense at sunrise' (TS 8–9). His mathematical speculation offers an experience – a witnessing, even – of the terrestrial envelope as a thin veil of life against a universe of immense extremes. These are existential questions, and certain of his estimates seem to shudder in disbelief at the implications of his argument.

Fourier anticipates the insulating properties of the atmosphere, which allow visible radiation from the sun to pass much more easily than the 'dark radiation' which radiates back to space from Earth's surface. This was cutting edge science: Herschel had discovered infrared radiation only in 1800, and the very idea (as Herschel put it) of 'invisible light' was a powerful provocation (Barr, 1961, p. 1). Fourier thoroughly integrated these insights into his analysis:

> [T]he heat emanated by the Sun has properties different from those of dark heat. The rays of this star [...] heat the air and the surfaces which contain it: the heat communicated in this way ceases to be luminous, and takes on the properties of dark radiant heat. (TS 12)

This same property relates to both the oceans and the atmosphere, and Fourier examines the implications of both. The atmosphere represents something of an enigma. 'The presence of the atmosphere produces an effect of [retaining dark heat more easily than luminous radiation], but which, in the present state of theory and owing further to lack of observations with which theory may be compared, cannot yet be exactly defined' (TS 5). An even stronger statement of the analytical predicament is thus: 'It is difficult to know just to what extent the atmosphere affects the mean temperature of the globe, and here the guidance of rigorous mathematical theory ceases' (TS 11). Such uncharted territory showed the emergence of a scientific problem with no clear solution. Specifically in considering the role of the atmosphere, he raises the question of its effect on the mean temperature of the planet.

Nonetheless, his reasoning on this point and his awareness of the possible role of the atmosphere are palpable. Fourier refers the question to experiments conducted by Horace Benedict de Saussure (1740–1799) – the great-grandfather of Ferdinand de Saussure – using an apparatus made with a box lined with black cork and covered with panes of glass and exposed to the noontime sun.[10] Temperatures inside the box could rise to 70°C or even 80°C. Visible light from the sun passes easily through successive transparent panes of glass, whereas dark radiation is unable to pass; 'the temperature rises to the point at which the incident heat is exactly balanced by the dissipated heat' (TS 12). From this he derives the importance of the accessory causes of the oceans and atmosphere.

Reasoning from this analogy, Fourier makes the exquisite claim that Earth's 'temperature is augmented by the interposition of the atmosphere, because the heat has less trouble penetrating the air in the form of light, than it has exiting back through the air after it has been converted to dark heat' (TS 13).

Ultimately, Fourier does not assign any great role to the atmosphere for maintaining Earth's temperature. Far more important for him is the speculative inference of the temperature of interplanetary space, which would have stood as a major prediction for a new field of theoretical physics. In other words, the Earth would be much colder if not for the communal temperature of the interplanetary space through which it orbits. The warmth of interplanetary space would be what remains after all other causes are accounted for. '[I]t would be impossible,' he concludes, 'for the action of the atmosphere to supplant the universal cause arising from the communal temperature of interplanetary space' (TS 11).

His language, once again, is worth attending to. 'The countless multitude of stars [...], the dark bodies which fill the universe, [...] the tenuous material strewn through the various parts of space, act together to form these rays which penetrate all parts of the planetary regions. [...] Thus, the Earth finds the same temperature of the heavens at all parts of its orbit. The same applies to the other planets of our solar system; they all participate equally in the communal temperature' (TS 10). The translator of this essay, Raymond Pierrehumbert, argues that his 'argument is qualitatively right but quantitatively wrong' (TS 10, n. 10). Fourier overestimated the temperature by about 200°C. And in this image of communion, this premise of stability and warmth, Fourier could *not quite* imagine a planet bereft of any protection, drifting anonymously in an infinitely cold expanse.

Geological speculation

Fourier's geological speculation neither fulfilled Enlightenment expectations that linked climate and history in a deterministic mode, nor inaugurated contemporary global climate discourse. Instead, while repeating ideas about the diversity of climates common to his times, his experimental and mathematical speculation opened scientific problems that he could not adequately address concerning the factors governing the temperature of the Earth. This tension between the continuity of the scientific problem and the discontinuity of its subsequent solutions situates Fourier's analysis of the temperatures of the terrestrial sphere squarely within a genealogy of contemporary global climate change sciences. In the context of examining the role of atmosphere in affecting the mean temperature of Earth and other planets, Fourier clearly articulated the difficulty with which infrared radiation could penetrate the atmosphere as a factor in augmenting the Earth's temperature. However, he balked at the idea that the heat-retaining properties of the atmosphere could explain the mild variation of temperatures at Earth's surface, and explained that variation instead by positing a comparatively warm communal temperature of interplanetary space.

Current interest in the socio-technical construction of facts within scientific practice rarely brings into view the practices of logical reasoning through which scientists sometimes imaginatively speculate on the possibilities of different worlds. However, in understanding current global climate models as computer-enabled processes of logical extrapolation, there is an urgent need to consider practices of thinking as public, materially specific modes of imaginative reason. The fact that climate scientists routinely refer to a plurality of potential Earth futures does not confirm the discredited claim that science can be reduced to literature. The speculative practices of Joseph Fourier are inherently materialist, in two distinct senses. First, Fourier's mathematical analysis depended on a complex experimental practice involving disciplined manipulation of highly specific physical relationships. That experimental process was productive and generative in its own right: the manipulation of an experimental apparatus is itself a process of 'thinking through things'. Second, rule-governed manipulation of the algebraic sign system, based on the expansion of plausible techniques for estimating infinite series, allowed for speculation upon and discovery of relationships that were neither simple expressions of experimental observation nor a re-statement of his original premises. This role of mathematical reasoning rested on plausible technique, not axiomatic proof, and demonstrates the protensive, imaginative dimension of an exploration of possibility rather than a foundation of axiomatic necessity.

For his part, Fourier did not imagine radically different futures, but instead found in the communion of interplanetary space a confirmation of a universal tendency toward relative warmth and stability. Some two centuries after Fourier's work, it is plausible to argue that pervasive anthropogenic carbon pollution has created vast new potential for imaginative speculation on different worlds. Today, material practices and their speculative dimensions continually seem to arise within geological and scientific domains. As a pollutant, carbon dioxide is historically novel because its danger is only apparent at the scale of the planet, and thereby it has introduced a striking discontinuity in the kinds of expectations it is possible to formulate concerning Earth's futures. This is true especially geologically, in the sense that fossil carbon results from the vast sequestration of chemical energy stored hundreds of millions of years ago in a biological permutation of the geological carbon cycle. The current geological extraction of chemical energy can similarly be interpreted as an anthropogenic permutation of the geological carbon cycle. To that extent, anthropogenic climate change problematizes the ecological dimensions of Earth as home, and poses a speculative, materialist question about what forms of existence may as yet become possible. In this, one can hear echoes of Fourier's attempt to provide a different viewpoint on the terrestrial envelope. Today we would call that viewpoint an achievement of climate modelling, which gives us not one but many viewpoints to consider simultaneously.

At the beginning of his standard textbook on climate science, David Archer introduces a very basic mathematical model of the climate. 'The first step,' he says, 'is to construct the model with no atmosphere, so that the only layer is the ground, a Bare Rock Model' (2012, p. 19). What would be the temperature of Earth without an atmosphere? As the very first lesson on modelling, its object is to teach an ethos. And what does this ethos of speculation entail? 'The layer model is a toy, demonstrating an idea.'

Yet speculation as a material practice comes full circle. Fourier took spheres of iron as Earth analogues and immersed them in media of different temperatures. By the mid-twentieth century a reversal had taken place, and the scientific experiment could be said to occur at the scale of the planet itself. What may be the most widely cited passage in climate change science comes from a 1957 paper by Roger Revelle and Hans Suess, the former of whom played a major role at Scripps Institution of Oceanography. They argued that 'human beings are now carrying out a large scale geophysical experiment [...]. Within a few centuries we are returning to the atmosphere and oceans the concentrated organic carbon stored in sedimentary rocks over hundreds of millions of years' (Revelle & Suess, 1957, p. 18). This statement perhaps more than any other has characterized the ethos of modern climate change science. Of course, global climate models are designed to model the future, but as the Arctic melts far faster than IPCC predictions, we know General Circulation Models are also trying to catch up with a planet that has outpaced the careful extrapolation of mathematical worlds. Myanna Lahsen (2005) has shown that sometimes climate modellers are seduced into confusing their models for the real world. But isn't it also the opposite, that the real world is sometimes treated as a model? Is the present such a generative moment that the Earth *per se* has become a model, meant to demonstrate an idea?

Who cannot sense the excitement in Revelle and Suess's anticipation of the planetary stakes of the moment? 'This experiment, if adequately documented, may yield a far-reaching insight into the processes determining weather and climate' (1957, p. 18). One way or another, we will no doubt learn more about the role of atmospheric carbon in governing the temperature of the Earth than anyone ever expected.

Notes

1 Translations of Fourier's words from the French here and in Grattan-Guinness (1972) are mine.
2 Partial differential equations and the Fourier series are the essential mathematical innovations that enable modern financial trading, contemporary climate modelling, and synthesized electronic music.
3 This 1827 paper is a reprint of a paper that appeared in 1824, much of which had been published already in his *Theorie Analytique de la Chaleur* in 1822 (Fourier, 1878) with the exception of the significant discussion of the temperature of interplanetary space. It seems much of the research was conducted prior to 1811 (Herivel, 1975, pp. 197, 202).

4 These two publications provide a synopsis of Fourier's treatment of issues related to contemporary discourses of the greenhouse effect, including a summary of the argument of his original 'On the Temperatures of the Terrestrial Sphere and Interplanetary Space', to which I am indebted.

5 Fourier would not have been able to make this calculation. On the previous point: 'In fact, the radiation of the sun in which this planet is incessantly plunged, penetrates the air, the earth, and the waters; its elements are divided, change in direction every way, and, penetrating the mass of the globe, would raise its mean temperature more and more, if the heat acquired were not exactly balanced by that which escapes in rays from all points of the surface and expands through the sky' (Fourier, [1878] 2009, p. 3).

6 Of course, if ideas can be owned as property, it is because they have been made rather than discovered. The debate here is between Neo-Platonists who view number and logical relations as ontologically prior to social relations (e.g. Badiou, Meillassoux) and a Wittgensteinian approach that views mathematics as the outcome of social processes. Harris's view is far from Fourier's own: 'Mathematical analysis has therefore necessary relations with sensible phenomena; its object is not created by human intelligence; it is a pre-existent element of the universal order, and is not in any way contingent or fortuitous; it is imprinted throughout all nature' (Fourier, [1878] 2009, p. 25).

7 The original reads '*températures soient devenues fixes*,' i.e. without using the phrase time-independent (Fourier, 1827, p. 576).

8 The tension between unvarying natural laws and the plurality of outcomes due to an array of contingent 'accessory' factors is a fascinating dimension of his analysis. Current climate science understands this tension as arising from coupled systems characterized by multiple feedbacks that can produce widely divergent results. Whereas Newtonian laws of motion are deterministic, Fourier recognizes that many of the relevant equations for heat analysis cannot actually be solved. He resolves the tension between determinism and contingency through the analysis of boundary conditions. 'While the complete solution of these differential equations depends on expressions which are difficult to discover, or on tables which have not yet been created, one can nonetheless determine the limits between which the unknown quantities are necessarily bounded. One arrives thus at definite conclusions regarding the object in question' (TS 20). However, an 1828 *précis* in the Bulletin des Sciences Naturelles et de Geologie claimed the article would 'establish a fundamental basis for a rational system of geology' (Anon., 1828).

9 The phrase is from Hélène Mialet, who takes Stephen Hawking as an extreme case of the myth of the disembodied mind. 'Inevitably, by depriving him of his hands, [Hawking's] disease has also deprived him of the ability to perform the gestural manipulations required for calculative work' (2012, p. 66).

10 Descriptions of heliometer experiments can be found in Fleming (1999) and Archer and Pierrehumbert (2011).

References

Anon., 1828. Geologie I. Fourier. *Bulletin des sciences naturelles et de geologie*, 14(1).

Archer, D., 2012. *Global Warming: Understanding the Forecast*. 2nd ed. London: John Wiley & Sons.

Archer, D. & Pierrehumbert, R. eds., 2011. *The Warming Papers: The Scientific Foundation for the Climate Change Forecast*. London: John Wiley & Sons.

Barr, S. E., 1961. The Infrared Pioneers – I. Sir William Herschel. *Infrared Physics*, Volume 1, p. 1–4.

Chang, H., 2008. *Inventing Temperature: Measurement and Scientific Progress*. Oxford: Oxford University Press.

Comte, A., 1875. *Course in Positive Philosophy*. 2nd ed. London: Trubner & Co.

Fleming, J. R., 1998. Charles Lyell and climatic change: speculation and certainty. In: D. Blundell & A. Scott, eds. *Lyell: The Past Is the Key to the Present*. London: Geological Society of London, Special Publications 143, p. 161–169.

Fleming, J. R., 1999. Joseph Fourier, the 'greenhouse effect,' and the quest for a universal theory of terrestrial temperatures. *Endeavour*, 23(2), p. 72–75.

Fleming, J. R., 2005. *Historical Perspectives on Climate Change*. Oxford: Oxford University Press.

Fourier, J.-P. J., [1807] 1972. Memoire sur la Propagation de la Chaleur. In: I. Grattan-Guinness & J. R. Ravetz, eds. *Joseph Fourier, 1768–1830*. Cambridge (MA): MIT Press.

Fourier, J.-P. J., [1824] 1837. General Remarks on the Temperature of the Terrestrial Globe and the Planetary Space (tr. Ebenezer Burgess). *The American Journal of Science*, 32(1), p. 1–20.

Fourier, J.-P. J., [1827] 2011. On the Temperatures of the Terrestrial Sphere and Interplanetary Space. In: D. Archer & R. Pierrehumbert, eds. *The Warming Papers: The Scientific Foundation for the Climate Change Forecast*. London: John Wiley & Sons.

Fourier, J.-P. J., [1878] 2009. *Analytical Theory of Heat*. New York: Cambridge University Press.

Fourier, J.-P. J., 1827. Mémoire sur les Températures du Globe Terrestre et des Espaces Planétaires. *Memoire d l'Academie Royale des Sciences de L'Institut National de France*, Volume 7, p. 570–640.

Freidman, R. M., 1977. The Creation of a New Science: Joseph Fourier's Analytical Theory of Heat. *Historical Studies in the Physical Sciences*, Volume 8, p. 73–99.

Grattan-Guiness, I. ed., 1972. *Joseph Fourier, 1768–1830 : a survey of his life and work, based on a critical edition of his monograph on the propagation of heat presented to the Institut de France in 1807*. Cambridge (MA): MIT Press.

Hacking, I., 1994. Styles of Scientific Thinking or Reasoning. In: *Trends in the Historiography of Science*. Dordrecht: Springer Netherlands, p. 31–48.

Haraway, D., 1988. Situated Knowledges: The Science Question in Feminism and the Privilege of Partial Perspective. *Feminist Studies*, 14(3), p. 575–599.

Harris, M., 2008. Why Mathematics? You Might Ask. In: T. Gowers, ed. *The Princeton Companion to Mathematics*. Princeton: Princeton University Press, p. 966–977.

Herivel, J., 1975. *Joseph Fourier: The Man and the Physicist*. Oxford: Clarendon Press.

IPCC, 2013. Why Are So Many Models and Scenarios Used to Project Climate Change?. In: *Climate Change 2013: The Physical Science Basis*. New York: Cambridge University Press, p. 1036–1037.

Lahsen, M., 2005. Seductive Simulations: Uncertainty Distribution Around Climate Models. *Social Studies of Science*, Volume 35, p. 895–922.

Mialet, H., 2012. *Hawking Incorporated: Stephen Hawking and the Anthropology of the Knowing Subject*. Chicago: University of Chicago Press.

Miller, P., 2004. Climate Science and the Making of a Global Political Order. In: S. Jasanoff, ed. *States of Knowledge: The Co-Production of Science and Social Order*. New York: Routledge, p. 46–66.

Montesquieu, C.-L. d., [1748] 1970. *The Spirit of the Laws*. New York: Simon and Schuster.

Rabinow, P., 1994. Introduction: A Vital Rationalist. In: F. Delaporte, ed. *A Vital Rationalist: Selected Writings from Georges Canguilhem*. New York: Zone Books, p. 11–24.

Rabinow, P., 1996. *Essays on the Anthropology of Reason*. Princeton: Princeton University Press.

Revelle, R. & Suess, H., 1957. Carbon Dioxide Exchange Between Atmosphere and Ocean and the Question of an Increase of Atmospheric CO_2 During the Past Decades. *Tellus*, 9(1), p. 18–27.

Said, E., 2003. *Orientalism*. London: Penguin Books.

Shapin, S. & Schaffer, S., 1986. *Leviathan and the Air-Pump: Hobbes, Boyle, and the Experimental Life*. Princeton: Princeton University Press.

4 Melancholy and the continent of fire

Tom Bristow and Andrea Witcomb

We live in the most fire prone landscape on Earth. Victoria has been shaped by fire over millennia. It is a natural and essential part of Australia's ecosystem and eucalypt landscape. As climate is becoming more variable and more people are living closer to bushland, fire will continue to impact our lives.

Department of Sustainability and Environment

Forest Gallery, Melbourne

The anonymous words that we have chosen for our epigraph invoke climate change in a gallery largely aimed at recreating the experience of human immersion within a vast living ecosystem. Their impersonality mirrors the elusive emotions of this gallery that we examine in this chapter. The tension between the scale and pace of evolutionary agency and the practices of human culture over time, are both named in this statement despite its flat affect. The words are located on the first information panel that visitors read as they access 'The Clearing', the memorial space at the end of the multi-layered Forest Gallery in the Museum of Melbourne, Victoria, Australia. The gallery is housed in an open-air, mesh enclosed area: 1,485 square metres, 27m wide and 55m long; the roof is 15m high at the lowest point and 35m high at the highest. This space is divided into three distinct zones: the subterranean entrance is dominated by a river and its amphibious life; the forest proper, of over-towering mountain ash, follows; then 'The Clearing' – perhaps inviting a Heideggerean rereading of the other two zones, as visitors exit, walking back down the hill through the forest and the river.

Visitors read this first information panel as they cross a threshold taking them out of an experience of seven indigenous seasons (indexed as 'climate' by the signage), stepping over a warning sign on the ground – a metal plate embossed with the words 'climate' and 'fire' – into an alluring and melancholic space that is a testament to fire. Here, a conflation of time and space conjoins references to climate change and landscape clearing, the physiological ecology of forest production, and fire ecology and succession. When visitors walk towards the edge of the forest, the gallery appears to be an organism shaped by environmental forces driven by human hands; an emergent museal amalgam of life forms and historical memory compresses relations between indigenous knowledge, settler practice and different forms and frequencies of clearing, regrowth and regenera-tion on the island continent throughout its troubled history. The space presents an endgame or political impasse, which can only be resolved by new configurations of memory and learning. Ultimately, it is a memorial with an aesthetic strategy to instruct the visitor on the aftermath of settler colonialism and its cultural and environmental clearance. Yet the gallery's ethical imperative is not told but per-formed in an affective threading together of distinct cultural practices and various climate change consequences. How, then, is this public pedagogy not to repeat history put together, and how is it presented?

To begin to answer that question we need to understand not only the rationale behind the gallery – its intellectual genealogy – but also the ways in which this genealogy is embodied in a range of interpretative strategies. We need, in other words, to attend to the gallery as a sensorial and emotional experience that is also a public medium of ecological knowledge of the ash forest and its history, and that of the troubled cultural engagement with the forest. After visiting The Clearing, visi-tors may exit the gallery into the top floor of the Museum, or walk back through the whole space in order to exit and so revisiting what has been seen, memories of creek-bed and forest are re-encountered through a filtering affective lens of loss, destruction and displacement – the experience of catastrophic fire, and of even more catastrophic colonization, which have been encountered through the gallery.

Emerging environmental histories

The Forest Gallery presents a complex amalgam of differing regimes of time, and different forms of expert knowledge alongside diverse relationships to a specific place, the ash forests of the Dandenong Ranges. Its origins lie in former Museum Victoria director Graham Morris' (1990–98) desire for a 'living space' in the heart of the museum to counteract the idea that museums were full of dead objects: the ambition being something like a museum of life itself. While the Forest Gallery was shaped by this specific historical moment, in which museums sought to overcome their 'dusty glass case' image by embracing experiential exhibitions, the idea also came at a time when Museum Victoria was experimenting with new approaches for engaging with indigenous histories, and new ways of thinking about the relation-ship between nature and culture (Rasmussen, 2001). These approaches were largely driven in Australia by the new modes of environmental histories then emerging, which contributed directly to the planning behind the Gallery (Griffiths, 2001, p. 198).[1] This general rise in academic and public prominence of environmental history built on arguments from the 1970s and 1980s that Australians needed to rec-oncile their historical experience with the places and peoples they had colonized, an as yet unachieved aim elusively evoked in the Forest Gallery's museal recrea-tion of an iconic Victorian landscape – the ash forests of the Dandenong Ranges – that seeks to reflect the perspectives of both the indigenous and settler populations that engaged with it, as well as stage the presence of a natural environment itself. Central to the interdisciplinary premise of environmental history as it is presented in the public space of the museum is then the desire to hold together the historical ecologies of vastly different human communities, along with their starkly different ways of understanding human relationships with non-humans.

This is an aim that Griffiths (2001) elucidates in his epilogue to the book that accompanies this Gallery. Griffiths argues that late twentieth-century forms of environmental history spring 'from a contemporary sense of crisis about the human ecological predicament' – the awareness that our activities have a deep impact on nature's own cycles of life and therefore on our own sustainability. In so doing, these histories often move 'audaciously across time and space and species and thereby challenge some of the conventions of history by questioning the anthropocentric, nationalistic and documentary biases of their craft' (194).[2] In these histories, nature has its own history, its own rhythms and biological processes, which we would do well to understand or simply acknowledge, as these rhythms and processes have their own impact on human lives (191).[3] An informed environmental history, then, can offer not only an understanding of the ecology of any given place, a perspective that enriches natural history, but also a warning – a warning given particular moral force by its treatment of fire as at once a natural regenerative force and a force of destruction with the power to change our environment – both human and non-human – that is itself being transformed by contemporary human societies. As one of the elemental forces this gallery engages with (the others being water and earth), fire certainly speaks to urban and rural demographics in distinct ways; yet ultimately, in this gallery, it is viewed as the agent before which our audacity to play with nature comes back to haunt us, forcing us to consider environmental change alongside our relationship to nature as defined by our cultural practices. That specific hauntological poetics does not offer a pastoral dialogue between urban and rural spaces but invites the visitor to entertain a generalized metaphor for change: to feel a specific desire for a future wherein climate is not premised on our indulgence in fossil fuels. That the warning comes in the shape of three memorials – to the forests, to indigenous people, and to those who died and suffered as a result of catastrophic fires – points to the ways in which our understanding of the issues at stake can involve a reappraisal of our relationships and entanglement in colonial attitudes to both the natural world, and indigenous people and their knowledge. For it is these memorials that give new meaning to the three histories that together constitute the eco-cultural foundations of environmental histories in Australia – ecology, indigenous and settler histories.[4]

Moving through time

A cross-section of kauri pine (*Agathis robusta*) dominates the external gallery entrance; over six hundred years old and eight foot six inches in diameter, the north Queensland tree's countable rings remind visitors of change and its lived measurements as they step into this extensive and living space.[5] A monument of growth over the centuries as well as a monument of widespread logging in the late 1800s and 1900s, the smooth-barked coniferous tree refers to two of the gallery's five timescales: the appearance of Earth's first life forms (3.8 b.y.a.), the emergence of the ancient supercontinent Gondwana (510–180 m.y.a.) and its distribution of eucalypts (from the early Eocene, 51.9 m.y.a.), indigenous settlement (40–80,000 y.a.), the colonial period (1788–1850), and the post/neo-colonial present. These timescales are threaded through the thematic zones depicting specific agents of change: water, earth processes, climate, fire and human intervention.

Entering through a liminal space that protects the rest of the museum from the green moist forest beyond, exposed as it is to the external climate, the visitor is suddenly in the fresh, moist air of the rainforest. Before them is a creek cascading over some rocks into an inviting pool: riverine and plant life enclosed by lush green ferns (see Figure 4.1). Turning the corner and passing through an underground space built into the hill that is the Forest Gallery, the path runs beneath the creek. On the cold August day we visited, this steamed into the air of the underground passage. In the midst of this mist and the murmurs of inland water appeared two accounts of the creation of the Yarra river, which the creek above references. One, from a geologist, describes the formation of the landscape of the Dandenong Ranges, as water carved its way through soft rock to the sea. The other tells of the creation of the river by Wurundjeri Elders, Barwool and Yan-yan, against attempts to stop them by Baw Baw and Donna Buang.[6] Both accounts embed us in far-distant times. Emerging then out of the darkness, from water into earth, we also seemed to move in time and physical scale. Here it was the minutiae of life that confronted us, rather than the grandeur of rivers and mountains, as we peered into the life of the creek by means of little windows set into it – museum peepholes into a dioramic watery lost world. Frogs hid on moss and liverwort covered rocks. Birdsong intermittently called us to look up, to the high trees arching above us. Walking up the hill past the threshold

Figure 4.1 Water Zone, Forest Gallery, by Jon Augier, with permission of Museum Victoria.

that divides the museum zones of water and earth, the intricate design of nature seemed to stand out: peculiar insects lay camouflaged against leaves; lizards hid in and basked on the rocks that lined the creek. On the banks, birds scratched for worms; butterflies danced in the air. The delicate balance between all living things, micro and macro, was there for us to witness, nature exhibited in the museum, the tight and dynamic relations between various forms of life folded into presentations of geological formations and the composition of the earth's atmosphere, conditions set down for potential localized ecologies to emerge later in time. The experience was both sensual and cognitive, the mind challenged to think of a set of relationships and also to feel them out, to envision and be affected by a stretched matrix of life spread over a slowly changing and elasticated space of ecological presence and representation.

Fire is a critical element for the reproductive survival of mountain ash trees, which require intense heat to germinate. While fire largely destroyed the ancient Australasian beech forests – surviving relics from the ancient Gondwanaland that linger on in moist, dark nooks – eucalypt developed a mechanism to thrive in increasing climatic heat and aridity. In the gallery, fire appears as a power that shapes and will shape the landscape, an agency that may never be fully determinable. A word of caution is provided: the mountain ash, *Eucalyptus regnans*, is only adapted to withstand occasional intense fires – by implication, frequent fires lead not to its regeneration but its destruction – an implication that comes back to haunt us in full force, in 'The Clearing'.[7]

The aesthetically framed experience of the forest, with its invitation to look closely into the daily life of its non-human inhabitants while moving through a staged mimesis of geological time, presents a disjointed experience. The creek flows, the forest grows, and outside the city traffic murmurs, just on the edge of audibility. Connections are presented without being consolidated, in a story that stretches comprehensibility. The gallery thus begins to emerge not just as a recreation of an environment but as a form of storytelling, operating in the same evocatory vein as Graham Huggan's understanding of storied atmosphere, which he sees as 'blend[ing] the phenomenological idea of *landscape*' – facts experienced by a sensitive being – with that 'of *climate*[,] the intuitive apprehension of a larger reality' (Huggan, 2015, p. 96). Drawing from Julian Knebusch, Huggan understands this narratively rich ambience as an ensemble that involves the 'opening [up of] an atmospheric relation to the world' (Knebusch, 2008, p. 247). But which world is that here, in the museum? Climate change belongs to the spheres of both human and non-human experience. Larger, non-human forces are present in the Forest Gallery, but they are also gallerised, presented in a space of visitor experience. In evoking an absent world in its exhibition of a forest, the constructed natural landscape introduces the possibility of other senses of time in its discontinuous references to the temporal and discursive layering of where we stand.

Climatic seasonal encounters

At this point, the gallery turns to seasons, an engagement already signalled by the presence of Dreamtime stories at the beginning of time itself when we first encounter the creation of the Yarra River.[8] Here, annual cycles of energy, atmosphere and oceans are registered in highly localized place-based oral histories of nuanced habitable conditions that connect micro-events with the larger process of setting the earth's climate. The gallery's climate zone runs horizontally from one side of the portrait-shaped rectangular space to another, leading to the fire zone and ultimately into 'The Clearing'. This route is structured by a wooden pathway edged by a single curve on the upper side, and a winding and turning series of curves on the lower. The shape to the path reflects the course of the creek through the landscape, connecting the climate path to the watery life of earlier zones; however, the series of curves most directly mirrors a flowing glass ribbon inserted into the forest, presenting the Aboriginal seasonal calendar of the Upper Yarra Valley (see Figure 4.2). This connection, in turn, refers to a local culture that is located between two historical periods referred to by the Kauri Pine at the gallery entrance (the distribution of eucalypts in Gondwana, and the colonial period) that run on into the present: the Kulin peoples, a loose confederation of five Aboriginal groups with commonalities in language, custom, traditions, burial rites and trade, and who identify themselves as a nation. For the Kulin, the interrelationships between weather patterns, star movements, and the changes in life cycles of plants and animals 'form the seasonal markers used to determine when a particular event may occur or when it was necessary to relocate' (Allen, 2001, p. 58).[9] Local ecologies resulting from or influenced by the prevailing seasons appear in the gallery as examples or fragments of a natural world, referencing changes in the larger cycles of Earth's life.

Figure 4.2 Visitors on Boardwalk, Forest Gallery, by Rob Blackburn with permission of Museum Victoria.

In the Kulin imaginary, 'this country enjoys an annual cycle of seven seasons and two non-annual seasons – the Fire season that occurs about every seven years; and the flooding season that has a cycle of approximately 28 years' (Allen, 2001).[10] For Bill Gammage (2011), an 'ecological philosophy' compelled the earliest Australians to care for country: 'Knowing which plants welcome fire, and when and how much, was critical to managing land. Plants could then be burnt and not burnt in patterns, so that post-fire regeneration could situate and move grazing animals predictably by selectively locating the feed and shelter they prefer' (1). The gallery is leading us towards a narrative of fire within a fire-prone landscape wherein, according to Gammage, 70 per cent of Australia's plants need or tolerate fire. Accompanying this narrative is a coupling of human and natural systems, which the gallery then places within an ethical context for reviewing our practices. This very coupling is based on an agential and experiential model of public culture – particularly the residual public intertwinings of colonialism and indigeneity. Shifting to the human time of the seasons invites a reappraisal of the relations between different temporal scales: of the intensity of our human activities, as of the slow rhythms of geological and climatic time. A corner of Carlton – an inner-city, highly urbanised neighbourhood – models a section of a continental, fire-ridden tapestry increasingly under pressure from the external driver of human-induced global climate change.

'Luk' is defined by the ceasing of hot winds, as cooling temperatures and the flowering of the Binap Manna Gum signal the time for harvesting eel: Eel season. This is followed by Waring, or wombat season, with the highest rainfall and lowest temperatures. Orchid season is known as Guling, and this comes when the ae-noke caterpillars of the common brown butterfly feed on grasses at night and orchids flower. Poornet, or tadpole season is next, with temperatures rising but rain continuing in a land of pied currawong calls and flowering flax-lillies. Then Buath Gurra, or glass flowering season, is present when bullyong bats catch insects in flight while kangaroo grass is flowering. Finally, the changeable thundery weather of kangaroo-apple season arrives, populated with fruiting bali (cherry ballart), apple bushes and active goannas.

All these events are rhymed with the appearance of constellations, which are offered equal representation on the ribbon. The Southern Cross, the most represented asterism of the southern hemisphere, has guided travellers on the dry continent for thousands of years, and has entered the cultures of Australia and New Zealand, Papua New Guinea and Samoa, Chile and Brazil. This young constellation (8–11 m.y.a.) is referenced as high in the south at sunrise during the final season, Biderap, the dry and dangerous season, when the tussock grass is long and dry, with high temperatures and low rainfall. Beyond the ribbon lie reference points that include the farming of orchids, which can be seen to be stimulated by the autumn temperature, signs for the stick insect's lifespan across the seasons, and labels for the rarest plants of the tall forest ecosystem. For the gallery is a forest even as human culture is ever present, and it presents a network of references even where those references are non-human, woven into an unnamed global fabric that the cosmological signage points to, not in terms of origins but of general structure.

In direct allusion to intergenerational stories that pass on knowledge, cultural values and belief systems, known as The Dreaming,[11] the ribbon presents four indigenous voices bringing into view their relationship with the seasons.[12] Martha Nevin speaks of when her foraging band would set up a line for eels in the lagoons, and provides instructions to catch a codfish with a frog; Jessi Hunter remarks on the similarity between meat samples from wombat, pork and echidna and how her Granny Jemima would pick and boil orchids as a remedy for headaches. Local history and the excitement of learning from local culture is picked up by Brian Paterson who recounts how swagmen, drovers and stockmen made damper (soda bread) from seeds, while also commenting on how to predict a storm two or three days in advance by listening to the birds who descend from the mountains. Dot Peters remembers, and almost makes tangible, the sensation of tussock grass growing tall enough for her to hide inside when playing games as a child, while her story also leaves the visitor to ponder the fate of grasslands in the Melbourne area, one of the most critical endangered ecosystems in Australia, with only a few percent remaining of its recent geographic coverage.[13] For Deborah Bird Rose, ecological knowledge is organized by indigenous peoples' 'observation and experience of interactive local events' and a 'patterned communicative domain of ecological time' (2005, p. 39). In this pedagogical space, where life in the forest is linked to the changing seasons and also to the changes too of seasonality, and of how climatic time has been organised in this place, Kulin accounts of land formations, animal behaviour and plant remedies are set in dialogue even with structures of museal signage, the museum's traditional labelled cabinets. They appear within the museum as voices that invoke 'human ways of communicating about a communicative system formed through connectivity' (34). Such nested connectivity, drawing from deep time and tens of thousands of years of human culture, disturbs our feelings as it says nothing about our climate futures.

This extensive moment of oral history depicts cultural knowledge and action calibrated to diverse dimensions of natural time: seasonal, climatic, geological. It presents a model of explanation and storytelling attuned with eco-cultural practices of collective memory. But it also addresses inhabitants of a dry continent subject to increasing doubts and large-scale fires owing to human-induced climate change. The ribbon, therefore, is a hybrid narrative of natures and cultures, a thread of disjunctive differences and unreconciled grammars. As a preface to 'The Clearing', the complex ribbon ends with three words forecasting the coming climatic moment: Biderap, 'hot dry weather'.

Melancholic environmental memorial

'Hot dry weather' in the collective settler imagination means drought, and the fires that come with extended dry spells: 'Black Friday' in 1939; 'Ash Wednesday' in 1983; 'Black Saturday' in 2009. This tradition of publicly naming intense fires that destroy entire communities seeks to recuperate within a community the possibility of its own annihilation, if only at the fragile level of language.[14] Increasingly, it is modern Australian society's role in the creation of these fires that is now being recognized, as the implications of human relationships with ecologies are better understood. In 1939, the Commissioner for the Royal Inquiry into the Black Friday fires could say that Australians had not yet lived long enough to appreciate the need for collective knowledge on the role of fire in the Australian ecology and our own role in causing them (Griffiths, 2001, p. vii, 136). But today, potential shortfalls of collective experience are no longer only retrospective: climate change would seem to require learning from the future, or at least from imagined memories of it. 'The Clearing' interweaves multiple lines of remembrance, a model, perhaps, of what such a learning experience might be: there is the clearance of these forests and, alongside it, the dispossession of indigenous peoples from their lands; but there is also the delicate balance of an exhibited forest ecology, a historical recreation, perhaps, of elements of a sustainable use of the forest that was historically devastated in the colonial and post-colonial periods. And fire is part of this history, not least as one of its Consequences.

In the gallery, this realisation starts with a memorial space to the impact of fire. Linked to the previous climate band by the continuation of the sinuous path that divides 'The Clearing' from an ashen memorial space to the mountain ash trees, it is here that we come to appreciate, for the first time, the regenerative and destructive force of fire. The image of the world's end is conjured up in the words 'hot dry weather' in two video presentations built into the trunk of a fire blackened tree, the first in a series of such tree trunks that, collectively, make a memorial to the loss of the ash forest through increasingly intense fires that do not allow the seedlings to reach full maturity. While the first video explains the regenerative power of fire, the second makes manifest the association between fire and fear, collapsing time and collective memories in a rendition of historical footage of destruction, devastation, loss and survival from the three major fires within living memory. There, the speed and intensity of these fires are repeated as if anew to each community, on whose faces can be perceived the mediated horror of a devastated relationship to place. The blacked trees stand like totem poles on a grey, ash-like ground, their blackened surfaces a silent testimony to the destructive force of fire; but horizontal stellae beneath them house little seedlings, symbolic of the regenerative power within fire. In one of them, we are told that an ash tree does not reach maturity until it is 300 to 400 years old. At another 'gravesite' we are told that if fires are too frequent the saplings will not reach the stage where their seeds will germinate again, making fire a permanent killer. Griffiths (2001) reminds us that 'mountain ash forests perversely need a catastrophe to survive' (188). The increased frequency of fires and the changing conditions of forests in the last two hundred years signals danger: they are now 'especially vulnerable' (28). The real possibility that permanent ecosystem death by fire might be occurring is implied in the list of fires over the last two centuries at a memorial for the most recent of these – a lone chimney that is all that remains from a nineteenth-century homestead in the Kinglake area of Victoria, one of over two thousand houses burnt in 2009. Added to the gallery as an impromptu memorial following those fires, it makes unavoidable how regular catastrophic fires have been since colonisation: 1851, 1865, 1898, 1926, 1939, 1983, 2009… The sequence is clearly unfinished.[15]

The increasing intensity of fires, however, is not the only pressure point affecting these forests. For on the other side of the sinuous curve defining the memorial to the after-effects of fire, 'The Clearing' houses its own memorial – this time to the loss of trees through deforestation as a result of human activity. A series of grey ironbark trunks, with notches cut into them, stand as silent memorials to the practices of loggers who could only see the forest as a resource to be harvested. On those tree trunks are a number of historical images, documenting our admiration of the sublime nature of these forests or a sense of fear in a dangerous landscape, in addition to reflecting our hope that knowledge might show us a way out of this conflicted emotional space backlit by cultural disorientation. There is something comforting about melancholy. It is a feeling of pensive sadness in which one can dwell; it is a state of being enveloped, not unlike the immersive experience of the gallery. Unlike numbness through depression, or hopelessness in grief, sorrow has purpose beyond its fleeting feeling of enclosure. This very purpose, illuminated by thick stasis in The Clearing, can be understood as a sustained directionless mood that is open to, or receptive to knowledge. At times it is invoked, or called upon as an aesthetic emotion that follows cultural disorientation but which does not speak to an obvious cause for the feeling (cf. Brady, 2003). The Forest Gallery contextualizes ecological melancholy, relating the emotion to publically symbolic dimensions of loss in 'The Clearing', creating what Witcomb (2015) has called a 'pedagogy of feeling'.[16] This pedagogy is given its final twist in the final memorial – this time to the displacement of indigenous people – a memorial that affects the appraisal of this pensive, melancholic aesthetic emotion.[17]

At the centre of the very back of the gallery lies an alluring plaque that the visitor comes across while looking out onto the open green space behind the museum and drawing in the sometimes fresh air of north Melbourne with their back to 'The Clearing', the darkness cast aside temporarily. But is it a plaque, an informational panel, or a tombstone? It is hard to tell. It is one of only three horizontal registers in the space dominated by the two groups of incredibly tall tree trunks (above) that draw the eyes up into the rainforest canopy and out into the sky.[18] This slate-black elongated diamond-shaped sign is raised two feet off the ground, requiring the visitor to bend down towards the stories inscribed on the surface. There are two semantic spaces on the plaque's surface. Divided by a flowing line representing the local river and evoking the season ribbon, and a jagged line remarking upon colonial cartography and indigenous dispossession. On the left-hand side is a photomontage of homesteads and Aboriginal labourers in the forest clearing industry of the late eighteenth century.[19] On the right-hand side is a timeline, running vertically from 1835 at the top (when an unlawful treaty was signed between indigenous groups and the Australian grazier John Batman) to 1998 at the bottom (marking the purchase of the last freehold property of a former Aboriginal station, Coranderrk, by the Indigenous Land Corporation). It presents a narrow slice of the history of a colonial conflict that had such profound effects for the damaged landscape that surrounds it: from the founding of the settlement in Melbourne and the establishment of a new colony, through indigenous resistance to forced removal from their ancestral lands, to a point when it was possible for the Kulin to purchase title to a piece of their territory – and by implication not yet possible for them to claim that title. Key dates are numbered with supporting sentences offering a glossed account of land clearance and indigenous displacement. The two forms of clearing are brought together while the looped video footage of bushfires run on the TV screens that visitors must turn away from when reading the inscriptions.

It is our understanding that the gallery repoliticizes the representation of nature and the inherently dualistic discourse of colonialism. A long quotation, typographically tilted, runs along the timeline, which, when the body is adjusted to read it, enables the trees marked by bushfire to enter into the visitor's peripheral vision: 'You got to know your father's country. Yarra is my father's country. There's no mountains for me on the Murray.' This is the voice of William (Ngurungaeta) Barak, the last traditional elder of the Wurundjeri clan, famous now for his artworks that depicted indigenous life and early encounters with Europeans, for his reported presence during John Batman's 'purchase' of Melbourne, and for his role as a major figure in Aboriginal resistance. The soundscape is of birds and fire, the view is of burnt trees and memory poles, the voice is one displaced. The gallery instantiates public memory as an overwhelming melancholic memorial to change: change of climate, of peoples, of place. It is worth slowing down here. Brady (2003) argues that melancholy 'is no less complex a phenomenon than sublimity'. And it is true: in the Forest Gallery, we find ourselves contracting these two feelings simultaneously. Loss, extended into openess, suggests something to be mourned and something to be celebrated. Visitors are thus situated in a site that bears analogy to the experience of the sublime: located within a material representation not only of a value judgement, but of a 'state of mind' (Shaw, 2006, p. 1). This confusion of ashes, of trees and cinders, juxtaposes signifiers of life and death; their co-presence troubles the borderlands of reason and feeling. Such affective dissonance points to a 'discontinuity of the subject's conscious experience with the non-intentionality of emotion' (Clough, 2010, p. 206). 'The Clearing' thus stimulates conflicted emotions – sadness, puzzlement, hope, guilt, anger – in a site of environmental witness. Its melancholic acknowledgement of states of emergence and loss leaves the visitor dispossessed of security. Reproduced within a museum space that challenges its own boundary conditions, the autopoetics of the forest ecology spills into a site of destruction circulating outside and between bodies and organisms. The museum forest's secret resides within this uncloseable gap between property and belonging: a forest, partially burnt, within walls. Within the historically specific mode of organisation of the museum, the 'forest gallery' compound is an experience that scaffolds and elongates emotional processes for the visitor; as an installation, it engenders a model of curatorial practice transformed into a living witness of change, of climate and fire. Placing these two coordinates together, the gallery is an imminent intersubjective technology grasping the imperceptible dynamism of ecological affect.

Conclusion

Graham Huggan (2015) negotiates an all too common ecocritical persuasion – that the sources and manifestations of climate change are difficult to represent – to argue that 'climate change lends itself to a *futural aesthetics*'.[20] Huggan's position arises during his examination of Ursula Heise's sense that apocalyptic and risk perspectives on climate change raise different sets of aesthetic as well as ethical questions. The former emphasizes uncertainty and indeterminacy, while the latter invokes holistic communities, harmony and self-regenerating ecosystems (Heise, 2008, p. 142; Huggan, 2015, p. 88).[21] The Forest Gallery in Melbourne oscillates between these positions, between indeterminacy and regeneration. In our analysis, this situates the visitor in a complex site of mixed emotions and ideas: about colonial relations, about fire and life, and about culture and climate. The lone chimney

Figure 4.3 The Kinglake Chimney installation, Forest Gallery, by Benjamin Heally with permission of Museum Victoria.

in 'The Clearing' (see Figure 4.3) attempts to bring this ongoing, understated site of cultural conflict and emotional turmoil back home, as it were. One of the problems with climate change discourse is that it is hard for people to relate their personal life stories and idiosyncratic symbolism to distant and vast earth processes. To clarify the role for museums here, Newell et al. (in press) argue that 'People need to find ways to speak of change that they relate to their lives':

> *Change* is as crucial as climate, and we need more participants to enrich this big conversation of our times. Change... highly affective – often threatening, worrying, stressful. Economic changes, environmental changes, technological changes and social changes are all multiplying and cross-magnifying, and these are very hard to make sense of from within the moment. We need a historical sense of where they are coming from, numerical ways to compare them, and emotional support to live with them (6).

Concrete examples and oral histories of changes within the first three bands of the Forest Gallery set up the emotional exploration of changes to the climate in the Melbourne museum; the catalyst for linking these being the ribbon that defines and shapes the 'climate' section of the gallery. The season band, once read in the context of 'The Clearing', might suggest 'a tale of remnants of indigenous biodiversity and cultural memory' (Dawson, 2013, p. 104). It also suggests one way, as Huggan has remarked regarding a different medium, 'of illustrating the scale effects currently being produced by global warming, and of suggesting – without falling into a limiting form of moral prescriptivism – the ethical responsibilities that come with increased awareness of the possible consequences of climate change' (2015, p. 101). And it is this capacity for re-reading and re-interpreting separate sections of the gallery that allows the ecosystem to function as a museal site of an ecological public to come, remaining open to the future and visitors that will have passed through more fire and experienced more climate change. Here, historical connection in the gallery are made in concert with larger intellectual and affective connections: of emotions to reason, aesthetics to politics, and history to environmental change. Perhaps these all allude to a larger metaphor that the gallery embodies: the non-representational differences and the ethical entanglements of natural evolution and social construction. Environmental history, then, offered the Melbourne Museum a way in which to bring a wide variety of disciplinary knowledge together within the one space in ways that enable visitors to learn not only about the ecology of the mountain ash forests within a history of change, but also to connect these to the ways in which our own species – humans – has played, and continues to play, a key role in the process of climate change. In doing so, the Museum attempts to represent the unrepresentable, and consequently opens itself to aesthetic practices of historical legibility that have as much recourse to the future as to the past.

Notes

1   See for example Rolls (1981); Griffiths (1992).
2   They do so, in part, by treating nature as an agent, as a subject in its own right, rather than simply as the object of human activity. It is partly ironic, then, to read an image of Griffiths's book on a carbon sink exemplar: embossed on the bark of an interpretation of the mountain ash forest east of Melbourne, his text marks one of the cluster of trees in 'The Clearing' that is a history of the entanglements between humans and non-humans, forming an intricate web of carbon fluxes.
3   The gallery does not cover the rural/urban distinction, which is a significant omission owing to the issue of mountain ash forests on the periphery of the city of Melbourne.
4   For these particular foundations we draw inspiration from Beattie et al. (2015).
5   These trees grow in the rainforests of the Atherton Tableland in Queensland, a fertile plateau some 3,000km from Melbourne, and a World Heritage listed area. The IUCN places the tree within the 'least concern' conservation status category. Melbourne Museum signage reads: 'this specimen symbolises the loss of "big trees", once common in Australian forests.' The tree is cousin to the equally widely felled New Zealand Kauri (a Maori word that endures in Australia).
6   Donna Buang and Baw Baw form part of the Dividing Range, a mountain range that divides the eastern coastal lands of Eastern Australia from its drier western regions.
7   Bill Gammage argues that Aboriginal use of fire was planned and precise, suppressing insect plagues and regulating kangaroo populations. It 'was scalpel more than sword, taming the most fire-prone country on earth to welcome its periodic refreshing, its kiss of life. Far from today's safe and unsafe fires, campfire and bushfire were one; far from feared enemy, fire was the closest ally' (2011, p. 185).
8   The creek connects to the Yarra, a perennial river which flows over 240 kilometers from its source in the Yarra Ranges (eastern and northeastern suburbs of Melbourne) to Hobsons Bay in northernmost Port Philip; the river name is understood to be mistranslated (rather than adapted) from 'Yarro Yarro' meaning 'ever flowing' in the Boonworrung language.

9 The Kulin nation is the Wurundjeri People, the Bunurong or Boonerwrung People, the Wathaurong People, the Taungurong People, and the Dja Dja Wurrung or Jaara People. Lindy Allen provides a complete outline of the season band in her piece 'Coranderrk Calendar' in Griffiths (2001, p. 58–59). Ribbon signage reads: 'The Kulin have a detailed local understanding of the seasons and the environment. Each season is marked by the movement of the stars in the night sky and changes in the weather coinciding with the life cycles of plants and animals.' Rose (2008) and Toussaint (2008) contend that while daily Aboriginal experience is not alert to climate change, their communities will be shaped by climate change.

10 NB the cyclic calendar represented by the season ribbon does not strictly correlate with a 12-month calendar. This installation was produced by the Melbourne Museum in association with Woi wurrung and Daung wurrung people (Allen, 2001).

11 The Dreaming, or 'Tjukurrpa' – a translation from the Arrernte word 'Altyrrenge' – means 'to see and understand the law'.

12 These are the results of Museum Victoria interviews with the Kulin peoples. At the time of writing, Jessie Hunter, Martha Nevin and Brian Paterson had passed away.

13 Charles Dawson's reading of Gammage places the idea of grasslands as one part of the Australian aboriginal ecology that was 'managed': once palatable, they attracted large marsupials that were hunted (Dawson, 2013, p. 96–97). Nearly 250 million acres of the outback are carpeted by grasslands, one of the few remaining large-scale natural areas of the Earth containing some of the most vulnerable patches of our environment, now threatened by mining, invasive species, the pastoral industry and of course, fire. Aboriginal and natural ecologists are working together to promote biodiversity in northern and central Australia – see Rose (1995).

14 Since the nineteenth century, devastating bushfires in Australia have been named after the day of the week and year in which they occurred.

15 See Dale-Hallett et al. (2015) for an account of the collecting project that occurred in the immediate aftermath of this fire, one of whose aims was to 'establish a chronology that could challenge the concept of "unprecedented," "would never happen again," and "one in a 100 year event" – terms that have appeared regularly in public discourse since February 2009.' (534).

16 For Witcomb, a 'pedagogy of feeling' in the context of museums is an interpretative strategy that turns the civil space of the museum towards a critical engagement with the ways in which collective narratives and memories disable the construction of our futures. Alternatively, visitors might take their affective experiences into the realm of citizen action; essential to this pedagogy is the use of affective immersive spaces to open up visitors to engage in critical modes of thinking through feeling one's way towards complexity.

17 Ute Frevert (2012) argues that melancholy is a 'lost' emotion: along with other emotions, its prominence changes throughout historical periods, and it has been 'lost in translation to a new emotional state called depression' (36).

18 The other horizontal markers are a table dedicated to maps of the area which doubles as a workspace for educational programs, and rectangular seed boxes (described above as stellae), which lie beneath each charred tree trunk.

19 One photograph, 'The Yara Tribe starting for the Acheron, 1862' by Charles Walter commemorates one of the crossways of the Blacks' Spur by the Kulin people. Griffiths (2001) writes that this corridor is named after the Woi wurrung and the Daung wurrung people 'who used it to travel between their territories and who, in the early 1860s, made the journey several times through the tall forests in quest of a permanent home, a safe refuge amidst the maelstrom of European invasion' (50).

20 This is Huggan's understanding of an understatement in Beck. He is drawing from Brady's sense of climate change speaking not to our present, but to our pasts and our futures (Brady 2014).

21 Heise is unpacking Buell's (1996) sense of dwelling in crisis.

References

Allen, L., 2001. Coranderrk Calendar. In: T. Griffiths, ed. *Forests of Ash: An Environmental History*. Cambridge: Cambridge University Press, p. 58–59.

Beattie, J., Melillo, E. & O'Gorman, E. eds., 2015. *Eco-Cultural Networks and the British Empire: New Views on Environmental History*. London: Bloomsbury.

Brady, E., 2003. Melancholy as an Aesthetic Emotion. *Contemporary Aesthetics*, Volume 1.

Brady, E., 2014. Aesthetic Value, Ethics and Climate Change. *Environmental Values*, Volume 23, p. 551–570.

Buell, F., 1996. *From Apocalypse to Way of Life: Environmental Crisis in the American Century*. Cambridge (MA): Harvard University Press.

Clough, P. T., 2010. The Affectve Turn: Political Economy, Biomedia and Bodies. In: M. Gregg & G. J. Seigworth, eds. *The Affect Theory Reader*. Durham: Duke University Press, p. 206–227.

Dale-Hallett, L., Carland, R. & Frazer, P., 2015. Sites of Trauma: Contemporary Collecting and Natural Disaster. In: A. Witcomb & K. Message, eds. *Museum Theory: Vol 1. of The International Handbooks of Museum Studies*. Oxford: Wiley Blackwell, p. 531–552.

Dawson, C., 2013. Field Guide for 1788 (Review of Gammage 2011). *Australasian Journal of Ecocriticism and Cultural Ecology*, Volume 2, p. 96–106.

Frevert, U., 2012. *Emotions in History: Lost and Found*. Budapest: Central European Press.

Gammage, B., 2011. *The Biggest Estate on Earth: How Aborigines Made Australia*. Sydney: Allen and Unwin.

Griffiths, T., 1992. *Secrets of the Forest: Discovering History in Melbourne's Ash Range*. London: Allen and Unwin.

Griffiths, T., 2001. *Forests of Ash: An Environmental History*. Cambridge: Cambridge University Press.

Heise, U. K., 2008. *Sense of Place and Sense of Planet: The Environmental Imagination of the Global*. Oxford: Oxford University Press.

Huggan, G., 2015. Australian Literature, Risk, and the Global Climate Challenge. *Literature Interpretation Theory*, Volume 26, p. 86–105.

Knebusch, J., 2008. Art and Climate (Change) Perception. In: S. Kagan & V. Kirchberg, eds. *Sustainability: A New Frontier for the Arts and Cultures*. Frankfurt: Verlag fur Akadmische Schriften, p. 242–261.

Newell, J., Robin, L. & Wehner, K., in press. Introduction. In: J. Newell, L. Robin & K. Wehner, eds. *Curating the Future: Museums, Communities and Climate Change*. London: Routledge.

Rasmussen, C., 2001. *A Museum for the People: A History of Museum Victoria and Its Predecessor Institutions, 1854–2000*. Melbourne: Scribe, in association with Museum Victoria.

Rolls, E., 1981. *A Million Wide Acres: 200 Years of Man and an Australian Forest*. Melbourne: Nelson.

Rose, D., ed., 1995. *Country in Flames*. Canberra and Darwin: Biodiversity Unit, Department of the Environment, Sport and Territories, and the North Australian Research Unit, Australian National University.

Rose, D., 2005. Rhythms, Patterns, Connectivities: Indigenous Concepts of Seasons and Change. In: T. Sherratt, T. Griffiths & L. Robin, eds. *A Change in the Weather: Climate and Culture in Australia*. Canberra: National Museum of Australia Press, p. 32–41.

Rose, D., 2008. Love in the Time of Extinctions. *Australian Journal of Anthropology*, Volume 19, p. 81–84.

Shaw, P., 2006. *The Sublime*. London: Routledge.

Toussaint, S., 2008. Climate Change, Global Warming and Too Much Sorry Business. *Australian Journal of Anthropology*, Volume 19, p. 84–88.

Witcomb, A., 2015. Toward a Pedagogy of Feeling: Understanding How Museums Create a Space for Cross-Cultural Encounters. In: A. Witcomb & K. Message, eds. *Museum Theory (Vol 1. of The International Handbooks of Museum Studies)*. Oxford: Wiley Blackwell, p. 321–344.

5 The Anthropocene and the long seventeenth century

1550–1750

Linda Williams

This chapter investigates the emergence of the Anthropocene by considering some of the dynamics between European cultural values and natural history in early modernity, and their relations with climate change. In particular, it seeks to disentangle the ways in which certain social processes that emerged in the long seventeenth century from 1550 to 1750 not only exacerbated global climate change, but also provided a robust foundation for ecocritical responses to the advance of global climate change in the twenty-first century.

The concept of the Anthropocene as a process of global transformation is generally conceived as a development coeval with the industrial revolution in the late eighteenth century (Steffen, et al., 2007). It is a model that has gained considerable critical traction in the environmental humanities, where it is largely understood as a term used to gauge the unforeseen ecological consequences of the progress of western-style modernity in the global context. Recently, there has also a focus on the 'great acceleration' of the Anthropocene in the mid-twentieth century, based on the intensified use of fossil fuels and worldwide fallout from the frequent testing of nuclear weapons, which have left indelible signatures on the chemistostratigraphic record (Zalasiewicz, et al., 2015). Coeval with the potentially destructive capacity of its technology, the twentieth century was also an era of world wars, violent political regimes and the perpetuation of global economic inequality that surely justify Eric Hobsbawm's claim that the last century was an age of extremes (Hobsbawm, 1996). These historical extremes reconfigured the socio-cultural values that people have inherited as a basis for meeting the global environmental challenges we face today, and thus demand the kind of careful scrutiny we bring to avoiding the worst errors of history.

However, in relation to catastrophic historical transition, profound environmental transformation and global climate change, I argue that the seventeenth century is also a period that we should be scrutinising carefully: certainly for its impact on the Anthropocene; for how the seventeenth century was itself an age shaped by significant climate change; and also for how the *longue durée* of its socio-cultural formations continue to shape present-day values. In the following account of the long seventeenth century as a complex age of both crisis and enlightenment, such historical transitions are considered from the perspective of what the Australian environmental philosopher Val Plumwood described as 'The set of interrelated and mutually reinforcing dualisms which permeate western culture' and 'forms a fault-line which runs through its entire conceptual system, (Plumwood,1993, p. 42).

Early modern poetic and philosophical critique

In the seventeenth century, certain cultural and philosophical concepts of nature were deployed in a form of innate critique of how the non-human world was generally conceived. There is, for example, an English poetic tradition arising in this period that criticised the exploitation of nature in ways that anticipate some of the affective and critical responses to environmental degradation in our own era. And for all the contrasts between the generally lowly status of woman's lot in the seventeenth century (Fraser, 1993) as against the spirited ecofeminism of later modernity, seventeenth century women writers had much to say on the subject of ecology (Bowerbank, 2004) that resonates very clearly with readers today.

Here, for example, is Margaret Cavendish, Duchess of Newcastle in a poem called 'Earths Complaint' written in 1664:

> O Nature, Nature! Hearken to my Cry,
> I'm Wounded sore, but yet I cannot Dye;
> My Children which I from my Womb did bear,
> Do dig my Sides, and all my Bowels tear,
> They Plow deep Furrows in my very Face,
> From Torment I have neither time nor place;
> No other Element is so abus'd,
> Or by Mankind so Cruelly is us'd.

A similar empathy for a violated Earth is also heard in the poetry of Aphra Behn, who in a work called *The Golden Age* imagined a time when:

> The stubborn plough had then
> Made no rude rapes upon the virgin Earth;
> Who yielded of her own accord her plenteous birth,
> Without the aids of men;
> As if within her teeming womb
> All Nature, and all sexes lay,
> Whence new creations ev'ry day
> Into the happy world did come;

These are two of many such examples of voices raised against the more intensive processes of early modern agriculture, Acts of Enclosure, and instrumentalist views of the land that were widespread by the mid-seventeenth century (Lowry, 2003). Cavendish's poem speaks plainly enough about the kind of expedient exploitation of nature with which are also familiar today. It was, moreover, a response to what at the time was regarded as the rapid encroachment of deforestation in England to which John Evelyn's *Sylva; or a Discourse of Forest Trees* ([1662] 1908) was dedicated.

Evelyn's book, the first published by the newly formed Royal Society, was also the first western publication on forest conservation,[1] just as his *Fumifugium* of 1661 was the first book published addressing the problem of urban air pollution. As such, these were the foundational precursors of late modern conservation literature.

The historical ecologist Oliver Rackham has called into question Evelyn's perception that English forests were particularly endangered, along with the more recent popular view that vast areas of medieval Britain were covered in ancient pristine wildwoods. Rackham argues instead, from evidence in the Domesday book and other sources, that Britain was not particularly well wooded, and further, that during the medieval and much of the early modern period the woods were managed intensively and conservatively as a part of everyday life (Rackham, 1990). In the political sphere, both Evelyn and Cavendish were conservative royalists, of the kind for whom as the historian Keith Thomas (1983) has pointed out:

> The depredations wrought in the 1650s upon the states of the Crown, Church and supporters of Charles I were exaggerated by the Royalist propagandists after the Restoration in such a way as to create an association between the wanton felling of trees and republican politics (209).

And there is certainly much in Cavendish's poetry and her strangely spectral novel *The Blazing World* (1666) that suggests a profound longing for a world of vast medieval forests to which only kings and nobles such as the Lord and Lady Cavendish had unrestricted entry. Behn's poem is recognizably derived from an older literary tradition that, as Raymond Williams (1973) pointed out, had long been preoccupied with an imaginary golden age. This was a powerfully nostalgic, essentially Edenic model of nature in which the distant past was represented as an unsullied, primal site to which one could never return.

On the face of it, it may seem that this early-modern nostalgia for a golden age of unblemished nature has no parallels in the present period of the Anthropocene, yet it seems to me that it has mutated in contemporary culture and now presides in advertising imagery, representing all that is left in the world that is pure and pristine. This is an imagery evoking a very deep current of human desire that is now leveraged towards the products with which it has become associated, such as bottled water from the 'purest' mountain streams, the imagery of luxury travel to tropical 'paradise', and the freedom to explore 'wilderness' in big four-wheel drives.

If both the call of a paradise lost and the relatively unsullied royal forests of feudal England imbue Cavendish and Evelyn's works of the 1660s with a nostalgia for the royalist traditions heightened by the Restoration, the establishment of Parliament had nonetheless ensured that England was not an absolutist state. In France, Colbert's forest ordinance of 1669 was designed exclusively to manage forests in the service of the *ancien régime*, but in England (despite Evelyn's *Sylva*) the development of democratic rights led to further depletion of English forests. In response the Crown, Navy, and industry turned increasingly to the use of coal, and to 'New England' in the colonised Americas (Grove, 1997, 57) where, as we will see, forests were more abundant than they had been for many centuries.

Poetic reconfigurations of Eden, abundant before the fall, were also imagined as part of the colonial project conveyed in the imagery of a *New World*. Of these images, Andrew Marvell's vision of the Americas is one of the most vivid as he evoked the bounteous beauty of *Bermudas* written in the 1650s:

> ...He lands us on a grassy stage
> Safe from the storm's and prelates' rage.
> He gave us this eternal spring
> Which here enamels everything,
> And sends the fowls to us in care,
> On daily visits through the air.
> He hangs in shades the orange bright,
> Like golden lamps in a green night;
> And does in the pomegranates close
> Jewels more rich than Ormus shows.
> He makes the figs our mouths to meet
> And throws the melons at our feet,
> But apples plants of such a price,
> No tree could ever bear them twice...

This is the European fantasy of a lush, uninhabited paradise, which despite the palpable sense of relief in its distance from the 'storms' of seventeenth century religious controversy nonetheless conveys a biblically inspired image of nature conceived purely for the pleasure of mankind. Here birds are living gifts God has sent carefully on the wing to men, while luminous fruits are perfectly designed for human pleasure. Marvell takes imaginary delight in the island's verdant abundance in ways that contemporary readers can also recognize as a familiarly anthropocentric vision of nature. It is a desire for opulent abundance that, as it were, deflects early modernity back to us in ways that are familiar enough to a late modern culture of conspicuous consumption.

This is especially the case since there is something about the poem's excessive anthropomorphism and a self-conscious abandonment of restraints that might seem amusing, perhaps even to Marvell, whose inchoate, shrewd allusions to excess point to the possibility that this may, after all, be just a fantasy.

In reality, colonial Bermuda at the time Marvell wrote this poem was a place of food scarcity, the abject enslavement of Africans and Amerindians, and of white indentured workers – mostly miserable Irish exiles from Cromwell's colonial campaigns in Ireland.[2] But whilst the poem may have been a fantasy derived from a dualist model of nature divinely created for the betterment of man, it could hardly be described as the result of seventeenth century mechanistic philosophy. Marvell's fruits pulsate with light and colour, and his birds may be sent to visit men by divine providence, but they are not Cartesian bird-machines.[3] And as we will see, this is but one example of a common view of the world that has an important bearing on the contemporary 'dead nature' thesis, which holds that the seventeenth century mind conceived nature as inert matter (Merchant, 1989).

It is precisely such early modern fantasies that are now said to have collapsed with the advent of postmodern incredulity, as if the colonial project or anthropocentric models of nature have been simply banished by the preferences of poststructural theorists. Yet it seems to me highly unlikely that the 'metanarratives' that Lyotard (1984), for example, claimed were the redundant formations of early modernity, have in reality collapsed. Moreover, zealous post-structuralist attempts to overturn all early modern humanist narratives perhaps too often elide those worth retaining.

As against claims for a general postmodern rejection of a 'failed' Enlightenment project, for example, the socially transformative effects of seventeenth century philosophy contributed an important and enduring intellectual foundation for the preference for reason over the affective qualities of faith as a crucial, if still contested, foundation of late modern western thought. Similarly, early modern speculation on the advantages of separating church from state remains at the bedrock of contemporary democracy along with the emergence of the early Enlightenment view that, with access to education, reason could serve women as ably as men.

This last provided an important legacy for eco-feminist philosophy and critique. It is one not always given due recognition as a significant catalyst of recent ecocritical discourse, which can accept too casually an intellectual history of reason in the early modern period as the severing of rational thought from feeling, and the assertion of an instrumentalist view of 'dead nature' involving a lack of empathy for the non-human world. But this version of intellectual history is belied by important developments in early modern science, as well as by significant shifts in the history of affective responses to nature. Progressive developments in seventeenth century economies of affects produced a *longue durée* of ideas and transformations in emotional life that are not yet sufficiently well recognised, especially as the foundations of Romanticism and later ecocritical thought (Williams, 2008).

This is not to suggest that the well-known late twentieth century eco-feminist critiques of the discourse of 'dead nature' in seventeenth century mechanistic philosophy are entirely mistaken (Merchant, 1989; Mathews, 1990; Plumwood, 1993). On the contrary, they have been crucial for identifying a turn in early modern rationalism that could be so readily adapted as a singly instrumentalist view of the non-human world as something entirely subject to human self-interests. Clearly, the gentlemanly and thus putatively impartial pursuit of knowledge represented by Royal Society figures such as Robert Boyle did not mean that the Royal Society was immune from the mercantile thrust of the age. The recognition of how shrewd businessmen invested in the new knowledge is unmistakable, for example, in Robert Hooke's reference in the preface to his *Micrographia* to:

> ...the *Real* esteem that the more serious part of men have of this Society, is, that several *Merchants*, men who act in earnest (whose Object is *meum* & *tuum*, that great *Rudder* of human affairs) have adventur'd considerable sums of *Money*, to put in practice what some of our Members have contrived....

[T]heir attempts will bring Philosophy from words to action, seeing the men of Business have so great a share in their first foundation (Hooke, [1665] 1938).

And as I discuss below, Val Plumwood's concept of the human self-interest evident in dualism as the primary logic of colonisation is particularly germane to my argument that the roots of our current climate predicament in the age of the Anthropocene lie in the long seventeenth century.

However, although the perceived turn towards a more systematic instrumentalization of nature was coeval with certain seventeenth century rationalist theories of matter, and more aggressive forms of economic rationalism, it does not, of course, necessarily follow that the perceived 'death of nature' at this time was an inevitable or sustainable consequence of seventeenth century philosophy, or even of rationalism as such.

To take mechanism as a case in point, though a mechanistic concept of nature initially proved effective for certain endeavours such as Robert Boyle's well-known experiments with air pressure (Buyse, 2010), it has been pointed out that 'However mechanical philosophy is defined, its ambition was greater than its real successes' (Garber & Roux, 2013, p. xii). A unified mechanistic theory of an essentially inert material world comprised of 'discontinuous bits of hard matter' (Gaukroger, 2010, p. 331) was particularly limited when applied to the natural sciences, where it often failed to provide satisfactory accounts of phenomena (Gerber & Roux, 2013, p. xv), and indeed had become more or less redundant by the by the end of the seventeenth century. Further to the advent of experimental natural philosophy developed by Boyle and others,[4] this was largely due to a range of investigations from the 1670s into gravitational forces and magnetism – including physical, if not material, action at a distance in Newton's theories of gravity. This was followed by subsequent research on the volatility of electricity (which also later led to theories of action at a distance), and on the agency of chemical reactions.

While in medical experiments a mechanical model was undoubtedly useful to Harvey's discovery of the circulation of the blood, which as Merchant correctly points out, also legitimised vivisection in Harvey's experimental methodology (Merchant, 2006, p. 530), it is also important to keep in mind that Harvey's methods were essentially a form of Aristotelian comparative anatomy that extended to Harvey's use of vitalist analogies in which the heart in the body could also be compared to the role of the Crown within the body politic (Williams, 2009, p. 233). Harvey's extensive use of vivisection that led to the publication of *De Moto Cordis* in 1627 predated the spread of Cartesian mechanistic philosophy. And in any case it was not based on the idea of animal bodies as mechanistic matter, but on a much older theological dualist order that endorsed the use of animals as instruments for the improvement of mankind.

Later in the century, the mechanist assimilation of living beings to non-living ones went entirely against the grain of the study of the generation and corruption of matter. And by the 1740s this field of study led Buffon to firmly reject the notion of lifeless matter (Gaukroger, 2010, p. 350), which like the comparative basis of early modern anatomy itself (Williams, 2008) engendered lines of enquiry that eventually informed the gradual emergence of theories of evolution. So, far from being an unassailable doctrine of dead white males who legitimated the idea of a universe of inert matter subject to their control, by the early eighteenth century the mechanist theory of matter had in effect become poor science, or rather poor natural philosophy – as it was known at that time.

Not that this was the only reason people rejected mechanism: the question of animal sentience as against the animal machine was for example debated passionately through the seventeenth and eighteenth centuries in France (Boas, 1933; Hastings, 1936; Maehle & Trohler, 1987). Despite the metaphysical debates engaging with mechanism such as those of the Cambridge Platonists (Fallon, 1991), Keith Thomas claims mechanistic philosophy never gained a strong cultural influence in England (Thomas, 1983). Margaret Cavendish, for one, had scoffed at the 'strange conceits' of mechanistic philosophers, who

> …rail against Nature's self-moving power. Condemning her as a dull, inanimate, senseless and irrational body' (Cavendish, [1666] 2001, p. 43–44)

Philosophically, even in Cartesian thought, mechanism shared common ontological ground with dualist theological values, but this was by no means the only influential discourse in seventeenth century philosophy. Along with a diverse range of theological positions on natural philosophy, there was also a strong interest in vitalist monism in such major figures as Milton (Fallon, 1991) and to a range of lesser writers. There was also a rigorous critique of substance dualism in the work of other influential philosophers such as Leibniz and, most importantly, Spinoza.

Spinoza's thought was shaped by the general turbulence of the seventeenth century: both as an era of crisis and of early scientific enlightenment. His family was one of many among the Sephardic Jews who had migrated to the Netherlands in the sixteenth and seventeenth centuries to escape religious persecution by the inquisition in Spain and Portugal. His father was a moderately successful merchant in Amsterdam, which from the mid-seventeenth century (following the protracted Dutch war of independence from Spain) was the wealthiest and most cosmopolitan city at the heart of the Dutch Republic, the world's largest commercial enterprise. Though an unusual degree of religious tolerance was practised in Amsterdam, Spinoza's critiques of traditional religion led to the formal cursing of his name from the city's Jewish leaders and his excommunication from Judaism.

Spinoza left Amsterdam to live in Rijnsburg near Leiden where he worked as a lens grinder refining lenses for spectacles, telescopes and the microscopes used by early Dutch microbiologists such as Christiaan Huygens, Jan Swammerdam and Antonie van Leeuwenhoek. It is clear from one of Huygens' letters referring to a conversation he had with Spinoza that he had also studied objects under the microscope,[5] and though there is no evidence to show Spinoza had witnessed movement in apparently inert substances, it is not unreasonable to suppose that he had heard of Swammerdam's research on the processes of generation in insects and van Leeuwenhoek's discoveries of cells and bacteria. Spinoza's general engagement with the intellectual climate of the Dutch Golden Age led Lewis Fuer (1987) to describe it as:

> ... a remarkable new world of what Leeuwenhoek called 'living atoms', which was replacing the cold mechanism which Descartes had imputed to the nonhuman world. The infinite diversity of living things, the omnipresence of life, the desire which animated the whole world – this was the vision which Spinoza felt confirmed by the new science of the small (239).

And though it is difficult to pinpoint more precisely the extent to which Spinoza's familiarity with Dutch scientific discourse might have shaped his philosophical thought, his approach to Descartes' rationalist method is much clearer. As Gaukroger (2010) astutely observes:

> Spinoza, who perfected what might be termed the 'Trojan Horse' strategy of adopting the language of his opponents and apparently playing by their rules, while at the same time substituting new meanings for central terms, took metaphysics as seriously as he took the Cartesian criterion of clarity and distinctness. Starting from Descartes' first definition of substance he is quickly able to show that there can only exist a single substance, and that traditional distinctions between God, mind, and matter do not make sense in metaphysical terms. The result was a metaphysical system of extreme religious and moral heterodoxy (25).

The cultural historian Jonathan Israel (2001) disputes the view proposed by nineteenth century historians that Spinoza's works had very little influence on the early Enlightenment (159), instead proposing that Spinoza's thought represents a radical, influential alternative to seventeenth century dualism:

> In fact, no one else during the century 1650–1750 remotely rivalled Spinoza's notoriety as the chief challenger of the fundamentals of revealed religion, received ideas, tradition, morality and what was everywhere regarded, in absolutist and non-absolutist states alike, as divinely constituted political authority (159).

In his most important work *Ethics* (published posthumously in 1677), Spinoza raised the radical monist proposition of *Deus Sive Natura* (God or Nature) in which God or nature is an eternal, single substance with infinitely varied attributes in matter and thought. Rather than the old theological dualist distinction of the soul and the body, or Descartes' dualist conception of mind differentiated from inert extended matter, Spinoza conceived our bodies and minds as one and the same substance coextensive with nature, or God, as the one self-subsistent universal substance, a position of enduring philosophical inspiration for later revaluations of nature, whether Romantic, as with Shelley (Lea, 1971, p. 84), or in twentieth century philosophy (Deleuze, 1988; Mathews, 1990). Much more recently there has been something of a rush for the philosophy of the new (or is that early modern?) materialism (Coole & Frost, 2010). In particular, the Deleuzian concept of an ontological 'plane of immanence', in which the world is embedded in a monist substance which offers neither an idealist nor theological means of *transcendence,* owes much to Spinoza, and as such is a seventeenth century concept prefiguring the ecological model of the world such as Mathews' in which the human is situated in a web of enmeshed relations with other life forms (Mathews, 1990).

While the twentieth century eco-feminist 'dead nature' thesis located an important turn in seventeenth century thought, it has become something of a critical 'dead end' insofar as it presents too partial a picture of the variety and resilience of seventeenth century thought. A more nuanced understanding of this moment is important because within early modern traditions, as with those in late modernity, the minor, though potentially powerful legacies of immanent critique provide important critical resources for combating the indisputably more influential cultural values of human exceptionalism and their corrosive effect on both non-human and human ecologies.

Nevertheless, though the socio-political turmoil of the seventeenth century provided fertile ground for the seeds of radical critique that had been sown in natural philosophy and poetry, they fell a long way behind the dominant urges to gain wealth, power and a callous indifference to both colonised peoples and non-human life forms.

These are the paradoxical legacies of seventeenth century modernity, raising the question of how we might gauge the relationship between the model of a world aligned with instrumentalist colonialism and the radical challenge of non-dualist critique. The problem does not lie within the domain of reason and scientific experimental culture as such, but instead in values arising from seventeenth century capitalism, economic globalisation and the world's first multi-national companies that continue to shape the prevailing values of our own age.

The seventeenth century age of crisis

Only the twentieth century rivals the prevalence of war and violent upheavals in the seventeenth century, when all that was promising about the minor tradition of European Enlightenment critique was tested by the moral crises of the age that led to profound long-term effects far beyond the limits of Europe itself. One of the most violent European conflicts of the era was the Thirty Years War of 1618–1648 that grew initially out of religious controversy and became an international struggle for supremacy across the Holy Roman Empire in which Northern Italy, the Netherlands, Denmark, Sweden and Spain also became involved.[6] It has been estimated that the war resulted in over seven million deaths in the German region (Wedgwood, 1938), along with many others in subsequent serious wars in France and England, and by the 1640s there were virtually no European states that had avoided war (Parker, 2013, p. 27). It was also a time of witch-hunts, inquisitions, censorship and recurring epidemics of the Black Death, particularly in outbreaks of plague in Italy, Spain, the Netherlands, England, Germany, Norway and Sweden.

The revaluation of the prevalence of turbulent political change, frequent wars, famine, disease and general instability in seventeenth century Europe led to a twentieth century historiographical debate on how to define the crises of the era. Some referred to the seventeenth century as a necessary phase of economic crisis required by the progress of modernity (Hobsbawm, 1954). Others pointed to a more 'General Crisis' of the early modern world wrought by the often violent socio-economic struggles in the formation of modern nation states along with profound shifts in religious and intellectual values (Trevor-Roper, 1959; Parker & Smith, 1997). More recently, in a substantial extended study, Geoffrey Parker has argued the General Crisis of the seventeenth century was global in scale, and one severely exacerbated by the conditions of global climate change known as the Little Ice Age (Parker, 2013).

The Little Ice Age is broadly defined as a shift in global climate occurring from the late sixteenth to the early nineteenth centuries, with the most severe cold intervals in the seventeenth century, especially from 1650 to 1700. It is generally understood that this was caused by two major environmental circumstances. The first was increased seismic activity around the Pacific Ocean leading to a number of massive volcanic eruptions in the southern hemisphere.[7] The ash expelled from these blocked solar radiation, and the sulphur dioxide gases emitted into the stratosphere turned into sulphuric acid particles that then reflected solar radiation, reducing its capacity to reach the earth.

The second likely major factor that is often cited as affecting the European climate in the seventeenth century was an unusually prolonged period in which sunspots were at a minimum, which led to changes in terrestrial climates resulting in colder and longer winters. The period, known as the Maunder Minimum, when sunspots were unusually rare, lasted between around 1645 and 1715, coinciding with the increase in volcanic activity in the southern hemisphere. Climate change in this period has been noted as a general cooling with increased processes of glaciation,[8] which was at its most severe in European winters from around 1650, adding greatly to the suffering of the common people already afflicted by war, political turmoil, and the poverty that inevitably followed such instability.

During the hardest winters, the rivers, coastal seas and ground froze, often to a depth of over a metre, and even large trees were splintered by the cold. There was a succession of poor or failed harvests across Europe, followed by severe famines leading to disease and death. Travelling through Europe during the Thirty Years War, William Harvey lamented the fate of local wildlife with a sardonic reference to missed opportunities for medical science:

> I can only complain that by the way we could scarce see a dog, crow, kite raven or any other bird, or anything to anatomise, only some few miserable people,

the relics of the war and the plague, where famine had made anatomies before I came (cited in Keele, 1965, p. 36).

The renowned English diarists of the era later observed the severe weather conditions of the mid-century, as Samuel Pepys complained of the treacherous business of walking home across the ice in London in January 1667, and at several points John Evelyn wrote of the bitter cold, particularly in 1658 when ice and snow enveloped the land:

> This has been the severest winter that any man alive had known in England. The crows feet were frozen to their prey. Islands of ice inclosed both fish and fowl frozen, and some persons in their boats ([1662] 1908, p. 331 [March 7th, 1658]).

Towards the end of the century when the young English aristocrat Anthony Ashley Cooper, the Third Earl of Shaftesbury, made his *Grand Tour* of Europe, his sense of the sublime and divinely inspired majesty of nature were tempered by his Whig sentiments when he witnessed how such intense cold affected the common people:

> How tedious are the winters there! How deep the horrors of the night and How uncomfortable even the light of day! The freezing winds employ their fiercest breath yet are not spent with blowing. The sea, which elsewhere is scarce confined within its limits, lies here immured in walls of crystal. The snow covers the hills and almost fills the lowest valleys. How wide and deep it lies, incumbent over the plains, hiding the sluggish rivers, the shrubs and the trees, the dens of beasts and mansions of distressed and feeble men! – See where they lie confined, hardly secure against the raging cold or the attacks of the wild beasts, now masters of the of the wasted field and forced by hunger out of the naked woods! (Cooper, [1711] 1999, II, p. 313).

In his study of what he called 'The problems of the Little Ice Age' the *Annales* school historian Le Roy Ladurie (1971) based his account on a careful examination of such human cultural records of changes in climate, together with numeri- cal information on crop failures and food prices, paintings and other material resources such as archaeological evidence. Le Roy Ladurie also thought historians should be able to draw on quantitative methods less encumbered by 'anthropo- centric prejudice' (1971, 17). In Geoffrey Parker's recent study it is precisely such quantitative data derived from ice cores and glaciology, phenological studies of pollen and spore deposits, the histories of tree growth rings, or from the slow annual deposits made by groundwater in underground caves forming stalactites which provides the means from which changes in climate can be traced. Hence in response to the challenges of historiographical methodology, Le Roy Ladurie was prescient in anticipating Chakrabarty's observation that the social ramifica- tions of the Anthropocene dissolve the classic distinction between natural history and human history, and between the natural and human sciences (Chakrabarty, 2009). Though the inexact differentiation of seventeenth century science from other coeval theories of knowledge is often regarded as a measure of the fact that science was simply undeveloped, contemporary calls for a dissolution of hard and fast distinctions between the arts and sciences in the comprehension of nature were anticipated in the seventeenth century.

Parker observed that in the mid-seventeenth century, 'the earth experienced some of the coldest weather recorded in over a millennium. Perhaps one third of the population died' (Parker, 2013, p. xv). He shows how severe weather conditions occurred in countries such as India, China and Japan. But although China, like Europe, was afflicted by deep social and political discord, this did not necessarily extend globally.[9] Hobbes infamous remark on the lives of Europeans as 'solitary, poor, nasty, brutish and short' (Hobbes, [1651] 1996, p. 89) was a dour socio-political observation that may well have included a grim sense of climatic extremes, as Parker suggests. But Parker also sees that this does not *necessarily* imply that there is a causal relation between climate and socio-cultural histories. Instead he opts for what he calls a 'fatal synergy' between human and natural disasters in Europe, especially in the earlier part of the century (Parker, 2013, p. xxiii). Parker follows the processes of how cooling affected food supply, and how war then exacerbated these conditions, leading to crises in the imbalance between supply and demand. This process recurred repeatedly in the first half of the century, but then dissipated to some extent towards the end of the century despite the persistence of severe weather conditions. Hence Parker's 'fatal synergy' began to weaken as the weather was at its most extreme, though it is not altogether clear why.

Wolfgang Behringer, on the other hand, suggests that the 'cool sun of reason' developed in response to the Little Ice Age was a necessary condition of the Enlightenment and describes 'the struggle for greater stability as a crisis-handling strategy' (Behringer, 2007, p. 146). Hence he sees the struggle for the consolidation of nation states, along with procedural rationalization and regulatory systems, as broad social processes generated by the severity of the climate and ensuing natural disasters. On this largely determinist view of the way climate shapes history, Behringer holds that the broad social process of Enlightenment that prioritised reason was also heightened by the demise of religious fanaticism, as it became increasingly evident that 'holy wars and witch hunts improved neither the weather not the harvest but merely caused additional suffering', and hence provided a context conducive to what he describes as the 'fencing in of passions' (149).

In Norbert Elias' compelling account of early modern European history, the normative internalisation of behavioural restraints was a far more complex civilizing process than a response to climate (Elias, [1939] 2000), just as Keith Thomas' study of popular religious beliefs at this time shows that the persecution of witches didn't stop merely because it didn't improve the weather or rescue harvests ([1971] 1997). Nevertheless, it is clear that the extreme weather events of the seventeenth century exacerbated socio-political conditions in ways that very likely provided the grounds for a more complex shift in cultural and intellectual values.

What neither Parker nor Behringer consider, however, is the question of how anthropogenic factors may also have contributed to the Little Ice Age. Their focus is on how the natural causes of extreme weather events intensified socio-economic crises. On the other hand, palaeoclimatologists (Nevle & Bird, 2008; Ruddiman, 2005), and geographers (Lewis & Maslin, 2015; Dull, et al., 2010) have focused on how seventeenth century European social values in themselves led to significant environmental changes on a global scale. Social historians are beginning to draw on the findings of science in understanding global change, but as Chakrabarty's call for a new epistemology of climate change makes clear, the dissolution of generic distinctions between natural history and human history, and between the natural and human sciences, is by no means an easy task. I shall turn now to how such complex entanglements of human and natural histories in the long seventeenth century produced the world-changing event of the Columbian Exchange.

The Columbian Exchange

As hard as things were for the weakened and diminished populations of mid-seventeenth century Europe (De Vries, 2007), they had been far worse for the indigenous peoples of the Americas where the full impact of mercantile colonialism reached an inevitable crisis following the arrival of Europeans in the Caribbean in 1492. Faced with the ineluctable forces of Eurasian diseases, war, famine and the miseries of enslavement, the Amerindians were subject to the biggest eradication of human populations in the past 13,000 years (Mann, 2011; Crosby, 2003). From a robust indigenous population recently estimated at 61 million before 1492, by 1650 there were approximately six million indigenous people left in the Americas (Mann, 2011; Kaplan, et al., 2011). Population change on this scale cannot be isolated from its wider ecological consequences, hence the claim that 'the history of globalization and imperialism is integral to understanding contemporary environmental issues' (DeLoughrey, et al., 2015) gains particular credence when applied to the Columbian Exchange.

The term 'Columbian Exchange', first coined by Alfred Crosby (1987), is now widely used to describe the global bio-political transfer of peoples, animals and plants between the western hemisphere and the Americas following the European colonisation of the 'New World' from the late fifteenth century. While Afro-Eurasian plants such as coffee, grapes or citrus were transported to the Americas, by the mid-seventeenth century American cocoa was being consumed as chocolate in Europe. Similarly, potatoes had become food for the poor in England and a field crop in Ireland, while tomatoes from the Andes quickly became popular in Spain and Italy. There were fewer domesticatable animals in America than in Europe, but turkeys were exported to Europe, while a range of species from honeybees to cattle, sheep and pigs were introduced to the Americas. Horses, which had first evolved in America and then become extinct there, had long before made a journey across the Bering Strait land bridge to Eurasia, and were subsequently returned to their continent of origin ridden by Spanish conquistadors.

Most of these exchanges were a result of the European capitalist endeavour to colonise the Americas and exploit its resources, but the most profound bio-political consequences of colonisation were the result of unintentional biotic transmission of the Eurasian diseases that devastated indigenous Amerindian populations. Before the European conquest, the Amerindians had controlled the land with fire (Pyne, 1997) to the extent that the landscapes of North America reminded the first colonists of parks rather than untamed wilderness (Mann, 2011, p. 39). As pandemics of smallpox and a wide range of other diseases to which Amerindians had no immunity effectively destroyed whole societies, CO_2 emissions from widespread burning fell significantly and the forests regenerated throughout the Americas. Further biotic instability was introduced by insects that had been transported in European ships, along with the plants intended for the introduction of mono-cultural agriculture to be planted where previously indigenous people had encouraged the growth of mixed species.

In a recent article in *Nature* on the Anthropocene, Lewis and Maslin (2015) argue that the multiple biotic transfers of the Columbian Exchange, including those that were accidental, constituted 'a swift, ongoing, radical reorganization of life on earth without geological precedent' (174). Moreover, it was, they argue, the extreme reduction of human populations that made the most indelible impact on global ecologies, when the:

> ...near-cessation of farming and reduction in fire use resulted in the regeneration of 50 million hectares of forest, woody savannah and grassland with a carbon uptake by vegetation and soils... resulting in an observable decline in CO_2 of 7–10 ppm between 1570 and 1620 documented in two high resolution Antarctic ice core records (175).

In his call for a historiography of the *longue durée*, the environmental historian Tom Griffiths conveyed a palpable sense of the preciousness of such ice core records kept in stations in the remote regions of the diminishing polar ice caps (Griffiths, 2010). They provide the crucial indices of the decline in CO_2 in the early seventeenth century when further to a significant diminishment of the CO_2 that had been caused by burning, the flourishing forests in the Americas combined with the environmental signatures of volcanic and solar activity to produce the Little Ice Age. Further to William Ruddiman's findings in paleoclimatology (2005), the geographers Lewis and Maslin argue that the Columbian Exchange was a crucial causal factor in what they call the 'Orbis' or world spike in various stratigraphic records which mark the year 1610 as one of two dates they see as most convincing as the beginning of the Anthropocene – the other being 1964 with the anthropogenic forcings of 'the great acceleration' (2015, p. 175). The argument that the Anthropocene began in 1610 is persuasive not only because it is grounded in the material evidence of global climatic change, but also because rather than being approximated with the effects of the industrial revolution, it provides a more effective lineage of the deeper socio-cultural conditions which led to the Anthropocene.

By the seventeenth century the European landscape itself had also changed significantly from the medieval period, not least as a result of deforestation due to early land enclosures such as those that had developed in England and France from the sixteenth century (Polanyi, [1944] 2001; Bloch, 1960) and the trees from Northern European forests needed for the tall ships used in naval warfare and expansion in trade. And it is surely one of the bleaker ironies of history that the countervailing environmental effect of the reafforestation of the Americas was due to the results of the same European dream of capitalist growth and bio-political mastery that led to the depletion of forests in Europe. The violence of the Columbian Exchange was, at least initially, partly unintentional, but there can be no question that the colonial process rapidly became a murderous regime in its inexorable drive for expansion and mastery.

The colonial drive, like many other dominant aspects of political agency in early modernity, was generally constituted by what eco-feminist philosopher Val Plumwood identified as a politics and bio-politics of mastery (Plumwood, 1993). It was, after all, predominantly 'guns, germs and steel' (Diamond, 1997), rather than the innate critiques of philosophy and poetry that the Europeans, also armed with Bibles and the promise of redemption, brought to the Americas. Plumwood was probably right to suggest that the sedimentary layers of socio-cultural processes that inform modern dualist thought may have prehistoric origins (1993, 43–44). She also correctly identified the radical exclusions of Platonic dualism of classical antiquity as seminal, and suggests they were heightened in the rationalism of the Enlightenment.

The historical foundations of dualist values that underpinned the European colonization of the Americas drew on other sources, too: they were also clearly based in Christian theological doctrine forged in the thirteenth and fourteenth centuries that, at its best (in Evelyn's *Sylva* for example), led to the stewardship of nature, but far more often simply advocated dominion, and at worst ruthless violation. In the rapid colonial advances of the sixteenth century, the Cartesian concept of mechanism would have been essentially redundant, since insofar as non-human life forms were conceived as beings with agency, they were unequivocally different *in kind* rather than degree, because only humans were believed to possess souls and hence supernatural status.

Subaltern peoples presented a more complex problem, but this too proved a largely redundant issue for Europeans because colonized people could always be subjugated to the natural rights of vastly superior human souls redeemed by the one true God.

In *Feminism and the Mastery of Nature* (1993), Plumwood developed a sustained dialogical critique of hierarchical dualism by adapting post-colonial theory to a social feminist reappraisal of ecology. Plumwood took great care to distinguish this eco-feminist critique of dualism from any essentialist biological connection between women and nature, and her critical strategy lay precisely in deconstructing dualism as 'the logic of colonisation'. Notwithstanding this refutation of essentialism, she nonetheless made it clear that the cultural connections between women and nature are intimate rather than arbitrary, since they were based on clear historical parallels between the status of subaltern peoples, degraded nature and disempowered women. She thus refuted post-structuralist accounts of the concept of 'woman' as an entirely fluid state of meaning because they weakened feminist politics or even claims that women are oppressed. For Plumwood, just as the subordinates of colonised countries are backgrounded by the controlling logic of colonisation, the domination of nature ensures it is kept in the background as a means of legitimising and naturalising the subjugation of those intimately associated with nature, such as women or tribal peoples.

Despite the prevalent hierarchical dualisms of culture over nature, human over animal and male over female, which seemed well established in colonial discourses, the hierarchy of colonisers over subaltern people and animals of the New World still raised certain historiographical problems for early modern writers. Colonial encounters with the New World unsettled existing ideas about human origins and histories in ways that led eventually to the development of a more scientific approach to natural history. The question of whether Amerindians were the descendants of Adam, for example, or whether the unfamiliar animals of the New World had been amongst those rescued from the flood in Noah's Ark, inspired early attempts at providing a history of the world beyond the canonical accounts of Europe, the Middle East and North Africa.

Mathew Hale's *The Primitive Origination of Mankind* (1677) attempted to address the problems presented by the American people and animals through the old Judeo-Christian narratives of origin. And while the English parson-naturalist John Ray in 1691 in *The Wisdom of God Manifested in the Works of the Creation* had not resolved the ethically tricky question of the inequalities of human history in the divine plan, he marvelled at the diversity of creation manifest in the vast array of unfamiliar species. The roots of botany and zoology, and more obliquely, anthropology, emerged from these early modern accounts. They also led to an interest in the effects of climate itself, evident in Shapin's account of Boyle for example, who in order to more accurately study the effects of extreme cold in 1665, invested in the Hudson Bay company so he could ensure direct, rather than second hand traveller's accounts of Arctic regions (1994, p. 251).

While these early modern histories of 'new' lands were clearly shaped by discourses of dualism and capitalist intstrumentalism, it is also clear that a countervailing tendency gradually emerges in which the processes of reason later begin to erode such conventions. One ecocritical approach to Enlightenment science suggests that its foundations in ontological dualism were simply secularized into a more modern scientific approach to achieving the same aims. Yet the ontological ground of enquiry was gradually changed profoundly by science in ways that clearly challenged the hierarchical dualism of human exceptionalism. Just as the Copernican revolution had profoundly shifted the figure of man as the hub of the universe, so the Darwinian revolution eventually shifted even more profoundly the supernatural status of humans as beings distinct from other life forms. And yet, people in earlier phases of modernity were as capable of ignoring the findings of science as we are today. As Plumwood observed, there remains a deep-rooted persistence of the 'the set of interrelated and mutually reinforcing dualisms which permeate western culture [and form] a fault-line which runs through its entire conceptual system' (1993, 42). And since it appears, if erroneously, to so many people that this is the only legacy that will protect human interests, it remains stubbornly resistant to change at the level of affects.

The Anthropocene

The challenges posed today by climate change draw in complex and sometimes contradictory ways on the legacies of a long seventeenth century that extends from 1550 to 1750. The processes of globalizing capitalism that multinational Dutch and British trading companies established in the seventeenth century can be identified as the foundations of the contemporary global economy, just as the processes of biotic transfer and genocide in the Columbian Exchange consolidated a colonial process that has led to profound global inequalities in our own time. And as Lewis and Maslin (2015) argue, it now seems increasingly likely that the bio-political impact of European expansion in the Columbian Exchange combined with natural events in ways that led to significant climate change in the seventeenth century.

In Chakrabarty's account of the 'Four Theses' of history, 'Thesis One' aptly describes the epistemological challenges to which scholars of climate change must adapt in order to traverse what Crosby (1995) called 'the concertina wire that divides the humanities from the sciences'. Yet given that findings on the climatic impact of the Columbian Exchange are quite recent (despite Ruddiman's anticipation in 2005), neither Parker, Crosby nor Chakrabarty consider how the colonial drive for mastery was itself an early modern form of biological agency powerful enough to gain geological momentum, at least in combination with other geological and solar factors. Though this biological agency was a largely unintended consequence of European colonialism, it was nevertheless constituted by the colonial project. It was a process designed to subjugate subaltern peoples that, as Plumwood saw, was inextricably enmeshed in the project to ensure nature remained in its theologically ordained place of inferiority in a binary order of the world privileging the human above all other life forms. And in similar ways, contemporary climate change is also an unintended consequence of the privileging of human interests conceived within the same ontological framework.

As I have argued, however, there was also a countervailing, if minor, humanist tradition that radically called into question this dominant legacy of dualism and its relentless anthropocentrism. I do not say that this is the foundation of post-humanism, but instead see it as a far more promising legacy of an enlightened human self-interest that could conceive of anthropocentrism as a model of a world impoverished by human exceptionalism. The processes of human expansion, capitalist growth and biotic exchanges that began in the early modern period are now accelerating at an unprecedented rate in forcing global climate change, while continued global biotic exchanges, erosion of habitats and a general attrition of bio-diversity seem poised to precipitate extinction on a scale unprecedented in human history. It is difficult to calibrate the complex historical junctures in which non-dualist philosophy or cultural forms of empathy for the non-human world were shaped by the General Crisis of the seventeenth century and the Little Ice Age, but they are now critical factors prefiguring the revision of ontological and cultural values in the way we grapple with the challenges of contemporary climate change.

What then, might early modern critiques of the exploitation of nature offer eco-critical responses to the conditions of late modernity? Though it could be argued that pointing to a dynamic progression in environmental degradation from early to late modernity merely demonstrates the inefficiency of immanent critique, this underestimates its cultural potency in the Anthropocene as an age of crisis. In the 'time poor' context of current climate change, understanding the history of innate critique offers a critical tool for understanding the dynamics of the Anthropocene, perhaps not primarily as a way of immediately addressing the global complexity, but instead as a means of analysing the origins of such complexity in order to better understand its more fundamental dynamics. The innate critiques of seventeenth century poetics or philosophy may seem fairly marginal instances of opposition to what have undeniably been more successful models of modernity based expediently on pre-modern concepts of dualism, but they nonetheless provide robust historical and ontological foundations for a more carefully reasoned ethics of environmental engagement.

Though historical parallels between the seventeenth century and late modernity are not exact, nor represent an unbroken line of development, they are nonetheless persuasive enough to suggest how a careful scrutiny of early modern values can be useful in understanding present day problems. While the seventeenth century sense of wonder in gaining a more enlightened understanding of nature combined with the potency of early modern immanent critique has not led to a departure from the dominant values of modernity, it does hold potential in the Habermasian sense of early modern enlightenment as an 'unfinished project' (Habermas, 1983). In this account I have touched on instances of critique in poetics and philosophy as the vibrant currents of resistance to human exceptionalism that emerged in early modernity. Undoubtedly they constitute part of only a minor tradition, but it is difficult to find persuasive reasons why this should continue to be the case.

Notes

1 Richard Grove notes that by the end of the seventeenth century forest conservation, water and soil management also appeared in Western India, China and Japan (1997, p. 61).
2 In 1653 Marvell was employed as a tutor in the house of the Anglican divine John Oxenbridge who had been to Bermuda, and in 1653 was appointed as English commissioner to the Bermudas.
3 By 1650 Cartesianism was already being taught at Cambridge by Henry More and others of the Cambridge Platonists, and *The Discourse on Method* was available in English.
4 Shapin & Schaffer (1986) show how a social conservative like Hobbes made clear his opposition to Boyle and others in the experimental community of practice because it represented a new model of independent thought that he regarded as a threat to the

theological and political order. Because Boyle and the Royal Society prevailed it is clear that it was not generally a threat to the social order, though in the longer term Hobbes was correct in identifying experimental philosophy as something that effectively undermined theological order.

5   'It is true that experience confirms what is said by Spinoza, namely that the small objectives in the microscope represent the objects much finer than the large ones' ([OC4, 140, May 11, 1668], cited in Klever, 1996, p. 33).

6   The Holy Roman Empire encompassed Germany, Austria, Czechoslovakia and Slovenia, as well as parts of modern France and Poland.

7   Mt. Billy Mitchell in Papua, New Guinea, erupted in 1580, followed by Huaynaputina in Peru in 1600, Mt. Villarica in Chile in 1640, Mt. Parker in the Philippines in 1641 and Long Island in Papua New Guinea in c.1660.

8   NASA identifies 1650 as the first glacial maximum of The Little Ice Age. http://www .giss.nasa.gov/research/briefs/shindell_06/ (accessed. 22, 1. 2016). NASA also identifies the Maunder Minimum when sunspots were at a minimum leading to lower terrestrial temperatures. (A later period of rare sunspot activity known as the Dalton Minimum from 1790-1820 resulted in a 2 degrees Celsius fall over a 20 year period recorded in Germany.)

9   Parker cites Moghul India and Japan as cases where significant climate change and subsequent imbalances between food supply and demand did not lead to war and revolt, but was contained by different approaches to social organisation.

References

Behringer, W., 2007. *A Cultural History of Climate*. Cambridge: Polity Press.

Bloch, M., 1960. *French Rural History: An Essay on its Basic Characteristics*. London: Routledge and Kegan Paul.

Boas, G., 1933. *The Happy Beast in French Thought of the Seventeenth Century*. New York: Octagon.

Bowerbank, S., 2004. *Speaking for Nature: Women and Ecologies of Early Modern England*. Baltimore(MD): Johns Hopkins University Press.

Buyse, P., 2010. Spinoza and Robert Boyle's definition of Mechanical Philosophy. *Historia Philosophica*, Volume 8, p. 73–89.

Cavendish, M., [1666] 2001. *Observations upon Experimental Philosophy*. New York: Cambridge University Press.

Chakrabarty, D., 2009. The Climate of History: Four Theses. *Critical Inquiry*, Volume 35, p. 197–222.

Coole, D. & Frost, S. eds., 2010. *New Materialisms: Ontology, Agency and Politics*. Durham(NC): Duke University Press.

Cooper, A. A., [1711] 1999. *Characteristic of Men, Manners, Opinions, Times*. Cambridge(UK): Cambridge University Press.

Crosby, A. W., 1987. *The Colombian Voyages, the Columbian Exchange, and Their Historians*. Washington DC: The American Historical Association.

Crosby, A. W., 2003. *The Columbian Exchange: Biological and Cultural Consequences of 1492*. Westport(CT): Praeger.

Crutzen, P. J. & Stoermer, E. F., 2000. The 'Anthropocene'. *Global Change Newsletter*, Volume 41, p. 17–18.

De Vries, J., 2007. *European Urbanization 1500–1800*. London: Routledge.

Deleuze, G., 1988. *Spinoza: Practical Philosophy*. San Francisco: City Lights Books.

DeLoughrey, E., Didur, J. & Carrigan, A. eds., 2015. *Global Ecologies and the Environmental Humanities: Postcolonial Approaches*. London: Routledge.

Diamond, J., 1997. *Guns, Germs and Steel: The Fates of Human Societies*. New York: Norton.

Dull, R. A. et al., 2010. The Columbian encounter and the Little Ice Age: Abrupt land use change, fire, and greenhouse forcing. *Annals of the Association of American Geographers*, Volume 100, p. 755–771.

Elias, N., [1939] 2000. *The Civilising Process*. Oxford: Blackwell.

Evelyn, J., [1662] 1908. *Sylva: A Discourse of Forest Trees*. London: Doubleday.

Fallon, S., 1991. *Milton among the Philosophers: Poetry and Materialism in Early Modern England*. Ithaca(NY): Cornell University Press.

Fraser, A., 1993. *The Weaker Vessel. Woman's Lot in Seventeenth Century England*. London: Phoenix.

Fuer, L., 1987. *Spinoza and the Rise of the Liberals*. New Brunswick(NJ): Transaction.

Garber, D. & Roux, S. eds., 2013. *The Mechanisation of Natural Philosophy*. Dordrecht: Springer.

Gaukroger, S., 2010. *The Collapse of Mechanism and the Rise of Sensibility: Science and the Shaping of Modernity 1680–1760*. Oxford: Clarendon Press.

Griffiths, T., 2010. A humanist on thin ice. *Griffith Review*, Volume 29.

Grove, R., 1997. *Green Imperialism: Colonial Expansion, Tropical Island Edens and the Origins of Environmentalism, 1600–1860*. Cambridge(UK): Cambridge University Press.

Habermas, J., 1983. Modernity: An Unfinished Project. In: H. Foster, ed. *The Anti Aesthetic*. Seattle(WA): Bay Press.

Hale, M., 1677. *The Primitive Origination of Mankind*. London: Shrowsbery.

Hastings, H., 1936. *Man and Beast in French Thought of the 18th Century*. Baltimore(MD): Johns Hopkins University Press.

Hobbes, T., [1651] 1996. *Leviathan, or the matter, forme, and power of a common-wealth, ecclesiasticall and civill*. Cambridge(UK): Cambridge University Press.

Hobsbawm, E., 1954. The crisis of the 17th century II. *Past and Present*, 6(1), p. 44–65.

Hobsbawm, E., 1996. *The Age of Extremes: A History of the World 1914–1991*. New York: Vintage Books.

Hooke, R., [1665] 1938. *Micrographia*. Oxford: Oxford University Press.

Israel, J., 2001. *Radical Enlightenment: Philosophy and the Making of Modernity 1650–1750*. Oxford: Oxford University Press.

Kaplan, J. O. et al., 2011. Holocene carbon emissions as a result of anthropogenic land cover change. *Holocene*, Volume 21, p. 775–791.

Keele, K., 1965. *William Harvey*. London: Nelson.

Klever, W., 1996. Spinoza's Life and Works. In: D. Garrett, ed. *Cambridge Companion to Spinoza*. Cambridge(UK): Cambridge University Press.

Landström, B., 1967. *Columbus: The Story of Don Cristóbal Colón, Admiral of the Ocean*. New York: Macmillan.

Le Roy Ladurie, E., 1971. *Times of Feast, Times of Famine: A History of Climate Since the Year 1000*. New York: Doubleday.

Lea, F. A., 1971. *Shelley and the Romantic Revolution*. New York: Haskell House.

Lewis, S. & Maslin, M., 2015. Defining the Anthropocene. *Nature*, 12 March, Volume 519, p. 171–180.

Lowry, S. T., 2003. The agricultural foundation of the seventeenth century English oeconomy. *History of Political Economy*, 35(Annual Supplement), p. 74–100.

Lyotard, J.-F., 1984. *The Postmodern Condition: A Report on Knowledge*. Minneapolis: University of Minnesota Press.

Maehle, A. H. & Trohler, U., 1987. Animal Experimentation from Antiquity to the End of the Eighteenth Century: Attitudes and Arguments. In: N. A. Rupke, ed. *Vivisection in Perspective*. London: Routledge.

Mann, C. C., 2011. *1493: How the Ecological Collision of Europe and the Americas Gave Rise to the Modern World*. London: Granta.

Mathews, F., 1990. *The Ecological Self*. London: Routledge.

Merchant, C., 1989. *The Death of Nature: Women, Ecology and the Scientific Revolution*. San Francisco: Harper Collins.

Merchant, C., 2006. The scientific revolution and the death of nature. *Isis*, Volume 97, p. 513–533.

Nevle, R. J. & Bird, D. K., 2008. Effects of syn-pandemic fire reduction and reforestation in the tropical Americas on atmospheric CO2 during European conquest. *Palaeogeography, Palaeoclimatology, Palaeoclimatology*, Volume 264, p. 25–38.

Parker, G. & Smith, L. eds., 1997. *The General Crisis of the Seventeenth Century*. London: Routledge.

Parker, R., 2013. *Global Crisis: War, Climate Change & Catastrophe in the Seventeenth Century*. New Haven(CT): Yale University Press.

Plumwood, V., 1993. *Feminism and the Mastery of Nature*. London: Routledge.

Polanyi, M., [1944] 2001. *The Great Transformation*. Boston(MA): Beacon Press.

Pyne, S. J., 1997. *Fire in America: A Cultural History of Wildland and Rural Fire*. Washington(WA): University of Washington Press.

Rackham, O., 1990. *Trees and Woodland in the British Landscape*. London: Dent & Sons.

Ruddiman, P., 2005. *Plows, Plagues & Petroleum: How Humans Took Control of Climate*. Princeton(NJ): Princeton University Press.

Shapin, S., 1994. *A Social History of Truth. Civility and Science in Seventeenth Century England*. Chicago: University of Chicago Press.

Shapin, S. & Schaffer, S., 1986. *Leviathan and the Air-Pump: Hobbes, Boyle, and the Experimental Life*. Princeton(NJ): Princeton University Press.

Steffen, W., Crutzen, P. & McNeill, J., 2007. The Anthropocene: Are humans now overwhelming the great forces of Nature? *Ambio*, Volume 36, p. 614–621.

Thomas, K., [1971] 1997. *Religion and the Decline of Magic: Studies in Popular Beliefs in Sixteenth and Seventeenth-Century England*. London: Weidenfeld & Nicolson.

Thomas, K., 1983. *Man and the Natural World*. London: Penguin.

Trevor-Roper, H. R., 1959. The General Crisis of the seventeenth century. *Past and Present*, November, Volume 16, p. 31–64.

Wedgwood, C., 1938. *The Thirty Years War*. London: Cape.

Williams, L., 2008. Reflections on modernity, monkeys, and men: Edward Tyson and the revelations of enlightenment science. *Philosophy, Activism, Nature*, Volume 5, p. 3–11.

Williams, L., 2009. Modernity and the Other Body: The Human Contract with Mute Animality. In: Z. Detsi-Diamante, K. Kitsi-Mitakou & E. Yiannopoulo, eds. *The Future of Flesh: A Cultural Survey of the Body*. London: Palgrave, p. 221–239.

Williams, R., 1973. *The City and the Country*. Oxford: Oxford University Press.

Zalasiewicz, J. et al., 2015. When did the Anthropocene begin? A mid-twentieth century boundary level is stratigraphically optimal. *Quaternary International*, Volume 383, p. 196–203.

Part II

Climates of writing

6   Change beyond belief

Fictions of (the) Enlightenment and Simpson's 'climate change suite'

Jayne Lewis

Climate change is surely no laughing matter. So it is always enlightening to see it treated as one. Take Alan Barr, the inveterate climate-change denier at the centre of Helen Simpson's short story 'In-Flight Entertainment' (Simpson, 2010). During an ozone-depleting flight from London to Chicago, Alan's seatback monitor magically displays a 'shrunken globe with a jewel of an aeroplane – the one he was on' – but he ignores the globe, preferring to track his plane's progress through the stratosphere. When that gets old, Alan testily debates a retired atmospheric scientist over the 'big con-trick' of climate change (9). It's nothing but a 'fairy story' in Alan's opinion, 'nothing but hot air' (20), and his argument is clinched when the plane makes an emergency landing in the Arctic. 'Look at that weather,' Alan challenges the scientist. 'Don't tell me you still believe in global warming. It's fucking freezing out there' (20).

Simpson's broad satire cloaks a fine irony: snug on his 'aeroplane' and in touch even with its pressurized environment only from afar, Alan Barr firmly believes that 'it' is 'fucking freezing'. Yet he is not actually experiencing whatever is 'out there', any more than he experiences what he *dis*believes – that being climate change. The grounds of Alan's belief, like those of his disbelief, are equally nonexistent. This puts him in interesting synchrony with Simpson's reader, for of course it is only through the mediating form of a fiction that that reader can be said to experience either Simpson's climate-change denier or the change he is denying. These distances, and the peculiar order of experience that attends them, persist even as Simpson (surely) urges us to take climate change if not as a fact, then at least as not contingent upon our beliefs about it.

Simpson's story isn't 'just' a story. It's a reflexive study of the role that fiction plays in the making of climates, in the inhabiting of them, in their change, and potentially in changing belief about such change. In none of this, paradoxically, is it new. As much is, if peripherally, acknowledged in the fictional environment through which Simpson's stylized characters move, even as it moves them. The seats in first class are 'ranged in curved couples, like Victorian loveseats' (8), Alan watches a 'retro' film (*North by Northwest*), and an environmental group he earlier saw protesting against air travel's toll on the atmosphere is ridiculed for 'trying to turn the wheel back' (9). Even as they arise from it, such circularities counter the trajectory of an airplane whose flight pattern mimics the progress that is modernity's defining narrative structure.

This story's deepest affinities, however, lie with the Enlightenment, a period widely believed to have made progress both a formal requirement for reputable fiction and the dominant template of modern historical experience. Other stories in the collection to which 'In-Flight Entertainment' lends its title name-check Daniel Defoe, Fanny Burney and Alexander Pope. Well they might. What, if not the Enlightenment, can we thank – or revile – for the technologies and habits of self-absorption to which we attribute climate change? But we also owe it significant formal debts, including one for Simpson's brand of literary 'entertainment'. This is not just because her medium is the mass-market fiction that materialized over the long eighteenth century. Simpson also draws on complex literary conventions whose values were negotiated at that time – conventions of reflection and denial, feeling and flight, that regardless of their thematic and rhetorical objectives rely on peculiarly modern means of managing distance. Before returning to Simpson, therefore, it is instructive to consider just how the Enlightenment's formal models of make-believe alienated the senses to engender distinctively 'modern' conceptions of climate, air and atmosphere.

Enlightenment atmospheres of belief

Introducing their edited volume *This Is Enlightenment*, Clifford Siskin and William Warner define 'the' Enlightenment as 'an event in the history of mediation' (Siskin & Warner, 2010, 7). They mean that over the long eighteenth century such novel cultural phenomena as mass literacy made mediation itself an implicit condition of experience. Siskin and Warner's title thus indirectly references their book as it appears on the horizon of the Enlightenment that it attempts to define. Now that we are here, of course, the horizon does not present as one. Yet it is precisely this distanced immediacy that we should recognize as a signature of (the) Enlightenment: as Simpson's atmospheric scientist puts it, 'the nearer you get to a mountain, the less of it you see' (Simpson, 2010, 10).

Another, more precise signature is modern scientific discourse, which in the Anglophone context is traditionally dated to the founding of the Royal Society in 1662, and which manages to be empiricist in its claims while yet depending on technology and its distortions to produce and validate them. The resulting suspense between sensation and separation typifies the 'modern' scientific conceptions of climate, atmosphere and environment that were forged between 1660 – the year that Robert Boyle published his *New Experiments Touching the Spring of the Air* – and 1774, when Joseph Priestley's *Experiments and Observations on Different Kinds of Air* shifted scientific belief about the air from a Boylean physico-mechanical model to the organicist one that would prevail into the twentieth century. Both of these models were designed at the macro level, where they afforded quantifiable and objective pictures of 'the' air, as well as of atmospheric states, weather patterns and global climate zones. Meanwhile, at the micro level, such three-dimensional instruments as the thermometer, the hygrometer, the barometer and the eudiometer joined forces with two-dimensional ones – statistical tables recording rainfall and temperature, weather maps, and the like – to register atmospheric change by stabilizing it in representational space. Regardless of the number of dimensions involved, enlightened means of measuring atmospheres, climates, even air itself make those ephemeral (temporal) phenomena conceivable only through spatial (atemporal) representations of them. Vladimir Janković thus traces our peculiarly modern sense of environmental threat to the eighteenth century's 'topocentric' bias, and ultimately to its conflation of 'normative constructs' with 'volumetric spaces' (Janković, 2010, 3, 1).

The distance between representations of the atmosphere and the atmosphere 'itself' is further obscured because of those representations' fixture in graphic forms endowed with their own sensible properties. A page out of an early eighteenth-century astrological almanac looks very much like a page of meteorological observations from the same period; the resemblance reminds us that representations are free to attract varying degrees of belief. Thus they produce what we might call microclimates of their own: bubbles of mediated reality that individuals or subgroups may be said to inhabit both conceptually and physically. The distances between these bubbles match the 'modern' disciplinary divisions whose ultimate superficiality – notwithstanding their reputation as absolute – Bruno Latour ([1991] 1993) has influentially theorized. Each modern discipline, meanwhile, forms through the 'fusing of common space' between intimate experience and universal theory (Fleming, et al., 2006, xii).

Within any given bubble, conceptual and sensory experience necessarily interpenetrate. This interpenetration is visible in the case of 'atmosphere' itself, a word that first appeared in print in 1638, ironically in reference not to the earth but to the moon, now believed to have none. In a classic essay tracing the history of the idea of milieu or ambience to the ancient Greek *periechein* Leo Spitzer pointed out that 'the history of this word cannot be separated from that of *medium*' (Spitzer, 1948, 179–80). Spitzer's point is rounded out in the twentieth-century conception of the so-called 'noosphere', which Janković and James Rodger Fleming characterize as 'the anthropocentric layer [of the atmosphere] in which we express our opinions, the interdisciplinary sphere of human affairs, the most influential layer of our planet's atmosphere'. Despite its exclusion from scientific analysis, Janković and Fleming place the noosphere at the outer margin of the troposphere, where its very proximity renders it invisible, 'as intimately close as our next breath' (Fleming & Janković, 2011, 4).[1]

The presumption of change over time ('our next breath') is as crucial to the idea of the noosphere as the presumption that, not unlike climate, 'the' atmosphere is a 'biospatial frame of reference', one in which experience and belief converge. With respect to temporal change and the notions that apparently undergo it, Spitzer took the 'rise' of Newtonian mechanics as evidence of the Enlightenment's flight from the 'warm abstraction' of Greek, Roman and even medieval ambiance – the historical point of its definitive cooling into a mathematical, empirical and thus objective account of atmosphere. The temperature plunge corresponds to the 'disenchantment of the world' that, a few years before Spitzer, Theodor Adorno and Max Horkheimer ([1944] 1997) famously identified with the Enlightenment – a disenchantment that apparently motivated new convictions about what is in the air (carbon dioxide, oxygen) and what is not (fairies, ghosts). We retain the Enlightenment's representation of itself as a period of climate change but forget the attendant experience of suspense between literal and figurative, physical and conceptual kinds of change. Competing registers of experience balance – perhaps are interfused – in discourse about an 'aera' (the word's modern sense was coined around 1696) whose (con) sequential model of change sought to separate those registers from one another. For example, as Golinski considers, in the eighteenth century, the barometer was promoted as a 'recognized symbol of enlightened culture' even as its true relationship to 'change in the weather' remained mysterious. The barometer's persistent ties to archaic knowledge forms such as superstition and intuition made it 'a most equivocal tool of enlightenment, or perhaps an indication of the ambivalences inherent in the movement itself' (Golinski, 2007, 109, 116, 120).[2] Golinksi obliquely captures not only the barometer's peculiar power to gauge a mental climate, but the tension between ambivalence and movement that defines that climate.

Modern climate science identifies the Enlightenment with the end of the so-called Little Ice Age (ca. 1350–1850). Numbers say that consecutive summers in the eighteenth century could be the hottest and coldest on record; that springs cut themselves uncommonly short; that droughts alternated erratically with hurricanes. Contemporary interpretations of such changes, while oblivious of the larger change now believed to encompass them, hardly lacked the element of self-reflection that enlivens present-day representations of climate change. The journalist (and future novelist) Daniel Defoe's words in *The Storm*, his bestselling *Collection of …* *Disasters* published the year after the Great Storm of 1703, are apposite. 'Such a Tempest never happen'd before as that which is the Subject of these Sheets,' Defoe wrote ([1704] 2004, 25). As Robert Markley observes, in order to account for a radical change from precedent, Defoe's text mixes emergent protocols of knowledge based on measurement and objective comparison – the ascendant, seemingly value-neutral idiom of scientific empiricism – with residual explanatory systems such as divine retribution and demonic interference. Its suspense between different accounts of causation makes *The Storm* a literary example of what Markley calls a new 'eco-cultural materialism that saw everywhere reciprocal influences between English society and the natural world it was busy reshaping' (Markley, 2008, 117).

Defoe's absorption of the 'Tempest' into 'these Sheets' also betokens the conceptual reshaping that took place when new representational forms became the frames through which the environment itself was encountered as a knowable object. The transition is everywhere apparent in the eighteenth century. Piloted by Jonathan Bate's pithy observation that 'the weather is the primary sign of the inextricability of culture and nature', Golinski bases his definitive study of 'the climate of Enlightenment' on the coincidence in which 'the British first began to formulate ideas about their national climate based on accumulated records of the weather' at the same time that they started 'saying that the climate was changing' (Golinski, 2007, 3).

Cultural change, changing conceptions of the weather and conceptions of climate as itself changing support one another in enlightened talk about the weather.

Such talk was for the first time also *writing* circulated on an unprecedented scale, diffused through physical space to shape conceptions of that space from within it. Many historians imply that it was a specific medium, print, which privileged the centralized, metropolitan centres of knowledge that could distribute uniform, systematic pictures of the atmosphere at the same time across populations (Connor, 2010; Hamblyn, 2001; Johnson, 2008; Janković, 2000; Monmonier, 1999). Golinski notes that, as a specific and formalized writing practice, enlightened models of the climate displaced local, traditional, body-based ways of knowing the environment; these were at most personified in popular print icons like the celebrated Shepherd of Banbury, who never drew a breath yet starred in a dozen editions of 'his' collected weather maxims at mid-century. Also displaced were other graphic habitudes, such as personal weather journals, whose lyric idiosyncrasies once grafted the experience of linguistic and representational inadequacy onto that of climates, weathers, atmospheres (Golinski, 2007, 72–73, 17–18).

If changes in *writing* practice turned objective forms of expression into conditions of the lived experience of climates and their changes, those practices were also linked to new *reading* habits that were in turn bound up with new conceptions of 'fiction' in relation to 'fact'. Thanks in no small part to Defoe's own innovations in the form in the 1720s, the defining feature of eighteenth-century fiction is its vaunted rhetoric of matters of fact – a rhetoric that has been heavily scrutinized by (among numerous others) Ian Watt (1957), Lennard Davis (1983), John Bender (2009), and J. Paul Hunter (1990), the last of whom identifies it specifically with the style of Boyle's pneumatic chemistry. But the Enlightenment's factual fictions, as Davis evocatively calls them, were also theorized from within by writers who saw that such fiction's visual embodiment in 'different kind[s]' of books gave it a uniquely objective status, making immersion in the print medium as sensational as it was conceptual, as literal as it was metaphorical, even as static as it was dynamic. While such critics as Clara Reeve and Thomas Warton strove to institute anthropological distance from 'romance' (the title of Reeve's 1785 *The Progress of Romance* tells all), the early novel took a slightly different tack. Here a stock character type is the so-called Quixote, who experiences literary mediation as 'real' and suffers bodily harm because she inhabits a non-consensual reality derived from books. The official rebuke of such figures as Charlotte Lennox's eponymous Female Quixote (1752) is balanced by acknowledgment that the body is fully implicated in the forms of false belief generated by literary romance (Lupton, 2012). In contrast to the atmospheric states adduced in scientific writing, however, fictional forms and figures did not simply insulate readers and assist them in their flight from 'reality'. Correcting science's rhetoric of transparency, they made apparent the mediating forms through which reality is experienced. Its protocols forged in conversation with those of scientific knowledge of the atmosphere, modern popular fiction thus claimed legitimacy, indeed fitness, as a philosophical investigator of both atmospheric states and the reasons for their change.

Virginia Woolf's 1928 fiction *Orlando* registers such change in suitably atmospheric terms: 'a turbulent welter of cloud covered the city. [...] The Eighteenth century was over; the Nineteenth century had begun. [...] A change had come over the climate of England' (Woolf, [1928] 1998, 128–9). The nature of this 'change' does not appear to be linear:

> Rain fell frequently, but only in fitful gusts, which were no sooner over than they began again. The sun shone, of course, but it was so girt about with clouds and the air was so saturated with water, that its beams were discoloured and purples, oranges, and reds of a dull sort took the place of the more positive landscapes of the eighteenth century. [...] Thus, stealthily, and imperceptibly, none marking the exact day or hour of the change, the constitution of England was altered and nobody knew it. Everywhere the effects were felt. (129)

Just what has changed? The difference of the 'positive' eighteenth century would seem to be that in that clean, well-lighted space constitutional changes were knowable and 'effects' were 'felt' as such, their causes well within view. Formally, however, there appears to be little distinction between England's old 'constitution' and its new one: the same style – knowing, sensibly remote – conveys both. From this perspective, nothing has changed at all! No wonder there's no 'marking the exact day or hour of the change'. Woolf's style, as she of course wanted, can only be called modern. But Woolf herself identifies it with the eighteenth century. It is then, on a 'fine night early in April', that Woolf's time-traveling (yet circularly named) Orlando finds herself among 'buildings [that] had an airy yet formal symmetry' while 'the canopy of the sky seemed most dexterously washed in to fill up the outline of roof and chimney' (123). This 'sense' of environmental experience as aesthesis looks very much like a vital legacy of the Enlightenment; Woolf claims it so as to dispel the romantic 'climate' that *Orlando* places diegetically after that of the eighteenth century even while reconstituting it stylistically as its successor.

Ironically enough, Woolf's retro-progressive rendering of history as climate change revives that of a Victorian, the Irish moralist and intellectual historian W. E. H. Lecky, who applies the Victorian notion of the 'spirit of the age' to the Enlightenment, with interesting results. Anticipating Keith Thomas's still foundational *Religion and the Decline of Magic* (1971), Lecky interprets popular 'fluctuations of belief' (for example from belief in magic and miracles to disbelief in them) as changes in 'cast and tone of mind' which are themselves exhibitions and formal expressions that emanate from other formal expressions such as 'a sudden outburst of the most derisive incredulity', expressed variously as parody and ridicule (Lecky, [1865] 1955, ix, 127). In Lecky's book, such formal 'outburst[s]' give rise to climates of experientially realized belief, even as belief remains a form of expression – a manner or even simply a manner*ism*.

Lecky's picture of how beliefs aggregate and predispose, but seemingly change, persists subliminally in our own day. Consider Dror Wahrman's recent review of the Enlightenment's notorious 'belief' in climate as a cause of bodily difference, exemplified in Oliver Goldsmith's claim that 'variations in the human figure' arise from 'the rigour of the climate'. Wahrman, whose true interest lies in the politics of race, damningly ties this maxim to 'strongly held beliefs in the superiority of some groups of humans over others', then tempers his judgment on the grounds that Goldsmith wrote before the 'innate and stable ideas of race' that underpin what we call racism. This was, as Wahrman puts it, before 'the emergence of such ideas as widely resonant; a development that in the middle of the eighteenth century was as yet an insignificant blob on the horizon' (Wahrman, 2004, 91). This account of conceptual transformation hinges on a nonlinear figure of that transformation, albeit one that remains peripheral to what Wahrman states explicitly. Yet the resonant 'blob' on Wahrman's 'horizon' perpetuates one of the Enlightenment's subtler legacies: its capacity simultaneously to render and inform the extra-historical *experience* of belief while appearing only to specify belief's proper objects.

That experience is by definition every bit as formal as it is sensational. In the post-Lockean empiricist context, belief means little more than assent to a proposition – an apparent redefinition of the term that helps to explain how the intimate experience of enchantment could persist in the distanced form of 'entertainment' after science and history discredited its 'real' possibility (During, 2002, 45–51). For a glimpse of belief's reformulation in action, however, we could look to Locke's successor David Hume. Best known for its debunking of beliefs about causality that turn out to be nothing but misprisions of correlation, Hume's *Treatise of Human Nature* (1739) also takes up the thorny question of what belief might look like within the skeptical and empirical picture of reality that the book itself paints. Lamenting the inadequacy of philosophical language to say what belief is, Hume finds himself 'at a loss for terms to express my meaning' when he attempts to define what he, as a modern, must finally take to be an 'operation of the mind'. 'Belief' is 'one of the greatest mysteries of philosophy' less because its objects are not always empirically verifiable than because 'no one has so much as suspected, that there was any difficulty in explaining it' (Hume, [1739] 1978, 102).

Hume presents belief as 'a particular manner of forming an idea'. He specifies that it 'is a lively idea produc'd by a relation to a present impression' (97). 'An opinion, [...] or belief' he writes, making no distinction between them, 'does nothing but vary the manner, in which we conceive any object' (96). This 'manner' of conception is bound up with a protocol of sensation: 'An idea assented to feels different from a fictitious idea that the fancy alone presents to us.' How so? Well, it has a superior 'force and vivacity' (96). But if an idea assented to feels different from an idea not assented to, then it would seem that the performance of assent is what distinguishes feelings from one another. At least within the expository setting of Hume's *Treatise*, 'belief' no longer seems to arise from distinct feelings themselves; instead, it appears to press distinctions upon them. Conceived as manner, belief can now take shape outside the individual believer in custom and community, which is to say in the nebula of ever-altering human interaction rituals through which it is communicated. This context is recapitulated within individual experience insofar as a believed sensation itself is able to 'communicate [...] a share of its force and vivacity to related ideas'. In either instance, 'facility of transition' provides the inexplicit condition, if not the very horizon, of belief (99). Even the Humean philosopher must express himself under this condition, and thus he steps back from his own language, declaring it to be 'so unphilosophical' that he hesitates to avail himself of its resources. But if not philosophical, what is it?

If the answer might possibly be 'fictional', we can explain Hume's subsequent anxiety to distinguish between a 'fictitious idea, that the fancy alone presents to us' and 'an idea assented to'. The former simply 'feels different' from the latter, but feeling itself is bound up with a manner of conception. Left unaddressed is the question of how beliefs manage to change. But the answer to that also arises from Hume's enlightened formulation; they depend on a change of the very climate they create. Aptly, then, Hume illustrates the difference between a believable idea and a fictitious one through the literary example of two readers, one confronted with a romance, the other with a 'true history'. The second reader 'has a more lively conception of the incidents. He enters deeper into the concerns of the persons. [...] He even goes so far as to form a notion of their features, and air, and person. While the former, who gives no credit to the testimony of the author, has a more faint and languid conception of all these particulars; and except on account of the style and ingenuity of the composition, can receive little entertainment from it' (97–8).

Hume proceeds to disparage 'the loose reveries of the castle-builder' as he does not the seemingly grounded sensations of the historical reader, though both readers are obviously in it for 'entertainment'. His exemplum, strikingly, focuses so much on manners of thought as to leave room for both of these readers to be encountering the same book. The 'entertainment' that motivates each reader to open the book at hand devolves upon 'style' in the case of romance, and upon such 'particulars' as 'features', 'air' and 'person' in the case of true history. Yet these too are matters of style; 'air' alone introduces manners into believable history, just as the goal of 'entertainment' makes skeptical and empiricist belief a state of suspense – of remaining up in the air, literally entertained, in a condition hard to tell from the active flight presumably pursued by the 'castle-builder' (Kareem, 2012, 152–73).

Hume invokes literary belief states so as to make his reader feel, hence believe, how 'real' ones work. He thus participates in a literate culture primed to experience fiction and philosophy as reciprocal forms of entertainment. Samuel Johnson's philosophical 'tale' *Rasselas* (1759) famously fears self-insulating belief states, so dangerously fed by romance and indeed by fiction in virtually any form other than the didactic one that Johnson here practices. As described within *Rasselas* by the philosopher Imlac, a since-notorious astronomer unwittingly tests the Humean proposition that belief is nothing more than an 'operation of the mind'. To all appearances, the astronomer's mind works just fine: 'his comprehension is vast, his memory capacious and retentive, his discourse is methodical, and his expression clear' (Johnson, [1759] 1990, 142). He is, in fact, in possession of all the manners of knowledge (as opposed to mere belief), even its corrective sociability insofar as he has 'the air of a man who long[s] to speak' (144). Yet the astronomer is convinced that he possesses 'the regulation of the weather, and the distribution of the seasons', that 'the sun has listened to my dictates' and 'the clouds, at my call, have poured their waters' (144–5).

How has Johnson's astronomer arrived at the false belief that his very words have 'restrained the rage of the dog-star, and mitigated the fervours of the crab' (145)? The astronomer, to his credit, asks that question of himself. 'I reasoned long against my own conviction,' he declares, 'and laboured against truth with the utmost obstinacy.' Even now he will reveal his self-certainty only to a man 'capable of distinguishing the wonderful from the impossible, and the incredible from the false.' When Imlac points out that the astronomer 'call[s] that incredible, which you know, or think you know, to be true', the astronomer acknowledges that this is because 'I cannot prove it by any external evidence' (147). But the question is not what there is evidence for. Rather, what verbal conventions sanction the schools of internal evidence that we call beliefs? The astronomer does not expect to be believed. He knows 'too well the laws of demonstration to think that my conviction ought to influence another, who cannot, like me, be conscious of its force' (147). Aha! Consciousness of force is the basis of conviction. Indeed, in order to believe, 'it is sufficient that I feel this power'. The astronomer's belief that there is some 'concurrence' between a cloudburst and his command of falling rain is grounded in a notably ungrounded form of experience, one in which form itself can be experienced as sensation: 'One day as I was looking on the fields withering with heat, I felt in my mind a sudden wish that I could send rain on the southern mountains, and raise the Nile to an inundation' (146).

Imlac's (and probably Johnson's) didactic motive is to demonstrate the nature of misguided belief so as to guide his primary listener, the innocent Rasselas's proper 'choice of life'. In that context, our attention rests on the same mistake of contingency for causality that Hume found to be the foundation of false belief. But Johnson's astronomer, like Hume's frustrated philosopher, also registers an experience, a 'wish' that can be 'felt' as if it were physical. Conventions of expression render the wish notionally continuous with the sensation of withering heat. If such sensations were transferable, shareable, they would carry us beyond belief, where they would count as truth. Johnson's genre of moral fiction, where fantasy and sense experience are but mutually circumscribing spheres of belief linked to habits of sensation, thus opens an inquiry not just into the question of *why* individual beliefs change – *what* convinces a natural philosopher that he can alter entire climates? – but into that of *how* consensual ones do. Moralized as an exemplum of 'the dangerous prevalence of imagination', the astronomer's mistaken conviction is one to be felt by the enlightened reader even as it originates in fictional sensation: 'What must be the anxiety of him, on whom depend the action of the elements, and the great gifts of light and heat!' (148). While 'no man will be found in whose mind airy notions do not sometimes tyrannize', the astronomer's peculiar 'malad[y] of the mind' literalizes these airy 'notions'. Johnson's own interest as a moralist is served from within the confines of a sealed didactic fiction, one that only pretends to have nothing to do with the 'real' weather or his reader's experience of it.

Johnson's meteorology-mad astronomer does not elicit a uniform reaction from Rasselas, his sister and her female servant Pekuah. Rasselas is properly sobered by this spectacle of human insulation from reality and the 'anxiety' that arises from it. But 'the princess smiled, and Pekuah convulsed herself with laughter' (149). While they are reprimanded for it, and for the lack of empathy that it seems to imply, the reasons for their mirth are never actually explained. Johnson himself genders reactive levity female. And his protégées Charlotte Lennox and Frances Burney bore him out when they examined reciprocal fictions of mental and environmental change. Lennox's comic, if ambivalent, 1752 novel *The Female Quixote* encloses its protagonist in bubbles of idiosyncratic sense experience that arise from textually inculcated spheres of belief. Burney's first published fiction, *Evelina* (1778), references air a full 72 times as her 'goose' of a heroine, equipped only with laughter, experiments within the mixed social, physical and musical 'airs' of an eighteenth-century metropolitan 'world' to see just what she can and cannot believe to be true of it.

In-Flight Entertainment

Helen Simpson references Burney in *In-Flight Entertainment*, albeit not in any of the five stories scattered through the volume's fifteen to compose what Simpson has called 'my little climate-change suite' (Gharraie, 2012). In a *ceci-n'est-pas-un-pipe* flourish akin to the one executed by Warner and Siskin's *This Is Enlightenment*, the book's title declines to distinguish between generic marking and real-world application. The very short stories that that title encompasses facetiously cater to the cropped attention span that in-flight entertainment must also assume; at the same time, Simpson's title conjures the pressurized factitious climates in which her book expects to be read – a trick repeated structurally as the book's title ends up attached to a story inside it while still hovering over and around it. Although its paperback cover promotes *In-Flight Entertainment* 'as read on BBC 4' (on the air, as it were), Simpson's title also looks back to early popular print fiction and the complexities attendant upon fiction's once new cultural role as 'entertainment'. Fiction's prestige, Warner (1998) has shown, plummeted when 'during the decades following 1700, a quantum leap in the number, variety, and popularity of novels led many to see novels as a catastrophe to a book-based culture' (4). Part of the catastrophe accompanying this change, of course, had to do with fiction's perceived inculcation of solipsistic flights of fancy, its production of just the bubbles of self-convincing sensation in which Johnson captured his mad astronomer. Johnson's example, however, reminds us that Enlightenment writers fought fiction with fiction.

We no longer entertain quite their worries, except of course when we do. One time we do is in relation to the denial of environmental realities. This fiction presumably keeps us from confronting, not least by means of its seductive, alternative and hermetic sensualities, the 'feeling[s] on the brain' that it stimulates. Simpson foregrounds this problem while reversing its centripetal force. Her climate-change stories mingle with external 'reality'. The French medieval tapestries at the centre of

'Geography Boy' can be researched on Wikipedia (a cyber-trip well-worth taking). 'Ahead of the Pack' was commissioned for a December 2009 climate change conference in Copenhagen. From within its own premises, then, Simpson also examines reality's reciprocity with non-empirical constructions of it. Fictional form becomes experimental design, as it was in the Enlightenment's virtual literary worlds.

Simpson traces the modern shape of belief as she objectively displays, in rotation, multiple ancient and modern genres of persuasion. One story takes the shape of a sales pitch bedecked with Ciceronian tropes; in other stories, maxims and slogans commodify wisdom discourse. Characters less argue or opine about the environment's present or future than make sensible the self-contained verbal postures – pontification, opinion, aphorism, argument, consensus, creed – through which this is done. Consequently, all of those postures present as propositions of equal (and equally negligible) value. Assent to any one proposition would appear to be optional, though in Simpson's plots choice is typically driven by self-interest or consumer desire.

When Simpson suspends beliefs before a reader compelled to entertain all such 'operation[s] of the mind', she risks selling herself short: who, even for a time, is going to 'believe' the stories in her 'climate-change suite'? But Simpson wants to rethink what belief might be outside the realist contract. The setup of her title story has about it the air more of a joke than of reality: a climate-change skeptic and an atmospheric scientist walk onto an airplane. Simpson puts their 'stationary' (yet moving) bodies literally in midair so as to consider how sense experience might at once inform and be informed by fiction. At the same time, she considers the role that a free-floating linguistic medium might play in realizing a cycle of mutual (dis)information. 'Global warming,' she writes of Alan Barr. 'He was sick of the sound of it, he had only to see those words and a massive wave of boredom engulfed him.' Seen words are heard as sickening sounds, felt as massive waves, even as they are held at arm's length; synesthesia simultaneously distances Simpson's fictional world as a rhetorical conceit and turns its constitutive 'words' into elements of experience. In this manner, Simpson's fiction revives an enlightenment dialectic of atmosphere in which critical distance mutually informs sensed immediacy. The twenty-first-century symbolic 'climate' changes back to that of the eighteenth, reintegrating micro and macro levels of experience under the umbrella of sentiment.

Because modernity itself is entirely mediated – 'all you needed for the modern world was to know how to work a remote control' (Simpson, 2010, 7) – it is composed of mutually exclusive spheres of opinion. Jeremy's insistence that the experts have 'reached a consensus' is as full of hot air as Alan's creed that climate change is 'all a big con-trick' (9). How then to move beyond the unanswerable 'question of belief'? Because belief has been linked to choice – even to what Johnson's *Rasselas* presented as 'choice of life' – this is also a moral matter. Yet Simpson seems to offer no true moral compass, at least with respect to the question of what it is right to believe. Jeremy may be exactly what Alan finds him to be, 'a moralising old wise guy in the middle of nowhere' (16). But he is far from the ethical centre of the story; whatever he might believe about global warming, he is making sure it happens, 'flying', as he states, being 'far and away the fastest-growing source of man-made greenhouse gases' (17). So what difference is there between him and Alan Barr, so skeptical that he doesn't even 'believe' he is moving at 500 miles per hour? 'He accepted this on a superficial level, but deep down did not believe it' (20).

Perversely, Simpson supposes that the only way to take her reader 'deep down' is via the 'superficial level'. So in 'Geography Boy', two university students are 'cycling' through the Loire Valley in modern end-times. They stop to visit the medieval apocalypse tapestries at Angers. Apocalypse? *Plus ça change, plus c'est la même chose.* The tapestries integrate Simpson's fiction with the 'real' world without forcing her to sacrifice aesthetic distance. Simpson is certainly interested in what the tapestries depict, from wormwood's poisonous rain to the City of Jerusalem and assorted monsters. But she is also interested in what has happened to them as textile moving through history. Bits were 'chopped off' in the French Revolution (74), the remains rescued during the nineteenth-century's medieval craze only to have their grass turned blue by zealous, if well-intentioned, launderers. It has been for the twentieth century to 'house them' (74). In this history of depredations, the Enlightenment's murderous dissections, its instrumentalism, come off no better or worse than the nineteenth century's hygienic nostalgia or today's aggressive cura-tion, which carries its own environmental price tag. Neither natural nor manmade, the tapestries' fantastic sky-blue grass triples as evidence of history's progress, a sign of its regressive arc, and proof it never changes.

This triplet moves Simpson's reader to participate (ultimately self-) critically in the mutual constitution of reality's many spheres. Angers, the castle that 'really' houses the tapestries, seems to have been 'set in an illuminated meadow of grass and flowers with the shining river beyond [...] like the ones in fairy-tales' (70). But like a fairy tale, this world is held together by belief. It's also rent by it: Adele and Brendan share the conviction that 'it's no longer a case of crying wolf, [...] the end of the world really is nigh' (71). But while it is Adele's 'considered opinion as a historian' (71) that 'we're the last generation' (83), Brendan's 'one-track mind' makes him appear more optimistic. He 'had faith in the world's adaptive powers whereas Adele didn't, it seemed' (71). But Brendan's 'faith' is impelled primarily by the superstitious force of his desire for Adele, his magical thought that 'if you really want something to happen, to change, then that definitely improves the chances of it actually coming true' (84). Should we really entertain Adele's hard 'opinion' over his romantic 'faith'?

Who can say? Even as the lovers' opposing beliefs are aired, their tensions are potentially resolved in the 'microclimate' (84) produced by waking love. Brendan wants to tell Adele what he wants (her, presumably) and she implores him not to because 'it's too soon. [...] It might not be true' (84). But 'something had shifted in his voice, in the temperature of the microclimate that enveloped them, and it roused her to pull away and hold him at arm's length' (84). Words mix with the body world that has already mixed with the man-warmed climate. Yet it is by distancing themselves from the compromised 'microclimate' they create — by 'checking and clashing and counterbalancing' — that Brendan and Adele are able to 'lea[d] each other into unanticipated fields of fresh thought and feeling' (80). In the end, Brendan 'lift[s Adele] into the air', and so into a state of suspense that converges with the reader's own. Suspense is the sensory aspect of wonder, and wonder moves beyond isolation and denial into the entertainment of possibility. 'For then' – the word could mean earlier or next or both or neither – 'exhilarated, they leaned into a mutual embrace, this time for balance as much as anything. Then they stood in the fathoms less dark and stared saucer-eyed beyond the stratosphere into the night' (85).

In contrast to the hovering omniscient narration in 'Geography Boy', 'Ahead of the Pack' speaks in the first-person of a rapid fire, present-tense sales pitch. 'The next big thing' (31) is global warming, the speaker firmly believes, jauntily likening 'people who say it isn't really happening' to his weight-loss clients, who 'insist that "It's glandular" or "I've got big bones." What they're really saying is, they're not ready to change.' Simpson's motivational speaker is professionally invested – which is to say self-interested – in questions of cause. He weaves his empty weight-loss analogy out of the conventionally bodily nature of belief, proposing a purely metaphorical solution to the ('surely real') problem of global warming: a 'global swimming club' to reduce a 'huge communal spare tyre of greenhouse gasses' (32). The only real problem is what to call it. Why not 'Ahead of the Pack'? So is Simpson's reader implicated in the hyper-metaphorical 'motivational world' she believed herself to be observing from afar.

Simpson's speaker pretends to specialize in inconvenient truths but has only mastered the sleight of hand that we have agreed to call realism. When the speaker's patter is interrupted, we hear only the speaker's sycophantic response, which, appropriately, is 'Really? Oh. Oh.' The unheard question dents the speaker's speech bubble so as to reveal that the questioner has objected to the selling of any second homes, having invested in one near romantic Perpignan because 'you can get there for twenty-nine pounds' (34). But the speaker speedily assures him (or her) that there is 'no reason' to do that: 'No reason, no reason. O reason not the need, as Shakespeare says! As long as you know of course it means that, globally speaking, in terms of your planetary profile, you've got an absolutely vast arse' (34). The speaker's insult falls short of the pun it rises above. Too literal to be figurative and too figurative to be literal, it hangs between the speaker's irony and Simpson's own. This suspense, however, makes the story's true context, its living reader – you – visible, especially if you happen to be on a cheap flight yourself, as Simpson supposes you are.

What of Simpson's academic readers? We're an embarrassment. 'The Tipping Point' shifts stylistically to Woolfian stream-of-consciousness as a romanticist, one Dr Beauman, drives into the drenched Scottish Highlands for a conference (62). Insulated from the elements by a 'windscreen', Beauman broods over the pathetic fallacy ('the reading of one's own emotion into external nature, child' [62]). Smarting from a failed love affair, Beauman finds the nature of the text has changed, eliminating all 'residual belief that rain is in any way cleansing'. Oh, no: 'As you so painstakingly taught me, Angelika, our sins of pollution lock into the clouds and come down as acid rain' (65). Angelika, for her part, turns out to have been an environmental realist whose 'constant state of alarm' and didactic bent have broken romance's narcissistic contract: 'I wanted you to talk about me, about you and me, but the apocalyptic zeitgeist intruded' (65).

Beauman identifies environmental damage with this bad relationship, but as dead metaphor – incredibly pathetic fallacy – not living cause. 'The oceans have warmed up and turned acidic. [...] Sweetheart, what can I do to melt your heart?' (66). Angelika, by contrast, seems to be awake to causal links between human desire and environmental catastrophe, having ended her long-distance relationship with Beauman because of the planetary harm his frequent flying has inflicted. Yet it is clear too that she has done so only rhetorically, that this is only what the repellent Beauman chooses to believe. Beauman also 'believes' Angelika's opinion about the environment but has nonetheless scheduled four international flights in the near future: 'You used to have to join the Foreign Office if you wanted to travel on anything like this scale. Now everybody's at it. The budget airlines arrived and life changed overnight. Sorry, but it's true. The world's our sweet shop. We've got used to it, we want it; there's no going back' (68).

A finger points at the Enlightenment's vaunted 'rise' and widening of the middle class, citing it as a cause both of change and of resistance to it. Beauman identifies himself with that class, and shares its desires, even while, as an academic, he professes to stand outside it. For instance, at the end of 'The Tipping Point' the sky clears into a 'truly theatrical spectacle' (67). 'Look at those schmaltzy sunbeams backlighting the big grey clouds,' Beauman enjoins himself, backing away from them. But the kind of enlightenment that the clouds afford is real too – not in the 'sorry, but it's true' sense but in its power to register the mind's implication in its own environment. Simpson's irony checks any easy worship of that power. Beauman sees the 'perfect scenery for the arrival of a *deus ex machina*' – 'a far-fetched plot device to make everything all right again. [...] An unlikely happy ending in other words' (68). Simpson's reader is deprived of such an ending precisely because he *is* the ending.

Simpson's climate-change suite ends with 'Diary of an Interesting Year'. The story revives the form of the early eighteenth-century weather journal, one kept in a dysphoric future that literally expresses itself through the female body. Entries scribbled by Simpson's nameless narrator in the days after the 'Big Melt' of 2040 return writing to its most material form; the story ends with the diarist burying her notebook with the fetus she has aborted. The diary's 'last lines' ('Good luck, good luck, good luck, good luck') are absorbed into a drowned, maimed earth that we understand to be of a piece with the narrator's own body. Unlike the self-shielding, Schiller-spouting Beauman, Simpson's diarist directly transcribes the 'very humid' atmosphere around her: 'Air like filthy soup, plus we're supposed to wear our facemasks in bed too but I was running with sweat so I ripped mine off just now' (117). She also records the words of a husband, G, given to 'wall-to-wall pontificating'. 'I saw it coming,' he claims. 'Thresholds crossed, cascade effect, hopelessly optimistic to assumer we had till 2060, blahdy blahdy blah' (117). G is a living anthology of Enlightenment truth genres, from maxims ('"The Earth has enough for everyone's need, but not for everyone's greed" was his favourite') to formulas ('Every one of us takes about 25,000 breaths a day… Each breath removes oxygen from the atmosphere and replaces it with carbon dioxide'). Purely formal, his verbal gestures are equally divorced from bodily experience and the mythic contours that shape it. Simpson's narrator at once reunifies and critiques these: 'Well, pardon me for breathing! What was I supposed to do – turn into a tree?' (119).

This is no Daphne. Simpson's narrator is a selfish modern woman and, no, she cannot 'turn into a tree'. Her spiral-bound pages once were one; the problem is that the natural world which gave rise to them no longer seems to exist in its generative and protective – its maternal – form. It has changed into a barter economy in which men have gone Neanderthal, women mutely drudge, and the class system mimics atmosphere, with 'the top layer on inside their plastic bubbles of filtered air while the rest of us shuffle about with goitres and tumours and bits of old sheet tied over our mouths. Plus, we're soaking wet the whole time. We've given up on umbrellas, we just go round permanently drenched' (117). Given her refusal to provide any umbrella against these sensations, Simpson's title, 'An Interesting Year', would seem to distance the 'real' story from the diary it only pretends to be. As Sianne Ngai (2011) explains, 'interesting' always bespeaks the disengagement born of contradictory responses to objects in a consumer economy. The end of consumption – which Simpson's narrator guiltily misses in the form of one-click Internet ordering – is also the end of fictional entertainment. The half-imagined elements absorb the narrator's written artefact back into themselves.

Simpson's self-consuming method of 'doing fiction' defies both realist and romantic protocol. This may explain the hostility of many of the reviews that *In-Flight Entertainment* has received. Michiko Kakutani's in *The New York Times* is representative, pronouncing Simpson's climate-change stories 'stilted and contrived, and in some cases tendentious' as they take on a 'subject matter that seems almost wilfully heavy and self-important' (Kakutani, 2012). But Kakutani is dead wrong. Simpson offers modern 'entertainment' if not in its purest form, then at least in the one it assumed in conjunction with modern conceptions of the environment. Desire for what (let's say) she believes fiction to be has caused Simpson's reader to pick up *In-Flight Entertainment* in the first place. This desire's frustration is why that reader might hold the book at arm's length. But all Simpson wants is for her to notice what she's doing – to entertain herself. Unable, however, to assume the entertaining kind of reader that they could in the Enlightenment, Simpson has had to make one up. If her success has been limited, it is really not her fault.

Notes

1 Fleming and Janković extend Peter Sloterdijk's formulation of the air itself as 'a medium that allowed humans to realize the fact that they are always already immersed in something almost imperceptible and yet very real' (p. 11). Emerging from its lexical affinity with 'atmosphere', 'noosphere' is a neologism coined in 1922 by the Jesuit philosopher Pierre Teilhard de Chardin following the Ukrainian geochemist Vladimir Vernadsky.
2 See also Castle, 1995.

References

Adorno, T. W. & Horkheimer, M., 1997. *Dialectic of Enlightenment*. London: Verso.

Bender, J., 2009. The Novel as Modern Myth. *The Eighteenth-Century Novel*, Volume 6–7, 67–78.

Castle, T., 1995. *The Female Thermometer: Eighteenth-Century Culture and the Invention of the Uncanny*. Oxford: Oxford University Press.

Connor, S., 2010. *The Matter of Air: Science and Art of the Ethereal*. London: Reaktion.

Davis, L. J., 1983. *Factual Fictions: The Origins of the English Novel*. New York: Columbia University Press.

Defoe, D., 2004. *The Storm; or, A Collection of the most Remarkable Casualties and Disasters Which happen'd in the Late Dreadful Tempest*. London: Penguin.

During, S., 2002. *Modern Enchantments; The Cultural Power of Secular Magic*. Cambridge(MA): Harvard University Press.

Fleming, J. R. & Janković, V., 2011. Revisiting Klima. *Osiris*, Volume 26.

Fleming, J. R., Janković, V. & Coen, D. R., 2006. Introduction. In: J. R. Fleming, V. Janković & D. R. Coen, eds. *Intimate Universality: Local and Global Themes in the History of Weather and Climate*. Sagamore Beach(MA): Science History Publications.

Gharraie, J., 2012. Helen Simpson on 'In-Flight Entertainment'. [Online] Available at: www .theparisreview.org/blog/2012/02/28/helen-simpson-on-%E2%80%98in-flight-entertainment%E2%80%99/ [Accessed 30 June 2015].

Golinski, J., 2007. *British Weather and the Climate of Enlightenment*. Chicago: University of Chicago Press.

Hamblyn, R., 2001. *The Invention of Clouds: How an Amateur Meteorologist Forged the Language of the Skies*. London: Picador.

Hume, D., 1978. *A Treatise of Human Nature*. Oxford: Clarendon.

Hunter, J. P., 1990. Robert Boyle and the Epistemology of the novel. *Eighteenth-Century Fiction*, Volume 2, 275–91.

Janković, V., 2000. *Reading the Skies: A Cultural History of English Weather, 1650–1820*. Chicago: University of Chicago Press.

Janković, V., 2010. *Confronting the Climate: British Airs and the Making of Environmental Medicine*. London: Palgrave.

Johnson, S., 1990. *The History of Rasselas, Prince of Abyssinia (The Yale Edition of the Works of Samuel Johnson)*. New Haven(CT): Yale University Press.

Johnson, S., 2008. *The Invention of Air: A Story of Science, Faith, Revolution, and the Birth of America*. New York: Riverhead.

Kakutani, M., 2012. Fretting over Carbon Footprints: Helen Simpson's 'In-Flight Entertainment'. *New York Times*, 22 March.

Kareem, S. T., 2012. Lost in the Castle of Skepticism: Sceptical Philosophy as Gothic Romance. In: Y. Baksaki, S. Mukherji & J. Schramm, eds. *Fictions of Knowledge: Fact, Evidence, Doubt*. New York: Palgrave.

Latour, B., 1993. *We Have Never Been Modern*. Cambridge(MA): Harvard University Press.

Lecky, W., 1955. *The Rise and Influence of Rationalism in Europe*. New York: George Braziller.

Lupton, C., 2012. *Knowing Books: The Consciousness of Mediation in Eighteenth-Century Britain*. Philadelphia: University of Pennsylvania Press.

Markley, R., 2008. 'Casualties and Disasters': Defoe and the Interpretation of Climate Instability. *Journal for Early Modern Cultural Studies*, Volume 8.

Monmonier, M., 1999. *Air Apparent: How Meteorologists Learned to Map, Predict, and Dramatize Weather*. Chicago: University of Chicago Press.

Ngai, S., 2011. *Our Aesthetic Categories: Zany, Cute, Interesting*. Cambridge(MA): Harvard University Press.

Simpson, H., 2010. In-Flight Entertainment. In: *In-Flight Entertainment*. London: Random House.

Siskin, C. & Warner, W., 2010. This is Enlightenment: An Invitation in the Form of an Argument. In: C. Siskin & W. Warner, eds. *This is Enlightenment*. Chicago: University of Chicago Press.

Spitzer, L., 1948. Milieu and Ambiance. In: *Essays in Historical Semantics*. New York: Russell and Russell.

Wahrman, D., 2004. *The Making of the Modern Self: Identity and Culture in Eighteenth-Century England*. New Haven (CT): Yale University Press.

Warner, W. B., 1998. *Licensing Entertainment: The Elevation of Novel Reading in Britain, 1684–1750*. Berkeley and Los Angeles: University of California Press.

Watt, I., 1957. *The Rise of the Novel*. London: Chatto & Windus.

Woolf, V., 1998. *Orlando, A Biography*. Oxford: Blackwell.

7 Fuels and humans, *bíos* and *zōē*

Karen Pinkus

Kathyrn Yusoff (2013) writes of fossil fuels as 'dead matter' that 'animates life in the engines of the Anthropocene' (784). This 'fossilized materiality', she argues, is active within the 'reproductive, creative, and technological possibilities' of late capitalist subjectivity; active, too, in their expiration, and as such can be understood as a form of 'geologic immanence'. But as Yusoff also notes, 'Fossil fuels are life that comes back to us, as it were, to take up new life forms and make new geopolitical subjectivities' (790). These different ways of qualifying fossils – as geological immanence, as the reanimating return of the dead, as the nonvitalist materiality of contemporary life – point to the complexity of the sense in which, in the Anthropocene, carbon *is* life. What kind of life might carbon be equated to? How might fossil life line up with the terms *bíos* and *zōē*, introduced most notably by Giorgio Agamben into the discussion of biopolitics? And then, how should fossil life be qualified in relation to the extinction and death brought about through climate change? As it turns out – perhaps counter to intuition – narrative literature (dead letters?) provides a significant way of beginning to respond to such questions.

Certainly, 'before literature', before language comes onto the scene to mark some forms of life as 'good', 'worthy' or enjoying rights as distinct from others that exist as 'bare', fossil fuels – fossilized sunshine – are 'natural', that is, they come from plant and animal life compressed underground in deep time. Such fuels have been on the planet much longer than humans, but there is no necessarily essential material difference between them, since humans too, given enough time and under the proper conditions, could turn into fuels. Given that in the broadest terms animals, plants and humans are all forms of life (leaving aside the ethical and philosophical issues associated with pinpointing the precise beginning or end of a *particular* life), fuels converge with the category of 'life' itself – and not just fossil fuels, but even some non-fossil fuels too, by proxy or by metaphor or metonymy. True, fossil fuels take millions of years to gestate, to change form. Yet isn't change a key ingredient if not a definition of life itself?

Found on every continent, coal is 'used up' in being used. Yet it does not completely dematerialize. There is a by-product, a part of it that remains: carbon dioxide. This remainder is also 'natural', not something manufactured by man. Given enough time, deposits of carbon buried in earth would weather away, releasing carbon dioxide – invisible to the human eye – into the atmosphere. But this process is so slow it exceeds human perception. Perhaps even our (literary) languages, evolving relatively slowly, are not up to the task of authentically engaging with the time of carbon. That such a lack might trigger mechanisms of compensation is a fascinating question potentially reaching far beyond discussions of the relative distance of reader from text or of the 'death of the novel' or the status of genres.

The project of the investigation of human life that is the (realist) novel comes to flourish in a period of industrialisation, during the early years of the acceleration of greenhouse gas emissions through the burning of coal (and then, of course, oil). The most instrumental sort of literary criticism, taking the novel to be an attempt of control or mastery, might recognize in language and/or form an awareness of coal's dirtiness, its destructive and life-giving powers. Or the novel might be troubled by coal's limited quantities and the aftereffects of shortages. But the history of science does not precisely run parallel to literary genres, and until very recently the novel is also precisely *not* aware of the cumulative and temporal effects of anthropogenic climate change. Given this, what does it mean to read a nineteenth-century novel (to read the end of Zola's *Germinal*, say) in the time of climate change – and so to entertain the idea of coal not simply as a dirty and abject mass distinct from the human user, but rather in a more complex frame: coal as life, as an informing vital force, as substance brought up from the earth and consumed by humans, with an invisible by-product that causes massive alterations to the earth's biogeochemistry?

Many important works have emerged in recent years on questions of life, the Anthropocene, geohumanity, transcorporeality and so on. The aim of the present chapter is to help think about some of these issues through literature. Why literature? Perhaps because literary narrative of the most rigorous sort offers an irreducible way to think about life and life forms. Literary language places the reader in a peculiar position with regard to the human subject and the surrounding/interpenetrating geological matter that cannot achieved through other forms of representation, and especially not through normative descriptive prose or what we might call 'science communication'.

To be sure, Emile Zola was interested in geology and he wrote during a crucial, even a revolutionary period for reevaluating the age of the earth. His 1885 novel *Germinal* does much more than describe the process of mining. It is profoundly engaged with the earth and with carbon. The author visited the Anzin mines in Northern France during a strike in 1884 and immersed himself in the culture of coal.[1] His phenomenology of the mine is precise. It should be noted that this novel is not entirely autonomous – it was part of the planned twenty-volume 'Rougon-Macquart series' focused on questions of illness and heredity.[2] Zola believed firmly in the idea of milieu or ambiance (environment) as inextricable from the human.[3] 'One no longer studies man as simple curiosity…detached from ambient nature (*nature ambiante*),' he wrote (Spitzer, 1968, 216). Thus, while in the novel those who dwell above ground and tend gardens, for instance, may enjoy relative health and economic independence, Zola also makes clear that the collier adapts to life below and makes of it his proper home. While Zola's contemporary Jules Verne imagines the subsurface as a place of magical vitality (in *Les indes noires* of 1877 most notably) the author does not go there and engage with it. The subsurface is simply another one of Verne's realms to be colonized by adventurous men of science – along with the deep sea, deserted islands or the skies, among others.[4] Earlier, in the fantastical tale of the 'mines of Falun' (E.T.A. Hoffman's version was published in 1819), the subsurface sustains (maleficent) life as it also preserves the human cadaver from aging at the rate of his betrothed on the surface.

Zola is a literary author, of course. Modelled in part on the epic voyages below the surface of the earth (Dante in particular), *Germinal* ([1885] 2004) enjoyed an afterlife beyond its material borders. It is, above all, a novel about the struggle between labour and capital – embodied in the absentee directors, the petty bourgeois managers, and small business owners around the fictional town of Montsou (money mountain).[5] Zola describes mining in free indirect discourse, through the eyes of the protagonist, Etienne. In this way, Etienne is the focus of the reader's attention, but not fully identified as the empathetic hero, and this has significant implications for the way language, the human and coal are made inextricable. It is imperative that we arrive on the scene with Etienne. The reader enters the world of the novel from outside, as a newcomer who has everything to learn. But even as we become acclimated with him to the world of the mine over the course of the novel, or as we learn about socialism, communism and anarchy with him, we are prevented by this flexible syntax from ever fully losing ourselves in his particular struggle to survive.

Soon after Etienne arrives he understands (so we understand) how the mines enter the bodies of the miners, who are also consumed by it. The mine entrance is a mouth; tunnels lead to its insatiable belly: 'The pit gulped down men in mouthfuls of twenty or thirty and so easily that it did not seem to notice them going down' (37). Underground the colliers tap on the rock face, loosening coal into tubs. After a seam is opened, they fill in the voids with timber, moving *another* natural substance – another fuel – from the surface down into the caverns.

Etienne meets Bonnemort, an old-timer who is now assigned to surface duty. Over the course of his years in the mine, Bonnemort has become a geological being. As he speaks flaming coals 'cast a gleam of blood-red light across across his pallid face' (11). He is prone to coughing fits. 'Is it Blood?' asks Etienne. Bonnemort replies 'It's coal...I've got enough coal inside this carcass of mine to keep me warm for the rest of my days. And it's five whole years since I was last down the mine. Seems I was storing it up without knowing. Ah well, it's a good preservative' (12).

Through the labour process – and let us recall that one of the central grievances in the novel is that the miners are paid only for coal taken from underground, not for the ancillary but necessary activities such as timbering – bodies are intertwined with the coal to a degree that they cannot be said to exist as separate entities. For instance:

> Each man hacked into the shale bedrock, digging it out with his pick. Then he would make two vertical cuts in the coal, insert an iron wedge into the space above, and prise out a lump. The coal was soft, and the lump would break into pieces which then rolled down over his stomach and legs. Once these pieces had piled up against the boards put there to retain them, the hewers disappeared from view, immured in their narrow cleft (39).

The miners merge here with the mine itself. Their bodies are transforming into its body, and vice versa; the sense of any separate representational of ontological difference between the two disappears as they burrow into the soft carbon past. Labour for Marx involved the manipulation of inorganic nature: through labour, the appropriation of nature confirmed 'man as a conscious species-being, i.e. a being who treats the species as his own being or himself as a species-being' (1964, p. 127). But in the material labours described in Zola's syntax, this distinction between species-being and inorganic nature becomes more difficult to sustain. 'Ghostly shapes' move in the coal, 'and chance gleams of light picked out the curve of a hip, or a sinewy arm, or a wild-looking face blackened as though in readiness for a crime' (40). Fossilized materiality seems spectral here; its edges are soft, illuminated only intermittently and by chance. The miners become coal – affectively, perceptually, representationally – as the mine itself takes on the properties of a living organism, a mortal body vulnerable to attack.

Toward the end of the novel, when the revolutionary, Souveraine, goes underground to undermine quite literally the past work done, the existing works, the enduring structures of past labour, he is possessed:

> He attacked the tubbing at random, striking where he could, with the brace, with his saw, suddenly determined to rip it open and bring everything crashing down on his head. And he did so with the ferocity of a man plunging a knife into the living flesh of a person he loathed. He would kill it in the end, this foul beast that was Le Voreux, with its ever-gaping maw that had devoured so much human fodder (463).

The mine, this vast man-made machinic apparatus of fuel and subjective life, of geological time and labour time, finally collapses in what we might call a geo-anthropogenic catastrophic event:

> Le Voreux shook slightly, but it was stoutly built and held firm. But a second shock followed at once and a long shout came from the astonished crowd... From then on the earth never ceased to shake, and there was tremor after tremor each time the ground shifted beneath the surface, like the rumblings of an erupting volcano...In less than ten minutes the slate roof of the headgear fell in, the pit-head and the engine-house were split asunder, and a huge gap appeared in the wall. Then the noises stopped, the collapse halted, and once again there was a long silence...It was all over: the vile beast squatting in its hollow in the ground, gorged on human flesh, had drawn the last of its long, slow, gasping breaths. Le Voreux had now vanished in its entirety down into the abyss (480–2).

We do not witness the collapse of the mine through Etienne, who is buried below. Rather, this is an occasion for Zola, author, with a genuine interest in geology and a fascination with new ideas of geological time, to express a more globalizing vision of his Neptunist, catastrophist theory. Le Voreux's end, he explains, is 'a reminder of the ancient battles between earth and water when great floods turned the land inside out and buried mountains beneath the plains' (504).

Philip Walker argues convincingly that *Germinal* reflects a 'new faith' vision of a catastrophic geology described by a young Zola in an article of 1865: 'He wanted to believe that more nearly perfect lands and beings were already taking shape in the deep recesses of the earth and in mankind's dreams' (1982, p. 2). The catastrophes of the mine were linked to both great natural upheavals and class struggles. The shift in narrative perspective out to geology serves to counterpoint and distance our reading from our immersion in the immediate struggles of the miners, our too empathetic engagement in the melodrama of Etienne, Souvarine, Catherine and Chaval.

Throughout *Germinal*, the distinction between human and animal is also constantly blurred. In part this is due to the particular conditions of labour in the mine, but it is also a broader condition of labour and life itself. A group of men going down to the pit is called a 'meat load' (28). The miners storm past the Hennebeaus (family of the salaried manager of the mine), who fail to pick out any individual faces: 'It was indeed true that anger and starvation had combined, after the past two months of suffering, and this wild stampede from pit to pit, to turn the placid features of the Montsou miners into the ravenous jaws of wild beasts' (352). Etienne fears violence (in part because of his inherited disease), but Souvarine remarks, 'Oh, blood. What does that matter? It's good for the soil' (244). We could mention numerous other moments in the novel when Zola undoes any easy distinction between human, animal and land itself: blood, semen, tears and bodies sink into the ground, immediately fusing with and melting into the earth as carbonised vital fluids, fuel for the life-world of Montsou. Zola achieves this fluidity not through metaphors or other figures of assimilation, but in a prose that is itself fully suffused with the geo-biomorphic, in its syntactic ambiances and mobile transformations of narrative perspective.

In Zola's language, coal and human/animal flesh meld to create a cyborg hybrid, a figure that is at once *zōē* (the simple fact of living common to all living beings – in Agamben's influential definition) and also *bíos* (a form of way of life proper to an individual or group). One cannot live without the other – they are literally geo-biodependent. Coal cannot be used without using it up (it is not a renewable source of energy); the miners cannot live without work, without using up their lives.

The miners are not only producers of coal. They also consume it directly, albeit in controlled circumstances. 'Every month the Company gave each family eight hectolitres of *escaillage*, a type of hard coal collected off the roadway floors. It was difficult to light but, having damped down the fire the night before, the girl had only to rake it in the morning and add a few carefully chosen pieces of softer coal. Then she placed a kettle on the grate and crouched in front of the kitchen dresser' (22). The miners' homes are filled with the smell and dirt of coal. They are immersed in it at all times, whereas the bourgeois enjoy a central heating system, and when they do have coal burning, it is contained 'cheerfully' (76) behind a grate in a kitchen that smells of freshly baking brioches.

Like his model Zola, Upton Sinclair spent time in the mines: in the case of Sinclair, in the Rocky Mountains where he witnessed labour disputes before composing his 1917 *King Coal*. Like Etienne, Sinclair's protagonist Hal is an outside observer, an intellectual who comes to immerse himself in the mine. And like Etienne, Hal surveys the surface of the landscape and contemplates geological time before his journey down:

> As one walked through this village, the first impression was of desolation. The mountains towered, barren and lonely, scarred with the wounds of geologic ages. In these canyons the sun set early in the afternoon, the snow came early in the fall; everywhere Nature's hand seemed against man, and man had succumbed to her power. Inside the camps one felt a still more cruel desolation – that of sordidness and animalism. There were a few pitiful attempts at vegetable-gardens, but the cinders and smoke killed everything, and the prevailing colour was of grime' ([1917] 1921, p. 21).

The miners here are living in the past, in a dehumanised condition of fossilized materiality.

Sinclair, in the third person – focused on, but not entirely fused with Hal – reports of miners as 'a separate race of creatures, subterranean, gnomes…stunted creatures of the dark' (22). The figure of the dwarf has a long and complex history in relation to mining. In some mythologies, the dwarf was assumed to have his home underground where he guarded treasures.[6] Sinclair references this tradition in a modern context. Life in the mines appears chthonic, diminished, and less-than-human: 'After Hal had squatted for a while and watched them at their tasks, he understood why they walked with head and shoulders bent over and arms hanging down, so that, seeing them coming out of the shaft in the gloaming, one thought of a file of baboons' (22). And here too, coal fuses with the human. As in *Germinal* the mine disaster is 'a thing of human flesh and blood' and miners lay on their backs, trying to catch drops of water from the ceiling to keep alive. Sinclair seems less interested than Zola in imagining subterranean life as Bergsonian or Deleuzian. In a book aptly titled *Germinal Life*, Keith Ansell-Pearson writes that Deleuze was interested in the complex relation of organismic and inorganic life, and in the indeterminacy of 'life' itself that is suggested by these complexities: for Deleuze, 'life is informed by the ability of its forms and expressions to hold chemical energy in a potential state and which serve as little explosives that need only a spark to set free the energy stored within them' (1999, p. 34). In comparison with the metaphysical and phenomenological horizons of this fossilised vitalism, *King Coal* is instead focused much more directly on manifest issues around actual politics. And yet in both novels, the biopolitical life form that develops is presented as a collective being, just as mining is a collective form of labour. No individual body can exist as such in the mine.

These narratives of the fusing of coal and human anticipate in powerful ways recent fables of bioengineering. Liao, Sandberg and Roache (2012) suggest that in confronting climate change, biomedical alterations to humans might be less risky than geo-engineering schemes and would work in tandem with behaviour modification and marketing strategies. They mention, among others, pharmacologically induced meat intolerance (to reduce the carbon hoofprint); height reduction (using growth hormones), cognitive enhancements (leading to lower birth rates), and pharmacological stimulation of altruism (leading, perhaps to sharing, sacrifice and practices of conservation). To be clear, the authors explain that they are not actually advocating such practices, only attempting to put into perspective the ethical questions that have arisen (or not) around proposed geo-engineering as a solution to climate change. Their proposal raises significant questions about 'creative evolution' and interventions on the genetic structure of individuals; they put to the question the nature of the human species – of 'conscious species-being' – linking subjectivity back to the slow geological processes of the fossil record.

Some carbon dioxide removal (CDR) schemes are already underway, but without carbon pricing they are likely to remain limited. That other broad category of geoengineering – solar radiation management – remains very controversial. Resistance to human engineering seems likely to be more powerful, offering a higher threshold to techno-utopian projects. One need only think of the writings of Habermas and Dworkin against biotechnology and genetic programming to get a sense of the profound embeddedness of a notion of the human as stable and autonomous. 'For Habermas,' Timothy Campbell writes in his exemplary introduction to Roberto Esposito's *Bíos*, 'symmetrical relations among the members of a group are homologous to the foundation of a moral and ethical community' (2008, p. xxxviii). In this sense, genetic manipulation is not only one among other problems of technoscience. For the modified humans it also 'jeopardizes how others will see them (as privileged, as escaping somehow from the natural development of characteristics that occur in interactions with others). These social foundations of society will be irreparably damaged when some members are allowed to intervene genetically in the development of others' (xxiv). Moreover, Campbell argues that, in his critique of biotechnology, Dworkin tends to conflate *bíos* and *zōē* as he calls for the ethics of the individual and personal values. Esposito (whom Campbell is introducing), converging with Jane Bennett's vitalism, deconstructs any notion of an absolutely normative system or baseline and argues instead for a difference among life forms: 'norm of life that doesn't subject life to the transcendence of a norm, but makes the norm the immanent impulse of life' (xxxix). For all that a critique of any sort of external intervention on the genes of a living subject may be warranted, what we learn from reading Zola and Sinclair is that coal miners, those who fuse with fossils fuels in producing them, are *already* altered. Mining literature presents different life forms, describing vital circuits of degeologisation and regeologisation. It presents a sense of life as already becoming fossilised, amidst geological irruptions of the past into the present.

Writing on the temporalities of the Anthropocene, Srinivas Aravamudan suggests that:

> the human is by no means the only subject or object. Endings are also mutations. The end of a singular species would still not be the end of all genres. There will be a post-ontological future of unnameable others, still new swarms that, once conceived, could fill many Chinese encyclopaedias. The Anthropocene sublime will yield its place both to the terrible and the beautiful. What began

as catachronism, the burdensome experience of 'living in the end times,' could morph into the birth of many brave new worlds populated by those that come after the subject. Those who come after will treat us as their version of Nature from which they will spell out their difference and articulate their critique (2013, p. 25).

Ian Baucom has similarly noted that, in the age of climate change we must begin to 'expand our sense of the ontological plurality of the human...we must now also recognize the post-natural actors, agents and actants of cyclones, heatwaves, and melting ice' (2014, p. 139). What if we were to agree that climate change has or will have so radically altered conditions, so sped up geological time, that we can no longer speak of a stable and unchanging human form? What if we already think of ourselves as becoming these others, those who will have come after? And how might that task be anticipated in the carbon narratives of writers like Zola and Sinclair?

Could Zola have imagined an *other*, like us, but not us, changed not precisely by revolution or reform but by geology itself? A great deal depends on how we read the end of the novel. To be sure, as Etienne moves on, on the surface of the earth revolution is still to come:

> Over to the right he could see Montsou in the distance disappearing down into the valley. Opposite him were the ruins of Le Voreux, the cursed chasm where three drainage-pumps were now working nonstop...while to the north, from the tall blast-furnaces and the batteries of coke-ovens, smoke was rising into the pure morning air ([1885] 2004, p. 531).

As he walks on, miners continue to work in the subsurface, which is not a place of death, but a womb generating life in all of its diverse forms:

> And far beneath his feet the stubborn tap-tap of the picks continued...The risen April sun now shone from the sky in all its glory, warming the parturient earth. Life was springing from her fertile bosom, with buds bursting into verdant leaf and the fields a-quiver with the thurst of new grass. Seeds were swelling and stretching, cracking the plain open in their quest for warmth and light...New men were starting into life, a black army of vengeance slowly germinating in the furrows, growing for the harvests of the century to come; and soon this germination would tear the earth apart (532).

Most critics, starting in Zola's time, believed he was expressing hope in this passage for the coming of a new Messianic time. Coal is dirty, black, difficult to extract. But someday, *Germinal* seems to suggest, the men who do the labour will be fairly compensated, perhaps even on a par with the capitalists who claim exemption from physical danger because of the financial risk they have made with their investments. Perhaps coal would be exhausted – this view was starting to be widely diffused in the period. Perhaps it would be replaced with another (clean) fuel available in the commons, outside of the structure of capitalism, outside of labour.

For Zola, coal is a form of life. For us, it is also one that we have displaced, from the subsurface to the atmosphere, through using and using it up, in a relatively brief period of human history, with consequences that are catastrophic for many life forms, including, potentially, our own. Zola's syntax tracks fossilized strata of carbon life that take on a transformed meaning in the Anthropocene present. While Sinclair's protagonist also leaves the mine with aspirations to fight capitalism, *King Coal* is a novel in which language remains on the surface, as political speech, rather than germinal life. Zola indicates other, more urgent, links, his language offering a more capacious political ecology for imagining climate change. As Etienne departs and the struggle continues – on the surface, for Zola, where plants face upwards toward the sun while also rooted in the soil, where coal also gestates – there, on the surface of language, life is ever evolving.

These plants could, some time long in the future, become coal. But Zola did not know this, or rather, not as we do now. That is a crucial difference: reading coal's life-cycle in our time – when geological time has been made human – the linguistic springing of life from the bosom of the Earth is also the dead hand of the past and present on the future.

Notes

1 Zola also drew on other strikes from the region. He set the novel earlier, in the 1860s. In part this allows him to point to some positive changes that did in fact take place in the intervening period, including the 1871 Paris Commune. By 1874 a law had been passed that made it illegal to employ women or children under twelve in the mining pit. Trade unions were made legal in 1884. Still, the technologies of coal mining that he described did not change materially in the period between his visit and the novel's publication and indeed they are much older.
2 The bibliography on Zola's 'Rougon-Macquart series' is vast. Etienne is the son of a laundry woman from *L'assomoir* (1877), and the brother of the title character of *Nana* (1880) and of Jacques Lantier in the 1890 novel *La Bête humaine*.
3 For a longer discussion of these terms, see Pinkus (2012).
4 Zola disdained what he perceived as the rather unliterary (commercial) qualities of Verne's prose.
5 This rendering perhaps underplays the smallness of the sou. One might think of 'penny-pinching mountain' [ed.].
6 See Pinkus (2008) for a more detailed discussion and bibliography on this topic.

References

Ansell-Pearson, K., 1999. *Germinal Life. The Difference and Repetition of Deleuze.* London: Routledge.

Aravamudan, S., 2013. The Catachronism of Climate Change. *Diacritics,* 41(3), p. 6–30.

Baucom, I., 2014. History 4°: Postcolonial Method and Anthropocene Time. *The Cambridge Journal of Postcolonial Literary Inquiry,* 1(1), p. 123–142.

Campbell, T., 2008. Introduction. In: *Bíos. Biopolitics and Philosophy (Roberto Esposito).* Minneapolis(MN): University of Minnesota Press.

Liao, S. M., Sandberg, A. & Roache, R., 2012. Human Engineering and Climate Change. *Ethics, Policy. and Environment,* 15(2), p. 206–221.

Marx, K., 1964. *Early Writings.* New York: McGraw Hill.

Pinkus, K., 2008. *Alchemical Mercury: A Theory of Ambivalence.* Stanford(CT): Stanford University Press.

Pinkus, K., 2012. Ambiguity. Ambience, Ambivalence. and the Environment. *Common Knowledge (Symposium: Fuzzy Studies, Part. 4),* 19(1), p. 88–95.

Sinclair, U., [1917] 1921. *King Coal.* Pasadena(CA): Georg Brandes.

Spitzer, L., 1968. Milieu and Ambience, in *Essays in Historical Semantics.* New York: Russell & Russell, p.179–316.

Walker, P., 1982. Germinal and Zola's 'New Faith' Based on Geology. *Symposium,* Fall, p. 257–272.

Yusoff, K., 2013. Geologic Life: Prehistory, Climate. Futures in the Anthropocene. *Environment and Planning D: Society and Space,* Volume 31, p. 779–795.

Zola, E., [1885] 2004. *Germinal.* London: Penguin Books.

8 The 'foreign grave' motif in Victorian medicine and literature

Roslyn Jolly

A striking motif in nineteenth-century texts concerned with the practice of travel for health is the image of the foreign grave. Signifying medical failure, the motif challenged the professional ethics of doctors who ordered patients abroad in search of cures that eluded them at home. It also raised broader questions about the unprecedented capacity of nineteenth-century men and women, armed with modern transport technologies and new scientific knowledge, to choose their preferred physical environment and to manage its effects upon them. In both medical and literary discourse throughout the century, the motif of the foreign grave functioned as a figure of irony deployed for the exposure of hubris – whether its target was the arrogance that led some members of the medical profession to carelessly recommend a fashionable therapy, or that of an entire social class, which increasingly took for granted its members' right to control the effects of climate on their bodies and minds.

The discourse of therapeutic travel provided a shared social context for the storytelling about climate in which a range of medical, journalistic and literary texts from the period 1825–1890 were involved. Close analysis of these texts reveals substantial common ground between different discourses and genres in their use of narrative forms, rhetorical techniques, and literary reference points. Yet the specific concerns and capabilities of literature are also evident in the way that later literary texts within this discursive field were able to break away from the origins of the debate about the measurable health benefits of therapeutic travel, and use the foreign grave motif to generate and explore states of feeling that were only indirectly connected with questions of illness and health. Nevertheless, although in such texts the therapeutic impetus may have become no more than a pretext for certain kinds of plotting or *mise en scène*, writers were still able to exploit the emotional charge associated with phrases from the medical discourse – phrases such as 'travelling South', 'doctor's orders' and, indeed, 'foreign grave'. Ideas about climate, change of climate and acclimatization, drawn from the shared Victorian context of telling stories about therapeutic travel, are redeployed in these literary texts to different ends, such as the exploration of personal identity and desire. New climate stories were created by exploring questions of personal identity and desire, more closely intertwining climate and culture.

The medical debate

'Change of air' was one of the most commonly prescribed environmental therapies used in the nineteenth century to treat symptoms, both physical and mental, which resisted pharmaceutical or surgical cure. Particularly popular was the practice of sending patients to the warm climates of southern Europe for relief from a range of ailments, including digestive disorder, menstrual dysfunction, nervous exhaustion and, most famously, pulmonary consumption. The idea that climatic factors could influence health and disease has its roots in classical medicine, and was discussed by both Hippocrates and Galen. However, the immense popularity and widespread application of climate therapies in the nineteenth century depended on distinctively modern forms of power and knowledge. 'It would be no new thing to insist on the influence which Climate exerts upon the health,' wrote D. J. T. Francis in his treatise *Change of Climate* (*1853*), 'but the continually increasing facilities for travelling, and the locomotive spirit of the present age, invest the subject, every day, with a fresh interest' (vi). The transport revolution created by the development of steam-powered technologies in the late eighteenth and early nineteenth centuries enabled patients to change their climatic environments faster and more cheaply than ever before. The practices of both travel and medicine in the Victorian period were affected, and affected each other, as a result. Increased medical investigations of climate shaped the habits of travellers. James Pollock (1850) observed: 'Of the numerous class of English travellers who are met with in almost all countries at the present day, a very large number have obtained the authority of some physician of note at home as a warrant for the efficacy of their experiment in search of health' (963). Conversely, greater opportunities for travel provided impetus for increased investigation in this burgeoning area of medicine. R. E. Scoresby-Jackson (1862) claimed that a new department of scientific inquiry – medical climatology – had been 'fostered by the remarkable facilities which now attend the traveller in his wanderings over every part of the world' (viii-ix).

Suggesting greater precision than the older notion of 'change of air', the new science of medical climatology purported to offer doctors and patients a systematic, rational and highly nuanced basis for understanding and applying the ancient therapeutic practice of travelling for health. Yet doubts persisted about the efficacy of climate therapies. In the realm of theory, scientists disputed whether 'acclimatization' was really possible (many rejected the term), and medical writers argued that risks as well as opportunities accompanied the exceptional 'cosmopolite' status of human beings within the animal kingdom (Burgess, 1850a, p. 593; Pollock, 1850, p. 964; Copland, 1858, p. 342–3; Scoresby-Jackson, 1862, p. 2–3). In the realm of practice, observers noted with disquiet that many patients ordered abroad for their health failed to return home and were buried in foreign graves, which stood as monuments to the shortcomings of contemporary medical knowledge or as reminders of the limits of human beings' abilities to control both their environments and their destinies.

Nineteenth-century medical writers offered three main explanations for the high failure rate of climate therapies: the progress of the disease was too advanced for any therapeutic intervention to succeed; or, the prescribed environment turned out to be positively harmful to the sufferer; or, death was caused by patients' inattention to therapeutic detail or by over-exertion resulting from their attempts to combine the roles of invalid and tourist. All three explanations enabled doctors to deflect blame for the foreign grave and the medical failure it signified from themselves and assign it to others, notably poets and novelists whose seductive descriptions of the warm South misrepresented its true climatic conditions (Linn, 1893, pp. 261, 277–8; Francis, 1853, p. 88), and patients themselves, who ignored instructions about accommodation, diet and dress attached to their prescriptions for 'change of air' (Scoresby-Jackson, 1862, p. 17; Lindsay, 1887, p. 873; Bennett, 1861, p. 57–58), especially when caught up in the excitement of the touristic environment (Francis, 1853, p. 45; Anon., 1875, p. 544–545; Young, 1886, p. 197–200; Bennett, 1861, p. 97–98). The last point, especially, attracted copious (and frequently censorious) discussion in medical writings on therapeutic travel, for as historian John Pemble has argued, the complex self-management required of the patient undergoing this style of treatment meant that medical climatology 'shifted the blame for failure to the invalid' and 'put the self-discipline of the patient rather than the skill of the physician on trial' (1987, p. 246).

Some medical writers, though, assigned ultimate responsibility to doctors themselves for creating situations that permitted the operation of these proximate causes. As early as 1828, in a letter to the editor of *The Lancet*, 'Phthisis' wrote: 'when one sees, as I have done, patients whose days, nay, whose hours, are numbered, daily expatriating themselves from their native land [...] one cannot help regretting, that medical ethics form no portion of the plan of education enforced by our medical and surgical professors' ('Phthisis', 1828, p. 517). The ethical questions raised by the consignment of so many English travellers to foreign graves centred on two issues: the needless suffering experienced by expatriated invalids, and the financial hardship imposed on their families by the expense of therapeutic travel. The latter consideration was often overlooked both by doctors, and by patients eager to reap the potential health benefits attached to the newly democratized conditions of travel. For, although European travel was no longer the exclusive privilege of the wealthy, the cost of relocating an invalid (and often his or her family) was considerable. In an 1860 essay on 'Luxury', English jurist J. F. Stephen identified health as one of three main objects upon which the comfortably off English spent their income (the others being refinement and a large family), noting also that the 'extreme costliness' of health was often forgotten in analyses of Victorian society and economy (1860, p. 348). A development from the eighteenth-century practice of domestic travel to spa towns for 'the cure', in the Victorian period travel abroad for health became one of the costliest ways in which the upper, middle and – as the century wore on – even the working classes of Britain affirmed their desire for control over their environments and their bodies. Awareness that this 'luxury' was increasingly demanded by and prescribed for patients who could ill afford it, together with scepticism about the medical value of such interventions, created a double ethical concern with regard to medical climatology. On the other hand, defenders of therapeutic travel protested that 'despite the obloquy that has been earned by repeated malpractice for this really useful remedial agent, we have evidence enough in its favour wherewith to repudiate this undeserved censure, and to determine its fitting rank in the list of therapeutics' (Scoresby-Jackson, 1862, p. 28).

The question of 'evidence' is relevant to an investigation of the foreign grave motif in the nineteenth century, because foreign graves were often made to function discursively as circumstantial evidence for the failure of climate therapies. 'The traveller, who bends over the lowly tombs in the burial ground at Leghorn, has melancholy testimony of [...] the too often injudicious recommendation of the physician, and the excessive and sudden vicissitudes [of climate] to which Southern France and Italy are so signally liable' wrote Robert Dunglison, M.D., in his textbook *Human Health* (1844, p. 146). Sir James Pollock (1850) agreed that 'many English inscriptions in these places [Montpellier, Nice, Rome] bring painful memories of a time which the medical philanthropist will often bitterly regret' (964), while Dr. Thomas Burgess, writing in *The Lancet* in 1850, approved English travel writer James Whiteside's view that '[t]he churchyards in the different towns in Italy, frequented by English invalids, teach a melancholy lesson on this subject' (1850a, p. 593). This way of 'reading' foreign graves was so common that one medical writer was moved to warn against over-interpretation of such supposed evidence of medical malpractice. 'It is hardly fair to make use of the evidence of misdirection of this kind which such cemeteries as those of Pau, Nice, Leghorn, & c., are supposed to afford, as an argument in condemnation of all foreign climates in the disease in question [consumption],' wrote D. J. T. Francis, M.D. (1853, p. 13). 'In counting, as some have done, the tombstones to our countrymen that lie beneath the shadow of the pyramid of Caius Cestius at Rome, or bask in many other of the sunny parts of Italy or France, we deal with a fixed record only of the dead. We lose sight in such calculations of those who have been relieved or cured, to the number of whom the former may bear but a small proportion' (41).

While the evidentiary value of the foreign grave might thus be questioned, its emotional, and therefore rhetorical, power was hard to resist. Even the doyen of medical climate theorists, Sir James Clark, invoked the motif when he wrote feelingly of the patient 'doomed shortly to add another name to the long and melancholy list of his countrymen who have sought, with pain and suffering, a distant country, only to find in it a grave' (1841, p. 53). Sir James Pollock (1850) used similarly emotive language when he described 'the foreign grave, how much dreaded by the many!' which 'might have been spared the wretched sufferer' if their doctor had been less ready to prescribe a faddish treatment (964). Through such rhetoric, these eminent medical writers contributed to a sentimental discursive formation, in which southern cemeteries – especially those that could be described as 'English' or 'Protestant' – carried an emotional charge in some ways similar to that of war cemeteries in the twentieth century: they focused feelings of pathos and regret; they offered a lesson in mortality and the vanity of human striving; and they were seen by some as bearing witness to historical folly and error.

Exchanges between literature and medicine

The motif of the foreign grave defines a point of intersection between literary and medical discourse in the nineteenth century. While doctors might condemn imaginative writers for misleading invalids with their selective and exaggerated depictions of southern climates, many medical writers nevertheless borrowed literary techniques in order to exploit the emotional and rhetorical charge of the foreign grave motif. Meanwhile, fiction writers drew upon the medical debate in which the motif featured in order to create stories of folly, pathos and irony. Such discursive traffic between the realms of literature and medicine (sometimes free-flowing, sometimes jammed on questions of ethics or evidence) is equally visible in C. H. Phipps's story 'Change of Air' (1825), and in a cluster of texts from the high Victorian period: the article titled 'Transportation by Order of Medicine', published in the *Pall Mall Gazette* (1872), and the immediate responses it drew from medical journals on both sides of the Atlantic. Comparison of these various texts reveals many rhetorical similarities between fictional and non-fictional treatments of the subject of failed therapeutic travel, while also demonstrating significant continuities in concerns around this subject over half a century.

Phipps's story begins by comparing the English 'practice of ordering patients to the South for "change of air"' (1825, p. 114) with the French habit of sending the terminally ill to ironically named *Maisons de Santé* so they would die out of sight of their friends and families. To be sent to such a place, Phipps maintains, 'is like an anticipated burial' (112); a patient thus placed amongst the dying, without hope of release, 'may be said to suffer burial twice, once at the hands of man's unkindness, before the last obsequies are to be gone through from necessity' (113). This Gothic motif of burial alive establishes the emotional tone of Phipps's story of young Bouverie, an Oxford undergraduate reduced to a state of nervous exhaustion by over-exertion in his studies. Bouverie's kindly parents, following medical advice, send him on a continental tour, but their son's health declines as he travels south; he eventually dies at Rome the victim of 'an idle counsel', 'southern air' and 'unbroken solitude' (135). The young Englishman's original complaint was not pulmonary consumption or any other organic disease, but generalised 'languor' (117) and 'debility' (133), which, the narrator suggests, time, rest and friendly society would eventually have cured if the patient had stayed at home. But his southern journey exposes him to continuous fatigue and solitude. Moreover, the role of tourist produces in the invalid a deleterious mental state, which mimics the notorious vicissitudes of temperature to which doctors routinely attributed the therapeutic unreliability of southern climates (116): alternating moods of 'depression' and 'elation' caused by the highs and lows of the tourist experience (120–21, 127) distemper the patient's mind as surely as the alternating heat and cold of Mediterranean winds unbalance his physical constitution. The 'slow fever' (129) that eventually kills Bouverie is as much mental as physical, caused by a combination of the exhausting role of tourist and the over-stimulating environment in which medical advice placed him.

The product of a more democratic era in travel, 'Transportation by Order of Medicine' shifts focus from the aristocratic to the middle-class traveller for health, while raising similar questions about medical ethics. The article questions the readiness of doctors to prescribe foreign travel without enquiring into the family or financial circumstances of patients, and without considering the relation of cost to benefit. 'We suppose we are bound to believe that physicians have a due sense of their responsibilities,' the article began, but it went on to demonstrate the irresponsibility of allowing a therapeutic last resort to generate false hope in the minds of dying patients. The article's polemic depends on a fictitious, present tense narrative that uses emotional language and lurid imagery. It tells the story of a young couple of moderate means, a consumptive woman and her devoted husband, who are persuaded to quit home, job and children in order to secure for the wife the supposed health benefits of a Mediterranean winter residence. But the patient is weakened by the 'exposure, fatigue, excitement, mental anxiety' of her journey and her condition further deteriorates in the 'bleak villa', lacking all the comforts of their English home. 'Then there is the end [...] and there is another grave with its little white cross in some Mediterranean cemetery, and a solitary mourner thinking of that consultation six months before, and all that has come of it.'

The *Pall Mall Gazette* article drew swift responses from the major medical journals on either side of the Atlantic. In Britain, the flagship publication of the medical profession, *The Lancet*, promptly endorsed it, even claiming that it did not go far enough in condemning the 'perfectly inexcusable' yet widespread practice of prescribing overseas climate therapies for patients whose suffering would only be increased by the rigours and expense of foreign travel (1872, p. 729). In America, by contrast, the *Boston Medical and Surgical Journal* called the *Pall Mall Gazette* article 'cynical in spirit, exaggerated in descriptive detail, and prejudicial in its reflections on physicians' (1873, p. 32). It accused the writer of going 'to the edge of falsehood' when he 'left his readers to infer that all people who travel for their health inevitably die before they reach home, or that all doctors are in the habit of exiling their patients indiscriminately' (33).

These two medical journals responded differently to the *Gazette's* use of emotive and connotative language. The British respondent admitted to feeling 'much sympathy with the tone of [this] interesting and even pathetic remonstrance'; adopted, without critical analysis, its central 'transportation' metaphor; and even employed the same rhetorical strategy of sentimentally narrating a fictitious generalizing case study: 'hundreds of patients die the miserable death of the exile who feels that his banishment has hurried him to the grave and broken the hearts and half-ruined the fortunes of the dear friends among whom he would have been only too glad to die in peace' (1872, p. 729). The American respondent, on the other hand, accused the *Gazette* writer of 'aim[ing] at the sensational' and called instead for further dispassionate investigation of '[t]he science of climatology as applied to medicine' (1873, p. 33). Thus, the literary qualities of pathos and sensation are valued quite differently in the two responses. While *The Lancet* praised the use of pathos as an effective means of engaging sympathy for the plight of misdirected patients, the

Boston Medical and Surgical Journal scorned the substitution of sensational writing techniques for scientific debate. Such differentiation of emotive modalities is unsurprising, for whereas pathos had a respectable literary pedigree in poetry and drama, sensation, associated as it was with the sensation novel, carried almost entirely negative connotations in contemporary critical discourse.

Indeed, the *Gazette* article not only employs a sensational tone but also – like Phipps's story a half century earlier – draws upon Gothic techniques. The sinister proleptic vision of the young wife arriving in the south at 'the house she is to die in'; the haunting sound of gusts of wind 'howling up the stairs and along the passages' of the southern death-house (the English were convinced that only they knew how to keep out draughts); and the 'ghastly show' made by the Sister of Charity who arrives to nurse the dying woman – all these touches invest the *Gazette*'s little narrative with the emotional atmosphere of an eighteenth-century Gothic novel. The portrayal of the young Englishwoman as the victim of combined conspiracy and neglect is intensified by the introduction of two further figures of institutional betrayal: the local doctor in the southern town, who behaves toward his patient 'with the air of a man who sets himself half-heartedly to a thankless duty'; and the local English clergyman, who is depicted as either a pariah ('a man of the stamp that the Church appoints to these foreign stations') or himself an invalid who selfishly avoids contact with anyone who reminds him of his own likely fate.

Phipps's 1828 story and the *Pall Mall Gazette*'s 1872 article carry the same warnings about the dangers of environmental medicine; in doing so, each writer presents a fictitious case study from which he extrapolates a general principle. 'An acquaintance with one victim especially of this medical edict,' the narrator of Phipps's story states, 'has led me to bestow a few pages upon it, as hastening in many instances the catastrophe, which it professes to ward off' (1825, p. 116–117). The extrapolation from 'one victim' to 'many instances' is not substantiated; rather, the writer relies on the emotional impact of his narrative to encourage his readers to question a whole area of medical practice. Like the *Gazette* contributor, Phipps also uses legal language to suggest that credulous patients and their families have ascribed an exaggerated authority to medical practitioners. In 'Change of Air', the doctor's 'idle counsel' has the force of an 'edict' (116) or 'one of those warrants, at once of death and exile' which, the narrator argues, should never have been 'passed upon the member of a happy family' (114). The *Pall Mall Gazette* article uses the metaphor of 'sentences of transportation' to imply both the high-handed exercise of power by medical men and the injustice of treating invalids as if they were criminals. This legal metaphor would have had a particular resonance in 1872, only five years after the English practice of transporting convicts overseas was abolished. The idea that 'transportation by order of medicine' was still practised upon innocent citizens, when transportation by order of judges was no longer considered an appropriate punishment for convicted felons, intensified the *Gazette*'s attack on this therapeutic practice.

Such 'sensational' rhetorical devices as the likening of invalid travel to convict transportation prompted the *Boston Medical and Surgical Journal* to pronounce the *Pall Mall Gazette* article 'harmful', because it allowed the techniques of popular literature to obscure the protocols of scientific enquiry (1873, p. 33). Yet, in the broader nineteenth-century debate over the merits of environmental therapies, one often finds medical writers themselves using hyperbolic language and emotive imagery to intensify their arguments against overseas therapeutic travel. Doctors wrote of the 'unpardonable cruelty' of other doctors in separating dying patients from their families (Scoresby-Jackson, 1862, p. 28); and of 'spectacles of human misery' encountered in the resort towns of the South, including the sight of Englishmen 'crawling along the streets or dragged in invalid chairs – to see sights perhaps the last they will ever witness' (Burgess, 1850b, p. 700). Indeed, a rhetoric of doom and dread, misery and melancholy, pervaded the medical literature on this emotionally charged subject, at least for the first two-thirds of the century. Thereafter, the science of therapeutic travel tended to be discussed somewhat more dispassionately, at least by doctors. During this period, as Vladimir Jankovic (2006) has demonstrated, '[s]cientific writers presented their case [against therapeutic travel to the South] as a long-overdue audit of a complacent medical opinion that concealed professional idiosyncrasy, anecdotal evidence, and social prejudice' (290, see also 281). Yet, while 'the weapon of impartiality' could be wielded to great polemical effect in this debate (290, see also 272–273), the discursive field continued to be characterized by widespread use of emotive language, regardless of whether the writer was arguing for or against climate and travel as remedial agents. An 1887 article in *The Lancet* recommending permanent expatriation of consumptive patients – on the ground that climate cures are effective, but may be reversed by removal from the therapeutically beneficial environment – mentioned the 'distressing cases' of patients ordered abroad who, 'yielding to that piteous home-sickness which sometimes assails the stoutest heart', 'returned home, and returned to die' (Lindsay, 1887, p. 871). Here, instead of the motif of the foreign grave, we are given the narrative of a fatal *nostos*, a doomed return. Nevertheless, just as in Phipps's story and the *Pall Mall Gazette* piece, this medical argument relies upon such literary techniques as subjective interpretation, emotive language, and persuasive anecdotes, suggesting that it was more difficult than the writer in the *Boston Medical and Surgical Journal* would have liked to free medical discussion of this issue from the taint or charge of the literary.

The literary life of the foreign grave motif

Such was the emotive value of the foreign grave motif that by the 1870s it had taken on a literary life of its own, independent of attempts to validate or discredit the claims of medical climatology. Whereas, in texts such as 'Transportation by Order of Medicine' and its responses, literary techniques were used rhetorically to affirm or undermine medical values and practices, in later literary texts we find the exchange reversed: medical ideas about climate are invoked to give shape and intensity to literary exploration of states of being and feeling. Although divested of the didactic urgency that characterized earlier examples from the same discursive field, these literary texts are recognizable versions of familiar stories the Victorians told themselves about the benefits or dangers of changing one's climatic environment.

The difference is that the stories were now being told for different reasons – not to persuade readers to a particular course of action, but to entice them into emotional spaces that could be mapped onto established discursive frameworks for writing about climate. In what follows, I examine three literary texts from the 1870s that exploited the literary potential of the foreign grave motif in very different ways.

I. 'Ordered South'

Robert Louis Stevenson's well-known autobiographical essay 'Ordered South' was first published in 1874, just two years after 'Transportation by Order of Medicine'. The essay is a meditation on many things – death, pleasure, identity – its thinking focused by a *telos* that is never explicitly named but everywhere implied: the foreign grave that awaits the confirmed invalid who has been 'ordered south' and 'knows […] that he may not live to go home again' ([1874] 1926, p. 93). This sweetly resigned essay reworks both the legal language and the Gothic spaces common to Phipps's 1825 story and the *Pall Mall Gazette*'s 1872 article. Stevenson's invalid rails against the narrow scope to which his physician's 'sentence of banishment' has contracted his sphere of life, but he then accepts his fate. He becomes 'a contented prisoner' within this narrowed 'cell' of experience (91), which he calls 'the very vestibule of death' (94).

No summary of 'Ordered South' can capture the disorienting experience of actually reading the essay. As Penelope LeFew-Blake has observed, here 'Stevenson permits the reader to view all direction and space only in relation to the invalid's troubled imagination' (2004, p. 121). Noting Stevenson's attribution of a certain 'carelessness' of self to the invalid, LeFew-Blake argues that such '"carelessness" in terms of direction, destination, and movement creates a confusing mental labyrinth' (122). Alex Clunas observes similarly that, contradicting the directional and purposive simplicity of its title, 'Ordered South' traces 'a wandering, random, undetermined itinerary' (1996, p. 66). This sense of textual disorder is partly due to the difficulty the essay's central consciousness has in adjusting to his new geographical environment. Stevenson writes of the transported invalid's numbness of spirit and sensation, and questions whether it is 'the very softness and amenity of the climate' – that is, the qualities for which he was medically ordered to the south – that have sapped him of energy and interest. 'A longing for the brightness and silence of fallen snow seizes him at such times. He is homesick for the hale rough weather' ([1874] 1926, p. 86). But as he remembers how terrible the northern winter can be, his spirit recoils from nostalgic longing and clings to the southern present: 'He cannot be glad enough that he is where he is' (86). Yet he can still only engage with his new environment intermittently, rather than through a sustained process of settling in. A 'glad moment' may be found in the sight of a group of washerwomen and 'the harmony of faint colour that is always characteristic of the dress of these southern women' or in glimpses of 'tropical effects, with canes and naked rocks and sunlight' (88). But wholeness eludes the invalid; only fragments work, as when he writes that 'the opulence of the sunshine, which somehow gets lost and fails to produce its effect on the large scale, is suddenly revealed to him by the chance isolation – as he changes the position of his sunshade – of a yard or two of roadway with its stones and weeds' (88). He becomes entranced by climate's micro-effects: 'a snatch of perfume, the sudden singing of a bird, the freshness of some pulse of air from an invisible sea, the light shadow of a travelling cloud, the merest nothing that sends a little shiver along the most infinitesimal nerve of a man's body' (89). Nevertheless the south, as a totalized climatic environment, remains foreign to him.

Alongside this mixture of geographic engagement and alienation runs a continual movement, through the essay, from outside to inside, from sensory to spiritual. The reader gradually realizes that the essay's subject is being displaced; this is not a work about the south so much as it is a meditation on what it means to face death. In fact, the south is a metonym for death, being its 'vestibule' (94). The invalid not only comes to comfortably inhabit this 'vestibule', but also becomes able to adjust his thinking to the idea of the chamber beyond. Thus, the process of successful acclimatization the essay records involves adjustment to an emotional environment rather than a physical one. Having failed to acclimatize fully to the south, in the second half of 'Ordered South' the subject becomes acclimatized to his inevitable mortality. It is in this sense, and only in this sense, that I would take issue with Alex Clunas's claim that that this essay is 'nonteleological' (1996, p. 55), for in its preoccupation with death its telos is unmistakable.

To be ordered south, then, is not to find a cure, but to be required to face one's own mortality. There are no charges of medical malpractice in this essay, no wishing for an easier, more peaceful death at home; rather, the idea of dying abroad becomes a vehicle of philosophical and spiritual enlightenment. Transplanted from his home and physically imprisoned within his failing body, the invalid shrinks into himself, eschewing social contact; 'desire after desire leaves him' ([1874] 1926, p. 92). There is a 'prelude' to the condition of 'the grave' in the way he now 'looks on' at life 'with a patriarchal impersonality of interest, such as a man may feel when he pictures to himself the fortunes of his remote descendants, or the robust old age of the oak he has planted over-night' (91–92). With the prospect of his own life being cut short, his consciousness is freed from the temporal confines of the individual human lifespan: he feels as involved in the distant as in the near future, neither of which he expects personally to witness. Spatially, too, diminution of his range of movement through physical debility paradoxically expands the mind's geographic range, and he becomes capable of a kind of teleportation into other lives and other places. More and more, his centre of gravity shifts away from the 'central metropolis of self' (95), as interest, connection and meaning are dispersed into 'the outlying colonies' (94) and 'provinces' (95) of his emotional and spiritual existence. This vacation of home, core, or point of origin, and concomitant expatriation of the self to its margins, would become defining characteristics of Stevenson's writing life, given their clearest and most material expression in his move to Samoa – where, twenty years after the publication of 'Ordered South', he would die, and where his foreign grave would become a place of literary pilgrimage. Indeed, the motif of the foreign grave provides an apt metaphor for the processes of displacement and decentring that Stevenson would explore again and again in life and literature, but first in this early essay about changing climates on medical orders.

II. 'Longstaff's Marriage'

'Ordered South' is a literary exercise in pathos, redeemed from sentimentality by its mystical speculations on the nature of selfhood. Henry James's story 'Longstaff's Marriage' ([1878] 1999b), by contrast, proceeds boldly, and somewhat coldly, under the literary banner of sensation. James uses two therapeutic environments, Nice and Rome, to frame his story of irrational and doomed love. When English invalid Reginald Longstaff falls in love with American tourist Diana Belfield at Nice, he proposes a bizarre bargain to her: if she will marry him on his deathbed, she will enable him to die in peace and in return will inherit all his estates in England. Diana refuses, leaving the Englishman to die; but he does not die – rather, he gets well and forgets his strange obsession with her. Diana, meanwhile, discovers that she loves Longstaff as 'insanely' as he had once loved her (320) and, seemingly as a consequence or expression of this passion, contracts a mysterious wasting disease similar to that from which the Englishman had previously suffered. When the two meet again at Rome, the positions are reversed: he is the healthy tourist, young, strong, and desirable; she is the pitiful invalid, 'fading and sinking' (322) as she awaits her certain fate. The story ends with her asking, and receiving, the very favour he had begged of her – a deathbed marriage service performed as prelude to a foreign burial.

In James's story, obsessive desire is a communicable disease and the sanatoria of Nice and Rome are the environments in which it festers and consumes. The motif of the foreign grave focuses and coordinates a struggle between *eros* and *thanatos* which only one of the protagonists can survive. Longstaff, believing he is terminally ill, is at first hesitant to declare his love to Diana: 'To speak to her of what I felt seemed only to open the lid of a grave in her face' (305–6). But his older and wilier Italian servant realises that proximity to death can generate the 'interest' that, in James's imaginative world, may be the source of life: 'If you could see him, poor gentleman, lying there as still and handsome as if he were his own monument in a *campo santo*, I think he would interest you' (310). According to the uncanny therapeutic logic of this story, Longstaff is 'cured' by the 'hurt' Diana inflicts when she refuses his marriage proposal (320), while she is 'consumed' (320) by the unsatisfied 'interest' (310) generated in her by that proposal. The story's chiastic structure determines that the foreign grave initially meant for the young Englishman will eventually, and inevitably, be assigned to the young American.

Diana Belfield's Italian doctor 'recommended her to remain in Rome, as the climate exactly suited her complaint' (321). Yet the prescribed 'air of Rome' (322) evidently has no remedial effect at all. Rome does not bring a reversal in the decline of Diana's health, but rather an acceleration once she finds out that Longstaff no longer cares for her. Nor would this therapeutic failure have surprised any Victorian reader who was at all acquainted with the basic principles of contemporary climate theory. Diana's condition – the Italian doctor offers no diagnosis, merely affirming 'that she was ill' (321) – is characterized by weariness, languor, fatigue and stillness (319); very little engages her interest, and her sphere of activity contracts until it is reduced to a single room. Victorian climatotherapy, which was based on the balance of opposing forces, dictated that depressed patients such as Diana required tonic or stimulant climates, whereas those suffering from irritable, over-stimulated conditions of either mind or body would benefit from exposure to sedative, relaxing climates. 'Longstaff's Marriage' includes a classic example of each of these therapeutic environments. As James Pollock (1850) wrote in his 'Considerations on the Climate of Italy', 'let the everyday air of Nice and Rome be contrasted by any one in health, and the different effects of what are called the "stimulant" and "sedative" will be very perceptive' (964). According to Victorian climate guru Dr James Clark, the right medical advice for a patient such as Diana Belfield was exactly the opposite of that given by her Italian doctor: 'on persons of a torpid, or relaxed habit of body, and of a gloomy, desponding cast of mind ... the keen, bracing, dry air of Provence, and its brilliant skies, will often produce a beneficial effect' (1841, p. 197). The soft, humid air of Rome, on the other hand, was well known for its 'depressing effect on the animal spirits' (Johnson, 1831, p. 277; see also 265). Enervating, sedative and relaxing, Rome's climate could only be recommended for 'persons ... of a sanguine temperament, and a lively, imaginative mind, who never feel so well as when breathing an atmosphere of this kind' (Francis, 1853, p. 28–29) – it would certainly not have been prescribed for someone as low in spirits and lacking in energy as Diana.

James himself was aware of, and engaged with, the Anglo-American medico-climatic discourse on Rome. In a letter to his brother William James, written there on 9 April 1873, he commented that the only thing he objected to about 'pure Rome' (1974, p. 364) – as distinct from the expatriate American society in the city – was 'the influence of the climate'. This, he said, had reduced him to 'a state of ineffable languefaction. The want of "tone" in the air is altogether indescribable: it makes it mortally flat and dead and relaxing' (365). The word 'relaxing', when used in relation to climate, had by no means the positive connotations in the nineteenth century that it enjoys today. 'Relaxing' climates had the power to destroy moral fibre, leaving one listless and disengaged.

> The great point is that it is all excessively pleasant and you succumb to languor with a perfectly demoralized conscience ... It seems to me that I have slept in these three months more than in my whole life beside. The soft, divine enchanting days of spring have of course made matters worse and I feel as if, for six months past, I have been looking at the world from under half-meeting eyelids. But I am going to fight it out to the end ... (365).

James complained that the relaxing air of Rome made it difficult for him to work, but insisted that he would 'fight it out to the end' rather than give in to the condition of passivity induced by the climate. But in Diana Belfield's case, when Rome's enervating atmosphere confirms her lack of will to live, she puts up no resistance at all. Her physical sphere contracts to a single room, within which she remains 'tranquil' and 'motionless' ([1878] 1999b, p. 324).

'The old doctor was with her constantly now, and he continued to say that the air of Rome was very good for her complaint' (322). One is tempted to think that the doctor speaks for the novelist here: the Roman climate, with its melancholy airs and golden light, 'exactly suited her complaint' (321) from the aesthetic, imaginative and emotional points of view, and that is why the author keeps his character there. Perhaps foreshadowing the simplest aspect of the physician Sir Luke Strett's role in *The Wings of the Dove*, the doctor's function in 'Longstaff's Marriage' seems to be to authorize the positioning of the doomed heroine within a climatic and cultural setting that is rich in artistic resonance and association. (It could also be argued that in the Nice scenes of the story, Longstaff's Italian servant foreshadows another aspect of Sir Luke's role in *The Wings of the Dove*: the idea of carrying out an experiment to see if romantic 'interest' can keep a dying patient alive.) For James's story shares with Stevenson's essay a lack of concern with medical ethics and a readiness to exploit, rather, the imaginative possibilities of the doomed expatriate invalid as a figure of existential or narrative irony. In 'Ordered South' and 'Longstaff's Marriage', no therapeutic environment is shown to bring any health benefit to any invalid depicted. But, as writers, neither Stevenson nor James was really interested in the contemporary medico-legal debates generated by such therapeutic failures. Instead, these writers put the rhetorical techniques of those debates to different imaginative uses, drawing on the discourse of therapeutic travel and its compelling central motif of the foreign grave to explore the philosophical questions that interested them most: for Stevenson, questions about the complexities of individual identity, and for James, about the mysterious nature of desire.

III. 'Daisy Miller'

James wrote 'Longstaff's Marriage' straight after he wrote another, more famous, story about a beautiful American who dies at Rome: 'Daisy Miller' ([1878] 1999a). Unlike Diana Belfield, Daisy Miller is not an invalid traveller; she even goes so far as to say, 'I never was sick, and I don't mean to be' (292). Her motives for travel are conspicuous consumption, cultural improvement and, perhaps, the increase of matrimonial opportunities. But Daisy succumbs to one of the main health risks against which medical writers warned all nineteenth-century English and America travellers to Rome, invalid or not: fever caused by reckless exposure to the elements and over-indulgence in tourist activities. In his article on 'Malarial Fever at Rome', published in the *British Medical Journal* in April 1878 – the month 'Daisy Miller' was accepted for publication by the *Cornhill Magazine* (Edel, 1962, p. 303) – Dr Lauchlan Aitken wrote that

> ...visitors, who are careless of consequences and heedless of the ordinary warnings, often overwork themselves in sightseeing, become heated in the sun, and stand for hours in museums, galleries and churches, exhausting their nervous systems, or expose themselves more directly on the Campagna, or even within the walls of the city, to a chill which results in an attack of so-called Roman fever (1878a, p. 597).

Daisy goes to see the Roman Colosseum by moonlight because it is on her checklist of unmissable tourist experiences (James, [1878] 1999a, p. 292). Her baffled and reluctant admirer, the expatriate American Winterbourne, is lured to the Colosseum at the same time by a poetic precedent, the attraction of which, he soon remembers, runs contrary to received medical wisdom:

> As he stood there he began to murmur Byron's famous lines, out of 'Manfred;' but before he had finished his quotation he remembered that if nocturnal meditations in the Colosseum are recommended by poets, they are deprecated by doctors. The historic atmosphere was there, certainly; but the historic atmosphere, scientifically considered, was no better than a villainous miasma (290).

Winterbourne is shocked to find Daisy in this deserted spot near midnight, alone with her Italian friend Mr Giovanelli – first, because of the social indiscretion, but then even more so because of the risk to her health. 'Winterbourne had now begun to think simply of the craziness, from a sanitary point of view, of a delicate young girl lounging away the evening in this nest of malaria' (291). When Daisy exclaims about the prettiness of the place and the light, he replies 'you will not think Roman fever very pretty. This is the way people catch it' (292).

Like contemporary medical writers, James identifies lack of acclimatization as a predisposing cause for this illness. Laughlin Aitken wrote of 'the effects of the malaria on unacclimatized strangers, English or American', maintaining that 'acclimatized members of the nationalities mentioned' were almost never affected (1878a, p. 597). An unsigned 'Letter from Rome', published in the *Boston Medical and Surgical Journal* three years earlier, had similarly argued that in terms of health and lifestyle, a visitor to Rome 'cannot, in fact, do as the Romans do without the loss of his usual vitality, or even the risk of jeopardizing his very existence' (Anon., 1875, p. 542). Exposure to extremes of temperature, dirt and 'lively odors' might not harm the health of the Romans themselves, but 'innocent as are these phases of Roman life to the children of the soil, it will not do for the stranger to presume upon their harmlessness to himself. To their effects the Roman alone can afford to be indifferent' (543). In 'Daisy Miller' Winterbourne remonstrates with Giovanelli for taking the young American to such a dangerous place:

> 'I wonder,' he added, turning to Giovanelli, 'that you, a native Roman, should countenance such a terrible indiscretion.'
>
> 'Ah,' said the handsome native, 'for myself I am not afraid.'
>
> 'Neither am I – for you! I am speaking for this young lady' (James, [1878] 1999a, p. 292).

After Daisy's death he again questions the Italian: 'Why the devil ... did you take her to that fatal place?' (292). Giovanelli's 'imperturbable' answer is, 'For myself, I had no fear; and she wanted to go', to which Winterbourne can only retort, 'That was no reason!' (293).

Although Winterbourne is aligned with contemporary medical opinion when he affirms the susceptibility to fever of unacclimatized visitors to Rome, James's story runs contrary to realistic expectation when he has Daisy not only catch fever but also die from it, making his imagined Rome a 'fatal place'. In one of a series of articles on 'The Health of Rome' – this one published just a few months after 'Daisy Miller' appeared in 1878 – the same Dr Aitken who had warned visitors in Rome to moderate their behaviour if they wished to avoid malaria complained that his observations as a practising physician, resident in the city, were completely at odds with the 'stories' currently circulating about the unhealthiness of the Roman climate; for 'the thousands of victims of that mysterious complaint, the Roman fever, so perceptible to the journalists of London and New York, are quite invisible to me' (Aitken, 1878b, p. 383). The *Boston Medical and Surgical Journal's* 1875 'Letter from Rome' similarly criticized the amount of 'exaggeration and delusion' to be found in current rumours and reports about the health of Rome, and cited statistics 'which show that the impressions of the world in general are erroneous, and that Rome is by no means so unhealthy as has been imagined' (Anon., 1875, p. 543). Twelve years after the publication of 'Daisy Miller', David Young M.D. wrote:

> Writers of all nationalities, but particularly English and American, have vied with each other in their efforts to find language sufficiently strong to show their dislike of Rome and its detestable and deadly climate. Perhaps no city in Europe has been so abused in this respect as Rome has, or afforded a more favourite theme upon which authors have delighted to dwell (1886, p. 70–71).

In his depiction of Rome as a 'fatal place' James was no doubt influenced by both immediate gossip and literary example. At the expatriate salons of Rome, Dr Aitken wrote, any indisposition became the subject of dire predictions, while 'a genuine illness forms an inexhaustible source of invectives against the treacherous nature of the climate' (1878b, p. 383). Such salons were James's primary social milieu in Rome, and he also had before him the powerful literary precedent of Nathaniel Hawthorne's *The Marble Faun* ([1860] 2002), which offered a compelling imaginative vision of 'a climate that instils poison into its very purest breath' (79), making Rome a nest of malaria where 'Fever walks arm in arm with you, and Death awaits you at the end of the dim vista' (58). These influences encouraged James to plot a catastrophic consequence for Daisy's indiscreet behaviour, to which contemporary medical commentary on the supposed fatality of Rome's climate offers an interesting counterpoint. As the author of the 'Letter from Rome' wrote:

> Few superficial observers would believe how slight is the number of Americans – and these are, I regret to say, by far the most reckless and foolhardy of all the visitors to Rome – who have died here, and how much more scanty still the roll of those who have fallen victims to the much dreaded fevers (Anon., 1875, p. 545).

Of the so-called 'Roman fever', the writer claimed statistics showed there had been 'during the past six years, but one death of an American in Rome' (546). Lauchlan Aitken reported that, although malarial fever was commonly contracted by young and foolish visitors who over-exerted themselves in sightseeing, in six years' practice in Rome he had seen no fatal cases: 'None of the forty-five patients treated throughout by myself died; and only three … were very dangerously ill' (1878a, p. 598). David Young's analysis of statistical information of the causes of death among English and American visitors to Rome in the years 1876 to 1883 showed that out of 109 deaths, only two were from malaria (1886, p. 95). He argued that scanty evidence and large inferences lay behind the popular attribution of the deaths of so many travellers to 'fever caught at Rome' (73).

Following popular imagination rather than medical data about the city, James turns Daisy Miller's 'fever caught at Rome' into the fatal attack of a treacherous climate upon a young girl who lacks the knowledge or experience to defend herself. Of course, the illness is metaphorical, the fever standing for (amongst other things) the destructive power of the climate of opinion in Rome's expatriate salons, which turns so savagely against the innocent but socially clumsy American. The Roman fever served literary purposes well, being a wonderfully uncertain disease, a kind of floating signifier of the potentially disastrous effects of exposing oneself to the wrong climate. Lauchlan Aitken wrote:

> What this fever is the residents are often very puzzled to know, as strangers include under the generic term all kinds of ailments from a simple cold to a severe enteric fever; and it is sufficient to fall ill in Rome to be credited everywhere with being a victim of that strange disease. The result is naturally a wide divergence of views on the subject, and an alarm proportionate to the amount of confusion created (1878a, p. 597).

The author of the 'Letter from Rome' agreed that there was much confusion about this disease, which was often confused with typhoid (Anon., 1875, p. 545). He claimed that

> [t]he Roman fever *par excellence* … invariably takes the shape of chills and fever, and strongly resembles our ordinary fever and ague. At times it assumes an aggravated type, is very dangerous, and then is called '*perniciosa*.' This is fatal in about one third of cases…. Of this there has been, during the past six years, but one death of an American in Rome (546).

This is clearly the disease James had in mind for Daisy, as he makes explicit in a sentence of free indirect discourse focalized through Winterbourne: 'What if she were a clever little reprobate? That was no reason for her dying of the *perniciosa*' ([1878] 1999a, p. 291). But Winterbourne has the literary logic all wrong here: it is because she is not 'a clever little reprobate' but rather 'the most amiable' and 'most innocent' of women (294) that Daisy will be destroyed, like the early Christians at whose place of martyrdom she contracts her illness.

In the brilliantly compact ending to 'Daisy Miller', James extracts maximum value from the lack of a precise medical referent for the concept of Roman fever. The term came already loaded with an emotional charge, because it was associated with so much fear in the public's mind (Anon., 1875, p. 544; Aitken, 1878b, p. 362). Building upon this sense of its random, unpredictable, ill-understood power, James uses Roman fever to suggest various unstable and conflicting forces.

One is the force of unregulated desire that Winterbourne believes Daisy to feel for Mr Giovanelli. Another, as already suggested, is the poisonous atmosphere of gossip and judgement within the Anglo-American expatriate community in Rome. Ultimately, Roman fever seems to signify everything that is at stake, emotionally, between Winterbourne and Daisy, who are attracted to, but unable to understand, each other. '"I don't care," said Daisy, in a little strange tone, "whether I have Roman fever or not!"' ([1878] 1999a, p. 293). This is her last utterance of direct speech in the story. Structurally, the sentence parallels Winterbourne's exclamation a few lines earlier, 'I believe that it makes very little difference whether you are engaged or not!' (293). For, after discovering that she has spent the entire evening unchaperoned with Mr Giovanelli at the Coliseum, he feels suddenly that he can 'read' the 'riddle' presented to him by her strange manners. He believes he now understands the truth, that '[s]he was a young lady whom a gentleman need no longer be at pains to respect' (291). Daisy is deeply injured by his admission of his lack of faith in her, as she has been by the lack of chivalry shown in his failure to defend her against her detractors ('I shouldn't think you would let people be so unkind!' (289]). As Winterbourne realizes later – too late – 'She would have appreciated one's esteem' (295). Daisy's saying she doesn't care whether she has Roman fever or not is typical of her characteristic recklessness, but the 'little strange tone' in which she speaks the words also reveals how deeply she is affected by Winterbourne's behaviour towards her, just as the messages she sends to him from her deathbed, assuring him that she was never engaged to Mr Giovanelli, show how greatly she valued his good opinion. Roman fever, that much talked of, little understood disease of climate and travel – sometimes regarded as not a 'real' disease at all but more a state of mind – aptly symbolizes the whole collision of cultures and emotions in Winterbourne's and Daisy's relationship.

'Daisy's grave was in the little Protestant cemetery, in an angle of the wall of imperial Rome, beneath the cypresses and the thick spring-flowers' (294). This simple sentence is redolent with emotive associations. In the nineteenth-century medico-climatic discourse of the foreign grave, mention of any overseas Protestant or English cemetery tended to evoke feelings of pathos and regret. This particular graveyard had strong and precise literary associations as well, being the burial place of the English Romantic poet and invalid traveller, Keats, and later of his compatriot and contemporary, Shelley. In the preface to his elegy for Keats, *Adonais*, Shelley called the burial ground on the edge of Rome 'the romantic and lonely cemetery of the protestants' and wrote: 'It might make one in love with death, to think that one should be buried in so sweet a place' (Shelley, 2003, p. 529). But in his description of Daisy's newly dug grave James provokes opposite feelings of anger and futility at the waste of such a young life. We are told that Winterbourne 'stood staring at the raw protuberance among the April daisies' (James, [1878] 1999a, p. 295); this image of a foreign grave suggests what is ugly and unnatural in the thought of lovely, amiable Daisy rotting beneath the ground when she should be blooming above it, like the flowers whose name she bears.

Conclusion

In his essay on 'Luxury' (1860), J. F. Stephen wrote of contemporary Britain: 'Probably no nation was ever so rich, and it would be hard to mention one in which riches have had more power to confer everything which human nature desires, or in which that power has been more thoroughly recognized, or more devoutly worshiped' (347). Yet throughout the century, the failures of medical climatology exposed the limits of such power, and hence the elusiveness of such desires. The nineteenth-century medical debate about therapeutic travel highlighted the human hopes and fears bound up with the scientific aspirations of medical climatology, as did the literature that responded to that debate. Phipps's narrative, the *Pall Mall Gazette* article, Stevenson's essay and James's stories all use the motif of the foreign grave to mark out a space of ironic dissonance between the kind of control over bodies and environments that seemed to be promised by nineteenth-century science, technology and affluence, and the implacable 'decrees of Providence' ('Phthisis', 1828, p. 517) that signified the reality of human impotence in the face of imperfectly understood diseases.

That space of mingled hope and disappointment, where the curative and destructive effects of climate on human health contended for dominance, offered a suggestive emotional landscape to the literary imagination. In 'Ordered South', Stevenson took the idea of a failing climate cure as an occasion to meditate on the evacuation of the 'central metropolis of self' ([1874] 1926, p. 95) and the dispersion of personal identity into its own 'outlying colonies' (94). In 'Longstaff's Marriage', James used a depiction of the apparently 'harmless society' ([1878] 1999b, p. 298) of invalids seeking a change of air to mark out the uncanny and fatal path of a consuming desire. In 'Daisy Miller' he made a disease of climate, 'Roman fever', into the unstable and over-determined signifier of – simultaneously – natural feeling, the culturally specific manners that oppress such feeling, and the treacherous territory of a cross-cultural emotional encounter. As he wrote of his first Roman winter and spring, which had provided him with material for both these stories, 'it has all … been "quite an experience" and I have gathered more impressions I am sure than I suppose – impressions I shall find a value in when I come to use them' (1974, p. 365). Both James and Stevenson had, while travelling, gained impressions of the climates of the South of France and Italy, especially in their therapeutic or noxious aspects. These impressions acquired 'value' when put to work in the process of writing, and the results show in what very different ways the literary imagination contributed to the emotional experience and cultural construction of climate in the nineteenth century.

References

'Phthisis', 1828. Letter to the Editor of The Lancet. *The Lancet,* 30 December, p. 517–520.
Aitken, L., 1878a. Malarial Fever at Rome. *The British Medical Journal,* 27 April, p. 597–599.
Aitken, L., 1878b. The Health of Rome. *British Medical Journal,* 12 October, p. 383.
Anon., 1875. Letter from Rome. *Boston Medical and Surgical Journal,* Volume 92, p. 542–546.

Bennett. J.H., 1861. *Mentone and the Riviera as a Winter Climate*. London: John Churchill.

Boston Medical and Surgical Journal, 1873. Transportation by Order of Medicine. *Boston Medical and Surgical Journal,* 87(10), p. 32–34.

Burgess, T., 1850a. Inutility of Resorting to the Italian Climate for the Cure of Pulmonary Consumption, No. I. *The Lancet,* 18 May, p. 591–594.

Burgess, T., 1850b. Inutility of Resorting to the Italian Climate for the Cure of Pulmonary Consumption, No. IV. *The Lancet,* 28 December, p. 700–703.

Clark, J., 1841. *The Sanative Influence of Climate.* London: John Murray.

Clunas, A., 1996. 'Out of My Country and Myself I Go': Identity and Writing in Stevenson's Early Travel Books. *Nineteenth-Century Prose,* 23(1), p. 54–73.

Copland, J., 1858. *A Dictionary of Practical Medicine.* London: Longman, Brown, Green, Longmans & Roberts.

Dunglison, R., 1844. *Human Health.* Philadelphia(PA): Lea and Blanchard.

Edel, L., 1962. *Henry James: The Conquest of London 1870–1883.* London: Rupert Hart-Davis.

Francis, D. J. T., 1853. *Change of Climate Considered as a Remedy in Dyspeptic, Pulmonary, and Other Chronic Affections.* London: John Churchill.

Hawthorne, N., [1860] 2002. *The Marble Faun.* Oxford: Oxford World's Classics.

James, H., [1878] 1999a. Daisy Miller: A Study. In: W. L. Vance, ed. *Complete Stories 1874–1884.* New York: Library of America, p. 238–295.

James, H., [1878] 1999b. Longstaff's Marriage. In: W. L. Vance, ed. *Complete Stories 1874–1884.* New York: Library of America, p. 296–325.

James, H., 1974. *Letters, Vol. 1: 1843–1875.* London: Macmillan.

Jankovic, V., 2006. The Last Resort: A British Perspective on the Medical South, 1815–1870. *Journal of Intercultural Studies,* 27(3), p. 271–298.

Johnson, J., 1831. *Change of Air or the Diary of a Philosopher in Pursuit of Health and Recreation.* London: S. Highley.

LeFew-Blake, P., 2004. 'Ordered South': The Spatial Sense of the Invalid in Robert Louis Stevenson's Early Travel Essay. *Nineteenth-Century Prose,* 31(1), p. 121–132.

Lindsay, J. A., 1887. Climate as a Therapeutic Agent in Phthisis. 30 April, p. 871–873.

Linn, T., 1893. *The Health Resorts of Europe.* London: Henry Kimpton.

Pall Mall Gazette, 1872. Transportation by Order of Medicine. *Pall Mall Gazette,* 18 May, p. 10.

Pemble, J., 1987. *The Mediterranean Passion: Victorians and Edwardians in the South.* Oxford: Oxford University Press.

Phipps, C. H., 1825. Change of Air. In: *The English in Italy.* London: Saunders and Otley, p. II: 112–135.

Pollock, J. E., 1850. Considerations on the Climate of Italy, with reference to the Treatment of Chronic Disease. *London Medical Gazette,* Volume 11, pp. 963–966, 1015–1019.

Scoresby-Jackson, R. E., 1862. *Medical Climatology; or, a Topographical and Meteorological Description of the Localities Resorted to in Winter and Summer by Invalids of Various Classes, both at Home and Abroad.* London: John Churchill.

Shelley, P. B., 2003. *The Major Works.* Oxford: Oxford World's Classics.

Stephen, J. F., 1860. Luxury. *Cornhill Magazine,* Volume 2, pp. 345–353.

Stevenson, R. L., [1874] 1926. Ordered South. In: *Virginibus Puerisque and Across the Plains.* Oxford: Oxford University Press, p. 82–96.

The Lancet, 1872. Transportation by Medical Order. *The Lancet,* 25 May. p. 729.

Young, D., 1886. *Rome in Winter and the Tuscan Hills in Summer: A Contribution to the Climate of Italy.* London: H. K. Lewis.

9   Climate change and literary history

Thomas H. Ford

What does climate mean?

The Western history of the concept of climate is intertwined in quite complex ways with the history of the concept of meaning, which entails that even when controversies surrounding the contemporary scientific meaning of climate change are set aside, as I will largely do here, the answer to the question – what does climate mean? – is far from straightforward. Since the early modern period at the latest, climate has often been thought of as meaningful because climates have been understood to shape distinct cultural worlds, exercising a formative influence over the actions and lives of all those who dwell within them. Different climates, this old story runs, shape different national characters, dividing up the human species racially, politically, culturally, linguistically and so on. The intellectual history of this argument, from its classical sources in Herodotus and Hippocrates, through its re-activation in such modern disciplines as political science, anthropology, literary history and geography – by Montesquieu, Herder, Taine and Huntington Ellsworth respectively – is too well-known to need any detailed rehearsal here (Boia, 2005; Peet, 1985; Livingstone, 2002; Fleming, 2005). Equally well-established are the ideological functions that climatic determinism has often served, notably providing colonialist projects, for instance, with ostensibly natural and scientific legitimations (Frenkel, 1992). My focus in this chapter, to begin with, is restricted solely to the circular relationship this type of argument tends to set up between climate and meaning – the idea being that if cultural meanings are climatically determined, then climates must in some sense already be intrinsically meaningful. And climatic determinism is just one of a number of ways in which climate has functioned historically as a recursive concept – a concept, that is, the deployment of which has often entered into a circle, to become a reflection on the nature of conceptuality itself.

One of the principal ways in which the word 'climate' has been used since it first entered the English language, its cognates concurrently entering other modern European languages, was to designate the totality of meaning that shapes and colours all discourse in a given historical moment or delimitable cultural formation. In consequence, it often became difficult to disentangle thinking about the meaning of climate from thinking about the meaning of meaning, so that climatic theories retraced some familiar philosophical paradoxes of linguistic self-reference. In what follows, I describe this circular self-referentiality of climate as one dimension of a more general paradox of atmosphere, which I analyse first by looking at the semantics of 'climate' in the twentieth century, and then as it emerges in the linguistic philosophy of Ludwig Wittgenstein – a paradox that complicates any inquiry into the meaning of climate. Having linked this paradox back to climate's classical etymological roots, I then turn to Hyppolite Taine's *History of English Literature*, first published in French in 1863 and translated into English in 1871, for a model of literary history that sought to make this climatic paradox operational, locating in climate's semantic ambiguity a means for parsing the complex co-implications of writing and its environments.

Climate, *climat*, 'climate'

In a 1937 essay on the meaning of the French word *climat*, the Romance philologist Rosemarie Burkart identified what she termed the 'modern meaning' of climate in the word's shift from having a strictly natural scientific frame of reference to acquiring in addition an extended meaning evident in such phrases as 'the political climate' or 'the intellectual climate' (Burkart, 1937). She described this development as 'the transition from the concrete to the metaphorical meaning', dating it roughly to the early years of the twentieth century. 'Climate', in this figurative meaning referred to 'the characteristic atmospheric or moral conditions of a region, a personality, an ideology which as such establish and exercise a particular changeable agency over the individual exposed to them' (192). (The fact that Burkart in effect uses 'atmospheric' and 'moral' here as near synonyms is very much to her point.) For Burkart, climate's scientific meaning was overlaid in the early twentieth century by a more figurative and cultural significance, which may well have borrowed semantic elements from the word's primary sense, but which nonetheless remained metaphoric, and so derivative and indeed essentially separate. A metaphoric climate is cultural, not natural. But a closer survey of the philological record complicates Burkart's narrative, for it calls into question the sharp and somewhat ahistorical division that was assumed by Burkart to lie between climate's scientific and what she saw as its purely metaphorical meanings. And it also greatly extends that narrative in time, pushing the interplay between these two meanings of 'climate' back into the early modern period.

Writing a decade prior to Burkart, for example, Alfred North Whitehead stated that the true subject of his book *Science and the Modern World* was 'the climate of opinion' – a phrase, he noted, that he had first encountered in writings from the mid-seventeenth century (1926, p. 4). The expression 'the political climate' was in common use in English by the mid-eighteenth century at the latest. 'Moral climate', 'spiritual climate' and 'intellectual climate' were all well established in the lexicon by the early decades of the nineteenth century. The currency of these idioms perhaps helps account for the fact that, in the first appearance of 'climatology' in English – a translation of Herder's new German coinage, *Klimatologie* – the term was essentially equivalent to anthropology, being defined as the cultural and historical science of 'all the sensitive and cognitive faculties of man' (Herder, 1800, p. I: 174). The phrase 'climate of ideas' entered the language somewhat later, but appears to have been in frequent use by the mid-nineteenth century. Set against this background, the expression 'the cultural climate' appears rather anomalous, apparently not having been coined until the middle of the twentieth century. That comparatively late semantic development may well tell us more about the slow evolution of the word 'culture' than it does about the history of the word 'climate'. For the philological record makes clear that culture was understood in climatic terms long before the emergence of our modern concept of culture itself.

It remains largely true today, as it was for Burkart in the 1930s, that the meaning of such phrases as 'the political climate' or 'the economic climate' is circumscribed broadly by what are generally understood to be the limits of human culture. We tend to think of such climates as metaphors or figures of speech, and as referring to phenomena that occupy an ontological order quite separate from the actual climates studied by actual climatologists. But for us, unlike Burkart, this metaphoric understanding is increasingly unsustainable, given that climate and its human limits are amongst the most intensely contested political questions of our times, and given that the political climate is now widely recognised as influencing the physical climate. But again, rather than focus here on the contemporary collapse of metaphoric into literal climates, I want instead to recover some aspects of the history of this distinction: first, to suggest that it has always been blurrier than we might have thought; and second, to link this persistent blurriness or undecidability between literal and metaphoric climates, to which the philological archive testifies, to the formal paradox that results from the use of 'climate' as a term for a totality or encompassing environment of meaning. For Whitehead, for example, the 'climate of opinion' named the mentality or collective state of mind in which certain ideas first became thinkable, while others faded unnoticed from view. Whitehead's 'climate of opinion' is a useful term for historians, N. Katherine Hayles has more recently suggested, because rather than invoking mechanical or efficient models of cultural causation, it instead suggests an underlying and pervasive background of multidirectional and reciprocal influences (1984, p. 22). For Hayles, such a climate is best understood as an ambient social mood or shared framework of largely unrecognised presuppositions – collective ways of seeing and thinking that seem somehow to be simply 'in the air' at a given moment. 'Climate of opinion', that is, names the interconnectedness and diffuse unity of a world of meaning. Climate, while functioning as a singular element in the modern semantic system, has then also been used prominently as a name for any semantic system taken as a whole. And so to speak about climate is to encounter the set of paradoxes that ensue whenever we speak about the totality of what can be said, or speculate about what may lie beyond those limits: the unsayable. To illustrate how the language of climate so often folds into the self-referentiality of language, I want to turn now to Wittgenstein, before coming back to some of the ambiguities suggested by climate's semantic history.

Wittgenstein's atmospheres

More than any other modern philosopher, Ludwig Wittgenstein performed and so formalised the basic paradox of linguistic self-reference. Indeed, commentators have seen in this paradox the key philosophical problem that impelled Wittgenstein's intellectual career, which can be read as a series of attempts to forestall and prevent linguistic self-referentiality. The basic problem has been neatly formulated by Boris Groys:

> Of course an outright prohibition can be placed on speaking about the whole of language and about the *logos* as such, as Wittgenstein demanded. However, such a prohibition is not only unnecessarily repressive, but is also contradictory in itself, for one must speak about the whole of language to be able to prohibit such speech (2009, p. 11–12).

Philosophical Investigations might then be understood as an attempt to defuse this paradox. This is what motivates, for example, his famous definition of meaning: 'the meaning of a word is its use' ([1955] 2001, §43).[1] The guiding idea is that it is a mistake to think that we can appeal to some fact outside language in order to discover the meaning of a term within a language, and that this is particularly mistaken when it comes to such general terms as 'meaning' itself. By ceasing to speak about words like 'meaning' in this way, Wittgenstein suggested, we could then begin to see that traditional philosophical problems which had centred on such terms as 'knowledge' and 'being' were essentially misunderstandings of the nature of language. Metaphysics required us to somehow lift ourselves outside of language in order to speak about language as such, language as a totality. And the basic problem with such a belief, Wittgenstein argued, was that 'Language is not *contiguous* to anything else. We cannot speak of the use of language as opposed to anything else. So, in philosophy, all that is not gas is grammar' (1989, p. 112); language has no such 'outside', and attempts to push it beyond the limits of use produce only vapid 'gassing'. Wittgenstein's anti-philosophy was dedicated to exposing these airy metaphysical mirages as so much windy confusion: 'What we are destroying are nothing but castles of air, and we are clearing up the ground of language on which they stood' (PI, §118, translation altered). Gas, castles of air, atmosphere: Wittgenstein repeatedly turned to this aerial vocabulary to describe the metaphysical illusions he wanted to deflate. Linguistic atmosphere, in this account, is what is produced when we mistakenly try to talk about language as a whole, and to describe the limits of meaning as if from beyond them.

But this attempt to avoid the paradoxes of linguistic self-reference by re-grounding meaning in use in fact only succeeded in reproducing them. Considered as a definition of meaning, Wittgenstein's account is notably circular, as is clear when his famous aphorism is returned to the full sentence in which it first appeared: 'For a *large* class of cases – though not for all – in which we employ the word 'meaning' it can be defined thus: the meaning of a word is its use in the language' (PI, §43). We know that the meaning of a word is its use, this sentence claims, because that is how the word 'meaning' itself has been used. But to set out to discover the meaning of 'meaning' in this way, by looking at a set of actual cases, is already to presuppose what you want to find out. In order to determine the meaning of a word, Wittgenstein suggested, we should look to its use. And yet he also advanced this definitional strategy in order to disallow certain types of use that generate only atmosphere or gas – as when we talk, for example, about meaning as such, or about the use of language as a whole. This is to treat some types of use as meaningful, and to rule out other types as giving only an illusory atmosphere of meaning. A prior judgement about what is properly meaningful would appear to delimit the field of use that is supposed to explain, in turn, what meaning is, and to distinguish meaning from mere gassy atmosphere. The circularity of Wittgenstein's definition of meaning leads to an infinite regress, as has been shown, amongst others, by Graham Priest (1995, p. 228–235).

And yet, throughout Wittgenstein's life and works there is a line of atmospheric thought that runs counter to his critical attacks on linguistic atmosphere. Wittgenstein, whose first academic job had involved testing kites at the University of Manchester's Kite Flying Upper Atmosphere Station, reportedly said that he saw his philosophy as having been written 'for people who would think in a quite different way, breathe a different air of life, from that of present-day men' (Wright, 1955, p. 527). One of the intellectual dangers of Cambridge, he once remarked, was that it was effectively airless: but 'it doesn't matter to me. I manufacture my own oxygen' (Monk, 1990, p. 6). In his *Philosophical Investigations*, Wittgenstein had sought to prohibit self-reflexive meta-statements – statements, that is, which described, as if from outside, the limits of the language in which they were formulated: 'You can never get outside it, you must always turn back. There is no outside; outside you cannot breathe' (PI, §103). Beyond the common ground of language lies only asphyxiation – or the intoxications of metaphysical gas. Yet Wittgenstein's self-reflective remarks hint, conversely, at an abiding desire for atmospheric transcendence, potentially orienting philosophy to the manufacture of new linguistic climates: to making its own oxygen, so to speak. Perhaps there is an outside, after all – or at least a blurrily liminal breathing-space on the atmospheric margin of language.

In some rather cryptic late comments, Wittgenstein appeared to retract his idea that atmosphere was what befell language when speech strayed beyond meaningful use. Instead, he proposed atmosphere to be a linguistic means for communicating an encompassing non-linguistic field. Atmosphere then figures a potential way of speaking meaningfully about the limits of language. In the manuscripts published as *Last Writings on the Philosophy of Psychology*, Wittgenstein suggested that the expression 'the word has an atmosphere', although figurative, was nonetheless comprehensible, a point he advanced in considering slight phonemic and graphic variations of common words. 'For example, the word "knoif" [*Sabel*] has a different atmosphere from the word "knife" [*Säbel*]. They have the same meaning, *insofar* as they are both names for the same kind of objects' (1996, §726). By twisting the word 'knife' into 'knoif' – an invented variant with the same denotative meaning, but which looks and sounds slightly different – Wittgenstein introduces his notion of a word having an 'atmosphere' that is non-identical with its meaning. This atmosphere relates to the word's sonorous and graphic particularity as illustrated in the difference *knife/knoif*, rather than to its referential scope, which in this case remains unaltered by an atmospheric difference. But while linguistic atmosphere appears to reside in the non-signifying specificity of the word as a distinct vocalised and inscribed object, it also evokes more loosely associated elements of feelings, moods and memories, invoking the haze of recollection and emotion that seems to cluster around certain words. Perhaps significantly, Wittgenstein's example for this involves music: 'The "atmosphere,"' he wrote,

> is precisely that which one cannot imagine as absent. The name Schubert, shadowed around by the gestures of his face, of his works. – So there is an atmosphere after all?…these surroundings seem to be fused with the name itself, with the word (1994, p. 4).

As such, the word 'Schubert', Wittgenstein suggested, could be associated with the atmosphere of Schubert's music: 'I feel as if the name "Schubert" fitted Schubert's works and Schubert's face' (PI, §183e). 'Schubert' then seems to subsist in a connotative swirl of half-remembered melodies, and so to communicate a singular historical experience of music, although this is one that may well lie beyond the realm of fully articulable meaning. These remarks position atmosphere as something that is conveyed by language and that takes place in language, something shaped and tinged by words, and yet that is bound up with the asemantic material specificity of the word. Indeed, Wittgenstein would even suggest it is not in fact meaning but rather 'the atmosphere of a word' that is its use (1994, p. 38). Atmosphere, rather than being what language generates in the absence of meaning, comes instead to resemble meaning, and even to convey meaning, for it is without question positioned here as a communicative dimension of language. As we have seen, 'climate' has often functioned as the name for the enabling (or constraining) totality of linguistic uses, the whole historical set of what can meaningfully be said. Wittgenstein's late notion of linguistic atmosphere suggests another way in which such a linguistic climate may be understood: atmosphere is what reaches beyond that set or climate of meaning to articulate, however fuzzily, the unnameable and the inexpressible, what lies on the other side of meaning, what cannot yet be said.

However provocative or far-reaching the implications of Wittgenstein's rethinking of atmosphere, he was careful nonetheless to insist that, in speaking of the atmospheres of words, he was not speaking literally. 'The word has an atmosphere,' he wrote, '– A figurative expression' (1996, §726). Linguistic atmospheres were seen to be comprehensible only as figures of speech. They remained bound up by a specific limiting context: namely, the language-game of metaphor and figure. In effect, Wittgenstein appealed to the same semantic distinction described by Burkart. On the one side, there are literal and scientific climates and atmospheres; on the other, figurative, fictional and metaphoric climates of meaning. But while Wittgenstein's late remarks on atmosphere distinguish the atmospheres of language from those of the world, they also serve to identify this distinction as the site of a paradox. Indeed, atmosphere in Wittgenstein's account makes for a notably vague, mobile and elusive boundary-object. It seems, for instance, to be transmedial: in atmosphere, language merges with recollections of music in a haze of meaning enveloping the word 'Schubert'. It is generated by language, and is even writable – the atmosphere of 'knoif' differs from that of 'knife', for instance – but it also works to blur and fray the limits of language. Wittgenstein's atmospheres are at once singular and vague, particular and indeterminable, communicable yet outside of meaning. They point to a paradoxical and para-linguistic dimension that erodes away the foundational distinction between figurative and metaphoric that Wittgenstein had previously instituted in order to introduce the notion of linguistic atmospheres into philosophy.

Climate, *clima*, clinamen

Despite these late and suggestive comments, atmosphere remained a relatively minor category for Wittgenstein, as it has arguably been for most modern philosophers of language. Indeed, Luce Irigaray ([1983] 1999) went so far as to convict the tradition of Western philosophy of a wholesale 'forgetting of air'. But while this may have been true when Irigaray was writing in 1983, air seems no longer to be forgotten by philosophy today, with a growing number of theorists proposing atmosphere to be an indispensable category for the philosophical comprehension of the present (Böhme, 1995; Sloterdijk, 2004; Anderson, 2009). One of the speculative appeals of atmosphere for these writers is precisely the way in which it seems to blur – or even entirely disallow – any firm distinction between figurative and literal climates. Wittgenstein's late notion of atmosphere describes both aspects of this complex and ambiguous structure of meaning. On the one hand, it takes the distinction between figurative and literal atmospheres to be foundational. On the other, it erodes this distinction from within, for figurative atmospheres spill beyond the limits of language to draw non-linguistic experiential qualities – tones, sounds, memories of music, raw elements of the texture of being – into the realm of communicable meaning. In formalising this paradox, Wittgenstein gave philosophical description to the doubled function that climate had long served in self-descriptions of modern knowledge: of at once marking a distinction between figurative and literal language, and of erasing that distinction in the same breath. And this paradoxical logic of atmosphere can be found at work in a much wider cultural history of climatic and aerial writing.

In a recent essay on 'The History of Air' in *Hamlet*, for example, Carla Mazzio reads early modern theatre as an technology or medium for exhibiting the aerial limits of instrumentality, including language (Mazzio, 2009). As Prospero remarks of theatricality in *The Tempest*, 'these our actors / As I foretold you, were all spirits, and / Are melted into air, into thin air.' On Mazzio's reading, the fact that this most metatheatrical of Shakespeare's plays is also the most meteorological is no coincidence. Steven Connor similarly describes seventeenth and eighteenth century figures of air in similar terms as 'recursively self-designating', involving a 'reflexive doubling' (Connor, 2010, p. 63). Early modern reference points such as these serve to remind us that the period when climate first began to be constructed scientifically as an atmospheric zone or dynamic and fluid system was also the same moment in which the term first came to be employed in its ambiguously figurative sense, as in 'the climate of opinion'. Indeed, the self-referential paradox of atmosphere often marked air's appearance as a troubling and liminal dimension on both the technical margin of early modern scientific knowledge, and on the aesthetic margin of the secularising humanities (Shapin & Schaffer, 1986; Lewis, 2012). Climate's ambiguity thus played a central part in the modern discursive formation of these diverse fields of knowledge, and of their differences from each other. But for all their singular modernity, these shifts in meaning also reactivated a semantic potential latent in earlier understandings of climate, which had linked climate to the ambiguities and slippages of meaning itself.

Prior to this early modern moment, the word 'climate' had been primarily a technical term of geometric and geographical knowledge, not a term connected to the weather or to the aerial environment. The etymology of climate is well-established: the word stems from the Latin *clima*, which in turn developed from the Greek verb κλίνειν, which meant to lean, slope or deviate – such words as 'decline', 'inclination' and 'clinic' all come from the same Greek root. Climate named the differing inclinations at which the sun's rays strike different points on the Earth's surface: climate was, in effect, a solar and geometrical expression of latitude. And this meaning persisted as the term's primary scientific frame of reference well into the nineteenth century, when it was finally replaced by our current sense of climate as a global thermodynamic atmospheric system. Dictionaries and encyclopedias from the early nineteenth century continued to distinguish between what they saw as climate's correct, geometrical meaning, and its merely 'vulgar' sense of a region defined by the prevailing temperature of the air.

These etymological and philological continuities, which run far into the modern period, relate our word 'climate' to the Lucretian term 'clinamen', which derives from this same Greek root-verb κλίνειν. Clinamen has become a familiar term within contemporary critical theory thanks to its recuperation by some influential post-structuralist thinkers, including Derrida, Deleuze, Lacan, Althusser, Badiou, Serres and others. Here, I want only to note how Lucretius' own description of the clinamen (and its associated vocabulary: *declinare, inclinare*) resonates with his description of the climate, which he understands in its ancient, geometrical sense. In the clinamen, Lucretius writes,

> When the atoms are carried straight down through the void
> By their own weight, at an utterly random time
> And a random point in space they swerve a little,
> Only enough to call it a tilt in motion.
> For if atoms did not tend to lean, they would
> Plummet like raindrops through the depths of space… (Lucretius, 1995, p. 63)

The language of swerving here is rejoined later, in Book 5, when Lucretius recounts how there is, in his words,

No reason, simple and direct...
For how the sun from his summer quarters swerves
To his midwinter turn in Capricorn
Then veers back into Cancer... (176)

The clinamen, the infinitesimal swerve that was for Lucretius the locus of human freedom and also, by leading to the concatenation of different atoms, the source of all natural phenomena, is linguistically correlated here to climatic difference, to the swerves of the seasons and the changing inclinations of the Sun's appearance in the sky. And this Lucretian connection of climate and clinamen was recovered in modernity, according, at least, to Louis Althusser, by Montesquieu, who in effect brought modern political science into being by refiguring climate as a concept of political analysis. Montesquieu's category of climate, Althusser argued, marked the first appearance in the modern understanding of politics of a conception of history as 'the concatenation of heterogeneous political forms and the contingent encounters between them' (Peden, 2015). Notoriously, Montesquieu is also the person who gave climatic determinism its modern canonical form. But if we re-read Montesquieu's climates via Lucretius, as Althusser suggested, it would seem that climatic determinism may actually involve a paradoxical rethinking of determinism as clinomatic indeterminacy (Althusser, 2006). This is because, for Althusser, Montesquieu's theory of climate gave expression to the central problem of modern political history, which is that of the intelligibility of contingency, of the meaningfulness of the randomness of what happens.

Climate has then long named atmospheric conjunctures in which the distinction between human systems of meaning and their material media grow vague. Climate has meant meaning – meaning in its swerves, silences and unpredictable shifts, in the unanticipated intersections it effects, in its irreducible ambiguities, in its undecidability between literality and metaphor. It describes language's tendency to lean, veer or slope when it is used to describe itself. Climate is not the smooth fall of atoms in the void, but the chaotic deviation through which those distinct elements come into sudden conjunctions with each other, giving rise to new forms. Climate designates the historical indeterminacy of meaning as the meaning of history's own indeterminacies. Climate has then always also meant change, naming both shifts within semantic structure and also those more paradoxical transitions from semantic systems to whatever may lie beyond them. Understanding climate in light of this philology might help restore to critical legibility a whole series of apparently now moribund literary and cultural theories that took it as a central term for their analysis of the social field: Taine's *History of English Literature* (1871), for example.

Writing climatic culture

Taine is a figure who has almost entirely disappeared from contemporary literary critical discussion. Although he was a vital touchstone for cultural thought of the later nineteenth century – his followers and admirers included Zola, Nietzsche and Bergson – when he is not forgotten altogether, he now tends to be seen as trivial and redundant. But Taine's ideas still shape the practice of literary history, if in selective and often unnoticed ways. Indeed, for Peggy Kamuf, it is precisely because Taine is no longer read that we risk uncritically perpetuating aspects of his intellectual program – specifically, of his ambition 'to make of art the object of a methodical science', in the interests of legitimising literary study as a discipline within the modern university (1997, p. 89). Kamuf touches here on questions about the social functions of literary research, and about its relationship with the hard sciences – questions which are being asked with renewed urgency in the era of climate change, which appears to be overturning the traditional disciplinary settlement or division of labour between the sciences and the humanities. But whatever appeal the synthesis of science and literature may now have, or may once have had in an earlier moment, Taine's own attempt at this synthesis has long appeared to present an intellectual dead end. The consensus view is that he is radically incoherent, at once too scientifically systematic – too committed to the discovery of law-like regularities within literary production – and too impressionistic, romantic and stylistically florid: in short, too literary. Kamuf's deconstructive reading pushes this sense of inconsistency further. The tension between Taine's methodological claims and his rhetorical techniques, she states, indicates 'a fundamental instability in the scientific foundation of the modern university' (1997, 91). Trying to make art scientific, Taine ends up demonstrating that science is actually a kind of art. We might refine this point for our own climatic moment: Taine's literary history suggests that the production of knowledge can never be finally disambiguated from the politics of inquiry in any discipline, whether of the sciences or the humanities. To me, that suggestion seems quite relevant to our current situation, in which something as apparently value-neutral as the measurement of air temperature has become a matter of political dissent.

The borders of climate change are notoriously indefinable: it is, in Sheila Jasanoff's words, 'everywhere and nowhere' (2010, p. 237). Climate change renders cause and influence diffuse and indeterminate. Today, any cataclysmic weather event – hurricane, drought, heatwave or cold-snap – will swiftly be followed by a public controversy over its cause. Does this strange weather fall within the parameters of natural variability? Or can we identify some element of human responsibility? Logically, the same controversy could equally erupt at every moment of every day, about the weather we barely even notice and almost immediately forget, as well as about the great tele-mediated collective weather events of a globalising public sphere. If climate change is the new normal, it is because it can be very normal indeed, as well as extreme and hyperbolic. And because the carbon logic of climate change infiltrates every moment of our lives, and is implicitly at work in every action we take, however trivial, it becomes very difficult to tell where climate change really starts, or ever finally comes to an end, in its causes as well as its effects, and in cultural and intellectual formations as much as in more purely physical processes. Ecologists are fond of the maxim that correlation does not imply causation. But climate change introduces the disconcerting suspicion that we might need to reverse this slogan: it hints at forms of latent causation that may exceed or elude any contemporary perception of actual correlation. Once you start pulling the loose threads of climatic action at a distance, the fabric of causality never ceases to unravel. We cannot help but suspect that climate change is present in ways which are impossible to pinpoint, and that largely escape notice, even as we recognise these unknowable quantities as ultimately ours.

Part of the difficulty of analysing the subgenre of climate change novels, for example, is the impossibility of knowing where to draw the line. Take the case of Don DeLillo's *White Noise* (1985). The novel's central section is titled 'The Airborne Toxic Event'. More widely, it describes a pervasive postmodern atmosphere of anxiety, electronic mediation, finitude and consumerism. The vital element of contemporary life, *White Noise* suggests, is a manufactured affective atmosphere. All that was solid has melted into air conditioning. But the doom-laden climate of *White Noise*, at once physical and cultural, cannot be correlated with climate change via any one-to-one schema of indexical representation. The novel's airborne toxic event may well be anthropogenic, but it is clearly not global warming. And yet, on the other hand, this airborne toxic event can never be finally dissociated from climate change. *White Noise* describes our time as one of a generalised climatic anxiety, and so actively solicits being read with a type of conspiratorial or premonitory logic, through a hermeneutics of atmospheric suspicion. Climate change institutes a similar kind of ambiguity or fundamental undecidability within all our cultural signs. The glimpses we get of it hint murkily at unrepresentable changes just beyond our perception, perhaps projected into the future, perhaps withdrawing into the opacity of the present. By eliciting this kind of irreducible suspicion, climate change presents us with something like a collective material unconscious, a realm of self-inflicted but often unrecognisable determination and compulsion. Taine's term for precisely this type of all-pervasive yet elusive determination was, in fact, 'climate'. Climate for Taine was a realm of ineradicable yet obscure and ambiguous traces – material scripts which record our actions and shape our being and yet escape not just our control but also potentially the limits of our perception, whether they be understood aesthetically or scientifically.

One reason almost no one reads Taine today is because he is seen as a strong climatic determinist. He notoriously claimed that if we could measure and compute climate and the other environmental and social forces of literary determination, then 'we might deduce from them as from a formula the specialities of future civilization' (1871, p. 1:14). This is a type of predictive claim that literary historians today tend to discount harshly. But as Kamuf suggests, there is more play in Taine's system than may be at first apparent from determinist claims like this. Indeed, Taine immediately goes on to discount this claim himself, writing that the 'crudeness of our notations' and the 'fundamental inexactness of our measures' mean that we can in fact only ever hope for a vague prophecy of our future destiny, rather than any scientifically precise prediction (1:14). Writing and notation, understood as the inescapable material mediation of knowledge, distance literary history inescapably from predictive formulations, instead restricting it to spectral and uncertain prophecies. So what at first might appear as a hubristic claim to deterministic scientific knowledge in Taine might in fact be better understood as a moment of medial self-reflection, for writing is a medium that literary history shares with its subject matter, literature. The paradoxes of self-reference thereby entailed are part of the reason why literary history is often seen as an impossible discipline. And Taine seems more aware of these medial paradoxes of knowledge than he is often given credit for. He repeatedly positions writing as a medium of uncertainty and variability, locating within it a mode of self-differentiation that opens it to an unknown future. Taine tends to do this, particularly, in moments of disciplinary self-reflection, as in his discussion, in the methodological 'Introduction' to his *History of English Literature*, of whether literary history can predict the destiny of civilizations, in passages, that is, in which he reflects most directly on the challenges of writing history. If we take Taine's fundamental claim to be that climate determines literature – that climate determines writing – such moments suggest how Taine's own theory of writing unsettles this notion of determination. Taine co-implicates climate and writing; one determines the other. But is it his writing that first allows this claim to be advanced, or is it the climate in which he writes? Circularity and self-reflexivity are so built into the theory that a final answer to this question can never be given.

Although Taine is now often seen as an early and failed sociologist of literature, the scope of the determinative forces he considers extends well beyond the limits of human societies. 'Social history,' Taine declares, 'is but a prolongation of natural history' (Taine, quoted in Brown 1997, p. 60). The forces included within his tri-partite conceptual grid of race, milieu and moment – the system he presents in his 'Introduction' – are environmental as well as social and political, as the central case of climate makes clear. It is this ontological inclusiveness that led Kenneth Rexroth to credit Taine with the first 'ecological theory of literature' – in what appears to be the first appearance of that phrase in print (Rexroth, 1987, p. 294). 'Hyppolyte Taine,' Rexroth wrote,

> evolved an ecological theory of literature. He looked first and foremost to the national characteristics of western European literatures, and he found the source of these characteristics in the climate and soil of each respective nation (loc. cit.).

Nonetheless, Rexroth continued, 'It is doubtful that anyone today would agree with the simplistic terms in which Taine states his thesis' (ibid.).

I will return a little later to the reason why Rexroth thought Taine had been discredited – the reason, that is, why we cannot accept climate as the ultimate inter-pretative horizon of literary writing, at least as Taine formulated this position. But first I want to consider a possible reason Rexroth could have given for dismissing Taine, but didn't. It is a surprising omission, because what Rexroth left out has in fact been the primary argument over the last few centuries against climatic deter-minism. Simply put, the argument attacks the notion that climates shape cultures on the basis of its ahistoricism. More broadly, it asserts the primacy in human affairs of social communication over environmental influence. Perhaps the most celebrated example is David Hume's refutation of the idea that climatic differences cause dis-tinct national types of subjectivity. In his 1748 essay 'Of National Characters', Hume wrote that

> Our ancestors, a few centuries ago, were sunk into the most abject superstition, last century they were inflamed with the most furious enthusiasm, and are now settled into the most cool indifference with regard to religious matters, that is to be found in any nation of the world (Hume, [1764] 1985, p. 206).

The English people had changed, and changed again, while their climate presumably had not. And if radical social transformations could occur independently of any atmospheric alteration, then climate was effectively valueless as an explanatory category of historical understanding: no correlation, therefore no causation. Rexroth had good reason not to deploy this argument against Taine, however, for in Taine climate, rather than being history's determining other, is actually the hidden truth of history, an immanent, motive power of social and cultural self-transformation. To see how this is so, I want to look a little more closely at Taine's conceptual trinity of race, milieu and moment.

Climate, race, milieu and moment

Race, for Taine, is the site of biologically inherited predispositions, what he calls 'differences in the temperament and structure of the body' (Taine 1871, 1:10). The history of race may run slowly, over vast stretches of time, but remains historical for Taine. He writes, for instance, of the 'almost immovable steadfastness of [these] primordial marks' – a phrase in which I want to stress the word 'almost' (1:10). Race is only 'almost' unchanging, and what appears to change it, most significantly, are climatic changes. Taine writes:

> As soon as an animal begins to exist, it has to reconcile itself with its surroundings; it breathes after a new fashion, renews itself, is differently affected according to the new changes in air, food, temperature. Different climate and different situation bring it various needs, and consequently a different course of actions; and this, again, a different set of habits; and still again, a different set of aptitudes and instincts. Man, forced to accommodate himself to circumstances, contracts a temperament and a character corresponding to them; and his character, like his temperament, is so much more stable, as the external impression is made upon him by more numerous repetitions, and is transmitted to his progeny by a more ancient descent. So that at any moment we may consider the character of a people as an abridgment of all its preceding actions and sensations (1:10–11).

Race can then be understood as the agency of climate viewed over a long evolutionary timescale. For Taine, it is something like an indelible – or *almost* indelible – biological record of past climates, a reader's digest of genotypic prehistory.

Milieu occupies a middle temporality. It involves what Taine calls 'these prolonged situations, these surrounding circumstances, persistent and gigantic pressures, brought to bear upon an aggregate of men who, singly and together, from generation to generation, are continually moulded and modelled by their action'

(1:12). Milieu is the primary category within which Taine locates the cultural agency of climate. Indeed, Taine often uses these terms, milieu and climate, almost interchangeably. But alongside climate, the category of milieu also includes the force of political forms and social conditions, bringing together natural and cultural factors. In his essay on 'Milieu and Ambience' Leo Spitzer (1942) attributes the word's adoption outside the French language to the prestige of Taine's theory; he also attributes the introduction and consolidation in other languages of broadly equivalent terms, notably including the words *Umwelt* in German and 'environment' in English, to the influence of Taine's term 'milieu' – a semantic history that underlies and justifies Rexroth's description of Taine as an ecological theorist of literature. We can already begin to see how Taine's categories shift about and morph into one another, how they are beset by a series of fundamental ambiguities. Where does milieu end and race begin? Both seem equally to be dimensions of climatic time. The milieux of the past determine race, which in turn determines how a being relates to its milieu in the present, and so on, circularly.

Whatever the complexities of their interrelationship, when taken together, race and milieu form an enduring archive of environmental history. At the opposite end of the temporal spectrum is the microchronology of the moment, Taine's final determining force of history. Moment involves the way the traces of race and milieu are imprinted on the present. Marshall Brown (1997) notes that 'Taine regards organisms not as beings that can reproduce themselves but as beings that can differ from themselves' (76). Moment is the primary site of this capacity for self-differentiation. At any given moment, Taine writes, the forces of race and milieu act 'not upon a *tabula rasa*, but on a ground on which marks are already impressed. According as one takes the ground at one moment or another, the imprint is different; and this is the cause that the total effect is different' (Taine, 1:12). As a figure for cultural reproduction, this is rather difficult to read: there is a ground on which marks are impressed, and which then imprints or re-marks itself variably on the present. This seems to involve taking a print of something already printed, or making an impression of an impression. But if the causal lines are hard to disentangle, it is nonetheless easy to recognise a process of mechanical reproduction here, even of something like a printing press – albeit a press that does not produce invariant, identical copies, but is instead devoted to differential repetition and the creation of errata-strewn singular editions. Moment, Taine states, can be reduced neither to an exact nor to an approximate formula. Instead, he writes 'we cannot have more, or give more, in respect of it [moment], than a literary impression' (Taine, 1:13). So moment, which is how sedimented climatic history is impressed on the historical present, can only enter knowledge via yet another imprecise and differential impression – a specifically literary one, even. I have already mentioned how Taine has often been read as a deeply inconsistent literary critic, committed to an impossible fusion of scientific determinism and literary impressionism. Taine's concept of moment suggests how fundamental this contradiction is to his model of literary history. It is necessarily entailed by his sense of historical time as a multi-layered surface of inscription, a palimpsest or mystic writing pad.

In *The Nature of Things* Lucretius described the origin of the universe as atoms falling through the void, like raindrops falling through space. Clinamen names the sudden deflection or deviation of an atom from this path, which leads it to bump into other atoms, thereby giving rise, ultimately, to the atomic combinations that underlie the world of everyday experience. The clinamen is unpredictable, apparently uncaused, and irreducible to prior determination. As such, it is also, for Lucretius, the basis for the freedom of living beings. Without the clinamen, atoms would continue to fall infinitely, unswerving, and without collision, so that there could be no history, or indeed no nature, even no being whatsoever. Given the close etymological and semantic relationship between climate and clinamen, Lucretius's notion of the clinamen suggests that climate might be a factor not only of fixity and territorialisation, but also one of indeterminacy. For Taine, race and milieu are forces of climatic determination. Moment, by contrast, names this aspect of climatic indeterminacy: climate as tendency or inclination, a vector of movement or change from a pre-existing state to a new one. Together, race, milieu and moment describe how history is at once determined and undetermined – determined precisely in this variability or lack of determinacy. Moment is the way climate encounters an unknown future.

So climate for Taine cannot be understood as standing outside of historical time, as an unchanging stage-set, a static set of parameters to which all actions necessarily conform. Instead, history consists of underlayers of near indelible climatic inscriptions, slowly accruing and metamorphising, and a top surface upon which these traces become differentially legible in the present. History for Taine is fragmented, composed of the disjunctive yet interweaving climatic strands of race, milieu and moment – distinct temporal dimensions of deep time, middle time and momentary transience. It may be possible, even, to draw some fairly precise parallels between Taine's three-way division of historical temporality and the multidimensional model of time developed by the *Annales* school of the mid-twentieth century. Race, milieu and moment, that is, can be mapped quite neatly onto the *longue durée* of structure, the medium history of conjuncture, and the flickering, ephemeral history of the event, as described by Fernand Braudel (1980). Braudel's model of the multiplicity of historical time now forms something of a theoretical touchstone for historians trying to come to grips with the conceptual challenges of writing the history of climate change. For climate change appears to collapse these discrete temporal orders into each other. It stages jarring intersections between deep climatic time, for instance, and the rapid temporality of everyday politics. How do you mediate between ice cores and election cycles? As Tom Griffiths (2010) has recently noted, Braudel's *longue durée* deals in 'awesome geological eras', while his history of events takes its maximum 'chronological scale from a human lifespan. The climate change crisis challenges us to connect these dimensions, to work audaciously across time and space and species.'[2] For Griffiths and others, the absence of any fleshed-out vehicle of mediation between these different temporal forms in Braudel is what points to the difficulty we confront today: it is up to us to fill this gap, and to generate forms of historical understanding that will somehow embed geological eras within the fleeting transience of contemporary political discourse. But if we take our model of historical temporality from Taine instead of from Braudel, then the challenge looks quite different. For in Taine, this vehicle of historical understanding, which is capable of shuttling between the glacial pace of lithification and the feverish pace of political decision, between the geological timescales of continental drift and the communicative ones of the public sphere, is nothing less than climate itself: climate, which is already installed within each of Taine's discrete orders of time, because he understands it as possessing the disjunctive and fissured temporality of writing, of simultaneous slow erasure and lightning inscription.

For a literary history of climate change

Rexroth's criticism of Taine, as we have seen, is not the standard argument directed against climatic determinism; namely, that it is insufficiently historical. Instead, Rexroth attacks the unquestioned national and racial frame of his literary history. In some ways, it is not even Taine's category of 'race' that is the real problem, however much his use of this term may jar with us today. For Taine's notion of race is of something unfixed, mobile and discursive, a motor of self-differentiation rather than a monolithic and inescapable essence. But an assumed organicism – organicism in the bad sense – does creep back into Taine in the form of the category of 'English', and it is this that Rexroth picks up on, writing:

> modern civilization becomes more and more a world civilization, wherein works of all peoples flow into a general fund of literature. It is not unusual to read a novel by a Japanese author one week and one by a black writer from West Africa the next. Writers are themselves affected by this cross-fertilization (Rexroth, 1987, p. 294).

Rexroth is basically following Marx's account in *The Communist Manifesto* of how capitalism creates world literature – one of capitalism's ambiguously liberatory and even potentially communist effects. So my first point of conclusion is this: if the literary history of climate change is to borrow anything from Taine, it will first need to attend, critically, to these vectors of world writing. If climate determines writing because it is a kind of writing, then it does so in modernity as an ever more global climate, one that is deterritorialised, released from regional specificity into the flux of what Rexroth calls 'wholesale cultural exchange' (294).

My second concluding point is that this critical reformulation is worth undertaking. Taine gives us a vocabulary that might help us describe an important type of change that climate change is exercising on the literary field, including literary criticism – that insidious, partly unconscious change that eludes precise description. The overlay Taine identifies between climate and writing hovers somewhere between literality and metaphor. It is this in-between status that generates its ambiguity, its indeterminacy, and its suggestive power. Climate change makes the statement that 'we write the climate' much more literal. Pieces of writing – legislation, contracts, treaties, judgements, but also perhaps the types of writing I have been discussing here – quite literally change the climate. But this shift doesn't entirely erase climate writing's constitutive metaphoricity. It ramifies the indeterminacy of climate writing, rather than removing it.

My final point addresses the disciplinary specificity of literary history. There is a view that climate change erases disciplinary boundaries, and that we could adequately address it only through some kind of popular front of all the disciplines. This may well be true, but there may also be reasons to pause before diving into any interdisciplinary melange. Climate change often presents us with a kind of cognitive impasse or breakdown, exceeding our conceptual and imaginative capacities. But literary history is also impossible, and for some of the same reasons. One mode of its impossibility involves paradoxes of self-reference – the fact, that is, that for literary criticism there really is no metalanguage, and barely even the presumption of one. Like climate, there is no outside. Literary history shares a second mode of impossibility with cultural history more broadly; namely, the attempt to understand the transhistorical power of an artwork by historicising it. Taine embraces this paradox. For him, the historical categories of race, milieu and moment can return to us the vocal presence of the dead. Perhaps it is these impossibilities that might allow literary history to speak meaningfully of climate change, as a discipline that reconvenes past climates of writing, even as it hollows out our current climate with writing's non-presence and ambiguity, opening it to an alternative and as yet undetermined future.

Notes

1 Hereinafter, PI. Subsequent references are to this edition.
2 See also Chakrabarty (2009).

References

Althusser, L., 2006. *Philosophy of the Encounter: Later Writings, 1978–87*. London: Verso.

Anderson, B., 2009. Affective atmospheres. *Emotion, Space and Society*, 2(2), p. 77–81.

Böhme, G., 1995. *Atmosphäre: Essays zur neuen Ästhetik*. Frankfurt am Main: Suhrkamp.

Boia, L., 2005. *The Weather in the Imagination*. London: Reaktion Books.

Braudel, F., 1980. *On History*. Chicago: University of Chicago Press.

Brown, M., 1997. *Turning Points: Essays in the History of Cultural Expressions*. Stanford: Stanford University Press.

Burkart, R., 1937. Climat. *Archivum Romanicum*, Volume 21, p. 185–199.

Chakrabarty, D., 2009. The Climate of History: Four Theses. *Critical Inquiry*, Volume 35, p. 197–222.

Connor, S., 2010. *The Matter of Air: Science and Art of the Ethereal*. London: Reaktion Books.

DeLillo, D., 1985. *White Noise*. New York: Viking Press.

Fleming, J. R., 2005. *Historical Perspectives on Climate Change*. Oxford: Oxford University Press.

Frenkel, S., 1992. Geography, empire, and environmental determinism. *Geographical Review*, 82(2), p. 143–153.

Griffiths, T., 2010. A Humanist on Thin Ice. *Griffith Review*, Volume 29, p. 67–117.

Groys, B., 2009. *The Communist Postscript*. London: Verso.

Hayles, N. K., 1984. *Cosmic Web: Scientific Field Models and Literary Strategies in the Twentieth Century.* Ithaca(NY): Cornell University Press.

Herder, J. G., 1800. *Outlines of a Philosophy of the History of Man.* London: Joseph Johnson.

Hume, D., [1764] 1985. *Essays Moral, Political, and Literary.* Indianapolis(IN): Liberty Fund.

Irigaray, L., [1983] 1999. *The Forgetting of Air in Martin Heidegger.* London: Athlone.

Jasanoff, S., 2010. A New Climate for Society. *Theory, Culture & Society,* Volume 27, pp. 233–253.

Kamuf, P., 1997. *The Division of Literature: Or the University in Deconstruction.* Chicago: University of Chicago Press.

Lewis, J. E., 2012. *Air's Appearance: Literary Atmosphere in British Fiction, 1660–1794.* Chicago: University of Chicago Press.

Livingstone, D. N., 2002. Race, space and moral climatology: notes toward a genealogy. *Journal of Historical Geography,* 28(2), p. 159–180.

Lucretius, 1995. *De Rerum Natura (On the Nature of Things).* Baltimore(MD): The Johns Hopkins University Press.

Mazzio, C., 2009. The History of Air: Hamlet and the trouble with Instruments. *South Central Review,* 26(1), p. 153–196.

Monk, R., 1990. *Ludwig Wittgenstein: The Duty of Genius.* New York: Penguin.

Peden, K., 2015. *Personal communication.* s.l.:s.n.

Peet, R., 1985. The social origins of environmental determinism. *Annals of the Association of American Geographers,* 75(3), p. 309–333.

Priest, G., 1995. *Beyond the Limits of Thought.* Cambridge(UK): Cambridge University Press.

Rexroth, K., 1987. *World Outside the Window: Selected Essays of Kenneth Rexroth.* New York: New Directions.

Shapin, S. & Schaffer, S., 1986. *Leviathan and the Air-Pump: Hobbes, Boyle, and the Experimental Life.* Princeton(NJ): Princeton University Press.

Sloterdijk, P., 2004. *Sphären III: Schäume.* Frankfurt am Main: Suhrkamp.

Spitzer, L., 1942. Milieu and Ambiance: An Essay in Historical Semantics. *Philosophy and Phenomenological Research,* Volume 3, p. 169–218.

Taine, H., 1871. *History of English Literature.* Edinburgh: Edmonston and Douglas.

Whitehead, A. N., 1926. *Science and the Modern World.* Cambridge(UK): Cambridge University Press.

Wittgenstein, L., [1955] 2001. *Philosophical Investigations.* 3rd ed. Oxford: Blackwell.

Wittgenstein, L., 1989. *Wittgenstein's Lectures: Cambridge, 1930–1932 From the Notes of John King and Desmond Lee.* Chicago: University of Chicago Press.

Wittgenstein, L., 1994. *Last Writings on the Philosophy of Psychology, volume 2: The Inner and the Outer, 1949–1951.* Oxford: Blackwell.

Wittgenstein, L., 1996. *Last Writings on the Philosophy of Psychology, volume 1.* 2nd ed. Chicago: University of Chicago Press.

Wright, G. H. v., 1955. Ludwig Wittgenstein, A Biographical Sketch. *The Philosophical Review,* Volume 64, p. 527–545.

Part III
Climates of politics

10 Climate change

Politics, excess, sovereignty

Nick Mansfield

Climate change discourse clusters around a series of key terms. Primary amongst these are 'mitigation' and 'adaptation'. These terms mobilise certain assumptions about our relationship to nature, the global political system and where we are situated in history. Central to these assumptions is a logic of stabilisation, preservation and reduction. Ecosystems must be allowed to function with only minimal impact from carbon emissions by a concerted effort to reduce them to the level they were at a certain historical moment. The international political system based around the sovereign autonomy of independent states must be respected as the key negotiating context for all agreements about climate change. The evolution of developing societies towards greater equality and prosperity must be allowed to continue. In this way, climate change discourse prioritises a language of fixity, continuity and return. According to this logic, the carbon culture has to continue, but its impact must be reduced to the lightest possible touch on a nature, world polity and social economy that are unfolding along an inevitable, perhaps even unquestionable, trajectory.

The aim of this chapter is to argue that despite the emphasis on continuity and preservation, the future that climate change discourse imagines is not one that is being preserved, or left to evolve unhindered, but that is being invented. This invention enacts specific assumptions about the nature of the historical, the political and the natural. Fundamental to these assumptions is the idea that the climate system, the political order and human social goals can be discussed as total, complete or fixed. Even when the processes of historical and climatic change are recognised as dramatic and disruptive, the world in which they will occur is given a set of fixed valences. It is perhaps inevitable that such fixed points be identified, but the decisions that lie behind them and the fact that they *are* decisions are obscured. To draw attention to this is not to discredit the logic of climate change discourse. The priorities it sets are neither more nor less artificial than any other priorities that might be chosen, but they are artificial. They involve a set of political decisions, made not to serve the logic of nature but on human terms, in order to serve human goods. This anthropocentrism has been much criticised, yet as I argue, it is inevitable, even necessary. The problem arises not because human beings make decisions on a human scale (what else can they do?), but because this process is dissimulated.

This dissimulation has a number of consequences. Firstly, in terms of the future of climate change discourse, the fact that the stable reference point for climate change discourse is arbitrary deconstructs the opposition between climate change mitigation and adaptation, on which most future planning pivots. Secondly, the obscuring of the process needs to be analysed so that there can be a full and open acknowledgement of collective human responsibility for the future we are envisioning and the human nature of the possible future. If the future is being invented on human terms, it must be recognised as such. Most crucially, we must address the question as to whether the world-view that lies behind such decision-making is appropriate to the era of climate change, and the reconceptualisation of the relationship between the human and the extra-human it will involve. Not only are the decisions we make at stake, but do we need a new conceptualisation of what it is to make a political decision? This leads to the final consequence, which is that if some sense of collective responsibility is acknowledged, then it must be based in a construction of sovereignty: who takes decisions, and who are they responsible to and responsible for? What would such a new understanding of sovereignty be in the era of climate change, and what would justify it?

Politics

The objective of the *United Nations Framework Convention on Climate Change* (United Nations, 1992) is the

> stabilization of greenhouse gases in the atmosphere at a level which would prevent dangerous anthropogenic interference with the climate system. Such a level should be achieved within a time-frame sufficient to allow eco-systems to adapt naturally to climate change, to ensure that food production is not threatened and to enable economic development to proceed in a sustainable manner (9).

The 'climate system' in question is 'the totality of the atmosphere, hydrosphere, biosphere and geosphere and their interactions' (7).

Climate change action is governed by two key political principles:

- The primacy of the international system of nation-states as the forum in which discussion will lead to decision (the *Framework* '[reaffirms] the principle of sovereignty of States in international cooperation to address climate change' (2)).
- The importance of acknowledging inequalities between nations, both in terms of their state of development (any action must 'take into full account the legitimate priority needs of developing countries for the achievement of sustained economic growth and the eradication of poverty' (6), which remain 'their first and overriding priorities' (14)) and their responsibility for damage to the climate (the *Framework* notes 'that the largest share of historical and current global emissions has originated in developed countries' (2)).

The benchmark for action will be the level of emissions of carbon dioxide in 1990 (12).

What is the world being characterised here? First, it is a world we have inherited complete. It can be grasped as a single thing, a 'totality', and the state and the needs of that totality can be known. Because we can grasp this world as a single totality, we can think of it as both an ecological and political system. This abstraction of the world as a single system trumps all the perspectivisms of history. Traditionally, human subjectivity has been constructed in relation to place, family, language, race, class, and religion. In the modern era, all of these have been subsumed in the larger formation of the nation. Now, they are to be superseded by a subject capable of grasping the world as a single co-ordinated thing. The political existence of nations may be acknowledged but nationality as a perspective is overwritten by our generalised human ability to see the world as whole and in the same way as one another. This promises both a depersonalisation and universalisation of human subjectivity, and thus the possible objectification of the subject as the inhabitant of the planet, first and foremost, and eventually perhaps, nothing more than that.

On the other side of this relationship, the totalisation of the object of this human subject has a significant meaning: the world is a single total system. This system is in place already and more or less complete. Change is part of its natural processes, but this change is gradual, not sudden, and should be allowed to continue as a slow process of development and adaptation. This process of evolution is most important in the social domain of economic development, whereby societies can meet their human goals, primarily defined in terms of social justice and the eradication of poverty. Sudden rupture is unwelcome, and thus notionally not part of the normal operation of the system. It appears here largely as the catastrophic consequence of anthropogenic interference, not as a normal part of the operation of the totality.

The human situation here is complex. Firstly, human beings live inside this totality because it is the physical context that surrounds and contains human life. It is the context within which all human activities take place; it is our *environment*, in the most literal sense of the word. In that way, it is larger than us; it encompasses and includes us. However, this physical totality is also an object of human thought. We can conceive of it intellectually as a single idea, that we can name, measure and discuss as if it is a single specific thing. This idea of the world is defined, positioned and determined by human conventions of thought and representation. Reduced to a single idea, the vast and complex human environment is contained within and therefore lesser than human thought. This creates a complex double situation in which the environment is the rich and diverse, superhuman context of which we occupy a tiny part, but simultaneously a representation defined on our own terms. This means the system both does and does not unfold on a human scale. It can be thought of as a single thing, graspable by human representation, but we do not live in it that way. As living creatures, the totality is always beyond us, infinitely vast. To be able to think of the system as a totality is a very different thing from living inside of it, as part of it. Being part of the system means the world is not reducible, as it is for thought, but always in excess of us.

By emphasising the ability to model, grasp and plan the world, the *Framework* must deny the necessary excessiveness of the world as lived by human beings. The form this denial takes is the construction of a taxonomy of human social needs that are compatible with the proper operation of the system. These needs are fundamentally liberal: they converge on physical sustenance, personal fulfilment and equal social opportunity. They do not privilege the fulfilment of any historical, national, racial, political, religious or any kind of teleological truths, which are now irrelevant. The *Framework* does not seek to interfere with these truths, but they are now radically privatised at the level of the group or individual subject. Since almost all the institutions we are used to, from the smallest community organisation to our nations and parliaments and beyond to our morally justified international bodies, were instituted to reflect such truths, it cannot be emphasised enough what an innovation this thinking is, no matter how much it now seems obvious and inevitable to us.

In sum, the world envisaged by the *Framework* is not an objectification of the world as it simply is. It constructs the world in a specific way as the enactment of a specific understanding of what human beings are and how we are situated. The world is a single thing understood as a system. Human beings are part of this system yet they also define and control it. They are responsible for it, but the measure of their responsibility is whether they can maintain it in such a state to safely fulfil their ongoing needs, defined as basically physical and economic, in the narrow sense. At the moment, historically, our role is not to change or invent a new world, but to maintain it on the trajectory it is on, to stabilise it as it more or less was at the time the *Framework* was drawn up. There is no claim that this is the ideal world. It is a world riven by injustice largely understood as differing stages of economic development. But the world to be stabilised – the world of 1990, the post-Cold War world of the New World Order – is the point at which we can still imagine the dream of the world of gradual adaptation and improvement is still on track, where dramatic change and sudden rupture have become marginal if not alien to history, and are not welcome to return.

The logic by which climate change mitigation and climate change adaptation are seen as separable relies on the assumption that this historical point – 1990 – is somehow a fixed measure. However, if 1990 is seen as a construct of how human life within the world system is imagined and not simply revealed, then the difference between mitigation and adaptation is simply between keeping this system on the track it was on in 1990, on the one hand, and, on the other, making adjustments so these same priorities can remain in place even if 1990 conditions cannot be restored. They represent not alternative attitudes to climate change but two options for living the same dream. What governs them both is a certain construction of human being in a certain imagined world.

The point is not that this way of thinking is wrong, but it is the invention of the future in the guise of a recovery of a norm, a decision that erases itself by a language of stabilisation, return and so on. The political decisions that lie behind such a construct are themselves not explained nor held up for scrutiny.

As we will see, they perpetuate a logic of human self-construction that sees the future as something humans make in the fulfilment of their own self-defined ends. This is not merely to say that it is anthropocentric. It is not merely a question of perspectives. Its logic is purely and simply political, the result of certain decisions made by empowered human groups in an historical context. Its primary tactic is to deny its political nature by adopting the image of a self-contained ecological system. This double logic – establishing political goals while denying they are political by reference to the indisputable nature of nature – works by excluding, denying or containing excess.

Excess

It is here I would like to return to the issue of excess raised above, where excess was seen in terms of the excess of the world as lived over the thinking subject. As Heidegger pointed out long ago (Heidegger, 1977), the grasping of the world in a single 'world picture' is a late and highly artificial development. This does not mean that it is less objective than other possible ways of thinking of the world – it is objectivity par excellence! – but that there is nothing absolute about it. It does not trump all other possible constructions of the world, nor subsume them. Its logic of totalisation has arisen to allow certain economic and strategic arrangements to be modelled and discussed. Yet, the world will always be in excess of any particular statement of it, even if this statement attempts to grasp the world in its totality. Each instance of grasping the world as a totality – or anything less – will always be a reduction of the world. In this way, the 'world' is implicitly in excess of its own versions. Any statement about the climate system in its totality therefore refers implicitly to that which exceeds it. There will always be by definition something the statement cannot include, either semantically (no generalisation is without exception) or structurally (the statement is itself only a fragment of the whole system it attempts to describe). This excess is not because the statements in question are themselves inadequate or poorly executed. It is because 'nature', of which the climate system even in its totality is a reduction, will always be larger than it is possible for us to grasp. In sum, a statement that purports to say something about the world as a totality contradicts itself. It supposes a total system, but cannot actually describe it. It assumes a totality that it cannot know. In short, it posits what is in excess of it as its own justification, and then exhibits that excess by failing to be able to describe it. It can only emerge in relation to that excess, but remains overwhelmed by it.

This excess of nature takes two forms: scale and knowledge. Firstly, nature is always much larger than any possible model of it, because nature is potentially infinite in both space and time. Secondly, any act of perception is subsidiary to this excessive totality, and must be a reduction of it, occurring only in specific events under specific conditions. These events take place in relation to all the other similar events that are alternative to them, and of equal value for the purposes of deriving truth. Let us now look at two writers who attempt to grapple with these issues.

The aim of Nigel Clark's *Inhuman Nature: Sociable Life on a Dynamic Planet* (2011) is to explore how social and political thought could engage more comprehensively with the insights of late twentieth-century earth sciences. Preliminary to this argument is an evaluation of post-Enlightenment philosophy's understanding of nature. For Clark, in modern western thought, the earth has usually been assumed to be the stable ground on which human history unfolds:

> The convulsions of nature that so perturbed Kant and fellow Enlightenment thinkers subsequently drifted far out of philosophical focus. So far, in fact, that whole schools would embrace the solidity of the earth beneath our feet – and assume that this abiding base offered 'thought' (a synecdoche for all human endeavour) its best or only foundation. While such a sense of earthly certitude has been repeatedly and thoroughly problematized, it has been troubled most often on account of the way that certain kinds of human experience – especially those associated with techno-cultural change – mediate between 'us' and the earth we stand upon. Even in the midst of the revolutionary discoveries of late twentieth-century earth science, there has only infrequently been any real consideration about what the planet's complex dynamics might mean for rethinking the 'ground' (23).

For conventional thought, then, the earth functions as the platform of human endeavour. It is simply the fixed point on which we stand to move worlds. It represents a limit to human thinking because the fundamental orientation of humans is intersubjective, and human-being is fundamentally social and political. Since what counts to modern thought is the process by which human beings structure and develop social systems, nature represents the mere frame on which we turn our backs and which we take for granted while we focus on the true site of dynamism called history. When human beings have turned towards nature in order to understand themselves, it has been towards biology and genetics, our continuity with other species, especially 'the continuity between biology and human expressive capacities' (24). Even when the radical indeterminacy of nature as ground is acknowledged – say, for example, in corporeal feminism – it remains ground, simply a 'shifting' one (44).

Clark's aim is to draw largely on thinkers who have not merely tried to redefine the ground on which the human is based, but have embraced the idea of the radical openness of human systems and the human context to what lies outside of them. Georges Bataille is an example of such a thinker in his acknowledgement, in Clark's words, that 'the systems we compose for ourselves can neither be closed at their beginning nor at their end – and are thus destined to be perpetually energised and animated by their outside' (22). It is only by this kind of acceptance of the fundamental openness of our context that we can properly take into account the 'radical asymmetry' of our relationship with nature, the fact that we inhabit a world on which we depend for all sustenance and all our practices, but that is not dependent on us, indeed that is 'indifferent to us' (50). Human history could not happen without the physical context in which we find ourselves, yet this context is itself unfolding across a macro-historical time that makes history negligible and in the tiniest pocket of an infinite physical environment that makes our physical activity more or less minor.

By re-thinking the closed nature of our systems of thought, we can embrace the physical meaning of this environment, according to Clark. Post-structuralism's insistence that all systems are open to otherness, and include otherness, provides just the kind of openness Clark is arguing for. Material reality is, in fact, the definitive other:

> The dynamism that inheres in material reality plays a part in the genesis of otherness. The quite ordinary eventfulness of the universe carves rifts in the continuity of life – chasms over which others meet without ever being as one. This is why, I am suggesting, we need to bring together what Derrida is saying about thresholds as the sites at which selves and others come into proximity with the understanding offered by natural sciences … about the discontinuous and messy trajectories of real world physical systems. This is much more than a matter of occasionally recognising that we or others might be thrown off course by exceptional natural forces. It is about acknowledging that the deter-ritorialising of the earth is the primordial condition of our existence, that the instability of the ground on which we stand precedes, accompanies and will likely succeed any material fabrications or inscriptions of our own (215–6).

Here we have a contrast between a human construction of the world in which the natural context is mere background, the predictable if changing frame within which we define our own human purposes on human terms on the one hand, and, on the other hand, a world-view that recognises the limit of such a rigid construction of externality by allowing for the existence of an otherness that is not only different to the human but on an infinitely extended scale. In this way, thought acknowledges the radical asymmetry of the human context. The human representation of its context must exhibit this radical acknowledgement of the always excessive nature of where we find ourselves. All it can do is to gesture at this excessiveness. By definition, it cannot include it.

Yet, even this acknowledgement falls far short of a truly balanced recognition of the human context. The asymmetry Clark speaks of is so great, it reduces the human to the infinitesimally small, perhaps next to nothing. Such accuracy would, of course, be meaningless. It would totally undo the human. It would not be representation at all, a process in which the human cannot be inconsequential. In Clark's statement above, this human quality overflows in the almost dogmatic (un-Derridean) metaphysical gravity of the rhetoric. Even in acknowledging the context that dwarfs the human, the human is re-asserted emphatically. Even in the context of excess that overwhelms it, the human builds its world. Over and above this, the excess that so outrages the human remains excess *as thought*. The human cannot not be part of it. Even as we acknowledge how infinitely great the spatial and temporal context within which we find ourselves is on any human scale, we still appear as an irreducible part of our observation. Below I will develop this idea in terms of decisionism: the human may no longer be able to simply and confidently construct worlds within a frame that walls out the true scale of nature, but it will continue to decide on worlds given to it from a universe of massive excesses. It is the fact that such decisions are necessary and cannot be reduced to zero that keeps our response to climate change irreducibly political, even when we deny it, as the *Framework* does.

If the universe is huge beyond what it is possible for human logic to measure or even conceive, and if historical time stretches into spans that make recorded history a mere snap of the fingers, then no human thought will be able to grasp the human context on its full scale. It is not only systems of thought that treat 'nature' as a neutral frame or passive resource that are defeated by such asymmetry. No thought, no matter how aware it is of this truth, can accurately situate the human. All thought can do is recognise this situation, by emphasising its own indefiniteness and incompleteness, in Clark's terms, its openness to otherness. This does not make it any less artificial. It remains an invention, an apparatus, a product of human decision-making, both conscious and unconscious. Human thought is an apparatus constructed in the face of excess, irreducibly human but inevitably overwhelmed.

Whether it is acknowledged or not, human thought includes within its own logic some relationship to this excess. This may be in its historicity, its contingency and its ephemerality. It is also part of the constitution of human thought in general, even in relation to itself. It is here I would like to turn briefly to the work of Karen Barad. Barad builds her understanding of the human relationship to its context on insights derived from the work of Nils Bohr and quantum physics. Bohr's work challenges the logic of the self-identical factual world identified by Newtonian axioms:

> The lesson Bohr takes from quantum physics is … there aren't little things wandering aimlessly in the void that possess the complete set of properties that Newtonian physics assumes (e.g., position and momentum); rather, there is something fundamental about the nature of measurement interactions such that, given a particular measurement apparatus, certain properties, become determinate, while others are specifically excluded. Which properties become determinate is not governed by the desires or will of the experimenter but rather by the specificity of the experimental apparatus (Barad, 2007, p. 19).

The properties of an object are not fixed and inherent to that object. In a particular interaction with the object, a specific way of observing or measuring it, the object will emerge in certain ways. These attributes of the object are not invented by the process of observation, nor does the object get reinvented. It is only knowable by way of a certain process of observation, a certain apparatus. It thus can only emerge in relation to that apparatus as part of an observation-event. It is inseparable from this event. Each event may produce a different truth about the object, and these truths may even be contradictory to one another, but an object only reveals truth as part of a measuring process. This is not to say that the object is not objective. The apparatus does not turn the object into whatever it likes. The truths of observation are not fictions. They are simply inseparable from the processes of meaning-making. To Barad, meaning-making is not something simply contrived in human culture. It is sown into the very fabric of the universe itself:

> Matter and meaning are not separate elements. They are inextricably fused together, and no event, no matter how energetic, can tear them asunder. Even atoms, whose very name … means 'indivisible' or 'uncuttable,' can be broken apart. But matter and meaning cannot be dissociated, not by chemical processing, or centrifuge, or nuclear blast. Mattering is simultaneously a matter of substance and significance (3).

Any event in the universe involves relationships between various actants, which develop from their interaction whatever truths are necessary. This is a process in which meaning, as the process of identification and activation of what is significant about the object for the trajectory of that particular exchange, can never be reduced to zero. This is true, whether or not the actants involved are human. The universe cannot not make meaning.

Meaning-making is inevitable, therefore. It is what existants *do*. Yet, every event of meaning-making must take place in a double context: firstly, it takes place in relation to a universe that is saturated with meaning, in which meaning, not a particular or fixed meaning, but the intense potential of meaningfulness in general, is immanent. There is thus no passive world on the outside of human centred meaning-systems that we can suppress or ignore, that we can deem inert or passive, and that we can construct as we like, while we pursue our own self-constituting meaning systems. We are always exposed to the infinity of meaning. Second, each event of meaning is the result of a particular deployment of an apparatus – mechanical or conceptual. But the meaning it derives must acknowledge an infinity of possible alternative meanings that may be contradictory, but also (in Bohr's terms) complementary to it. What I measure to be true is true, but I must recognise that there are other truths possible for other subjects at other moments using other apparatuses. It is even possible, of course, that the difference between me, another observing subject, the time in which truth is developed and the apparatus used may be reduced to next to zero: it could be me a moment later, a meter away. The point is that any truth occurs in the context of an infinite reach of possible truths beyond us to infinity, both in space and time and in the face of an indefinite number of alternative truths, all of which are equally valid, even when they are incompatible with one another.

From both Clark and Barad, then, we derive the insight that human systems of truth and the truths that are their prize are apparatuses constituted in relation to that which exceeds them, materially, spatially, temporally and conceptually. The choice we make, again either consciously or unconsciously, is whether to deny or embrace this situation. In denial, we construct dogma. In embracing this contextualisation, we imagine possibility. Let us return to what we said about the *Framework* to see how its assumed truths about the human historical, political and climatic situation can be read in relation to these ideas about truth and excess.

In our reading of the *Framework,* we identified several key ideas. Key amongst these was the idea that the world is a single total climatic system, which is the object of a human subject who lives within it but is capable of grasping it as a single totality, and acting on it in ways that will fundamentally remake it. This human subject inhabits a stable system of sovereign nation-states, which are all on a common trajectory of social development, even though they are at different points on this trajectory. These views represent a stabilisation of a world at a specific moment in historical time, according to certain social priorities. The world conceived as a single, total system is already a reduction and abstraction of the nature Clark and Barad identify. It may be totally defensible as the most appropriate and digestible way of imagining the world, given the political context of denialism and vested interests. Yet it remains a specific way of conceiving the world as a subset of both the universe and possible other worlds. Even when the whole discourse of climate change rests on the assumption that the global system is not closed – we are in danger because it receives an open-ended quantity of energy from outside of it in the form of solar radiation – it chooses to define the world on a certain historical scale.

Yet, this discourse would lose its political purchase if it tried to represent the asymmetrical nature of the human/nature relationship, or the indeterminacy and complementarity of our knowledge of it. It would be seen as a mere construct; it has already been attacked for that. As Barad argues, in the world of quantum physics, the fact that there are many alternative possible ways of making meaning from the universe does not mean that that meaning is 'constructed' by human beings on human terms. The specificity of a particular meaning is the result of the interaction of an apparatus and a universe already saturated with potential meanings before the human encounters it or even arises. In sum, the version of the world in the *Framework* is a totally defensible one, but in order to be politically effective, it must deny the fact that there are alternative possible ways of representing the world. In the specific context we find ourselves in, threatened by cataclysmic environmental disruptions, this way of imagining the world couldn't seem more legitimate. Yet the fact remains, it operates by denying the excess in which it is inevitably situated, and which makes it possible. It is the result of political decisions made in a specific context, but must deny both these decisions and this context.

Sovereignty

What would a politics be that did not perform this kind of denial, that attempted to grasp the logic of excess as part of itself? Why would such a politics be important? To answer the second question first: it would be important because it would grasp the decisions we are making and the models we are developing as such, not as something fixed. This means the horizon of decision-making could be extended. We would not simply be recognising our future as our problem, but taking full responsibility for the fact that we are enacting political values when we attempt to deal with climate change. Responses to climate change have been much criticised for their anthropocentrism: we deal with climatic problems in service to human priorities. My aim is not to repeat this criticism, but to assert that we have no choice but to do this. If we gave the objective totality of the universe its due, both in space and time, the human would appear as so inconsequential as to be of no significance. We can only frame our problems in relation to the scale of the human, and what human beings identify as priorities. This mean our priorities can only be human-defined. This does not mean they can only have the human as priority. We are capable of developing our human value of justice in ways that insist on the rights of other living things, and even non-living things. These are also now starting to be recognised as political issues for us. The issue is not whether these decisions are human-centred, but whether or not they are properly recognised as decisions, and thus as political.

This returns us to the first question: what form would thinking take if it were to accept this political responsibility and fully recognise its relation to excess? As we have seen, what is at issue in the relationship to excess is what lies outside or beyond, the way in which any so-called system or identity, or in Barad's case, method, emerges in relation to something larger, further or alternative to it, so that systems can never be definitive, final or closed. As mentioned above, one of Clark's inspirations in developing models of systems that are not closed in upon themselves was the French thinker, Georges Bataille. I would like to provide a brief account of Bataille's understanding of how the universe – or what he understood as the cosmic system of energy – works, because not only does it provide a compelling image of an open system, but it also converges on political theory. In work that was amongst the first to break out of the closed post-Enlightenment human world, in which the natural was the mere resource for and background to human behaviour, Bataille saw a continuity between the solar system and human societies. What bound them together was what he understood as a general economics of energy. What does this mean?

Bataille was profoundly influenced by energeticism,[1] the view that all material things are formations of energy, and that all changes are really shifts in the composition of energy. In his view, the earth is bathed in energy it receives from the sun. This energy gives rise to living things. Energy is absorbed into living things in order to sustain them. Energy not only gives rise to life, it is harnessed by living things to produce certain results. Bataille named each of these living things a 'restricted economy', a closed system turning in on itself, functioning to meet certain goals, to live on, or to make something. Yet, each living thing and the world in general continue to receive energy from the sun in the open 'general economy'. A fixed quantity of energy may be required to make each living thing live and each system work, but the energy keeps coming. It doesn't stop. It goes on indefinitely, in an open-ended consumption that knows no ends. The living thing continues to grow beyond the boundaries of its container or until the container shatters. For Bataille, the issue for the earth is not scarcity but excess: energy fuels systems, but energy keeps coming until it threatens to make each system explode. Every restricted economy is part of the operation of the general economy, a fragile fragment of that economy, dependent on it but threatened by it as well.

The restricted economy is thus not the opposite of the general economy. It is part of the flow of the general economy, and could not exist without it. Yet the excess of the general economy threatens each restricted economy, even as and when it gives rise to it. The restricted economy forms out of the general economy, and can only arise in relation to it, but the general economy also brings with it the threat of explosion. Each restricted economy becomes itself only in relation to the infinite abyss of the general economy. It must be in relationship to that general economy but constantly resisting its excess even as it draws on it.

To Bataille, the human world is no different. The pragmatic activities of human daily life involve a certain logical, means-and-ends thinking. We must contain quantities of energy in order to make them do work. We can only take this energy from the larger potentially infinite flow of energy, however. Bataille understood this as the human creating a discontinuity in the continuity of the cosmic flow of energy. We must make these discontinuities in order to live: we couldn't perform the pragmatic operations of feeding, sheltering and protecting ourselves if we did not. Yet, we know in some undefined unconscious way that the truth lies in the greater infinite continuity that exceeds all our practical, discontinuous operations. We remain drawn to this continuity. This is the function of religion. Acts of sacrifice, the transgression of taboos about death and sex, and our artistic practices all try to invent ways in which we can feel again that openness to the continuous flow of the universe. All our aspirations and emotions play out this tense and potentially explosive relationship between discontinuity and continuity. We seek access to the absolute freedom from the pragmatic, goal-oriented obligations of the discontinuous workaday world, by seeking to define ourselves in relation to the impossible world of absolute continuity, which holds out to us the promise of absolute freedom. Tellingly, Bataille's word for this absolute and uncontained possibility of freedom, which he saw as the primary drive of human beings, is *sovereignty*.

Bataille's thinking is provocative, even outlandish. Although it has an obvious political meaning, it defies adherence. Any attempt to turn this sovereignty into a programmatics would, for Bataille, be slavish following of a rule, an identification of a particular goal, and thus a return to the slavishness of means and ends thinking. It would thus not be sovereign at all. So Bataille both proposes and refuses a politics. Yet something much more fertile develops out of Jacques Derrida's work on sovereignty. Derrida acknowledged the importance of Bataille for him early on in his career. He doesn't do so explicitly in his later work on sovereignty (Derrida, 2005), though he does use Bataillean language. As he does with so many thinkers, Derrida radically de-literalises Bataille's energeticism, turning it into a much more abstract, philosophical account that has a clearer political meaning.

The crucial point to take from Bataille's theory of economies is that there is only one kind of energy, but the relations that it gives rise to are double. The energy that infuses the restricted economy is the energy of the general economy. Indeed, the energy of the general economy only manifests itself in restricted economies. What reveals the generality of economy is the movement within the restricted economy to overflow itself. The general economy is not something opposite or even different to the restricted economy. There is only one process of energy, but it is a double process: out of the general economy, restricted economies form, but only on their way to coming undone. The general economy is the principle of deformation latent, even inevitable, in the formation of restricted economies. This logic anticipates Derridean deconstruction, which is also a logic of doubleness. Derrida understands sovereignty as a double movement. Sovereignty is firstly a principle of autonomy and self-containment. The sovereign is sufficient unto itself. The canonical models of sovereignty from Bodin and Hobbes to Schmitt and Foucault all understand the sovereign as self-identical and transcending accountability. The sovereign in Hobbes guarantees the laws but is not answerable to them. In Schmitt, the lodestone of sovereignty is its prerogative to decide on the exception, in other words, to decide when the law will be suspended. The sovereign, then, is not bounded. In a world of limits, it is the one thing that is not restricted. In this way, the sovereign is always in excess of the law, open to that which is unmapped, to the open itself.

This openness to that which is beyond accountability also means that the sovereign is self-sustaining. It justifies itself. It is self-forming and self-identical, the very principle of ipseity or self-sameness. It is simultaneously the principle of self-forming and of openness to that which is beyond limits. The sovereign self forms only in relation to excess. It is here we can see the resonance with Bataille most explicitly. In Bataille, the restricted economy of the thing forms out of the energy of the general economy, but only as part of the trajectory of that energy towards its own undoing and inevitable re-making into something else. In Derrida, the self-sustaining self-identical thing forms only by reference to excess, to the imagining of something beyond and different. It develops itself and it gains its authority only in relation to the infinite abyss of unconditional sovereignty. A thinking that acknowledges the excess of the asymmetrical nature and infinite meaningfulness in which it is situated, therefore, is inevitably and necessarily a thinking of sovereignty.

Conclusion

In our analysis, we argued that the assumptions behind the *Framework* were of a climatic system that could be thought in its totality as a single thing: a stable international system of autonomous nations and fixed development goals, focussed on opportunity, prosperity and social justice. We argued that these assumptions implied that there was a stable received order of nature, history and society that the *Framework* was merely identifying. We argued, however, that this claim disguised the fact that each of these assumptions was the result of certain identifications and constructions that were produced by human decisions. They might have been the right decisions, but they were decisions nonetheless.

In a reading of Clark and Barad, we argued that each of these decisions necessarily involved some segmentation of the infinity of space and time, and a selection from the indefinite range of the possibilities of different knowledges. These decisions form only in relation to infinities that exceed them, even when each decision may attempt to deny this excess in order to present itself as fixed and objective.

In the end, we argued that a thinking that was able to grasp excess was inevitably a thinking of the sovereign. It involves human self-making by way of the thinking of the open-ended possibility of absolute freedom. This freedom is unrealisable, of course, indeed impossible, but it serves to orient thought as an open-ended human self-remaking by negotiation and decision.

The point of such an analysis is to argue that what we do collectively in response to climate change should not be understood as a mere response to natural conditions or a fixed global order. It involves decisions. These decisions are not at the level of the individual, who may or may not contribute to greenhouse gas mitigation by recycling more and flying less; what the individual does is a distraction. What matters is the negotiation of human goals collectively as an enactment of the possibilities of human sovereignty. It would be lovely to stay on the familiar ground of ideological debate, where the logic of the imagined free individual and the dreamed-of social democracy are pitted against one another. But the individual has evolved into the mere anxious and scrutinised biopolitical specimen, and social democracy has been weakened by endless compromise with the market, that will never fully trust or even tolerate it. These options arose in that post-Enlightenment world Clark castigates for its suppression of the natural beyond vain and closed human systems of thought. The era that allowed such closed systemic thinking is passing away, because in the era of climate change we must recognise again that our situation belongs to that which exceeds us. What is required more than anything is a renewal of the revolutionary promise of democracy, of what Derrida called 'democracy-to-come'. Democracy-to-come is not a realisable state, but the orientation of human politics to the possibility of that which is ever more open, free and just, that always requires a re-energising of the political as itself a good. Such a possibility opens the future as human self-construction in relation to that which always lies beyond. It is only by the self-conscious recognition that our action in the world is the result of decisions made in relation to excess that we can imagine a renewed orientation of the human project in the face of possible extinction.

The debate about climate change is not a debate about science. Scientists are tricked onto false ground if they believe climate change denialism is open to persuasion by scientific reason. Instead, the functional denialism that has paralysed political leadership in this area operates as an amalgam of forces and accidents long recognisable in the opportunistic and cynical, all-too-clever history of liberal appeasement: short-sighted and careerist politicians, encouraged and fed by vested interests, target their ideological enemies with a rhetoric infested with anti-intellectual *ressentiment*. This decadent and degraded mess is the hollowed-out shell of a political culture that has lost the priorities of general human sovereignty. By re-animating as necessary and defensible a logic of human sovereignty, politics can restore to humanity a destiny and a future.

Note

1   Key figures in energeticism were Georg Helm (1851–1923) and Friedrich Wilhelm Ostwald (1853–1932, Nobel Prize in Chemistry 1909). The 'school of energetics' held strongly to the First Law of Thermodynamics regarding the conservation of energy in the universe, but they read the Second Law of Thermodynamics to say that energy is transformed only between entities which have different intensities of energy, and that in any process the emission of energy at the outset always exceeds the capture of energy, at the end, and that energy is thus always lost or escapes in the process. See Hochroth (1995, p. 64–77).

References

Barad, K., 2007. *Meeting the Universe Halfway: Quantum Physics and the Entanglement of Matter and Meaning*. Durham(NC): Duke University Press.

Bataille, G., 1993. *The Accursed Share: An Essay on General Economy (Volumes 2 and 3)*. New York: Zone Books.

Clark, N., 2011. *Inhuman Nature: Sociable Life on a Dynamic Planet*. London: Sage Publications.

Derrida, J., 2005. *Rogues: Two Essays on Reason*. Stanford(CA): Stanford University Press.

Heidegger, M., 1977. The Age of The World Picture. In: *The Question Concerning Technology and Other Essays*. New York: Harper Torchbooks, p. 115–54.

Hochroth, L., 1995. The Scientific Imperative: Improductive Expernditure and Energeticism. *Configurations*, 3(1), p. 47–77.

United Nations, 1992. *Text of the Convention*. [Online] Available at: http://unfccc.int/key_documents/the_convention/items/2853.php [Accessed 2 July 2015].

11 Para-religions of climate change

Humanity, eco-nihilism, apocalypse

S. Romi Mukherjee

The Anthropocene is not a simply a scientific index of a new geological era typified by rapid environmental change. Nor is it simply a hermeneutic through which to diagnose the ills of *homo sapiens*, now newly cast as rapacious actors who have disrupted the Rousseauian Edens of the Holocene. On the contrary, the Anthropocene, the 'human epoch', is, in fact, the threshold of all human projects. As such, it has a certain relationship to death; it partakes in the great questions of religion and emerges as a religious object itself. The response to these questions is not, however, delimited by the world of 'organized religion'. It is also articulated from within 'para-religious' perspectives, many of which seek neither mitigation nor sustainable forms of redemption, but rather advance a hermeneutics of climate change as an inevitable, and often welcome, Armageddon.

The Anthropocene as object of (dis)belief

Ethical action in a changing climate can be difficult because it involves acting without being certain whether the agreed action will be truly beneficial, and whether the appropriate 'good' action is truly good. It seems to demand perseverance in belief – not least, belief in doing the right thing – despite the knowledge that any such human project might now appear arbitrary and radically inadequate at best. This is a space of radical disavowal or knowing-unknowing; here, one registers and comes to believe in the looming trauma of climate change only to repudiate the traumatic trace, a repudiation further sustained by the obscure and obscurantist nature of public 'knowledge' of climate change. But while human belief in a time of climate change – belief in climate change – might confront new difficulties, the religious impetus (broadly construed) continues unabated, even turning towards the Anthropocene itself. In popular and para-religious practices – in the ambiguous underside of the public sphere – climate change is imagined, variously, as an object to be overcome, negotiated or nihilistically embraced.

The para-religious construction of the Anthropocene contrasts with 'organized religious' interventions into the climate change debate. For instance, when faced with climate change, clerisies of religious leaders vie for positioning within the international system, claiming that they can adapt notions of divine justice and theodicy to the challenges of the Anthropocene while simultaneously deploying the disaster (past, present and future) as justification for their missions and initiatives. Such an abridgement runs contrary to a central theme in the great holy books of the monotheistic traditions, namely that God gave humans the Earth and the animals for their unbridled use. In their various injunctions, these leaders foreground their capacity to mobilize and sensitize their constituents to environmental change and, in the process, wage a silent battle against secularism which is held largely responsible for the warping of the divine natural order, straining to decouple Christianity (for example) from its implication in, arguably, its most glorious achievement – secular democracy. The Pope's recent encyclical, while valiant in its assailing of capitalism and the myth of unlimited growth, is a *political* and *ethical* counterpoint which does not (and perhaps cannot) marshal biblical or theological arguments in its pleas to 'save our common home'. Climate change and religion remains the site of a missed encounter.

In addition, the response of the 'major' religions to climate change reveals three overarching leitmotifs: (1) The monotheisms find themselves struggling to reread the Earth as not simply a 'waiting room', and strain to reread their traditions as always-already environmentally sensitive. Faith-based initiatives merge with environmental initiatives and moralize development as part and parcel of spiritual development. (2) The non-Abrahamic critique of Abrahamic religions, which conveniently argues that climate change is not only the fault of the secular west, but also of the religions of the secular west which have conspired to produce a noxious brew of consumption, rabid capitalism and a de-spiritualized world view. In the case of Hinduism, for instance, this religious riposte also takes on a colonial and post-colonial hue, particularly when, for instance, Indian politicians argue that, in light of colonial extractive economies and the occident's strong implication in environmental change, through the logic of distributive justice, they have the right to supra-develop at accelerated speed with little regard for carbon emissions and pollution and have no obligation to be concerned with the plight of vulnerable regions let alone the rest of the world. (3) When religious leaders from both camps assemble to 'dialogue', they more than often set their differences aside, preferring to create a religious environmental coalition whose solidarity is founded upon a shared suspicion of all that is secular, let alone atheist.[1]

Para-religious readings of the Anthropocene propose a different set of protocols from their more 'organized' counterparts. They are not religions confronted by the Anthropocene, but rather 'religions of the Anthropocene'. In these circumstances, climate change, and the Anthropocene more broadly, have become powerful centres of conceptual, semiotic and affective attraction for an array of new mythologies, cosmologies and symbolizing practices. In a general sense, the para-religious engagement with the Anthropocene can be organized along three dialectical movements: ecological humanism and 'sustainability' as religion/the sacred; green ecologies and eco-paganism; and 'anthropocentric apocalypticism'.

Global transformation and climate change jettison humanism out of its philosophical entanglements and transform humanitarianism into a world-forming cult of action animated by missionary zeal. For François Mabille (2007), 'humanitarian religion', crystallized in international nongovernmental organization (NGO) culture, is a post-secular religion that 'engenders a humanitarianism of the state or rather a global-state humanitarianism with NGOs as new churches of providence'. Mabille identifies, amidst the disarray of traditional political and religious discourses, an emergent transnationalizing conjuncture of discourses and institutions, a new 'bricolage based on the notion of the gift, sustainable development, the commons, ecology, and the suffering of the other, all in the name of a new global order'. Staunchly opposed to this para-religious humanitarisism is green mysticism and its anti-humanist derivatives. Green para-religions usually involve some combination of the following mythemes: a rejection of the 'west' in favour of an embrace of non-occidental, supernatural, indigenous and oriental world views which all refuse the separation between man and the cosmos; the insistence on the intrinsic value of nature and the embeddedness of man in nature, often justified by a principle of life which affirms the worth of all 'living things' (closely aligned with the no harm principle); an affirmation of nature's agency which does not preclude the possibility of spirits dwelling in trees and tricksters in forests; nature as ontology; a dismissal of the Abrahamic religions as complicit in environmental crisis; green, organic, vegan and macrobiotic practices of ethical consumption; a re-writing of global history from the perspective of nature with organicism, vitalism, geophilosophy and strategies of immanence, regularly deployed as privileged heuristics;[2] and calls to 'green' the world's religions and spiritual traditions.[3]

When pushed to their para-religious extremes, these humanitarian and 'green' religions produce a new dialectical stage, 'anthropocenic apocalypticism'. From Gaia movements to post-natal ethics to voluntary human extinction movements, anthropocenic apocalypticism 'goes to the end' in its engagement with the Anthropocene and welcomes the demise of the human species. The nihilistic commitment of these movements differentiates them from their normative, humanist and neo-pagan counterparts. At once militant and carnivalesque, these new apocalyptic cults are 'para-religions' insofar as they are religions of the outside that refuse all '*order*', '*tradition*' *and normativity*,[4] preferring to exalt nihilism (as religion) and revel in the *agōn* of the last man. Their emphases on the worst possible futures also provide a timely critical buttress against present-ism and the misplaced optimism that continues to pervade normative rational accounts of the collective human project. They effect – or, at least, attempt – a total devaluation of all existing values, including any that might be attributed to non-human nature. New climate change cults and apocalyptic religions are radical experiments in ethical foresight, efforts to reimagine human virtue for a changed climate. In doing this, para-religions call on a diverse and heterogenous series of narrative conventions and long-standing tropological traditions. Their concern to identify things that *might happen* (and how they might) is always shaped by the desire to tell a *story* that makes sense and dramatizes the event. Sociologically, in its public circulation, but also formally, in its futurological narrativity, climate change is both a scientific fact and a story with para-religious dimensions.

Is not/il y a

Apocalyptic para-religions of the Anthropocene inscribe themselves in the tradition of negative theology. Here, the Anthropocene appears as the ultimate horizon of language and thought, that is, as the most radical alterity and most absolute negativity. For Ilse N. Bulhof and Laurens ten Kate (2000), the Anthropocene condition of 'damage to the environment, overpopulation, and the threatened exhaustion of the Earth's regenerative abilities… presupposes a creative resumption of the heritage of negative theology' (31–32). In particular, what they resume from that heritage is negative theology's 'emphasis on the unknowable, the unutterable, and the deep darkness of transcendent being which elicits the idea that transcendence is best approached via denials, via what according to earthly concepts *is not*' (5). But negative theologies of climate change are also necessarily involved in the performative contradictions of negative theology more generally: those of saying of what cannot be said, for instance. This positions catastrophic climate change as something that is simultaneously conceivable and inconceivable, possible and impossible.

For religious and para-religious traditions of thought, climate change often appears as part of an ongoing disaster without clear beginning or end. Modern geopolitics is often characterized by the collapsing of the distinction between 'peace time' and 'war time'. Climate change similarly exceeds any sense of a narrowly time-bound event, rather invoking, for religious and political discourse, a wider culture of the disaster wherein the Earth and the socio-eco-techno systems that occupy it are typified by a catastrophic flux. The flux is 'managed' through apocalyptic imaginaries, new human security paradigms, disaster technologies, markets driven by catastrophe capital and governmental policies – various ways of framing hazard, risk and 'preparedness' in a world where nothing is certain. Here, the horizon of negativity theology is not God, but rather the disaster itself as a radical calling into question the human, as embodied, natural and moral being.

This negative theological construction of climate change as disaster, as unthinkable break, corresponds to the harrowing arrival of what French philosopher Emmanuel Levinas called the *il y a* (there is). For Levinas, the *il y a* is the radically contingent interference of the impersonal, an event that persists as a shadow of subterranean trauma that invests all purposeful activity. As total interruption, unanticipatable, wholly alien to what it interrupts, the *il y a* names for Levinas the

> …total silence of being, in all non-thought, in all withdrawal from being. *Il y a* (it is) like 'it rains' or 'it is nice outside,' – this 'it' marks the impersonal character of this stage where impersonal consciousness lives 'there is something,' without object, without substance – a nothing that is not nothing. In this horrifying experience of 'nothingisation,' the thematic of the *il y a* embeds the construction of a subjectivity…despite its annulling of it (1995, p. 109).

In a broad sense, *il y a* was, for Levinas, a means for grappling with the problem of how to think about the outside, what lies beyond thinking. It voices, without speaking, the negativity of contingency as the unravelling of being and consistency. It fashions a subjectivity whose parameters and constitution remain wholly 'negative', rather than being dialogically set into relation with an embodied other. Levinas's formulation points to an inescapable provisionality of being: *il y a* is lodged in the dimension that precedes and underlies the distinction between subject and object. Hence, *il y a* is the non-transcendent eruption of contingency into the system – a stuttering temporality, a foreclosing where the disaster 'no-things'.

Nonetheless, and despite its stringent impersonality, the negativity of the *il y a* cannot be divorced from the circulation and so potential recapitulatory dynamics of 'human negativity'. The *il y a* surges forth as the negative reflux of human violence in a spiral where human domination produces the domination of the human from within another *entre-deux* of misrecognition. Or, the *il y a* offers us with a philosophical grammar through which we can explain the 'weather' and how the weather is never given, but a product of human–climate interaction.

The *il y a* is the name for a form of negativity which forms the ground of the para-religious and apocalyptic reading of the Anthropocene. Here, the alien otherness of nature is born of human alienness and alienation (from itself, from the Earth etc.). In these metaphysical and social dynamics, the para-religions of the Anthropocene lodge themselves in the interstices and mirrorings of duelling negativities. Para-religions are intrinsically tragic or 'torn'. Or, as Zizek explains, the Anthropocene could be understood as

> ....the relation between two negativities, the negativity of nature as radical Other...and the negativity of human subjectivity itself, its destructive impact on nature... nature appears as a threatening Otherness from the standpoint of the subject who perceives itself as opposed to nature: in the threatening negativity of nature, the subject receives back the mirror image of its own negative relationship to nature (2011, pp. 336, n. 22).

Green and humanitarian faiths labour to suture the chasm named by Levinas and go to recuperate the negativity presumed to lie beyond the human. The former does so through various strategies of re-enchantment which flee the human and its negativity through dreams of total immanence with something called nature. The latter does the same through mythically re-elevating the human above the tragic ground of duelling negativities. Tragic negative theologies and apocalyptic para-religions, by contrast, reject their recuperating projects, basking instead in the painful encounter with the *il y a*. They recognize the Anthropocene as the historical product of arbitrary forms of human domination. There can be no metaphors here and no grand *récits* – humanity is revealed to be a convenient fiction whose deconstruction leaves only the 'open' empty chasm between modernity and the 'after-modernity' of the Anthropocene. As for nature, as S. Pickett and Richard S. Ostfield (1995) suggest, climate change disrupts our univocity, and forces us to recognize 'ecological systems to be open, regulated by events outside of their boundaries, lacking or prevented from attaining a stable point equilibrium, affected by natural disturbance, and incorporating humans and their effects' (274–275). Nature's non-equilibrium challenges metaphysical conviction in the One of Being, and so also points to a wholly other *il y a* which cannot be absorbed by paradigms of multiplicity. What apocalyptic and para-religious ecologies propose is that nature's non-equlibrium as negativity forms the material conditions for existence in the Anthropocene while suspending any conceptual schema driven by the grand significis of God, Being, Man, Futures etc. They re-imagine climate change as a total interruption of 'Being' thereby detaching religious thought from its human origins and all too human salvific imaginaries. It is thus not a question of 'rethinking the human', but of a progressive detachment from humanity to be accomplished through the sustained relation to negativity, *autrui* and *il y a*.

Gaia revisited

The high priest of anthropocenic apocalypticism is James Lovelock who, over the course of the 1970s, rewrote the story of the biosphere and named it Gaia. Gaia is the homeostatic Earth and also a goddess who predates man. She is a metaphor and a hypothesis, but also

> …a complex entity, involving the Earth's atmosphere, biosphere, oceans and soil: the totality constituting a feedback or cybernetic system which seeks and optimal physical and chemical environment for life on this planet….described by the term 'homestasis.'…if Gaia exists, the relationship between her and man, a dominant animal species in a complex living system, and the possibly shifting balance of power between them, are questions of obvious importance… the Gaia hypothesis is for those who like to walk or simply stand and stare, to wonder about the Earth and the life it bears and to speculate about the consequences of our own presence here. It is an alternative to the pessimistic view that sees nature as a primitive force to be subdued and conquered. It is also an alternative to that equally depressing picture of our planet as a demented spaceship, forever traveling, driverless and purposeless, around the inner circle of the sun (2000, p. 10-11).

The Gaia hypothesis, while eliding anthropocentric pessimism, is 'hopeful', but *only* from the perspective of the Earth. Lovelock writes on behalf of the goddess herself and appears delighted to be potentially rid of the nagging cough called humanity. His oeuvre, moreover, is epitomized by its ambivalence concerning the competing claims of Gaia as science and as religion. Whatever its scientific merits, the insistence on Greek-Earth-Goddess imagery replete with pantheistic echoes of cosmic wrath and human resignation has offered a vital framework for the wider reception of the Gaia hypothesis, so that its use of religious terms and concepts prove indispensable for its critical interpretation.

In other words, the hypothesis emerges within the interstices of the natural sciences and geo-cosmic polytheism and, at the risk of over-simplification, argues that the Earth does not need us (Lovelock, 1995, p. 212).[5] She does not care any more as, following the 'Earth's biography" we have long ceased to honour her. She is the self-regulating and living Earth who, stricken by the greatest of betrayals, turns away in apathy. She defends herself, fends for herself, and actually does not implore us to make reparations. Rather she asks us to reflect on a quick retreat from her vicious cycle of positive feedback (Lovelock, 2006, p. 7). Gaian desires should not be confounded with human sustainability.

She, macrocosm, eliminates the parasitic microcosm of humanity in a narrative of self-healing legible in terms drawn from conceptions of 'traditional' medicine. The time for rediscovering immanence has passed (Gaia may be an Earth goddess, but her religion is not necessarily 'green' or re-enchanting). And, as Lynn Margulis, Lovelock's colleague and co-creator of Gaia, exhorts:

> For me, the human move to take responsibility for the living Earth is laughable – the rhetoric of the impotent. The planet takes care of us, not we of it. Our self-inflated moral imperative to guide a wayward Earth, or heal our sick planet, is evidence of our immense capacity for self-delusion. Rather, we need to protect ourselves from ourselves (2012, p. 53).

In the Anthropocene, it is every organism for itself. The human organism appears furthermore ill-equipped to offer Gaia any salvation, not least because of its mis-guided moral egoism, but also because it is an organism whose secret longing for death diverges from the planet's will to live in spite of its inhabitants.

In other words, humanity's ejection from Gaia is not simply the result of a cognitive error, a mistake in thought that could be amended by thinking otherwise, by thinking about our place. To the contrary, one widely identified challenge of climate change is that it presents a wholly unprecedented type of challenge, one that falls outside the parameters not just of recent political history or religious imagining, but even perhaps outside the frontiers of the emergence of the human species itself. As Dale Jamieson argues, 'Evolution did not build us to see climate change as a threat, our ethical systems are not designed to confront this, our politics is not created to engage with this…we have not survived climate change, the Earth has.'[6] Once again, there appears something intrinsic to human 'systems' (epistemological, bodily, behavioural etc.) which instantiates the gulf between the human organism and Gaia's wholly other homeostatic ethos. Extinction is trauma deferred into a final future, disavowed under the auspices of 'carrying on'.

Lovelock is less concerned with following up such speculative explanations for the phenomenon of human violence to the Earth, treating it instead largely as a *fait accompli*. Lovelock's Gaia apocalypticism becomes almost giddy in its embrace of the end: 'Humans are too stupid to prevent climate change from radically impacting on our lives over the coming decades… Even the best democracies agree that when a major war approaches, democracy must be put on hold for the time being. I have a feeling that climate change may be an issue as severe as a war. It may be necessary to put democracy on hold for a while.'[7] In the name of pluralism, democracies – all too human constructions – lapse into cacophony and actually prevent the necessary action, which may indeed be a total state of exception, a total suspension of all democratic law. And, as Michel Serres observed, 'the Earth was not invited to Copenhagen,', resulting in a participatory democratic paradigm that was quite exclusive. Yet, it is not clear that neo-Schmittian climate decisionism would offer any firm solutions, as even a super-league of climate change experts would be necessarily unable to confront their own human limitations. According to Lovelock's own prophecies (apparently wryly delivered with a smile), climate change activism and legislation are nothing more than feelgood deterrence mechanisms: 'Most of the things we have been told to do might make us feel better, but they won't make any difference. Global warming has passed the tipping point, and catastrophe is unstoppable. It's just too late for it... Enjoy life while you can. Because if you're lucky it's going to be 20 years before it hits the fan.'[8] For Lovelock, environmental ethics, ethical living, and moralizing prove to be nothing but 'scams', stories we tell ourselves about ourselves to guarantee a modicum of hope where there is none. If we take him at his word, his earth poetics foreclose the very possibility of action be it efficacious or useless.

Gaia creates a new world of moral equivocation where the good is suspended in a cosmic balance, unidentifiable and impossible to act upon. She represents a consummation wherein the binaries of good and evil, fragmentation and totality, and life and death are entirely superseded by an altogether other order. What Lovelock implicitly gestures towards in his hypothesis qua theology is Gaia as messianic principle. But she is not *our* messiah. Gaia signifies the total displacement of human spatio-temporal existence, duration and remembering. This total displacement bears comparison with the paradoxical nature of traditional politico-religious messianisms, which tend to posit an event that is entirely outside secular human history, but which nonetheless completes and renders meaningful that history. With Gaia, the emphasis falls on the first fork of this paradox, on the sense of total rupture with the past. 'Nothing historical can relate itself on its own account to anything Messianic,' Walter Benjamin wrote in his Theses on the Philosophy of History: 'the Kingdom of God', therefore, 'is not the *telos* of the history dynamic; it cannot be set as a goal' (1978, p. 312). Gaia is in this sense is non-epochal, an end that liberates the human organism from its own 'ends'. Gaia has no meaning as she exists in complete removal from all human activity, and so stands even outside historical schemes, such as that of the Anthropocene, which aim to break with the purely human limits of historical understanding. While humans co-exist with Gaia, Gaia exceeds the normative domain of the political, foreclosing any possibility of 'anthropocenic subjectivity'.

And yet, the claims of Gaia on public attention – its existence as an idea, a figure circulating in complex paths that link scientific knowledge to the para-religious underside of contemporary public life – suggest ways that it must always defer this total messianic rupture with the values of human history: it can never finally break with human perspectives, even as it demands this break to have been always already achieved. For either the movement ceases to be properly apocalyptic, or it *collapses* as a *movement*. Perhaps a few of the faithful will persevere in their commitment and postpone the final date. But if the apocalypse does not come, its alarmism also tires. Others may cease to believe, postpone, or be enthralled and simply go back to things as they always were...

Gaia is something of a para-religious performative contradiction. Its circulation and status as an 'object of faith' is unjustifiable in its own self-concealing terms. It remains a dark wager.

The last man's party

The Gaia hypothesis implores us to reflect on our ultimate event – human extinction. What is at stake here is less the ethical injunction engendered by the possibility of extinction, but the ethical dimensions of extinction itself. The ethics of extinction is necessarily para-religious; it crystallizes in an anti-scientific realm beyond normative modes of reasoning, for it calls into question the sustainability of reasoning itself. When refracted onto the Anthropocene such an ethics qua para-religion introduces a cold distance to humanity, preferring to treat it as an aberration.

Themes and variations on this line of questioning have become the dark obsessions of a new breed of apocalyptic ethicists who ask about humanity's worthlessness. The most 'extreme' ethics of the apocalypse emerges in the recent work of the guru of the anti-natalist movement, David Benatar, whose 2006 treatise on the matter, *Better Never to Have Been: The Harm of Coming into Existence*, laments not only humanity's ineptitude, but argues that such ineptitude merits the end of all human procreation. Benatar dreams of a world of zero population [?] and admits the logical implication that he should commit suicide himself, carrying on, nonetheless, only to make other humans aware of the damage they do to the Earth (Kooten, 2013, pp. 273, n. 43). Benatar's theses offer a strong version of person consequentialism, the ethical and philosophical extension of para-religious negative theologies and apocalyptic anthropcenism. In a broad sense, consquentialism refers to a school of ethical theory, which – in opposition to virtue ethics, for instance – establishes the parameters of the good in relationship to the ends of human activity. Within consequentialism, one also finds strains of 'negative consequentialism' which insist that the good is bound in the diminishing of pain amongst human actors. Person consequentialism, a variant of negative consequentialism, argues that humans may actually be quite inconsequential insofar as they are, by and large, incapable of reducing their own pain in the present, and in the future, climate change and the Anthropocene providing compelling evidence for such a position.

Based on these principles, the Benatar syllogism, then, takes a familiar form: in giving life to someone, we harm them and are ultimately responsible for the accumulated suffering that they will most probably endure. On the other hand, we cannot legitimately be held responsible for whatever happiness they may experience and, in any case, in terms of cost/benefits, the suffering will inevitably outweigh the joy. The majority of human lives are replete with suffering, not only not ideal, but even not worth living at all. By bringing someone into this world we cannot help but be responsible for their suffering and, considering that most are bound to suffer, it is unethical to give them existence. This suffering, moreover, is imbricated in not only the degraded planet that we leave for future generations, but the high probability that future generations will not only suffer more, but inflict more suffering on the planet and others and also future-future generations. Following the logic of asymmetry – that we are responsible for the sufferings of others when we generate the possibility of their existence, but not for their joys – bringing other humans into the world is clearly bad in light of this. Insofar as humans are able to inflict the least amount of pain on others (present and future), they are bad, despite their good intentions. Procreation is morally wrong.

In Benatar's view then, 'Non-existence has an advantage over existence…the pleasures of the existent, although good, are not an advantage over non-existence, because the absence of pleasure is not bad. For the good to be an advantage over non-existence, it would have to have been the case that its absence were bad' (Benatar, 2006, p. 41). If we take him at his word, existence is morally reprehensible, as all life will in some manner be poor and therefore, non-life is always preferable. In non-existence no one can be in any way 'worst off', and hence, 'coming into existence cannot be *worse* than never coming into existence' (20–21). Of course, no clear measure of 'worse', 'better', 'good' and 'bad' could be advanced to measure the force of such arguments empirically. Nevertheless, as it is generally admitted that future generations in a changed climate will be likely be *worse off* than present ones, non-existence therefore appears to be preferable to 'this'.

For these reasons, those who do procreate do so in full cognizance of the fact that their offspring will not only suffer (which is bad), but suffer potentially more than they did (which would appear to seem 'worse'). And while one may bet on the possibility of a 'life worth living', such a hope does little to remedy the fact that most lives do not appear 'worth starting' (23). In other words, our understanding of temporality, informed by personal and civilizational 'trajectories', has moral implications. On the level of existence, deferred pleasure in a future life does little to parry the trauma of suffering in the present life. The fallacy is found in how we subtract the bad from the good in order to determine a hazy future standard of well-being. Once existence is understood as a 'trade-off' or series of cost-benefit calculations between duelling asymmetries, the possibility of identifying any firm ethical principles which could legitimize it as a having intrinsic worth has been foregone. Existence appears more and more like a confidence game. Extinction or non-existence are heuristics with which to problematize existence as speculation. According to Benatar, most people do change their minds about being 'glad to be born', but persist in their gladness nonetheless. Here lies the power of speculation and confidence (faith): 'Why so few people do change their minds is explained, at least in part, by the *unduly rosy picture* most people have about the quality of their own lives' (59).[9] A good deal of 'work' goes into sustaining the fantasy that our lives and our world are much better than they really are.

With a view to building on Benatar's misanthropic realism and cutting through post-modern cultures of rosiness, Peter Singer (2010) calls for the immediate end to the species and the celebration of this end in one glorious *fête infatigable*, a last hoorah for a truly Last Man. Grappling with population overload, resource depletion and the potential irreversibility of harm to future generations, he has given up on the human race. His ethics of care has shifted from a concern for others to a concern for the yet to be born; he contends that the non-existant have rights and that assuring their dignity may paradoxically require that we respect their right to not be born. Such care reaches its paroxysm in the form of a party:

> Most thoughtful people are extremely concerned about climate change… But the people who will be most severely harmed by climate change have not yet been conceived. If there were to be no future generations, there would be much less for us to feel to guilty about. So why don't we make ourselves the last generation on Earth? If we would all agree to have our-selves sterilized then no sacrifices would be required – we could party our way into extinction!… Is a world with people in it better than one with-out? Put aside what we do to other species – that's a different issue. Let's assume that the choice is between a world like ours and one with no sen-tient beings in it at all. And assume, too – here we have to get fictitious, as philosophers often do – that if we choose to bring about the world with no sentient beings at all, everyone will agree to do that. No one's rights will be violated – at least, not the rights of any existing people. Can non-existent people have a right to come into existence?

The question, of course, is would it really be a party? In the slow-motion nuclear apocalypse imagined in Nevil Shute's *On the Beach*, end-of-the-world hedonism quickly cedes place to a resigned ethics of keeping up appearances, and of keeping on keeping on. As if nothing so brilliantly maintains the status quo than its immi-nent and unavoidable demise.

Dark temples, sordid churches: 'new religious movements'

Extinction religions have already appeared, well before the kick off to the big party. These new frames of non-belief in the human foment religions that have little therapeutic or emancipatory value. Nonetheless, they are 'critical religions' inso-far as they are religions without redemption, religions guided by the imperatives 'stop human' and 'stop the world'. The Voluntary Human Extinction Movement (VHEMT), described by Stephen Hicks (2010) as being 'firmly in the grip of zero-sum anti-humanist environmentalism', is perhaps the most vocal of apocalyptic cli-mate cults. It rigorously attempts to institutionalize the ethics of Singer and Benatar (the latter's opus serving as its unofficial bible). The movement's unofficial slogans are 'may we live long and die out', and 'thank you for not breeding'. It goes without saying that its adherents hold humans and themselves in low esteem.

The movement's founder is Les U. Knight, a former Vietnam vet and Oregon high school teacher whose disgust with humans led him to get a vasectomy at the age of 25. Repulsed by our species' intractable penchant for destruction, Knight maintains that 'zero humans is the only safe number. As long as there's one breeding couple we could be right back where we are now' (Miller, 2011). VHEMT aspires to prevent the extinction of animals and the Earth itself by promoting human extinc-tion. Moreover, such logic is the natural product of human rationalism itself; it is paradoxically our 'humanism' or capacity to deliberate on the right action which should lead us to the conclusion that 'distributive justice' in the Anthropocene requires that the human species voluntarily phases itself out: if our intelligence cannot lead us to ameliorate the eco-system, it can surely lead us to 'save' it through eliminating its greatest scourge (us). However absurd or impertinent para-religions of the apocalypse may appear, they are, at least, quite stringent in their reasoning, one that they share with the most 'respectable' moral philosophies, philosophies which they supplement in their own epistemo-theological fashion.

The most rational and rationalized means of accomplishing the phasing out of the human is through a total moratorium on all 'human breeding' and 'people husbandry'. In principle, Knight's reasoning seems justified if we accept the Intergovernmental Panel on Climate Change's and UN's recent findings. The United Nations estimates that the human population, currently at 6.5 billion, will reach 9.1 billion in 2050. Many estimates place a sustainable global population level at between one and two billion; meanwhile, almost 16,000 new humans are born each hour. The natalist ethos, for VHMET, appears to be not only irresponsible, but narcissistic. More broadly, following Knight, having a child is an implicit *endorsement* of the idea that it is possible to have a sustainable ecosystem that includes humans – that it is possible to find a way out of the mess we have created. Having children then is the last illusion that sustains us in a world after god, after science, and after the dream of a perfectable society. Yet, the movement is less gloomy than it is optimistic:

> We're not just a bunch of misanthropes and anti-social Malthusian misfits, taking morbid delight whenever disaster strikes humans… Voluntary human extinction is the *humanitarian alternative* to human disasters. We don't carry on about how the human race has shown itself to be a greedy, amoral parasite on the once-healthy face of this planet. That type of negativity offers no solution to the inexorable horrors which human activity is causing. Rather, the movement presents an *encouraging* alternative to the callous exploitation and wholesale destruction of Earth's ecology. As VHEMT volunteers know, the *hopeful alternative* to the extinction of millions of species of plants and animals is the voluntary extinction of one species: Homo sapiens… us. Each time another one of us decides to not add another one of us to the burgeoning billions already squatting on this ravaged planet, *another ray of hope shines* through the gloom…[10]

As with Singer, part of the euphoric vision of this 'humanitarian solution' involves its commitment to a non-reproductive sexual hedonism that would usher in the 'end'. VHEMT is thus firmly on the side of the sexual revolution, gay rights, the dissolution of the traditional nuclear family, and anything that does away with priggish morality and what Knight calls 'reproductive fascism'. In opposing such morality the movement, also, at least implicitly, opposes the long-standing relationship between the reproduction of populations and the reproduction of capital and labour power in human societies. Stated otherwise, in rejecting the human, Knight also awards little value to the most primordial source of capital, the human body and its capacity to labour. If humans are worth nothing, the same can be said for their work and works. In addition, women here are not defined in terms of their procreative capacity, a view advanced by a multitude of radical feminisms and the litany of critical theorists who have pleaded for the social construction of sexuality.

This intervention in population overload and breeding gone awry could also potentially intervene into the geo/bio-politics of the transnational population movements buoyed by demographic booms and economic inequality. And voluntary 'extinctionists' are indeed sensitive to comparisons between their movement and other projects and politics of extermination and eugenics. Yet, as Vanessa Baird remarks, VHEMT does not discriminate and refuses to 'identify "the problem" with Africans or Asians with high fertility rates but applies its logic to all of us – and especially to the US which, while having only five percent of the world's population, manages to consume a quarter of the world's resources' (2011, p. 120). For Knight, better to rush towards extinction than attempt to reform the distribution of resources through global policy measures. This principle that extinction *is* simply extinction also entails treating the refugee or immigrant from a developing region as a problem as opposed to a potential victim of a series of systemic conditions of marginalization. In other words, if humans are the problem, there can be no moral distinction between the climate refugee and the polluter whose activities have uprooted the refugee. For VHEMT, everyone is equally culpable and everyone must go.

Knight often delivers sermons at the Church of Euthanasia. A more flamboyant variant of VHEMT, the church understands itself to be a non-profit educational foundation devoted to restoring the balance between humans and the remaining species on Earth. Founded in 1992 by a transvestite who calls himself the Honorable Reverend Chris (Chrissy) Korda, the Church boasts a full clergy. Amongst its patron saints is 'Saint Kevorkian'.[11] As for the movement's mantras, one finds: 'Eat people not animals', 'Save the Planet, kill yourself', 'Eat a queer fetus for Jesus', and 'Fuck breeding'. These imperatives also correspond to the more general commandments and pillars of the religion: 'The Church has only one commandment, and it is "Thou Shalt Not Procreate." In addition, we have four "pillars" or principles, which are Suicide, Abortion, Cannibalism and Sodomy. Note that cannibalism is only required for those who insist on eating flesh, and is strictly limited to consumption of the *already dead*. Also note that, for the Church, sodomy is defined as any sexual act not intended for procreation: fellatio, cunnilingus, and anal sex are all forms of sodomy.'[12] Driven by the spirit of dada, porn, and Sadean performance art, the church shares the same core tenets as VHEMT. However, it infuses them with *inter alia* a quasi-libertarian politics, a belief in extra-terrestrials,[13] and an aesthetic of 'cannibal whores'. The church's icon is 'Brigitte', a crucified transvestite sex doll with taped nipples. She is often paraded to protest various pro-life rallies, Planned Parenthood openings (next to a sign which reads 'Fetuses aren't people. They aren't even chickens. Who cares?'), sperm banks, Earth days (brandishing a banner that says 'Stupid Monkeys') and traffic. In addition, she is regularly invited to the Church's fetus barbeques where children's dolls are grilled in parking lots and bustling thoroughfares.[14] The Church's second in command, Pastor Kim, also regularly marches in public with a cross of 'carnivorous babies' delivering the Church's 'good news': 'Eat People, Not Animals.'[15] In terms of liturgical literature, the Church publishes a quarterly journal, entitled *Snuff It*, which details the church's myth of origins, cosmology and ritual practices. It encourages the downtrodden to kill themselves, and offers advice on performing the perfect suicide. The journal is ambitious and hitherto has contained pieces on UN overpopulation data, the art of drinking one's own urine, the Unabomber, vasectomy confessions, and critiques of media and surveillance society, amongst other heterogeneous and counter-cultural topics. Apropos ritual itself, the church makes it very clear that abortion is a sacred rite (Kerr, n.d.). In addition, part of the church's interest in abortion also concerns food depletion. For Korda, there is simply no reason that aborted foetuses cannot be eaten.

The church represents species consciousness at its limit point and synthesizes its rabid anti-humanism with an anti-capitalist, anti-modern and anti-Christian agenda. In fact as Kristen Hatten (2013) notes, 'It is dangerous to dismiss these people as mere extremists. The truth is, they're only carrying a pro-abortion, pro-euthanasia mentality to its logical end. If abortion is a responsible and acceptable act – as it is, according to pro-choicers – then what is abortion's exact opposite, procreation?' Which is all to say that its crucified dolls and rubber chickens, in all of their flamboyant performativity, participate in the most serious of critiques. As a 'church', moreover, it parodies conventional notions of 'churchiness', and, in a broader sense, the current composition of organized religion and their epistemological foundations. Regardless of its 'antics', the church now boasts several thousand members across the globe, all of whom commune during their regular fetus barbecues. Nonetheless, in all of their hatred for the human, most of the members of the church have yet to kill themselves.

Moral panic, apocalypse and other bourgeois pastimes

Apocalypse is a hermeneutic, a way of watching ourselves as we move towards an array of tragic ends unleashed by 'something-we-know-not-what' (Leslie, 1996, p. 9). Or rather, it is a set of possible hermeneutics, different ways of conceiving of the self-reflective subject and his or her finitude, for the political and religious desire for catastrophe is always embedded in a certain regime of contemporary knowledge – within major strains of eco-ideology, for instance – that creates the socio-epistemological conditions that generate and shape any given apocalyptic imaginary. That imaginary is not a sui generis structure that thinks the beyond of the world and being, but a material point of relay for a series of political interventions, a series that is shaped by its pre-existing discursive and social parameters. And it is one shot through by paradoxes of belief and 'turning away', of collective Eros and Thanatos, and of presentism and the uncertainties of what may transpire. For the apocalyptic ecological imaginary, these paradoxes are operationalized in modes of 'believing' in the cataclysmic end while getting on with your business – a way of being scared without being scared. The registration of the imminent catastrophe runs against the grain of capitalist infinity, a culture of fulfilled desires and perpetual growth that resists any symbolic challenge launched by the forces of the disaster, thus relegating these things to the apocalyptic imaginary. Ecological responsibility cannot be understood simply by interrogating the rapport between human animals and nature, but instead needs to be reconsidered in terms of the critique of contemporary capitalism and its life cultures not least because these are cultures that secretly rejoice in apocalyptic fantasy. The fantasy is neurotic; undergirding infinity is the silent desire to be burned by the event.

In the public sphere, one is bombarded by headlines which speak of 'Global Warming and Ozone Loss: Apocalypse Soon', 'Apocalypse Now: Unstoppable Man-Made Climate Change', 'Global Warming: 2014 May Be Apocalyptic'. Etymologically, the Greek term *apokalytein* has its roots in *apo* (from) and *kalyptein* (to cover and conceal), signifying a process of unconcealing or revelation. Religious apocalyptic eschatology sought to pierce the veil of matter and point the way to the world of redemption of *eschaton* that exists underneath/beyond this one. For many an ancient Gnostic, this meant accelerating historical time to its cataclysmic breaking point where a redemptive universe would open up and deliver the politically marginalized of this world. Millenarian eschatology was a means for the marginal to 'bargain from a position of weakness' and triumph over earthly alienation through the positing of another world. As I.M. Lewis thus argued, religious ecstasy and messianism have often worked to 'help the interests of the weak and downtrodden who have otherwise few effective means to press their claims for respect' (2003, p. 32). The apocalyptic lays claim to eschatology to produce authority. It also offers marginalized groups a narrative through which to comprehend their abjection as part of a redemptive and heroic cosmic teleology. As Norman Cohn further remarks, 'The world of millenarian exaltation and the world of social unrest, then, did not coincide but did overlap… the usual desire of the poor to improve the material conditions of their lives became transfused with phantasies of a world reborn into innocence through a final, apocalyptic massacre' (1972, p. 16).[16] For Cohn's primarily Christian millenarians, the 'last times' usher in the purging of 'evil' (the clergy, the rich etc.) and the real possibility of the poor inheriting the Earth in a triumphant new order. Conversely, 'evil' would lament this final epoch as a moment of decadence and the loss of authority. For those who profited from social hierarchy the 'last times' truly signalled a fall (quite literally), while the poor saw in this a flight from a sordid social position.

What distinguishes contemporary eco-apocalyptic narratives from these religious traditions is the relative absence of narrative communities bound together by the struggle against evil (unless we take statements like 'Humans are evil' to be neo-gnostic in nature) and, more specifically, the simple fact that *we do not really* believe the narratives themselves. In addition, *they, the vulnerable, do not construct nor speak through them*. The champions of the apocalyptic climate imaginary are not the population at the greatest risk or those who stand to be imminently effected by climate transformation, but rather the comfortable global middle class who, from within relative material and intellectual luxury, can theorize and watch the apocalypse as a post-politics or as extinction porn. The new ecological 'millenarianism' is also by and large secular; and unlike its primitive counterparts, posits no world after this one. In other words, metaphysics, eschatological utopianism and the dreams of the golden age are no more than allegorical resources that have been 'overcome' through both the critique of religion and the desacralization of the political. Even the apocalypse itself is exhausted and unable to really imagine or achieve its completion. Nonetheless, contemporary apocalypticism is the perfect space of absorption for the secular, the religious, the consumerist, the post-religious and everything in between. It is everything and nothing, something to burst forth in a distant future and also something that already happened.

It is no coincidence that the Church of Euthanasia is so attached to porn; the apocalypse is an obscene and pornographic *mis en scène* and, as hyper-modern spectators bereft of all empathy, our own death in the near future is something 'I like to watch'. But this obsession also betrays the presence of another disavowal; eco-apocalyptics may be asking the wrong question. In lieu of seriously engaging with questions of mitigation and adaptation, eco-apocalyptics chooses to 'go to the end' in extinction daydreams. The apocalyptic imaginary may be born in part of collective anxiety about the end, but is surely also inspired by the will to surpass actual political impotence, and to break heroically, at least in the imagination, with the drab realities of 'post-politics', by foreclosing these entirely in apocalyptic resignation. The result is what Susan D. Moeller (1999) describes as 'compassion fatigue', a lurching numbness that sets in with the mediatized apocalypse, annulling the possibility of all critical thought on the realities, and repercussions of the event; there are simply too many disasters and apocalypses occurring at once, dulling the psyche and rendering imperatives to action empty phrases that meld into the general din (11–13).

Apocalypticism is a liminal strategy for liminal times. Paradoxically, it undermines the real horizon of the disaster; in lieu of understanding narratives about the future as a series of interpretative and practical tools, it settles on one overarching narrative that silences others. While the apocalypse is a site of discursive struggle, it is also one that is strangely non-agonistic and un-nuanced. Perhaps, this is because the apocalypse comes as a relief. It is a tidy means of imposing a temporal narrative on post-historical time, a way to project all negativity into the homogenized space of the end of man. The apocalypse, like religion, is a symptom, a cause and a solution. There is giddiness in abnegating control and rapture in deferring responsibility in the face of something as unmanageable as climate change. In its overdetermination of fatalism, the apocalyptic imaginary may be just as arrogant as the myth of unlimited progress. In its smugness, it refuses to ask where responsibility comes from. It prevents the enlightenment of apocalypticism, if such a process were possible, which would not necessarily deny that we may be a pestilence, but would also ask how such pests should deliberate on their actions. This mode of engagement would take seriously the apocalypse, exorcising it from the domain of the imaginary. It would surpass apocalypticism and, following John Leslie, it asks 'what our duty would be in a situation where absolutely nothing could be done...if the human race manages to survive for the next couple of centuries, it will quite probably be in a position to start spreading right across the galaxy. It could have a very strong duty to do so' (1996, p. 182–183). Or maybe a strong duty not to do so... Uncertainty remains the ground, not the dilemma. We certainly may go extinct (through voluntary or involuntary means). We may also go to outer space. We may be already cursed to obsolescence. The fact of the matter is we don't really know. But this was always an experiment.

Notes

1 On the normative construction of religion, see Bruce Lincoln (2012). On the 'religious climate change coalitions', see Keith Runyon (2013). On various monotheistic ecological re-readings of religion, see Deutsche Welle's portal 'Religion and Climate Change' at www.dw.de/top-stories/religion-and-climate-change/s-100334. For a general treatment of religion and climate change, see Gerten & Bergmann (2013). On Christianity and climate change, see Conradie et al. (2014). On the heavily acerbic critique of Abrahamic religions, enlightenment universalism, and human rights, from a non-Abrahamic perspective, see Roy et al. (2010).

2 Contemporary post-Bataillean and post-Deleuzian theories of immanence find perhaps their most pronounced iterations in the recent work of Bruno Latour (1991, 2012); Isabelle Stengers ([1997] 2003); and Phillipe Descola (2005, 2011).

3 See Bron Taylor (2005, 2009); Mary Evelyn Tucker & John A. Grim (1994); J. Baird Callicott (1994); Catherine Albanese (1991); and Joanne Pearson, Richard H. Roberts & Geoffrey Samuel (1998).

4 José A. Prades (1987, p. 171). Originally a Durkheimian term and a pejorative one at best, according to Prades, para-religious phenomena are constituted by a proliferation of themes and practices, amongst which one finds Alchemy, Angelology, Astrology, Cartomancy, Shamanism, Popular Beliefs, Ancestor Cults, Demonology, Esoterism, Ecstasy, Fable, Fanaticism, Fetishism, Folklore, Geomancy, Gnosticism, Hermeticism, Heroes, Idols, Incantation, Initiation, Kabbalah, Legends and Fairy-Tales, Levitation, Masonry, Magic, Metaphysics, Metapsychosis, Mysticism, Secret Societies, Sorcery, Spiritism, Superstition, Syncreticism, Taboo, Tarot, Telepathy, Theosophie, Totemism, Transmigration and Yoga. Durkheim himself had long struggled with the relationship between the religious, nomo-religious, quasi-religious and para-religious, alternately claiming that $R=NR+QR$, $R=NR$ or $R=NR+QR+PR$, equations which belie his efforts to meld morality (QR), the sacred-social (NR) and rites and practices (PR) into a holistic apparatus of belief and institutional life (R – which, for Durkheim, was the sacred-secular version of NR). 'Religion' would always attempt to absorb the other terms which were subservient to it as pieces of its gestalt. Yet, not all para-religious phenomena could be so easily integrated into the Durkheimian edifice of the sacred, and hence, as Prades adds, Durkheim would come to elaborate a socio-morphologic distinction between NR and PR, which was furthermore a distinction between 'doing' and 'being', ethical social life and its dissolution in radical interiority, ecstasy, and a host of negations of the negation, cf. Prades op. cit., p. 180–189.

5 On Gaian religion and theology, see Anne Primavesi (2000, 2003).

6 Dale Jamieson, 'Biodiversity and Climate Change: Ethics and Politics', lecture given at conference on *Environmental Ethics, Biodiversity, and Climate Change*, Sponsored by UNESCO and the Principality of Monaco, December 8, 2011, Monaco. On humanity's cognitive and emotive block vis à vis the Anthropocene, see also Jamieson (2014).

7 James Lovelock quoted by Leo Hickman (2010).

8 James Lovelock quoted by Decca Aitkenhead (2008). Gaia Apocalypticism also finds a rousing crescendo in the work of John Gray, cf. Gray (2002).

9 Emphasis added. Anti-natalists contend that those who argue that human lives are infinitely better than they were in, for instance, the middle ages, are missing the point. Suffering still exists and this suffices to justify the anti-natalist position.

10 Voluntary Human Extinction Movement, 'About the Movement', http://www.vhemt.org/aboutvhemt.htm#vhemt. Emphasis added.

11 Church of Euthanasia, 'Resources'. See http://www.churchofeuthanasia.org/resources/resources.html.

12 Church of Euthanasia, 'FAQ'. See http://www.churchofeuthanasia.org/coefaq.html.

13 'The Church of Euthanasia was inspired by a dream, in which Rev. Chris Korda confronted an alien intelligence known as The Being who speaks for the inhabitants of

Earth in other dimensions. The Being warned that our planet's ecosystem is failing, and that our leaders deny this. ... Rev. Korda awoke from the dream moaning the Church's infamous slogan, Save the Planet – Kill Yourself' (Hatten, 2013).

14 Ibid.

15 Ibid.

16 On Millenarianism as strategy for political voicing, essential readings also include John Lofland (1977); Gary Trompf (1990); and Eric Hobsbawm (1965).

References

Aitkenhead, D., 2008. James Lovelock: 'Enjoy life while you can. Because if you're lucky it's going to be 20 years before it hits the fan'. *The Guardian*, 1 March.

Albanese, C., 1991. *Nature Religion in America: From the Algonkian Indians to the New Age.* Chicago: University of Chicago Press.

Baird, V., 2011. *The No-Nonsense Guide to World Population.* Oxford: New Internationalist Publications.

Benatar, D., 2006. *Better Never to Have Been: The Harm of Coming into Existence.* Oxford: Oxford University Press.

Benjamin, W., 1978. Theological-Political Fragment. In: P. Demetz, ed. *Reflections: Essays, Aphorisms, Autobiographical Writings.* New York: Harcourt Brace Jovanovich.

Bulhof, I. N. & Kate, L. t., 2000. Echoes of an Embarrasment. In: I. N. Bulhof & L. t. Kate, eds. *Flight of the Gods: Philosophical Perspectives on Negative Theology.* New York: Fordham University Press.

Callicott, J. B., 1994. *Earth's Insights: A Survey of Ecological Ethics from the Mediterranean Basin to the Australian Outback.* Berkeley: University of California Press.

Cohn, N., 1972. *The Pursuit of the Millenium: Revolutionary Millenarians and Mystical Anarchists of the Middle Ages.* Oxford: Oxford University Press.

Conradie, E. M., Bergmann, S., Deane-Drummond, C. & Edwards, D. eds., 2014. *Christian Faith and the Earth: Current Paths and Emerging Horizons in Ecotheology.* New York: Bloomsbury Academic.

Descola, P., 2005. *Par-delà nature et culture.* Paris: Gallimard.

Descola, P., 2011. *L'écologie des autres: L'anthropologie et la question de la nature.* Paris: Éditions Quae.

Gerten, D. & Bergmann, S. eds., 2013. *Religion in Environmental and Climate Change: Suffering, Values, Lifestyles,.* New York: Bloomsbury Academic.

Gray, J., 2002. *Straw Dogs: Thoughts on Humans and Other Human Animals.* London: Granta.

Hatten, K., 2013. *For the Anti-Humanist Group, Church of Euthanasia, Abortion is a Sacrament* [Online]. Available at: http://liveactionnews.org/anti-humanist-group-church-euthanasia-abortion-sacrament/ [accessed 21 October 2015].

Hickman, L., 2010. Humans are Too Stupid to Prevent Climate Change. *The Guardian*, 29 March.

Hicks, S., 2010. *Voluntary Human Extinction* [Online]. Available at: http://www.stephenhicks .org/2010/06/07/voluntary-human-extinction/ [accessed 21 October 2015].

Hobsbawm, E., 1965. *Primitive Rebels: Studies in Archaic Forms of Social Movement in the 19th and 20th Centuries.* New York: Norton.

Jamieson, D., 2014. *Reason in a Dark Time: Why the Struggle Against Climate Change Failed – and What It Means for Our Future.* Oxford: Oxford University Press.

Kerr, N., n.d. *Abortion is a Sacred Rite* [Online]. Available at: http://www.churchofeuthanasia .org/snuffit4/abortion.html [accessed 21 October 2015].

Kooten, G. K. v., 2013. *Climate Change Science and Economics: Prospects for an Alternative Energy Future.* Dordrecht: Springer Press.

Latour, B., 1991. *Nous n'avons jamais été modernes: Essai d'anthropologie symétrique.* Paris: La Découverte.

Latour, B., 2012. *Enquêtes sur les modes d'existence: Une anthropologie des modernes*. Paris: La Découverte.

Leslie, J., 1996. *The End of the World: The Science and Ethics of Human Extinction*. London: Routledge.

Lévinas, E., 1995. *Altérité et transcendence*. Montpellier: Fata Morgana.

Lewis, I. M., 2003. *Ecstatic Religion: A Study of Shamanism and Spirit Possession*. London: Routledge.

Lincoln, B., 2012. The (Un)Discipline of Religious Studies. In: *Gods and Demons, Priests and Scholars: Critical Explorations in the History of Religions*. Chicago: University of Chicago Press.

Lofland, J., 1977. *Doomsday Cult: A Study of Conversion, Prosetylization, and Maintenance of Faith*. New York: Irvington.

Lovelock, J., 1995. *The Ages of Gaia: A Biography of Our Living Earth*. New York: W.W. Norton.

Lovelock, J., 2000. *Gaia: A New Look at Life on Planet Earth*. Oxford: Oxford University Press.

Lovelock, J., 2006. *The Revenge of Gaia*. New York: Basic Books.

Mabille, F., 2007. L'humanitiare comme religion?. In: F. Champion, S. Nizard & P. Zawadzki, eds. *Le sacré hors religions*. Paris: l'Harmattan, p. 126–128.

Margulis, L., 2012. Gaia. In: É. Hache, ed. *Ecologie Politique: Cosmos, Communatés, Milieux*. Paris: Éditions Amsterdam.

Miller, A., 2011. *This Guy Wants You Dead* [Online]. Available at: www.vice.com/print/this-guy-wants-you-dead [accessed 21 October 2015].

Moeller, S. D., 1999. *Compassion Fatigue: How the Media Sells Disease, Famine, War and Death*. London: Routledge.

Pearson, J., Roberts, R. H. & Samuel, G. eds., 1998. *Nature Religion Today: Paganism in the Modern World*. Edinburgh: Edinburgh University Press.

Pickett, S. & Ostfeld, R. S., 1995. The Shifting Paradigm in Ecology. In: R. L. Knight & S. F. Bates, eds. *A New Century for Natural Resources Management*. Washington, DC: Island Press.

Prades, J. A., 1987. *Persistance et metamorphose du sacré: Actualiser Durkheim et repenser la modernité*. Paris: PUF.

Primavesi, A., 2000. *Sacred Gaia: Holistic Theology and Earth System Science*. London: Routledge.

Primavesi, A., 2003. *Gaia's Gift: Earth, Ourselves, and God After Copernicus*. London: Routledge.

Roy, J. S., Thorheim, C., Dorjderem, A. & Macer, D., 2010. *Universalism and Ethical Values for the Environment*. Bangkok: UNESCO Bangkok Press.

Runyon, K., 2013. *World Religious Leaders Urged to Fight Climate Change* [Online]. Available at: http://www.huffingtonpost.com/keith-runyon/world-religious-leaders-u_b_4337235.html [accessed 21 October 2015].

Singer, P., 2010. Should this be the Last Generation?. *New York Times*, 6 June.

Stengers, I., [1997] 2003. *Cosmopolitiques*. Paris: La Découverte.

Taylor, B., ed., 2005. *Encyclopedia of Religion and Nature*. London: Continuum International.

Taylor, B., 2009. *Dark Green Religion: Nature Spirituality and the Planetary Future*. Oakland: University of California Press.

Trompf, G., ed., 1990. *Cargo Cults and Millenarian Movements: Transoceanic Comparisons of New Religious Movements*. Berlin: Mouton de Gruyter.

Tucker, M. E. & Grim, J. A. eds., 1994. *Worldviews and Ecology: Religion, Philosophy, and the Environment*. Maryknoll: Orbis Books.

Zizek, S., 2011. *Living in the End Times*. London: Verso.

12 Litigation, activism, and the paradox of lawfulness in an age of climate change

Nicole Rogers

Climate change litigation, in which activists argue that legal doctrines and existing legislation should be applied to achieve either climate change mitigation or adaptation outcomes, has become an increasingly common occurrence in Western courtrooms.[1] But the wisdom of resorting to legal rules, which reflect values and principles antithetical to those held by many climate change activists, has been questioned.[2] As a well-entrenched form of cultural performance, litigation may struggle to challenge established codes of behaviour and values that have contributed and continue to contribute to anthropogenic climate change; in fact, climate change litigation has even been seen as supporting and reinforcing such codes and values.[3]

Climate change activism, by way of contrast, appears to offer more potent possibilities, particularly when it involves role-swapping, farce, and the arsenal of the trickster (Kershaw 2002, 128). Climate change activism can be most effective in generating a paradigm shift when it highlights instabilities in established structures, institutions and stereotypes. As a form of cultural performance it is often deliberately subversive; rather than reinforcing established social and political structures, it attacks and undermines such structures. It also raises an important question about legitimacy and lawfulness: what exactly is the meaning of lawfulness in the context of climate change?

Activists who initiate climate change litigation can find that lawfulness operates to prevent successful outcomes. Appropriating a phrase from authors Sam Blay and Ryszard Piotrowitcz, I have previously designated this 'the awfulness of lawfulness' (Blay and Piotrowitcz 2000, 1; Rogers 2013, 20). By way of contrast, lawfulness becomes a contested norm in climate change direct action.

In this chapter, I will consider the transformative possibilities presented in climate change litigation and climate change direct action, reflecting in particular on what these different forms of cultural performance reveal about the role and significance of lawfulness in the context of climate change.

Lawfulness and climate change litigation

Climate change activists who resort to litigation must operate within the constraints of the official discourse of law. They must deploy its terms and phrases, principles and values; since this discourse has evolved within the capitalist paradigm, they are operating on enemy terrain or in what Baz Kershaw would describe as a 'paradoxical landscape' (Kershaw 2002, 119). In fact, Kershaw points out that when activists take any form of 'cultural action', they 'risk recreating the pathology – endemic denigration of the "natural world" – that it is trying to eliminate' (Kershaw 2002, 119).

Litigation as a form of cultural action poses particular challenges for activists. Within the self-referential system which is law, the concept of lawfulness operates as a force for systemic inertia, encompassing as it does the requirement that judges decide cases according to precedents and established legal principles; the principle that legislation trumps judge-made law; and the structural and doctrinal barriers which prevent judges from making new law in response to shifting values and changing social norms. Thus lawfulness restricts opportunities for practical and systemic change through climate change litigation.

One important obstruction faced by activists lies in the existence of a vast body of authoritative judge-made law and legislation. Much of this body of law evolved before and outside the context of climate change awareness and has been shaped by the dominant 'tale of capital'.[4] Such precedents are readily available to support judicial interpretations which are consistent with a conservative 'business as usual' approach, rather than an approach which permits an innovative adaptation of the legal system to the ominous realities of climate change. This is illustrated in the *Macquarie Generation* case.

In this case, two climate change activists unsuccessfully argued that the 'licence to pollute' held by one of Australia's largest energy producers should be read, in its application to its greenhouse gas emissions, as subject to an implied condition relating to health and the environment. The New South Wales Court of Appeal applied legal principles relevant to the interpretation of commercial contracts in resolving this issue.[5] These included a requirement that the implied term 'be necessary to give business efficacy to the contract'.[6] Justice Handley held that he could 'see no reason why these principles should not apply by analogy to the implication of a term in a statutory licence, making due allowance for the differences the nature of the instruments.'[7] In his view, it was 'not necessary to imply any condition to make [the licence] effective, and the condition relied on would contradict the licence.'[8]

Ironically, even law designed to protect human rights can be ill suited to the resolution of climate change issues. Kiribati citizen Ioane Teitota unsuccessfully sought to claim refugee status under New Zealand law, arguing that Kiribati is rapidly becoming uninhabitable due to climate change impacts. A deciding factor for the judge was the absence of persecution as required under the 1951 *Convention relating to the Status of Refugees*. He concluded that:

> The optimism and novelty of the applicant's claim does not … convert the unhappy position of the applicant and other inhabitants of Kiribati into points of law.[9]

An additional obstacle to effective climate change litigation arises from the traditionally distinct functions of the different arms of government. According to the doctrine of separation of powers, the legislature makes law and determines policy, and the role of the judicial arm of government is to apply and enforce the law. Some judges have refrained from making controversial decisions in climate change litigation on the basis that the relevant issues are non-justiceable[10] or best left to the political sphere.

Admittedly, a 'suitable minded court' may be prepared to 'repurpose' a regulatory regime designed for other purposes in order to achieve climate change mitigation outcomes (Ghaleigh 2010, 41); one well-known example is the decision of the United States Supreme Court that greenhouse gas pollutants should be regulated as air pollutants under the 1990 *Clean Air Act*.[11] The interpretation and application of existing legislation is an accepted function of the judiciary. Regulatory agencies opposed to such 're-purposing' have raised the argument of climate exceptionalism (Heinzerling 2008, 416). Climate change activists have also expressed doubt as to whether climate change can be effectively addressed through existing regulatory regimes (Nagle 2010, 55, 75–76).

In fact the existence of a regulatory framework, irrespective of its operational inadequacies or even possibilities in the context of climate change, can deter judges from resolving climate change issues. For instance, an action in public nuisance against four electric power companies and the Tennessee Valley Authority was unsuccessful when the United States Supreme Court held, on appeal, that any common law right was displaced by the United States *Clean Air Act*.[12] An action in public nuisance brought by the Inuit Village of Kivalina against oil, power and coal companies failed for the same reason.[13] Another example can be found in the one of the first most well known of the myriad Children's Trust lawsuits and petitions.[14] In 2012, the United States District Court for the District of Columbia dismissed the argument that the United States government had a fiduciary obligation to protect the atmosphere under the public trust doctrine. The judge held that even if the doctrine were part of federal law, it had been displaced by the *Clean Air Act*.[15]

Furthermore, judges who are prepared to make progressive decisions directed towards climate change mitigation can find that the impact of such decision-making is negated or eroded by the subsequent enactment of legislation. For instance, after the Queensland Court of Appeal set aside on administrative law grounds a decision to approve the extension to the Newlands Coal Mine,[16,17] the Queensland government amended the relevant legislation within four days to ensure that the mine went ahead (McGrath 2007, 227). In 2013, after Justice Preston broke new ground in holding that the expansion of Rio Tinto's Mount Thorley Warkworth open-cut coal mine should be refused on the basis that the economic benefits did not outweigh the social impact on the community,[18] the New South Wales government amended an existing planning instrument such that the economic significance of the resource became the principal consideration in approving any mining project.[19] As a consequence, despite an unsuccessful appeal against Justice Preston's judgment,[20] the company lodged a new application for the mine extension which was assessed as 'approvable' by the New South Wales Planning Assessment Commission in March 2015.[21]

More comprehensive legislative schemes can prevent innovative judicial decision-making directed towards climate change mitigation. In the second Ulan mine case,[22] Justice Pain revisited her earlier unprecedented decision that conditions which required the offsetting of Scope 1 greenhouse gas emissions should be imposed on the approval of an extension to the Ulan coal mine at Mudgee in New South Wales.[23] She held that the conditions were not warranted in light of the subsequent enactment of federal greenhouse gas legislation.[24] In so doing, she implicitly conceded that policy and legislative initiatives, however short-lived, could replace the need for judicial innovation in the area of climate change mitigation.[25]

Structural barriers also adversely affect the outcome of climate change activist litigation. Common law standing requirements can deny activists access to courts.[26] Entrenched legal rules and statutory constraints, which limit the issues to be decided and identify relevant factors in decision-making processes, can confine the impact of judicial findings. Only in merits appeals can judges remake decisions;[27] in many other matters, they find themselves restricted to 'policing the procedural parameters of decisions' (Farrier 2007, 204). For instance, although in 2006 Justice Pain broke new ground in holding that environmental assessment of the proposed Anvil Hill coal mine in New South Wales had to include all greenhouse gas emissions, including Scope 3 emissions,[28] she had no decision-making power to prevent the approval of the mine itself.

The above examples demonstrate the 'awfulness of lawfulness' in the climate change context. However it is not my intention to downplay the significance of climate change litigation. Most commonly, commentators refer to the capacity of climate change litigation to 'transform or tweak the regulatory landscape' (Osofsky and Peel 2014, 303). Climate change litigation is often viewed as a driver for regulatory change (Preston 2009, 189).[29] Climate change litigation, even if unsuccessful, can also generate change by suggesting a new understanding or re-evaluation of key concepts in the legal system, including human rights, nuisance, intergenerational equity and even justice. The resulting debate can form part of a paradigm shift when the public imagination is captured by the symbolic and/or rhetorical significance of the litigation.

As I have discussed elsewhere, the use of children as plaintiffs in the Children's Trust lawsuits constitutes effective symbolism; they provide an embodied representation of the concept of intergenerational equity in the climate change context and their expression of personal grievance and deprivation through the lawsuits evokes both guilt and a sense of responsibility in adult spectators (Rogers 2013, 22–24). Osofsky and Peel have identified climate change litigation which changes norms and values as an indirect pathway to regulatory change and observe that such indirect pathways 'may often be some of the most significant and transformative' (2014, 326; 2013, 155).

The distinction between changing the way we interpret and apply particular concepts and norms, and changing legal rules, is important. Systems analyst Donella

Meadows identified a number of different places to intervene in artificial systems and called these leverage points, or points of power (Meadows 2008, 145). The rules of the system constitute 'high leverage points', but changing the rules of the system is less effective than changing the mindset out of which the system arises, for 'paradigms are the sources of systems' (Meadows 2008, 158, 163). Thus unsuccessful climate change litigation which engenders debate on the meaning of key legal concepts can be a more effective force for systemic change than climate change litigation which tinkers with legal rules.

The most powerful climate change litigation compels us to reconsider the fundamental concepts and assumptions which underpin the 'tale of capital' which is law. However activists who bring lawsuits must accept the way in which the legal system defines lawfulness and confers legitimacy upon certain activities and actors. In contrast, activists interrogate the meaning of the concept of lawfulness through climate change direct action. In the following sections I shall evaluate the political efficacy of climate change direct action and in particular, consider the challenges posed by climate change direct action to the concept of lawfulness.

Climate change direct action

A conference paper with the provocative title of 'Is Earth F★★ked?' was delivered at an academic forum in 2012 by complex systems analyst Brad Werner.[30] According to one commentator, the radical nature of the presentation lay in the author's references to environmental direct action or what he termed resistance.[31] In Werner's modelling of the coupled human-environment system, existing forms of environmental management constitute part of capitalist cultural dynamics; they may slow down the catastrophic end results of climate change but cannot prevent them. Resistance, however, involves the adoption of a certain set of dynamics antithetical to capitalist culture. According to Werner, 'the future sustainability of the coupled human-environment system may well depend on the strength of resistance and the ways that the society acts to suppress that resistance' (Werner 2012).

In evaluating the political efficacy of climate change direct action, it is necessary to acknowledge the broad spectrum of climate change direct action and to consider, furthermore, the legal response to this phenomenon. Certainly, environmental activists have always utilised the theatre of direct action to draw public attention to environmental issues. Greenpeace pioneered much of this theatre, staging 'image events for mass media dissemination' (De Luca 1999, 3-4). Environmentalists who deploy strategies such as lobbying and negotiation, and even litigation, remain within the parameters of institutional politics and the system which they are critiquing (De Luca 1999, 65, 71). Environmental activists who utilise direct action strategies are engaged in what Kevin De Luca describes as discourse politics; he contends that they are challenging 'the grand narrative of industrialism' (De Luca 1999, 64).

The images generated by direct action can arguably be powerful tools in deconstructing central ideologies and cultures in contemporary society (De Luca 1999, 92; Orenstein 2001, 151). However performance studies theorist Baz Kershaw is sceptical about the effectiveness of environmental protest image events. He draws a distinction between such events, exemplified in the Greenpeace occupation of a defunct oil rig in which the carefully orchestrated dramaturgy of the event ensured that 'human culture [was] still the primary focus of attention', and more spontaneous forms of environmental protest which draw upon 'the traditions of the trickster' (Kershaw 2002, 125, 128). Kershaw argues that protest events which fall into this second category manage to 'sidestep' the contradictions in traditional image events and pose a subversive challenge to entrenched institutions, stereo-types and cultural norms (Kershaw 2002, 128). Such protest events feature multiple references, satire and caricature through role playing, the subversion of traditional images, and irony.

Two examples from this second category can be found in the 'fraudulent' bidding for oil and gas leases by American activist Tim DeChristopher and the 2013 share market hoax perpetrated by Australian activist Jonathon Moylan. Both of these actions disrupted commercial activity through playful misrepresentation and the assumption of false identities, and the subversive impact of such actions is apparent in the subsequent response of those responsible for upholding the law and protecting the authority of the marketplace.

Tim DeChristopher presented himself as an authentic bidder at a controversial Bureau of Land Management oil and gas lease auction in Salt Lake City in 2008, in an attempt to highlight its serious climate change and other environmental implications. He successfully placed bids of almost $1.8 million. He was charged with and convicted of two offences and sentenced to two years in prison.[32]

In January 2013, Jonathon Moylan issued a counterfeit press release stating that the ANZ Bank had withdrawn $1.2 billion in funding from Whitehaven's controversial Maules Creek mine project. As a consequence, shareholders sold shares and Whitehaven's share price temporarily dropped by $314 million. Moylan was prosecuted by the Australian Securities and Investment Commission (ASIC) and faced a maximum penalty of $495 000 or up to ten years in jail.[33] He pleaded guilty to the charges prior to his Supreme Court trial and received a prison sentence of one year and eight months,[34] but was released on a good behaviour bond. His lawyer commented that Moylan had 'learnt a big lesson' and would continue to protest only 'as far as he can within the confines of the law'.[35]

The Bidder 70 and Whitehaven hoaxes highlight the weaknesses, corruption and falsehoods of the marketplace, the key capitalist structural institution.[36] DeChristopher's crime lay in the fact that he masqueraded as a legitimate bidder when he had no intention of exercising his rights under the leases and no money to pay for them. Since, however, the relevant market itself lacked legitimacy and was subsequently dismantled,[37] there was no real distinction between genuine and false bidders. His sham bids drew attention to the nebulous nature of that particular market and the surreal nature of all financial markets.

Moylan's hoax exposed the susceptibility of the share market to lies and both non-corporate and corporate fictions. Moylan himself did not envisage that his hoax would have such a dramatic impact on share prices or on investors.[38] The market's vulnerability to virtual representations indicates that it is itself a chimera and lacks material substance (McNevin 2013).

ASIC and commentators expressed alarm at the threat to 'market integrity' posed by Moylan's hoax.[39] Yet the hoax drew attention to the fact that investment decisions with large-scale climate change implications are generally made in an ethical vacuum; Moylan has maintained that he 'made the announcement that ANZ *should* have made'.[40] In Moylan's world view, the oxymoronic phrase 'market integrity' has quite different connotations than it assumes in the world of business and investment.

Moylan was engaged in an act of parody, which he compared at the time to the Chaser team's incursion into the APEC security zone in 2007[41] and the announcement on the part of United States 'culture jammers' the Yes Men that Union Carbide had shut down.[42] Those responsible for protecting the marketplace took Moylan's hoax seriously. They maintained that 'the credibility and functionality' of the financial marketplace is at stake (McNevin 2013). The zeal with which ASIC initiated legal action against Moylan, a non-corporate target, has been contrasted with its marked tolerance of corrupt behaviour on the part of corporate players.[43] The heavy-handed approach has been justified by ASIC as a necessary strategy to protect the market and reassure investors (Ker and Hawthorne 2013). The sentencing judge, in deciding to impose a sentence of imprisonment, also emphasised the serious impact of Moylan's actions on the market even while noting that he was not – unlike others – guilty of market misconduct, motivated by personal profit.[44] He described Moylan's actions as 'much more than some sort of public mischief offence',[45] stating that:

> …here, the market was manipulated, vast amounts of shares were unnecessarily traded and some investors lost money or their investment in Whitehaven entirely. These were not just 'day traders and speculators' as the Offender said to Mr Duffy – superannuation funds and ordinary investors suffered damage. It was intended that ANZ at least be embarrassed and that Whitehaven should be damaged or threatened, even if there was no intention to hurt shareholders and investors as such.[46]

The response of both ASIC and the sentencing judge to Moylan's hoax can also be explained by the subversive impact of parody, which Baudrillard has described as 'the most serious crime' since it 'cancels out the difference upon which the law is based: the difference between obedience and transgression' (1983, 40, 39). Parody is an affront to the literalness of law, to its 'deadly seriousness' (Davies 1996, 132). However some individuals and groups, who commit offences by engaging in acts of parody, escape prosecution by virtue of their role as the Fool.

I have argued elsewhere that the 'state's ongoing "discourse of self-legitimation" is ill-served by prosecuting the Fool' (Rogers 2010, 287). As Brian Sutton-Smith has put it, the Fool 'live[s] in the place where the "writ does not run"' (Sutton-Smith 1997, 212). Charges against the Australian Chaser team for breaching a section of the *APEC Meeting (Police Powers) Act* 2007 by carrying out their 2007 APEC stunt were eventually dropped. During the 2007 APEC meeting, the Chaser team in a cavalcade of cars and motorcycles, parading 'insecurity' passes and complete with jogging 'security guards', had found themselves unexpectedly waved through checkpoints in a restricted security zone to emerge, one audaciously impersonating Osama bin Laden, on Macquarie Street in Sydney's central business district. They were promptly arrested and charged with unauthorised entry into a restricted area. The United States Yes Men, who have both impersonated individuals in a process of 'identity correction' and maintained fake websites, have thus far escaped prosecution. In 2009, they were sued for trademark and copyright infringement by the United States Chamber of Commerce but the Chamber abandoned its lawsuit four years later.

Satirists such as the Chasers and the Yes Men, who have an established cultural following, enjoy a relative immunity from prosecution which climate change activists do not share. I have written that:

> The rational play of law is ill-suited to controlling the arbitrary and the frivolous, the satirical and parodic, the carnivalesque. The state cannot effectively assert its authority over satirists and comedians by recasting satire and parody as legal transgression (Rogers 2010, 307).

Despite the existence of a substantial network of supporters, who include David Suzuki and Noam Chomsky, Moylan did not have a recognised social role as a satirist, as a Fool. As an activist, he was vulnerable to prosecution for his act of parody. Moylan's plea of guilty meant that his Supreme Court trial did not proceed, but it is quite possible that his trial – particularly if the defence of necessity had been argued – would have amplified the political effectiveness of the hoax even while putting him at far greater risk of a non-suspended prison sentence.

Lawfulness and climate change direct action

From the above discussion it is apparent that climate change direct action encompasses image event and spectacle, performance and metaphor, satire and parody. The illegality of much climate change direct action contributes to its political efficacy by providing further transformative possibilities. Lawfulness becomes a contested norm when activists engage in acts of civil disobedience. Activists are prepared to break the law in order to change the law and in the ensuing legal performances, the court is compelled to re-evaluate the meaning of lawfulness.

Such legal performances are generally prosecutions, but corporations have also attempted to claim compensation for profits lost or corporate damages sustained as a consequence of climate change protests. In one such Australian case,[47] the magistrate warned activists that anyone who similarly entered coal loading facilities in order to protest would be liable for any resulting financial loss which could be proven and quantified (Higginson, 2011). In such lawsuits, victimhood becomes another contested norm in the context of climate change. Large emitting corporations present a narrative of victimhood contested by protesters, who maintain that such corporations are, instead, the perpetrators of crimes against humanity. The Rising Tide defendants in this particular lawsuit argued that 'the real victims here are those affected by climate change and Newcastle coal export'.[48]

In such cases we witness a surreal clash between two competing narratives of persecution and victimhood, and two opposing discourses: the alternative ecocentric discourse of the protesters and the dominant discourse of capitalism within which corporations have rights, markets have integrity, and all activities can be commodified and costed.

More commonly, climate change protesters appear in courts as defendants in criminal trials, prosecuted for offences against property or, as in Moylan's case, corporate offences. Such trials can be powerful political spectacles. Joel Schechter describes the trial of a protester as 'a continuation of the resistance that begins with civil disobedience' (Schechter 1994, 88). Importantly, as Robert Cover argued, 'by provoking the response of the state's courts, the act of civil disobedience changes the meaning of the law articulated by officialdom' (Cover 1983, 47).

An activist himself, Cover wrote eloquently on the intimate relationship between violence and law, reminding us that judges administer violence (Cover 1986, 1601). An ideological if not experiential distinction has been drawn between such violence, law-preserving violence in the typology of Walter Benjamin and Jacques Derrida, and the acts of lawmaking violence which overthrow existing legal systems and establish new ones, and which are constructed as acts of civil resistance and even terrorism at the moment of enactment.[49] Lawmaking violence acquires a belated legitimacy in the newly established legal system (Derrida 1992, 36). Law-preserving violence, which 'maintains, confirms, insures the performance and enforceability of law', is lawful at the time it is administered but its legitimacy may be retrospectively questioned if a new legal system with different norms and values is subsequently established (Derrida 1992, 31).[50]

This distinction is helpful because legitimacy and lawfulness are clearly portrayed as relative rather than absolute concepts. Other theorists have argued that civil disobedience can be justified through an invocation of 'the commonly shared conception of justice that underlies the political order' (Rawls 1973, 365); and as an expression of an individual's moral judgment (Allan 1996, 89, 93). These theorists have argued that existing legal systems can accommodate and should accept civil disobedience. Rawls states that civil disobedience operates 'within the limits of fidelity to law' (Rawls 1973, 366); and Allan suggests that the rule of law is entirely consistent with an individual's decision to disregard morally unjust 'laws' as non-laws (Allan 1996, 108).

Once it is conceded that the legitimacy of existing laws is not an absolute legitimacy, we can query the legitimacy currently conferred upon the activities of big greenhouse gas emitters and indeed upon our own often unthinking contributions to climate change, in a legal and social system dominated by the 'tale of capital'. Such activities may well be condemned as unethical, illegitimate and even evil (Newman 2014, 60) in an alternative normative universe and alternative legal system (Cover, 1986). On the other hand, the activities of climate change activists which are currently construed as unlawful or illegitimate may be viewed as lawful and legitimate in this alternative normative universe, in the same way that the activities of members of the Jewish resistance in Nazi-occupied Europe are no longer represented as crimes in contemporary Western societies.

A judge, confronted with civil disobedience, can choose to administer law-preserving violence and thus reinforce the official interpretation of what is law and what is lawful. However if a judge refrains from penalising or punishing protesters, he or she is thus implicitly and sometimes explicitly acknowledging the legitimacy of an alternative normative order, of alternative narratives and alternative paradigms.[51] It is at this juncture, when those responsible for upholding the existing system of law concede that alternative narratives and understandings of lawfulness might have validity, that we find possibilities for a fundamental paradigm shift. Hence such moments constitute significant leverage points in the artificial system which is law (Meadows 2008, 145).

Lawful excuse and necessity: legal avenues for renegotiating the norm of lawfulness

This moment of renegotiation of a fundamental norm is particularly powerful when climate change activists argue in a courtroom that it is necessary or even 'lawful' to break the law in an attempt to avert the much greater evils associated with climate change impacts. One of the most publicised cases in this regard involved the successful use of the 'lawful excuse' defence on the part of six climate change activists in England.

The activists were members of Greenpeace, who scaled the Kingsnorth power station chimney in 2007 with the intention of writing 'Gordon, bin it'. Their aim was to draw public attention to Prime Minister Gordon Brown government's imminent decision to approve a new coal-fired power station at the site. The protest caused a temporary closure of the power station and attracted nationwide publicity. The company claimed that it spent thirty thousand pounds to remove the graffiti.[52] The activists were charged with criminal damage; since the extent of the damage was more than five thousand pounds, they were entitled to a jury trial. If found guilty, they would have faced prison sentences.[53]

One important aspect of the case was that the relevant legislation made it permissible to commit the offence of destroying or damaging property in order to prevent the commission of a greater property offence.[54] The jury held that the global emergency of climate change justified otherwise criminal activity in the form of acts of civil disobedience and minor property damage.[55]

The jury reached this conclusion after listening to the compelling evidence of five expert witnesses, including eminent climatologist James Hansen and a former president of the Inuit Circumpolar Council, Aqqaluk Lynge. Hansen, who surprised Greenpeace by accepting the request to be a witness, explained to the jury how their own coastline in Kent would be affected by climate change.[56] Lynge told the jury that he had 'witnessed the effects of climate change with my own eyes right across the Arctic.'[57] Such testimonies were compelling. As Graeme Hayes has pointed out, the testimonies 'negotiate[d] climate change as proximate and material', thereby 'making the global, distant, abstract, and immaterial relevant to the concrete, material, local, and immediate concerns of the citizenry' (Hayes 2013, 220, 221).

After listening to this evidence, the jury was prepared to accept a new meaning of lawfulness in the context of climate change. The radical implications of this conclusion were clear; as one of the activists stated outside the courtroom:

> When twelve normal people say that it is legitimate for a direct action group to shut down a coal-fired power station because of the harm that it does to the planet, then one has to ask: where exactly does that leave government energy policy? (Broomfield 2009).

The corresponding defence of necessity has also been raised, but thus far unsuccessfully, by climate change activists on trial in Australia,[58] the United Kingdom,[59] the United States[60] and Canada (Tremblay 2012, 328); this defence similarly requires the court to reconsider the meaning of the norm of lawfulness in the context of climate change. Activists assert that it is necessary to break the law in order to prevent a greater imminent harm to life or property.[61] Judges have dismissed this argument on various grounds, including the remoteness or absence of the connection between the defendants' actions and the prevention of death or injury, and the fact that alternative legitimate avenues could have been adopted instead.

Judicial refusal to allow the defence of necessity to be argued at all by climate change activists[62] can be explained in light of the fact that the courtroom, when evidence pertaining to necessity is presented, is transformed into 'a privileged and uncontested space for the construction of political challenge' (Hayes 2013, 215). In arguing necessity, activists can draw on expert testimony about climate change impacts without such testimony being challenged. It is, in fact, a 'tactical mistake' for the prosecution to call its own expert witnesses, as the prosecution would thus concede that what is at stake is a 'policy contest' rather than a criminal prosecution. In climate change litigation directed towards mitigation outcomes, judges have been swayed by conflicting evidence on climate change impacts presented by experts employed by industry and/or government interests.[63] By way of contrast, the defence provides activists in climate change trials with a valuable opportunity to present an unchallenged political case about climate change impacts (Hayes 2013, 214).

Judicial resistance to the defence can also be explained by the fact that it poses such a profound normative dilemma for the legal system. It is the nature and magnitude of the alleged threat of climate change that contributes to this dilemma: as one commentator has put it, 'What acts might the law permit in fighting a threat of global, even catastrophic, proportions?'[64] Hugo Tremblay discusses the possibility that the invocation of the doctrine of necessity in the context of climate change might 'dissolv[e] … law's normativity' (Tremblay 2012, 351). He maintains that the use of the doctrine by climate change activists who break the law 'could indicate a threshold in the continuum between legal certainty and flexibility', beyond which 'law may become incapable of performing its function and ensuring its own normative power' (Tremblay 2012, 353). This was acknowledged by a New South Wales District Court judge, who dismissed the defence of necessity in an appeal brought by climate change protesters with the observation that it could lead to anarchy (Mills 2010).

Judicial resistance to the use of this defence is exemplified in Tim DeChristopher's trial. The judge refused to allow DeChristopher to argue the defence of necessity or to present evidence in relation to the Bureau of Land Management's possible violation of environmental laws, expressing reluctance 'to open [his] courtroom to a lengthy hearing on global warming and environmental concerns when this is a case based on simple criminal actions' (Morgan 2009). On appeal, this ruling was upheld.

In spite of the judge's refusal to hear political arguments of necessity, DeChristopher's trial created a forum for participants and onlookers to articulate and interrogate fundamentally different understandings of the meaning of lawfulness in the context of climate change. Sympathetic commentators heralded DeChristopher as a hero and emphasised the importance of civil disobedience in redefining both the law and the meaning of lawfulness.[65] DeChristopher himself made reference to an alternative normative order, stating that:

> The reality is not that I lack respect for the law; it's that I have greater respect for justice. Where there is a conflict between the law and the higher moral code that we all share, my loyalty is to that higher moral code.[66]

Statements made by the judge during the sentencing hearing indicated that he imposed a term of imprisonment partly as a consequence of DeChristopher's 'continuing trail of statements' about his 'civil disobedience' and his propensity to 'step to any bank of microphones that he could find to give a speech ... and advocate that it was fine for him to break the law'.[67] On appeal, Judge Baldock of the US Court of Appeal upheld the judge's right to take DeChristopher's widely promulgated views on civil disobedience and lawfulness into consideration in determining a sentence 'necessary to deter Defendant from future violations and to *promote respect for the law*'.[68]

In DeChristopher's view and the view of other climate change activists, lawfulness loses its moral authority when the government and legal system support the activities of major greenhouse gas emitters and fail to take effective steps to protect the community and the environment. Lawfulness assumes paradoxical dimensions in this line of reasoning, in that breaking the law is portrayed as a necessary means of obeying a higher law; through civil disobedience and the flouting of relatively minor legal rules, activists hope to draw public attention to the unethical and, from their perspective, unlawful conduct of governments and corporations.[69]

Conclusion

The concept of lawfulness plays a pivotal role in climate change activism. Lawfulness impedes activists in their pursuit of practical outcomes through climate change litigation. Climate change litigation can identify possibilities for policy reform and legislative changes; however it is arguable that regulatory modifications cannot generate significant climate change mitigation outcomes while our legal landscape continues to be shaped by the 'tale of capital'.

Some climate change litigation challenges accepted norms and assumptions, its transformative potential lies in the symbolic value of such litigation and the resulting rhetorical debates about the meaning of legal and cultural terms, rather than in the practical outcomes.

Climate change direct action is inherently more subversive in that it tells a different narrative to the tale of capital. Importantly, climate change direct action and related courtroom performances provide a forum in which the norm of lawfulness can be contested and debated.

Meadows wrote that people change paradigms by 'pointing at the anomalies and failures in the old paradigm' and 'speaking and acting, loudly and with assurance, from the new one' (Meadows 2008, 164). Climate change activists who engage in acts of civil disobedience are contributing to a significant destabilisation of what is currently considered lawful in the climate change context. They are doing this by compelling courts and the public to consider what is meant by lawfulness, and highlighting the contradictions and anomalies in the ways in which our current legal system legitimises the behaviour of those who contribute the most to climate change and criminalises the behaviour of those who seek to curb such activities.

Such a paradigm shift is imperative if we are to address effectively the looming crisis of climate change.

Notes

This chapter originally appeared as "'If you obey all the rules you miss all the fun": Climate Change Litigation, Climate Change Activism and Lawfulness' in (2015) *New Zealand Journal of Public and International Law*, 179–199.

1 The definition of climate change litigation remains contentious (Vanhala and Wilson 2013, 141). In this article, I am analysing trials of climate change activists and compensation lawsuits directed against such activists as a separate phenomenon to climate change litigation in which activists attempt to use existing legal doctrines and legislation to achieve climate change mitigation and adaptation outcomes.
2 Laurence Tribe has written that, in mounting lawsuits to protect the environment, 'a subtle transformation is likely to be occasioned by the philosophical premises of the system in which the effort is undertaken. The felt obligation will be translated into the terminology of human self-interest' (Tribe 1974, 1330).
3 The insidious impact of public interest environmental litigation was recognised by Tribe, who wrote: 'What the environmentalist may not perceive is that, by couching his claim in terms of human self-interest – by articulating environmental goals wholly in terms of human needs and preferences – he may be helping to legitimate a system of discourse which so structures human thought and feeling as to erode, over the long run, the very sense of obligation which provided the initial impetus for his own protective efforts' (Tribe 1974, 1331).
4 J. Thornton, 'Our World Needs a New Renaissance', *The Sydney Morning Herald*, 6 June 2009 (online).
5 *Macquarie Generation v Hodgson* [2011] NSWCA 424 at [61]; see my discussion of this case in Rogers 2013, 20–21.

6 *Macquarie Generation v Hodgson* [2011] NSWCA 424 at [61].

7 *Macquarie Generation v Hodgson* [2011] NSWCA 424 at [63].

8 *Macquarie Generation v Hodgson* [2011] NSWCA 424 at [65].

9 *Ioane Teitiota v The Chief Executive of the Ministry of Business Innovation and Employment* [2013] NZHC 3125 at [63].

10 As one United States commentator has expressed this, 'the courts of this country are not the appropriate forum in which to resolve these complex policy issues' (Hall 2009–2010, 266).

11 *Masschusetts v Environmental Protection Agency* 549 US 497 (2007).

12 *American Electric Power Company v Connecticut* (2011) 131 S Ct 2527.

13 The village will have to be relocated due to the impact of global warming on the sea ice which protected the village from inundation. The suit was dismissed by the United States District Court and an appeal to the Ninth Circuit Court of Appeals was unsuccessful on the basis that the claim was non-justiceable and displaced by legislation. In 2013 the United States Supreme Court refused to hear the case. The village of Kivalina also argued that the defendants were guilty of conspiracy in attempting to subvert the public debate on global warming.

14 In these lawsuits and petitions, young people are attempting to compel United States governments and government agencies to protect the atmosphere as part of the public trust; see <http://ourchildrenstrust.org/Legal>.

15 Memorandum opinion in *Alec L et al v Lisa P Jackson et al and National Association of Manufacturers et al* 11-cv-02235 (DDC 2012) 31 May 2012 at 6-7. In 2014 an appeal to the US Court of Appeals for the DC Circuit was unsuccessful. In December 2014, the plaintiffs' petition for a writ of certiorari was denied by the United States Supreme Court.

16 *Queensland Conservation Council Inc v Xstrata Coal Queensland P/L & Ors* [2007] QCA 338.

17 *Re Xstrata Coal Queensland Pty Ltd & Ors* [2007] QLRT 33.

18 The judge, in an innovative judgment, referred to the concept of 'sostalgia' or loss of place (at [404]) and held that the project's adverse impacts 'would exacerbate the loss of sense of place, and materially and adversely change the sense of community, of the residents of Bulga and the surrounding countryside' (at [18]); *Bulga Milbrodale Progress Association Inc v Minister for Planning & Infrastructure and Warkworth Mining Limited* [2013] NSWLEC 4.

19 *State Environmental Planning Policy (Mining, Petroleum Production and Extractive Industries)* 2007.

20 *Warkworth Mining Limited v Bulga Milbrodale Progess Association Inc* (2014) NSWCA 105.

21 New South Wales Planning Assessment Commission, *Warkworth Continuation Project Review Report*, 4 March 2015.

22 *Hunter Environment Lobby Inc v Minister for Planning (No 2)* [2012] NSWLEC 40.

23 *Hunter Environment Lobby Inc v Minister for Planning* [2011] NSWLEC 221.

24 *Hunter Environment Lobby Inc v Minister for Planning (No 2)* [2012] NSWLEC 40 at [17].

25 In 2013, the Abbott government was voted into power with the election promise that it would repeal this legislation and subsequently made good on that promise.

26 Rodgers and Moritz describe standing barriers as the 'most conspicuous' of the 'doctrinal barriers' which 'offer a constitutionalized hindrance to those so rash as to quarrel with perversion of science and destruction of nature unsubtly disguised as federal policy' (Rodgers and Moritz 2009, 309).

27 One example of a successful merits appeal in which an approval for the extension of a coal mine was set aside was *Bulga Milbrodale Progress Association Inc v Minister for Planning & Infrastructure and Warkworth Mining Limited* [2013] NSWLEC 4. Another example of a merits appeal in which the judge gave paramountcy to the reduction of global greenhouse gas emissions was the decision of Justice Preston in the Taralga wind farm case; *Taralga Landscape Guardians Inc v Minister for Planning and RES Southern Cross Pty*

Ltd [2007] NSWLEC 59. In holding that 'the broader public good of increasing the supply of renewable energy' should prevail over the 'geographically narrower concerns' of local residents (at [3]), Justice Preston approved the wind farm with more turbines than originally approved by the Minister.

28 *Gray v The Minister for Planning and Ors* [2006] NSWLEC 720.

29 See also Osofsky and Peel (2014, 2013), where the authors develop a model for understanding how climate change litigation influences regulation.

30 N. Klein, 'Why science is telling all of us to revolt and change our lives before we destroy the planet', *New Statesman*, 29 October 2013 (online).

31 J. Mingle, 'Scientists ask blunt question on everyone's mind', *Slate*, 7 December 2012 (online).

32 The offences were interfering with the provisions of Chapter 3A of the *Federal Onshore Oil and Gas Leasing Reform Act 1987* (30 USC § 195(a)(1)) and making a false and fraudulent material representation (18 USC § 1001).

33 Under section 1041E of the *Corporations Act 2001* (Cth).

34 The case was removed to the Supreme Court rather than to the District Court, at the request of the Department of Public Prosecutions, apparently due to the complexity of the charges. See L. Shanahan, 'Jonathon Moylan's Whitehaven Hoax Case to go to Supreme Court', *The Australian*, 24 September 2013 (online).

35 'Activist Jonathon Moylan Avoids Prison over Mining Hoax', *The Australian Business Review*, 25 July 2014 (online).

36 Such actions are markedly different to climate change activism directed at financial investment markets through legitimate channels, such as climate change shareholder activism and what has been described as risk-based corporate campaigning (Shearing 2012, 479; Ricketts 2013).

37 The leases were cancelled in 2009 when the Obama administration came into power, on the basis that environmental reviews had not been undertaken in relation to the relevant parcels of land. Bidders were refunded their money. See L. Kaufman, 'Drilling Leases Scrapped in Utah', *The New York Times*, 4 February 2009 (online).

38 Interview with Jonathon Moylan (SBS television, 9 January 2013).

39 ASIC's acting chairman Greg Tanzer stated in an interview that 'Our focus is on market integrity, and preserving market integrity, and we're concerned about threats to market integrity wherever they arise': see 'ANZ Hoaxer Facing Jail Despite No Profit Motive', *ABC News*, 10 January 2013 (online:); and P. Ker and M. Hawthorne, 'How Hoaxsters Hold Market to Ransom', *The Sydney Morning Herald (Weekend Business)*, 12 January 2013 (online).

40 Interview with Jonathon Moylan (SBS television, 9 January 2013) (emphasis added).

41 See Rogers 2010 for an analysis of this incident and the legal fallout.

42 P. Ker and B. Cubby, 'ASIC to look into Whitehaven Hoax', *The Sydney Morning Herald*, 7 January 2013 (online).

43 B. Keane, 'Double Standards as Gutless ASIC Targets the Little Guy', *Crikey*, 5 July 2013 (online).

44 *R v Moylan* [2014] NSWSC 944 (25 July 2014) at [101].

45 *R v Moylan* [2014] NSWSC 944 (25 July 2014) at [102].

46 *R v Moylan* [2014] NSWSC 944 (25 July 2014) at [103].

47 The case involved a claim made under the *Victims Support and Rehabilitation Act 1996* (NSW) in relation to a 2010 climate change protest at the Port of Newcastle and was unsuccessful due to lack of evidence of actual loss.

48 A. Branley, 'Rising Tide Activists Win', *The Newcastle Herald*, 3 March 2011 (online).

49 This distinction was made by Walter Benjamin in 'Critique of Violence', and is discussed by Derrida in his influential essay 'Force of Law: The 'Mystical Foundation of Authority' (Benjamin 1996; Derrida 1992).

50 For instance, Saddam Hussein was tried and executed for detaining, torturing and executing people believed to have been involved in an assassination attempt on his life. These

acts were legitimate under his regime at the time they were committed. He argued at his trial that '[t]hese people were charged according to the law, just like you charge people according to the law'. See Rogers 2007, 428, 435.

51 Cover expresses it thus: 'The community that disobeys the criminal law upon the authority of its own constitutional interpretation, however, forces the judge to choose between affirming his interpretation of the official law through violence against the protesters and permitting the polynomia of legal meaning to extend to the domain of social practice and control' (Cover 1986, 47–8).

52 'Climate Danger "Justifies Power Station Damage" Caused by Environmental Activists', *The Australian*, 12 September 2008.

53 *Criminal Damage Act 1971* (United Kingdom) section 4(2).

54 *Criminal Damage Act 1971* (United Kingdom) section 5.

55 M. McCarthy, 'Cleared! Jury decides that threat of global warming justifies breaking the law', *Common Dreams*, 11 September 2008 (online).

56 G. Bedell, 'Why six Britons went to eco war', *The Observer*, 3 May 2009 (online); James E Hansen, witness statement, <www.greenpeace.org.uk/blog/climate/kingsnorth-trial-witness-statements-full-20080912>.

57 Aqqaluk Lynge, witness statement, (www.greenpeace.org.uk/blog/climate/kingsnorth-trial-witness-statements-full-20080912).

58 Six protesters who were convicted of trespass on rail tracks at Newcastle Coal Terminal in 2008, and thus contributed to a delay in the export of 20 000 tonnes of coal, appealed their conviction to the District Court on the basis of this defence (D. Mills, 'Hazel Fights On', *The City Hub*, 3 March 2010 (online)). However the judge dismissed the appeal as the mining and exporting of coal are legal activities which should be protected from disruption.

59 M. Schwarz, 'Why did Ratcliffe defence fail where Kingsnorth Six succeeded?' *The Guardian*, 16 December 2010 (online); M. Wainwright, 'Drax protesters found guilty of obstructing coal train', *The Guardian*, 4 July 2009 (online); 'Manchester airport climate change protesters found guilty after judge says actions not justified', *Manchester Evening News*, 20 February 2011 (online); A. Hickman, 'Climate activism: is the trial more important than the protest?' *The Ecologist*, 25 August 2010 (online).

60 Nick Engelfried stated in January 2013 that he and other defendants intended to argue necessity at their forthcoming trial for trespass (N. Engelfried, 'Montana coal protesters argue necessity defense', *Waging non-violence* 14 January 2013 (online)). However, in April 2013 the judge refused to allow the use of this defence (S. Talwani, 'Coal protesters admit trespassing into the Montana Capitol', *Billings Gazette*, 18 June 2013 (online)).

61 This defence has been discussed in its application to environmentalists who engage in acts of civil disobedience (Hernandez 2007). Hernandez contends that it is easier to establish this defence when this greater harm is framed as a discrete threat rather than when it is something as 'amorphous' as climate change.

62 For example, in 2009, an English judge held that the defence of necessity could not be raised in the trial of twenty-two defendants who obstructed a coal train. See M. Wainwright, 'Drax protesters found guilty of obstructing coal train', *The Guardian*, 4 July 2009 (online).

63 See for instance *Xstrata Coal Queensland Pty Ltd & Ors v. Friends of the Earth – Brisbane Co-Op Ltd & Ors, and Department of Environment and Resource Management* [2012] QLC 013.

64 J. Mingle, 'The climate change defense', *The New York Times*, 12 December 2008, (online).

65 See, for instance, the commentator in *Rolling Stone* who described DeChristopher's conviction as a 'Rose Parks moment': J. Goodell, 'A Rosa Parks Moment: Climate Activist Tim De Christopher Sentenced to Prison', *Rolling Stone*, 27 June 2011 (online).

66 Statement of Tim DeChristopher (26 July 2011) <www.peacefuluprising.org/tims-official-statement-at-his-sentencing-hearing-20110726>.

67 Quoted in *US v DeChristopher*, Judge Baldock, 14 September 2012 at 23 <www.ca10 .uscourts.gov/opinions/11/11-4151.pdf>.
68 *US v DeChristopher*, Judge Baldock, 25 (emphasis added).
69 For instance, one protester at his trial stated: 'The law will eventually have to change and acknowledge the harm that carbon emissions do to all of us, by making them illegal'; quoted in M. Wainwright, 'Jury Retires to Consider Verdict in Drax Hijack Trial', *The Guardian*, 3 July 2009 (online).

References

Allan, R.S., 1996. Citizenship and Obligation: Civil Disobedience and Civil Dissent, *Cambridge Law Journal* 55:1, pp. 89–121.

Baudrillard, J., 1983. *Simulations*: New York: Semiotext[e].

Benjamin, W., 1996. Critique of Violence. In M. Bullock and M.W. Jennings (eds), *Walter Benjamin. Selected Writings Volume I 1913–1926*. Cambridge, MA: The Belknap Press.

Blay, S., and R. Piotrowitcz, 2000. The Awfulness of Lawfulness: Some Reflections on the Tension between International and Domestic Law, *Australian Yearbook of International Law* 21, pp. 1–19.

Broomfield, N., 2009. *A Time Comes*. Documentary film (http://nickbroomfield .com/A-Time-Comes).

Cover, R.M., 1983. Foreword: Nomos and Narrative, *Harvard Law Review* 97:4, pp. 4–68.

Cover, R.M., 1986. Violence and the Word. *Yale Law Journal* 95, pp. 1601–1629.

Davies, M., 1996. *Delimiting the Law. 'Postmodernism' and the Politics of Law*. London and Chicago: Pluto Press.

De Luca, K.M., 1999. *Image Politics. The New Rhetoric of Environmental Activism*. New York and London: Guilford Press, London and New York.

Derrida, J., 1992. Force of Law: The 'Mystical Foundation of Authority.' In D. Cornell, M. Rosenfeld and D.G. Carlson (eds), *Deconstruction and the Possibility of Justice*. London and New York: Routledge.

Farrier, D., 2007. Anvil Hill in the Land and Environment Court. In Tim Bonyhady and Peter Christoff (eds), *Climate Law in Australia*. Sydney: The Federation Press, pp. 189–213.

Ghaleigh, N. S., 2010. 'Six Honest Serving-Men': Climate Change Litigation as Legal Mobilization and the Utility of Typologies, *Climate Law* 1, no.1.

Hall, M., 2009–10. A Catastrophic Conundrum, but Not a Nuisance: Why the Judicial Branch Is Ill-Suited to Set Emissions Restrictions on Domestic Energy Producers through the Common Law Nuisance Doctrine,' *Chapman Law Review* 13, p. 265.

Hayes, G., 2013. Negotiating Proximity: Expert Testimony and Collective Memory in the Trials of Environmental Activists in France and the United Kingdom, *Law & Policy* 35, no. 3, pp. 208–235.

Heinzerling, P., 2008. Thrower Keynote Address: The Role of Science in *Massachusetts v EPA*, *Emory Law Journal* 58, p. 411.

Hernandez, C.C.G., 2007, Radical Environmentalism: The New Civil Disobedience?, *Seattle Journal for Social Justice* 289, pp. 315–321.

Higginson, S., 2011. Coal, Cimate Activism and the Law of Victims Compensation, *Alternative Law Journal*, 36:2, p. 131.

Ker, P. and M. Hawthorne, 'How Hoaxsters Hold Market to Ransom', *The Sydney Morning Herald (Weekend Business)*, 12 January 2013 (online).

Kershaw, B., 2002. Ecoactivist Performance: The Environment as Partner in Protest? *TDR/ The Drama Review*, 46:1, pp. 118–130.

McGrath, C., 2007. The Xstrata Case: Phyrhhic Victory or Harbinger? In Tim Bonyhady and Peter Christoff (eds), *Climate Law in Australia*. Sydney: The Federation Press, pp. 214–229.

McNevin, A., 2013. Market fraud or politics of the market? *Acts. The Archives Project* (www.enginfisin.eu/cms/market-fraud-or-politics-of-the-market).

Mills, D., 2010. 'Hazel Fights On', *The City Hub*, 3 March 2010 (online). See fn 58.

Meadows, D.H., 2008. *Thinking in Systems: A Primer.* White River Junction, Vermont: Chelsea Green Publishing.

Morgan, E., 2009. 'Judge rejects DeChristopher's "necessity defense"', *Deseret News*, 17 November 2009 (online).

Nagle, J.C., 2010. Climate Exceptionalism, *Environmental Law* 40:1, p. 53.

Newman J., 2014. Hannah Arendt: Radical Evil, Radical Hope, *European Judaism* 47:1, pp. 60–71.

Orenstein, C., 2001. Agitational Performance, Now and Then. *Theater* 31:3, pp. 139–151.

Osofsky, H.M. and J. Peel, 2013. Climate Change Litigation's Regulatory Pathways: A Comparative Analysis of the United States and Australia, *Law & Policy* 35:3, pp. 150–183.

Osofsky, H.M. and J. Peel, 2014. The Role of Litigation in Multilevel Climate Change Governance: Possibilities for a Lower Carbon Future? *Environmental and Planning Law Journal* 30:4, pp. 303–328.

Preston, B.J., 2009. Climate Change Litigation. *Environmental and Planning Law Journal* 26:169, pp. 169–189.

Rawls, J., 1973. *A Theory of Justice*. Oxford: Oxford University Press.

Ricketts, A. 2013. Investment Risk: An Amplification Tool for Social Movement Campaigns Globally and Locally, *Journal of Economic and Social Policy*, 15:3, p. 4.

Rodgers, Jr, W.H. and A.T. Moritz, 2009. The Worst Case and the Worst Example: An Agenda for Any Young Lawyer Who Wants to Save the World from Climate Chaos, *Seattle Environmental Law Journal* 17:2, pp. 295–335.

Rogers, N., 2007. Violence and Play in Saddam's Trial, *Melbourne Journal of International Law* 8:2, pp. 428–442.

Rogers, N., 2010. Law and the Fool, *Law Text Culture* 14, pp. 286–308.

Rogers, N., 2013. Climate Change Litigation and the Awfulness of Lawfulness, *Alternative Law Journal* 38:1, pp. 20–24.

Schechter, J., 1994. *Satiric Impersonations. From Aristophanes to the Guerilla Girls*. Carbondale and Edwardsville: Southern Illinois University Press.

Shearing, S., 2012. Raising the Boardroom Temperature? Climate Change and Shareholder Activism in Australia, *Environmental and Planning Law Journal* 29:6, pp. 479–497.

Sutton-Smith, B., 1997. *The Ambiguity of Play*. Cambridge, MA: Harvard University Press.

Tremblay, H., 2012. Eco-Terrorists Facing Armageddon: The Defence of Necessity and Legal Normativity in the Context of Environmental Crisis, *McGill Law Journal*, 58:2, pp. 321–364.

Tribe, L.H., 1974. Ways Not to Think About Plastic Trees: New Foundations of Environmental Law, *Yale Law Journal*, 83, pp. 1315–1348.

Vanhala, L. and C. Wilson, 2013. Climate Change Litigation: Symposium Introduction, *Law and Policy*, 35, pp. 144–145.

Werner, B., 2012. Is Earth F**ked? Dynamical Futility of Global Environmental Management and Possibilities for Sustainability via Direct Action Activism. Paper presented at the AGU Fall Meeting, San Francisco, 2–7 December (http://fallmeeting.agu.org/2012/events/ep32b-the-future-of-human-landscape-systems-ii-video-on-demand).

13   This is not my beautiful biosphere

Timothy Morton

Since roughly 1790, humans have been depositing a thin layer of carbon in Earth's crust. This layer can now be detected in deep lakes and in Arctic ice. The term now given for this by geology is *Anthropocene*, a disturbing moment at which human history intersects decisively with geological time (Crutzen & Stoermer, 2000, p. 17–18).

Since 1945, when humans began to deposit a layer of radioactive materials in Earth's crust, the Anthropocene has accelerated logarithmically, and we now live within a period called The Great Acceleration. Global warming and extinction are interrelated effects of the crossroads we have now reached, a crossroads at which geological and human time have intersected.

This intersection renders meaningless the very tools with which modernity has striven to talk about the nonhuman: concepts such as *nature*, *world* and even *environment* are now obsolete. Though they may be politically useful in some circumstances, they are not heuristically useful in any meaningful sense, and may indeed be part of the problem and not part of the solution.

Furthermore, we are now confronted with gigantic entities – *global warming*, *evolution*, *biosphere* – that cannot be seen directly by three-dimensional beings of limited intelligence. Rather, they can be inferred mathematically and logically, a fact that emphasizes that reason itself is not strictly human-flavoured, and that we inhabit a reality that is much larger, and more intractable, than we had supposed.

1790 was also roughly the moment at which Western philosophy decided that it could not talk about the real, but only about (human) *access* to the real. I see this moment and the fact of the Anthropocene as deeply related. What is required is a philosophy – and a corresponding ethics and politics – that can think of the nonhuman not simply as the adornment or correlate of the human. Modernity damaged Earth, but it also damaged thinking. Unfortunately, one of the damaged concepts is the very concept *nature*.

A crack in the real

Since the advent of the Anthropocene, a host of strange entities are thinkable by humans: thinkable, but not strictly visible. At present I make no distinction between those entities I myself hold to be real, and those that others do. It is just interesting to catalogue them, so we can think about them. I can't see or touch the unconscious. I can't see or touch evolution. I can't see or touch what Hegel means by world history. I can't see or touch Adam Smith's invisible hand. I can't see or touch the biosphere. I can't see or touch what Marx means by capital. I can't see or touch global warming.

I can see and touch this rain falling on my head, these huge drops of subtropical Houston rain. They fall on my head in 2015, which means that they fall as manifestations of global warming, which means that they fall as manifestations of the Anthropocene. But they are not global warming or the Anthropocene. Climate is real yet we can't point to it – and climate change is a still more vexed phenomenon, because it's even more real, in the same way that momentum tells you more about how a thing is moving than velocity, and inertia tells you more about movement than momentum.

There is a gap in reality, a crack – a disturbing blank. The blank is disturbing because it suggests something is incoherent or incomplete about our reality. It is even more disturbing, perhaps, that we can think about the gap, but that we can't directly see or experience what's in it. The name for thinking about this gap is reason and the trouble with reason is that it is caught in the technical and mechanical modes that have themselves given rise to the Anthropocene.

The very tools we use to discover what is going on as Earth warms are also part of the tools with which humans started to lay down carbon in Earth's crust. Thus ecological knowledge has the form of a noir fiction, which, in other words, means that ecological awareness is Oedipal. The detective discovers that he is the culprit – isn't this the essence of the Oedipus story? Thus the dilemma of an ecological era is that the era is at once the product of massively increased knowledge – but also that this knowledge is itself a component of a planet-scale machination that has profoundly damaged Earth.

Back to the crack, the gap in the real. I can count: one, two, three, four, five. But I can't tell you what number is. But counting presupposes a concept of number. There was always already what Kant calls an a priori, a condition of possibility for counting (Kant, 1965, p. 52–3). Yet when I try to show you number, I resort again to counting, to showing you my fingers, to counting them off. Thus what Kant discovered was a crack in the real. He discovered this at the very moment at which humans were beginning to lay down a thin layer of carbon in Earth's crust. The thin black layer of carbon has an uncanny, inverted resemblance to the thin, dark slit in reality, as if they were two versions of the same thing, the one solid opaque and unknown for two hundred years, the other open and clear and somewhere in my head, or perhaps better, behind the back of my head. As if, just to free associate for a moment, we were looking at a distortion that could be a slit or gap, or a thin black line.

Kant has a very evocative phrase for the dark slit and what lies behind it, in the *Critique of Pure Reason*: he calls it the 'Unknown = X', a phrase whose poetry and mystery is plangently vivid (51). Something is wrong with the real. The data just don't add up. Hume had shown that theories of causality could not account for cause and effect (Hume, 1993). All we have to go on are statistical correlations. Kant grounds this in what he calls pure reason and gives a deep explanation for it. Causality in contemporary science just is Humean – it is about bundles of data that correlate statistically. Causality, in other words, is *in the realm of appearance*, not some mechanical realm churning away underneath things. But what are the conditions of possibility for knowing that these rather than those data are accurate? There must always already be something in the back of our heads, something like a gigantic ocean right behind us, an ocean of reason we are unable to see or touch, yet an ocean which gives us the possibility of counting, of understanding number and numbers, and so on.

Our sense of reality shudders. Kant himself provides an example that is uncannily meteorological. We frequently feel raindrops on our head: they are wet, spherical, cold and so on. But there is no basis to regard this experience as the thing in itself – whatever we are sensing is merely a phenomenal display, an aspect of that Unknown = X (Kant, 1965, p. 84–5). Our concept of rain – the very physical, the very tangible experience of raindrops hitting our head – does not fully access the real. Prior to Kant, Hume had blown a hole in causality theories by reducing causality to mere statistical probability, which as I stated is how modern science operates. Kant provided the deep reason for this stochastic approach to causality – there is an Unknown = X in the world, there is a crack in the real, and this fissure marks the difference between phenomenon and thing.

For Kant, two kinds of being inhabit reality on either side of the fissure: humans (or rather, consciousness, but for the anthropocentric Kant these are very much the same thing) on the hither side of the crack; and everything else on the yonder side. Kant himself was disturbed by the fissure. In a sense, this is Kant's way of policing the fissure, restricting the movement of the genie he has released, the genie that comes to be known in the century that followed as *nothingness*. Something is there, yet inaccessible, something like a shadow that flickers across a thing, something we can only glimpse out of the corner of our eye.

Hegel's "solution" to the problem of nothingness that leaks out of the fissure is to paper over the crack. I cannot know the thing in itself, he argues, but there I am, realizing that – so I *can* know the thing in itself. For Hegel, nothingness is thus a form of illusion belonging to a primitive state of consciousness that doesn't realize this sublime Hegelian truth. This primitive state has a name for Hegel – it is called *Buddhism*. Hegel palms nothingness off on the supposedly inferior peoples of the East with their supposedly inferior religion, hobbling them in the grand march of history towards its inevitable outcome, which is becoming a Hegelian (Hegel, 1988, pp. 265 n. 183, 185, 266 n. 188, 504–5; Hegel, 1975, pp. 125, 127).

But what elsewhere I have called hyperobjects, massively distributed entities such as global warming, biosphere, evolution, electromagnetism – the discoveries of the nineteenth century and after – are precisely efficient in reopening the gap for us. Hyperobjects are things that one can compute and think, but not see or touch (Morton, 2013). It is as if in the case of hyperobjects, reason were capable of slapping us upside the head with a dose of reality, or better, as if through reason we figured out that we were not the greatest and final creatures on Earth, but rather that we were inhabiting all kinds of gigantic entities that are thinkable, yet invisible. The nineteenth century was the moment at which the hyperobject we call El Niño was conceptualized, a vast climatic system in the Pacific that affects weather – a gigantic being whose existence can be surmised but not directly seen, only indirectly and vicariously in phenomena such as rain and drought.

Hyperobjects reassert the fact that nothingness, once admitted into one's thinking, is incapable of being banished. Nothingness is here to stay. Thus the basic affect of an ecological era – that is, the era we have been realizing we have been inhabiting, namely the Anthropocene – is *anxiety*. Anxiety: a fear of existence, a fear that *is* existence – not a fear of something, but a fear that is precisely a kind of nothingness, nothingness as fear. Nothing-ness: not absolutely nothing at all, what one philosopher calls *oukontic* nothing, but a –ness, a something, a quality that can-not be objectified by definition (Tillich, 1951, p. 188); nothing-ing, or as Heidegger puts it, nihiliation. In response to this nothingness you could readily do what Schopenhauer did: Schopenhauer, that exemplary Kantian (and anti-Hegelian) who argues that behind the crack in the real is what he calls Will, an intractable drive to exist. The only way to subvert this intractable drive is to suspend its operation, and this is why Schopenhauer became his version of a Buddhist, and why the last word of *The World as Will and Representation* is *nothing* (Schopenhauer, 1969, p. I: 412).

Nietzsche thinks that the solution of Schopenhauerian quietism is just striving against fate, and that this means one has not fully accepted the nothingness. Thus Nietzsche develops his philosophy of flux and becoming and amor fati. But as Heidegger shows, *flux* is just a new and improved term for a version of metaphysical entity. In other words the flux theory relies on a notion of constant presence that Hume and Kant had made illegitimate (Heidegger, 1999, p. 332). Instead of solid static things, we have flowing gooey things, rhizomes, deterritorialization, life force. In such substitutes for the obvious squareness of the Aristotelian substance-and-accidents model, there remains a resistance to the cognitive openness required by the critique of metaphysics. Such an openness rests on the openness of reality as such that nothingness forces us to accept. No matter whether they seem to be flowing or static, we commonly think of things in that Aristotelian way: as formatted lumps of whatever, decorated with (superficial) accidents.

Heidegger himself nevertheless panicked about nothingness. His own embrace of nothingness is quite Kantian in its anthropocentrism. Heidegger's nothingness just is Dasein (being-there), which just means humans – and in some versions, German humans in particular. Nothingness is the dark question mark that inhabits the world in the guise of human being, strung out into the future with all its projects, projects that cover up the basic anxiety and the basic strung out-ness. Nothingness is still just the human–world correlate.

Let us now consider object-oriented ontology (OOO), the philosophical view to which I subscribe. What object-oriented ontology does is to multiply the cracks in the real everywhere. There are as many cracks in the real as there are things. Because reality just is things, and things just are riven from the inside between what they are and how they appear, even to themselves. There is a human–world gap. There is a toaster–world gap. There is a crack between octopuses and toasters. There is a crack between octopuses and octopuses: octopus thing and octopus phenomena are fissured from within. There is a crack between this octopus and this coral reef; a crack between this coral reef itself and this coral reef itself. Like some astonishingly beautiful piece of Japanese raku, reality is just riddled with trillions of cracks. OOO is thus the first western view to embrace the nothingness with no hesitation whatsoever. And thus OOO performs the task of overcoming nihilism – which as Nietzsche and Heidegger argued cannot be overcome by pushing or resisting but by going in and transforming from underneath.

Nothingness rules out the metaphysics of presence. Kant made sure that the factoids of presence were reduced to flimsy perilous islands floating on top of the giant ocean of reason. Things like cause and effect, things like primal substance, are no longer safe havens. If you can't have presence, then you can't have a void at the beginning of time – you can't shunt the void back there. To do so is not particularly scientific: it is just to conform to the Papal edict of 1277 that pronounced that since God was all powerful, he could have created an infinite void, and that therefore, he had (Casey, 1997, p. 106–16). But you also are incapable of restricting the nothingness to the human–world gap, since there is nothing in particular that makes humans special, and you know *that* because you are a post-Kantian who grew up in a world of science. You can't really palm nothingness off on the Buddhists either – people who live Over There in a primitive state of not knowing the beautiful circularity of Hegel.

Since nothing at all can coincide with its appearance, then, in the words of my title *this is not my beautiful biosphere.*[1] Anxiety arises as the spontaneous result of noticing that we are not at home in our home: the uncanny. The gigantic entities that human reason, assisted by prosthetic computing devices, has detected, will simply not fit into the human box, because they are not part of human phenomenal experience – and because human phenomenal experience is just that: it's simply what we touch and see and know.

Dark ecology

The Anthropocene collapses the difference between the human realm and so-called nature. Boundary collapse has resulted in what I prefer to call *the end of the world*, which is to say the collapse of a meaningful and stable background against which human events can become significant, as on a stage set. In turn, the loss of distance has resulted in a powerful sense of the uncanny and the strange.

The collapse of the human–nonhuman boundary is due, as we have been exploring, to the radical intersection of human history and geological time. As if to prove Jung's law of synchronicity, the intersection coincided with the restriction of philosophy to the human–world correlate. And yet the deep reasons for this restriction, the realization that there is a crack in the real, that there is a profound finitude to human being, means that there are things in heaven and earth that hadn't yet been dreamed of in philosophy. Thinking became more rigorous and restrictive, and discovered an entirely new dimension of the real, at the very same time and for the very same reasons.

The discovery of profound finitude is the discovery of an ineradicable nothingness. Beings no longer coincide with their phenomena. Things become misty, shifty, nebulous, uncanny. At the very same time reality becomes thinkable in a mathematical way in a manner hitherto unprecedented. Transfinite sets, discovered by Georg Cantor, are impossibly larger than infinity as previously thought, and strictly impossible to see or count. Yet one can see with one's naked eyes, in the brilliant diagonal proof of Cantor, the crack in the real, the gap in a certain way of explaining things. That is what is uncanny – it is as if you can see the gap, the nothingness. Imagine a grid on which are arranged all the rational numbers, in sequence from the first to the whateverest. Appearing down the diagonal of this incredible list is a weird, monstrous, deviant number that literally slants away from the others. It is not in the infinite set of rational numbers, by definition! No wonder there is a legend that Pythagoras, worshipper of the sacred integer, had Hippasus, who discovered pi, drowned.

We can think things that are counterintuitive and imperceptible yet incontestably valid. We can argue that this is because there is something uncanny about the human being – the human is the dark question mark that interrupts the smooth continuity of reality. This is Heidegger's solution, and in some sense it is also Kant's solution, though Kant would not have put it in those dark terms. The human makes reality thinkable, or real, or significant. This notion, plus the ineluctable movement of science, has defined the way philosophy and the humanities in general have construed themselves since the advent of the Anthropocene: become a Hegelian and close your ears to the nothingness like it never happened. Get high on the grand march of history.

Another, less predominant philosophical tradition – Schopenhauer is an early example of how to nudge Kant in this direction – is preoccupied with supposing that the gap in human cognition has to do with reality itself, not with the human or with cognition. Thinking has gaps, because things have gaps. Reality is full of cracks and holes. Since it is a hyperobject, global warming gives a very elegant example of a real entity that is riddled with gaps. So does evolution. Let us proceed down this path for a moment.

Cantor showed that there is a gap between numbers and sets of numbers. Likewise there is a gap between lifeforms and sets of lifeforms. We can think of these sets as ecosystems, biomes, biosphere – we can think of these sets at any scale, and there is no easy continuity between these sets. An environment just is a certain set of lifeforms. The way one does ecological research is to establish a somewhat arbitrary set – to define a boundary sometimes called a *mesocosm*, in which one observes lifeforms coming and going, reproducing, struggling. An ecosystem is vague, in the sense that paradoxes called Sorites paradoxes arise when one attempts to define them precisely. How many blades of grass do I have to remove for this meadow not to be a meadow? One – surely not. Two – still a meadow. Three, four, and so on – and the same logic applies until I have only one blade of grass left. I conclude, wrongly, that there is no meadow. These paradoxes plague sets of lifeforms at any scale, and therefore it is strictly impossible to think ecological reality via a metaphysics of presence, namely, a belief that to be a thing, you have to be constantly present.

It is paradoxically much better to think that there is a meadow and there is not a meadow at the same time. We seem to have violated the supposed Law of Noncontradiction, asserted but not proved in Section Gamma of Aristotle's *Metaphysics*. There is a meadow, but we can't point to it directly, because it's not constantly present. And yet here is the meadow, with the butterflies, the cowslips, the voles. Just as a vole is a set of things that are not voles, so the meadow is a set of things such as voles that are not meadows.

Thus a spectral strangeness that haunts being applies not only to lifeforms – a vole is a not-vole – but also to meadows, ecosystems, biomes and the biosphere. The haunting, withdrawn yet vivid spectrality of things also means that there can be sets of things that are not strictly members of that set, and this violates Russell's prohibition on the set paradox that arises precisely through thinking Cantor's transfinite sets. Transfinite sets are as we just saw sets of numbers that contain sets of numbers that are not strictly members of that set. There is an irreducible gap between the set of real numbers and the set of rational numbers – Cantor himself, like Gödel, drove himself crazy trying to find a smooth continuum between the two. This drive to find a continuum is a hangover from the Law of Noncontradiction, which has never been formally proved, but which has been accepted as a precondition for philosophy since Aristotle.

This means that contemporary thinking cannot cleave to a logic that assumes that things are rigid and brittle, whether those things are static entities or flowing processes – for processes can also be rigid, namely 'ontically given' in the Heideggerian lingo. Brittleness has to do with assuming that things do not contradict themselves. The deep reason for self-contradiction is that reality is ambiguous and contradictory.

Nothing makes this clearer than ecological awareness, which is simply human cognition coming up to speed with the fact of the Anthropocene. This coming up to speed is like tracing the contours of a Möbius strip. There we were, achieving escape velocity from the past, being modern – I would assert to the contrary that we have in fact been modern, contra Latour – when all of a sudden, we find out that we are shrink wrapped in the real. And, irony of ironies, this discovery is within reason and logic themselves. It was phenomenology, for example, that set logic back on a rigorous footing in Husserl's preface to *Logical Investigations* – wresting it away from the psychologism that had reduced logic to a function of (human) brains (Husserl, 2006, p. I: 1–161). Yet this very move discovers discrete entities, which Husserl calls intentional objects, swimming around like fish in the ocean of reason: hoping, hating, asserting, wishing. These intentional objects have autonomy: they are real in the sense that they are not simply reflections of our mind. They have a front and a back, as it were – my mental image of a mailbox (Husserl's example) has a front and back, I can turn it around in my thought, I can't see all of it all at once. This means that my thinking is chock full of things that are not reducible to the mind or the brain. This in turn suggests that reality is full of things like that. Spoons, clouds, ecosystems, hyenas, saltshakers. I can never grasp them in their totality. They themselves can never grasp themselves this way. Why? Because of the irreducible gap between what a thing is and how it appears, which goes all the way down into the object as such. This means that an object and indeed all objects whatsoever are impossible to totalize.

Ecological beings such as climate and biosphere and radiation are so immense both in spatial and in temporal terms that they defeat our habitual notions of constant presence. They are like physical, nonhuman deconstructive philosophers, pulverizing our ideas about what a thing is, what time and space are. They reduce our concepts about things, space and time to what they are: arbitrary constructs based on habitual reflexes that have not been questioned until the advent of modern measuring instruments that can discover, for instance, that Plutonium 239 has a half-life of 24,100 years, which is almost as long as all of human history all the way back to the Chauvet Cave. These hyperobjects force us to recognize that it is in fact impossible to peel reality away from ourselves. And yet they also force us to give up our prejudices about what reality is: constantly present things, whether those things are atoms or flows or static lumps, substances decorated with accidents; or correlates of some 'decider' such as Subject, History, human economic relations, will, Dasein or discourse.

Hyperobjects are irreducible to totalizing thought. Thinking itself discovers its nemesis in the form of hyperobjects. The better we think, the more we know about hyperobjects, which means the less we can assure ourselves that this is a human centred, human flavoured reality. Which means that thinking itself is not entirely on the side of human beings. Thinking itself contains alien presences, just as the idea that true (that is coherent) logical systems must contain statements that they can't prove, in order to be true on their own terms (Gödel's Incompleteness Theorem).

Since ecological entities defeat the possibility of a perfect metalanguage that would encapsulate them perfectly, ecological thinking is necessarily *dark*. This is why I call it *dark ecology*, which is almost a tautology: ecology as the thinking of darkness, darkness as the basic flavour of ecological thinking. This darkness does not have to do with ignorance, blissful or otherwise, but precisely with reason. The more we know, the more uncanny things become. To extend the metaphor, darkness doesn't mean that we are dealing with absolute blackness here. We are dealing with all kinds of gradations, twilight shades, moonlight and starlight.

This darkness has to do with mystery (Greek *muein*, to close the lips), which means secrecy and unspeakability. But the darkness does not have to do with mystification or stupefaction. It might have to do with realizing that we are stupid, or at any rate limited, or wounded on the inside by our necessary finitude, just like everything else. That is what Gödel showed: any coherent system must have an Achilles heel (Gödel, n.d.). And it applies to physical objects too. For any record player, there is a record called *I Cannot Be Played on This Record Player* – when you try to play it, it emits sympathetic vibrations that blow the record player to bits (Hofstadter, 1999, p. 76). Existence means being inconsistent, which means having what in Greek tragedy is called a hamartia, a tragic flaw.

This flaw is a wound, but it is a productive wound. Oedipus' hamartia is that he is so smart and so competent as the intellectual detective that he finds out that he is the criminal he has been looking for. It's a tight loop, a Möbius strip. Dark ecology means that we realize the truth of Oedipus, the primal myth of the agricultural age – the age we still live in, the age that is responsible for much global warming, the age that necessitated the industry that accounts for the rest of global warming. Necessitated it not only socially but also ontologically, because Mesopotamian agricultural logistics reifies Earth into domination-ready slabs of unformatted space waiting to be filled and ploughed: a reification that paves the way for patriarchy with its male seeds containing the essence of the human. An ecological age must necessarily be a post-agricultural age, which means that an ecological age must push against thousands of years of human history. Oedipus, king of the city-state that is the culmination of generations of agricultural development, discovers that he is the culprit responsible for the miasma (the physically and morally polluting plague) that plagues not only people, but also the environment itself.

The Möbius twist is this: the very reasoning that asserts that human access to reality is all philosophy can talk about is the passageway to an uncanny awareness that humans are the culprit; furthermore, following Darwin, humans are replicants, haphazard kludges of nonhumans, made of nonhumans and thus self-contradictory. Humans are collections of nonhuman tools as if we were witnessing Darwin shaking hands with Heidegger. We are human and not-human at the very same time. Under its own steam (pun intended) reason exits the anthropocentric sphere and begins to speak of strange, nonhuman entities.

Thus the dominant mode of ecological awareness is anxiety, the feeling that things have lost their seemingly original significance, the feeling that something creepy is happening, close to home. Through anxiety reason itself begins to glimpse what indigenous – that is, pre-agricultural – cultures have known all along: that humans coexist with a host of nonhumans. For reason reveals itself to be at least a little bit nonhuman itself. In turn, reason discovers global warming, that miasma for which humans are responsible. Through reason we find ourselves not floating blissfully in outer space, but caught like Jonah in the whale of a gigantic object, the biosphere. Such an object is not reducible to its members, nor its members to it; it is a set whose members are not strictly coterminous with itself. Since this entity cannot be known directly, it is known by intuition, by a kind of synthetic judgment a priori, as Kant calls it. It is dark, insofar as its essence is unspeakable. It is dark, insofar as illumination leads to a greater sense of entrapment. It is dark, because it compels us to recognize the melancholic wounds that make us up – the shocks and traumas and cataclysms that have made oxygen for our lungs to breathe, lungs out of swim bladders, and crushing, humiliating reason out of human domination of Earth.

Within logic, we discover things that contradict themselves. Via accurate instruments, we discover beings that far outstrip human temporality: the time of global warming is 100,000 years, at whose conclusion seven percent of remaining global warming effects will be slowly absorbed by igneous rocks. Western humans thought they were achieving escape velocity from their homeworld, while all the time they were burrowing more deeply into the mesh of things. Thus when David Byrne sings, 'And you may tell yourself – This is not my beautiful house / And you may tell yourself – This is not my beautiful wife,' he should also be singing, 'And you may tell yourself – This is not my beautiful biosphere.'[2]

Notes

1   The title alludes to Talking Heads, 'Once in a Lifetime', *Remain in Light* (Sire, 1980).
2   Talking Heads, 'Once in a Lifetime'.

References

Casey, E., 1997. *The Fate of Place: A Philosophical History.* Berkeley: University of California Press.
Crutzen, P. & Stoermer, E., 2000. The Anthropocene. *Global Change Newsletter,* 41(1).
Gödel, K., n.d. *On Formally Undecidable Propositions of Principia Mathematica and Related Systems (tr. Martin Hirzel)* [Online]. Available at: www.research.ibm.com/people/h/hirzel/papers/canon00-goedel.pdf. [Accessed 3 April 2014].
Hegel, G. W. F., 1975. *Hegel's Logic, Being Part One of the Encyclopaedia of the Philosophical Sciences.* 3rd ed. Oxford: Oxford University Press.
Hegel, G. W. F., 1988. *Lectures on the Philosophy of Religion.* Berkeley, Los Angeles, and London: University of California Press.
Heidegger, M., 1999. *Contributions to Philosophy (From Enowning).* Bloomington: Indiana University Press.
Hofstadter, D., 1999. *Gödel, Escher, Bach: An Eternal Golden Braid.* New York: Basic Books.
Hume, D., 1993. *An Inquiry Concerning Human Understanding; with Hume's Abstract of a Treatise of Human Nature and a Letter from a Gentleman to His Friend in Edinburgh.* Indianapolis: Hackett.
Husserl, E., 2006. Prolegomena to All Logic. In: D. Moran, ed. *Logical Investigations.* London: Routledge.
Kant, I., 1965. *Critique of Pure Reason.* Boston and New York: Bedford/St. Martin's.
Morton, T., 2013. *Hyperobjects: Philosophy and Ecology after the End of the World.* Minneapolis: University of Minnesota Press.
Schopenhauer, A., 1969. *The World as Will and Representation.* New York: Dover Publications.
Tillich, P., 1951. *Systematic Theology.* Chicago: University of Chicago Press.

Index

Printed in the United States
by Baker & Taylor Publisher Services